Reach for Paradise

*"You gotta have a dream,
if you don't have a dream,
How you gonna have a dream come true?"*

Oscar Hammerstein II – *South Pacific*

Among Pacific Islands

Reach for Paradise

Fragments of Perfection

ANDREW RAYNER

COMPANIONWAY PRESS
Maui, Hawai'i

Copyright © 2013 Andrew Rayner

All rights reserved.

RE-ORDERS
For further copies of *Reach for Paradise*, whether e-books or proper books, visit: www.reachforparadise.com or email andrew@reachforparadise.com.

ISBN (softcover): 978-0-9886748-4-4
ISBN (hardcover): 978-0-9886748-5-1

Library of Congress Control Number: 2013904325

Cover and text design by John Reinhardt Book Design

Printed in the United States of America

THE ART, THE PHOTOS, and THE MAPS

The twenty fine paintings illustrating this book, each marked RR, were created by Robin Rayner in acrylics on canvas. Robin also built the maps.

Most of the photographs were taken by the author. Some are attributable to Robin, and a few to other sources. If any recognition is inadequate, we would be happy to correct this.

No part of the world exerts the same attractive power...
The first experience can never be repeated. The first love, the first sunrise, the first South Sea Island, are memories apart and touch a virginity of sense.

>—Robert Louis Stevenson,
>*In the South Seas*, 1891–92

Stevenson said that one's first tropical island landfall touches a virginity of sense. So it does, and the tenth or the fifteenth. The purity of perception is not lost by repetition of the experience. There is a magic about these islands that is time-defying, that loses nothing of its power however long continued one's association with them may be.

>—James Norman Hall
>*My Island Home*, 1952

Contents

AUTHOR'S NOTE ix

1 RIPPLES 1

2 TAMELIFE 9
   The Galápagos: Genovese ~ Santa Cruz ~ Española ~ Santa Fe ~ Isabel

3 THE LAND OF MEN 19
   The Marquesas: Fatu Hiva ~ Hiva Oa ~ Ua Pu ~ Nuku Hiva

4 THE GREAT OCEAN 39

5 A DANGEROUS ARCHIPELAGO 51
   The Tuamotus: Makemo ~ Tahanea ~ Fakarava

6 THE SOCIETY ISLANDS 59
   Tahiti ~ Moorea ~ Huahine ~ Taha'a ~ Raiatea ~ Borabora ~ Maupiti

7 PARADISE PAST 83

8 THE ONE-FAMILY ISLAND 91
   Cook Islands: Palmerston

9 SAVAGE ISLAND 99
   Niue

10 WHERE TIME STARTS 105
   Tonga: Vava'u ~ Tapana ~ Euakafa ~ Foeata ~ Nuapapu

11	THE FRIENDLY ISLES 125	
	Tonga: Ha'apai ~ Tofua	
12	FIJI and the ASTROLABE 131	
	Taveuni ~ Vanua Levu ~ Yasawas ~ Viti Levu ~ Astrolabe ~ Kadavu	
13	KANAKY..143	
	New Caledonia: Grande Terre ~ Île de Pins ~ Ouvéa	
14	THE PANDEMONIUM 155	
	Vanuatu: Tanna ~ Efate ~ Epi ~ Maskelyns ~ Ambrym ~ Pentecost ~ Maewo ~ Espiritu Santo ~ Gaua ~ Vanua Lava ~ Ureparapara	
15	THE TERRIBLE SOLOMONS 189	
	Santa Cruz ~ Three Sisters ~ Guadalcanal ~ Russell ~ Mary ~ Marovo ~ Rendova ~ Munda ~ Vona Vona ~ Kolumbanggara ~ Gizo ~ Simbo	
16	JEWELS IN THE OCEAN 245	
	PNG: Budibudi ~ The Louisiades: Misima ~ Panapompom ~ Panasia ~ Motorina ~ Bagaman ~ Gigilia ~ Hessessai ~ Tagula	
17	THE KULA RING 263	
	PNG: Hummock ~ Tubetube ~ Alotau ~ d'Entrecasteaux: Normanby ~ Dobu ~ Trobriands: Amphletts ~ Kiriwina	
18	BISMARCK'S SEA 301	
	PNG: New Ireland ~ New Britain ~ Manus ~ Hermit: Luf ~ Maron	
19	A PACIFIC FESTIVAL 317	
	Palau: Koror ~ Babeldaob ~ Rock Islands	
20	REFLECTION 335	
	ACKNOWLEDGMENTS 341	
	GLOSSARY 343	
	SOURCES 349	
	INDEX 353	

Author's Note

IN MY ATTEMPT to convey a flavor of the islands of the Pacific in all their variety, a story bound together by the thread of a splendid journey, I am guilty of dreadful omissions. It takes not a book but a library to do justice to this enormous slice of our globe. Some islands are unfairly abbreviated; others do not appear at all. In particular, though they are an integral part of Pacific Ocean lore, I have excluded New Zealand and the Hawaiian chain, each well covered elsewhere.

I trust sailors will not use anything in this book for navigation. I'd hate to be suspected of leading anyone astray, for wayfinding is not its purpose.

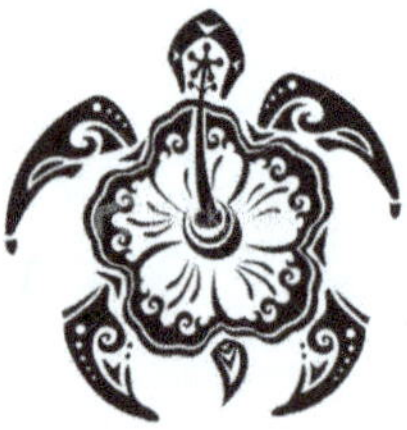

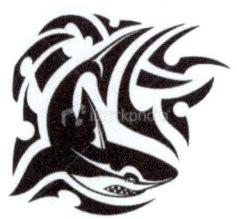

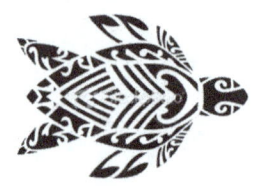

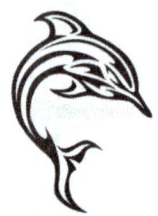

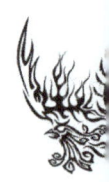

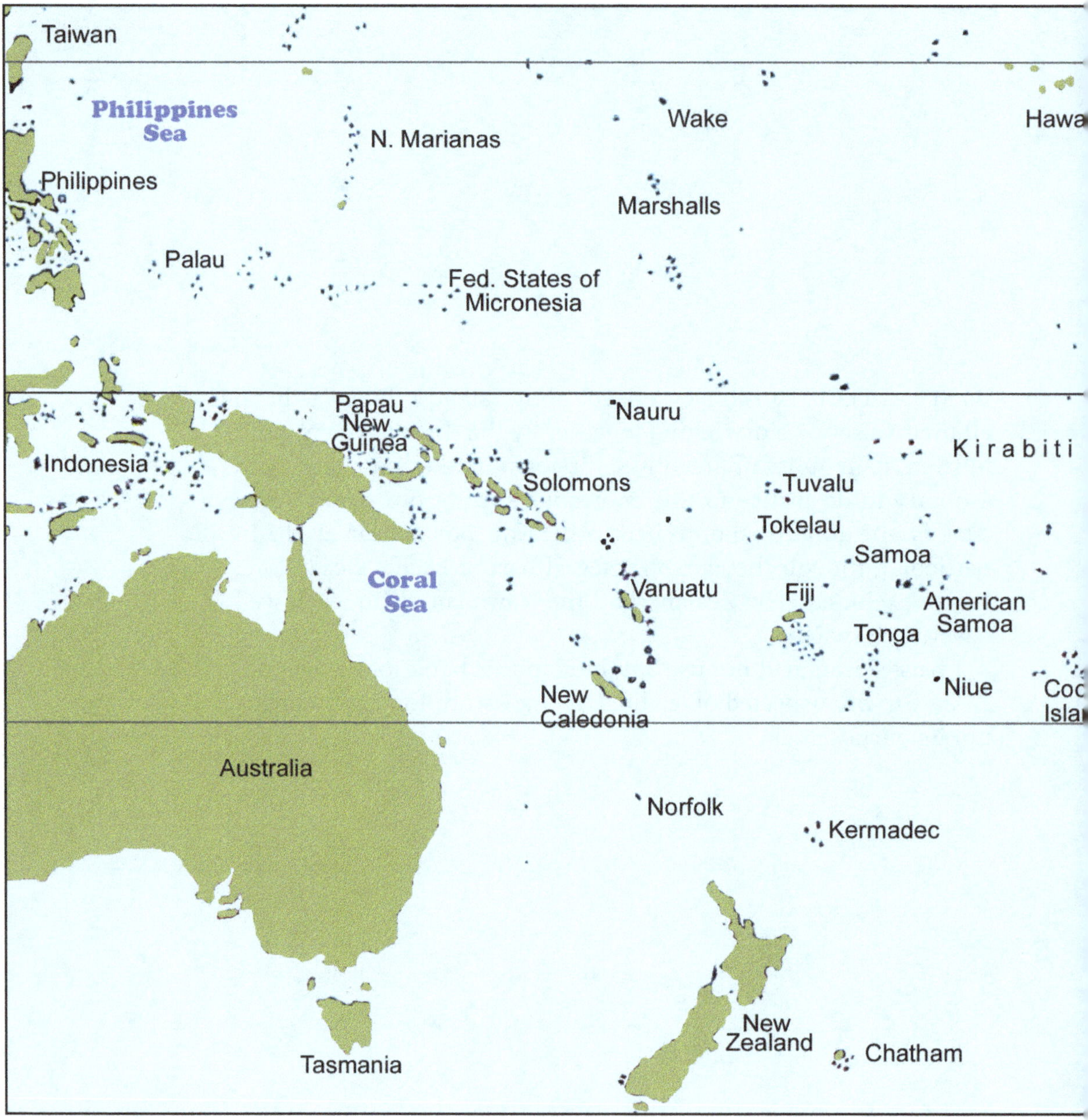

Taiwan
Philippines Sea
N. Marianas
Wake
Hawa
Philippines
Marshalls
Palau
Fed. States of Micronesia
Papau New Guinea
Nauru
Kirabiti
Indonesia
Solomons
Tuvalu
Tokelau
Samoa
Coral Sea
Vanuatu
Fiji
American Samoa
Tonga
Niue
Coc Isla
New Caledonia
Australia
Norfolk
Kermadec
New Zealand
Chatham
Tasmania

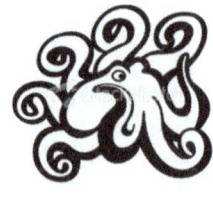

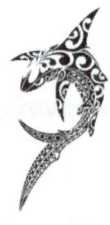

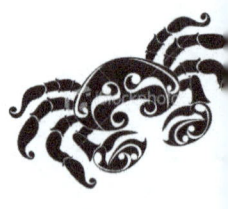

tropic of Cancer

Central America

Panama

the equator

Galapagos

South America

Marquesas

Tuamotus

Gambiers

Australs

tropic of Capricorn

Pitcairn

Rapa Nui (Easter)

Juan Fernandez

Ripples

THE IMMENSITY of the ocean is cloaked at night. Calm or turbulent, under stars or the beam of a full moon, the ocean is a pond fenced in black, our ship a toy upon it. As the eastern sky is tinged saffron and wave crests glow with the first tentative feelers of a new day, reality dawns with the light. The angle of the sun's ascent in the tropics is steeper than in higher latitudes, so twilight is short. Then oblique sunbeams shine briefly through the steeper waves, a carpet of backlit rolling green bottles. The helmsman lifts his eyes. Pivoting slowly on his heels, he scans the horizon.

Nothing.

He is at the center of an unruly disk, wet plowland in motion, empty. With his first mug of coffee comes the daily message of his infinite smallness on an infinity of unpunctuated sea.

Yet it is not so. Like a traveler in thick forest who sees neither glades nor villages nor streams until he is upon them, the Pacific sailor is blinded. Not by obstacles, but blinkered by geometry, for the curvature of the earth restricts his vision. Thus, from the deck of a small boat, the treetops on an atoll can be detected only from a distance of perhaps ten miles. All around him are islands that he does not see, for the forces that controlled the drift of continents and ordained that a third of the earth should be dedicated to a single ocean were generous in sprinkling on its surface abundant scraps of dry land. No one is sure of the number of these islands. A reasonable guess might lie within ten to twenty-five thousand.

Even five hundred years ago, none were known save to Pacific peoples.

Since the Great Ocean was mapped by the sailors of the late eighteenth century, reports of blue lagoons, dusky maidens and money to be made from coconuts have brought a trickle of outsiders to its atolls and islands. The explorers, the whalers, the soldiers and those who sought business here, God's as well as mammon's, were followed by the beachcombers, drifters and romantics who soon appeared once the existence of each scrap of paradise was announced. For most dedicated hedonists, it was a trap. Some found a welcome unmatched elsewhere in a shrinking world, but no arcadia. The limitations of life on a faraway speck in the ocean, the only company people of different background and language, often a loving woman who could not talk of things beyond her horizon, were soon apparent to even the most convinced refugees from civilization, while any sensitivity to injustice and deprivation diluted a suggestion that here was paradise for its own peoples.

Careful scrutiny of a world map, however, shows that only these small islands of the Pacific are both remote enough and pleasant enough for serious paradise potential as generally defined. For most, isolation has proved a protection from the ugly contagion of an urbanizing and traveling world. The climate is right, tourism is thin, and valuable mineral resources rare. The military or strategic value that was once attached to some of these places is almost gone. Most have proved insufficiently interesting for permanent takeover by outsiders, and are peopled by their old clans. And most are simply lovely.

"Paradise" is a suffering word, grossly overused and ineptly devalued in everyday hype and blurb. Yet, tired as it is, it will have to do. Nothing else conveys that sense of place that can inspire a blissful contentment. It seems unsurprising that, initially prompted by the tales of the loving welcome sailors received from the girls of the South Seas and the easy life of Tahiti, the idea of an earthly paradise has long focused on the Great Ocean.

It was a dream of childhood that matured into curiosity to discover whether Eden's heir, a last refuge from civilization's defects, is indeed somewhere beyond the western horizon that brought me to sail this ocean. Were the ravers right, recognizing something exceptional about Pacific islands; a blend of beauty, simplicity and climate that even the most cynical traveler seems to acknowledge? It started, as one day I chewed on a lunchtime sandwich at my London desk, with a reverie of sailing around the world. I would follow the trail of the redoubtable Captain Cook, find tropical islands without a footprint on pearly sand, feast with cannibal chiefs, swim with whales, dine on roasted breadfruits, and gather wild mangoes. I pictured my little ship riding at anchor in the blue waters of coral lagoons, canoes bringing leis of flowers and Polynesian beauties. There would be a peace and fulfillment, the achievement of reaching places unvisited and people uncorrupted. A life of compliance, cars and cares would be junked for gentle breezes on unpolluted oceans, horizons broken only by coconut trees, the company of frigate birds and dugongs, communication by message in a bottle.

The dream didn't go away. It became a hypothesis, and then grew to a scheme, accelerated by the notion of escape from the suffocating corporatist stasis that has taken over in Europe. The only way to find out whether anything that remains of the traditional Pacific can add up to a version of paradise for Western eyes chimed with my plan: a small boat. While it is possible to fly to a few islands, to buy passage on ferries to others, this is only scratching at the edges, constrained to find a resort or guesthouse to lay one's head where the port or airport village will be attuned to tourists. Cruise ships can damage innocence wherever they touch quiet backwaters. Roads to get around an island are rare; in most, the canoe is the only form of internal transport. Even a bicycle is of little use, for rocks, sand and jungle often ensure that any paths that connect villages to each other are seldom negotiable on two wheels.

But few villages in this vast ocean are far from the sea, which serves as an infinite bus-route. Before pacification by colonial navies and indoctrination by missionaries, it was too dangerous to dwell on the coast. Canoe-borne expeditions might descend without warning. Painted warriors armed with stone knives and wooden clubs stole the women and cooked up the defeated men with yams and hogs for a triumphal feast, perhaps reserving a few notable heads or jaw-bones as trophies. Villages accordingly moved inland, and fishing became a careful armed excursion. Now this has reversed; the hidden villages are abandoned, and almost everybody in the smaller islands lives by the sea, which is both their main food source and their highway. Thus, like snails, floating travelers can bring their lodging to a village and become a temporary part of the community, living with people who may have little outside contact. They are invariably welcomed warmly into the local scene, often guests in leaf houses, talking for hours. They will mend equipment and help as they can with medical problems, and are offered whatever the island has to give. Vegetables and chickens are traded for fishhooks and shirts; spare magazines and books meet a ubiquitous lack of reading material. Newspapers are often requested, for paper to roll homegrown tobacco once they've been read. Visiting boats are floating goody-boxes, able to provide all sorts of unobtainable things, and yet the tradition and generosity of the villagers demands no quid pro quo for the crayfish, flowers and fruits that arrive by canoe soon after an anchor splashes down in their yard.

I could meet the other essential too. A slice of life was needed for the transmogrifying change from a settled urban existence complete with business, family, friends and dogs to an exotically sequestered, wind-drenched ocean life on the far side of the world. With the children fledged and flown the nest, their mother soon to marry someone else, I had space to take off, time to cope with the boggling extent of the Pacific at average sailing speed, not much quicker than walking. Polynesia alone is larger than the United States plus all of South America.

Imagination flourished. I would feel the impact of unknown places on the spirit and learn to tread quietly ashore where my forbears thought only of planting a flag. I could gossip with the children of cannibals and headhunters and inspect their inheritance of skulls, discuss spells with sorcerers, watch boobies dance, evaluate bride-price payable in pigs, shells or banana leaves. I'd dine with island chiefs on megapode eggs and learn to quit fast if megapode flight signalled an eruption of one of the thousand active volcanoes in the Pacific Ring of Fire. Though my only baths might be waterfalls, I'd eat of the finest fresh food on earth.

And in the ocean, the marvels of whale song, of nudibranchs, dolphins, and the fantastic reefscape of sponges and corals would together instill a limitless sense of wonder. I'd meet turtles, manta rays, whales and sharks of all sorts, dugong, sea horses and a kaleidoscope of amazing fish.

I little guessed all these dreams would prove real. That I would swim with fourteen million jellyfish and a chambered nautilus from a thousand feet down. Or that I was to be kissed by the biggest fish in the ocean.

Though I'd sailed coastal waters since childhood, it took six months to learn enough about blue-water cruising and acquire a boat, and a few more days to discover how little I knew. The

Haul of reef fish, Luf lagoon.
RR Acrylic on canvas

boat had been sturdily built in Holland twenty years before by Nordia, a well-established yard. Comprehensively equipped and beautifully finished, she was a strong, well-found boat with the reassuring bonus of good looks. A steel hull supplied the strength to survive often unavoidable collisions with whales or awash containers, and to escape serious damage if ever we grazed the rocks. A ketch gave the flexibility of two masts; and a reliable engine would be indispensable in areas of little wind. It proved useful in getting off shoals, too, for we were to have several encounters with the seabed. And she possessed a dive compressor, which made it possible to explore the ocean hundreds of miles beyond the reach of commercial dive operations.

The boat arrived with a name derived from the previous owner's family, the sort of amalgamation that, from Wayne and Frankie, would proudly produce Wankie. It had to be changed, something many sailors regard as certain ill luck. Fortunately, despite a childhood under the eye of a nanny who warned direly about the certain

Nereus

disaster that would follow the introduction of a peacock's feather to the house, walking under a ladder or passing on the stairs, I was not superstitious. Touching wood, the boat was renamed *Nereus*, evoking one of the most ancient of the pantheon of Greek gods. Nereus was god of the sea, the grandfather of Achilles and the father of fifty stunning daughters, the Nereids, who pervade much early mythology. Unlike terrible Poseidon, whose power as Earth-shaker eventually increased his portfolio to include Nereus' ocean business, Nereus was an august, gentle sort of deity.

Nereus was provisioned for a long voyage and crew assembled, ever changing while I sought my Nereid, a freedom-loving spirit to appreciate the wonders of the South Seas with me. Once ocean-readied in South West England, *Nereus* sailed for the Pacific, down the coasts of Portugal and Spain, and then Gibraltar and across the Atlantic to Barbados. She wintered in the southern West Indies. After a cruise from Trinidad along the top of South America, successfully avoiding the active pirates of those parts, she emerged through the Bridge of the Americas, which spans the Panama Canal at Balboa, the threshold of the Pacific Ocean.

There was a curious link between my pursuit of paradise and Nereus. Hercules was given an extra labor by King Eurystheus who had found out that he'd done an unacceptable deal over the cleansing of the Augean stables, bringing in help, which, the king decreed, was cheating. It was his penalty labor to fetch apples from the Garden of the Hesperides, a sort of immortals' paradise. Hercules had no idea where to find this garden until he met up with Nereus, who fooled around a while, changing himself into a variety of birds and animals, but eventually calmed down and consented to show him the way. This tale from ancient Greek mythology seemed a propitious omen for my voyage.

Tamelife

EVEN AMONG THE ENDLESS DIVERSITY of Pacific islands, the Galápagos Islands are odd. If qualifying as a fragment of paradise, they are eligible for a particular marvel only, the tamelife. These lava heaps, six hundred miles off the closest bit of South America, are rough and uninviting; yet, there is no place like them to experience the St. Francis of Assisi vision of paradise. Nowhere else are the birds of the air, the animals on the land and the larger inhabitants below the waves tame. Or, rather, equal. Nothing defers to man.

Once, long ago, before the creatures of nature learned to fear the deadliest and most rapacious of them all, much of the world may have been like this—a Garden of Eden where St. Francis could imagine passing the time of day with rabbits and birds and talking the odd wolf out of eating a peasant. Children learning the legends of St. Francis at their mother's knee never guessed that the extraordinary privilege to be with unafraid wild creatures could be granted to ordinary folk. Galápagos iguanas walk over you; mantas and turtles play with you; the sharks and seabirds ignore you. Sea lion puppies are always happy for a game subject to parental consent. Magnificent frigate birds wheel above while boobies, the finest of streamlined divers, arrow into the water beside you from a hundred feet with barely a splash. Pelicans, shearwaters, petrels, Galápagos gulls, mockingbirds, go expertly about their business taking no notice of human interlopers.

Free-riding red-foot boobies

The islands are recently volcanic and rather inhospitable; lava and congealed ash lie everywhere with an occasional covering of thin soil where it has been able to accumulate over the last few thousand years. Several volcanoes remain active, erupting most recently in the 1970s. They are of the flat-topped, sawn-off shield variety with huge calderas and a rash of ash-cone hillocks where magma has escaped. Much of the scrubby endemic flora has now been displaced by introduced species, which find the rich minerals and the location on the equator to their liking. Rampaging passion flower vines are prominent among the invaders.

Half way from Panama, we acquire a number of passengers. One dawn a booby lands precariously on the pulpit after a few preliminary circuits and settles down for a passage home. Another red-foot booby comes in, wheels down, to join the first. Soon there are nine boobies, perched in two stacks on the pulpit rails at the bow, where they sit throughout the day, preening and gossiping between themselves and with each of the crew who go to pass the time of day with them. Come dusk we think we should wish them good-bye in case they were to waddle aft during the night, bringing smelly guano. My polite request, however, from a distance of a foot or so, meets with blank looks: "We will not be moved."

Direct action becomes necessary to break the sit-in. "Cleared for take-off," I say to each, tipping it under the tail so that it overbalances into a shallow dive off the bow. A couple of circuits and they're back again, unwilling to abandon their ferry, coming in at short intervals like a fighter squadron returning from a sortie. A portly lawyer aboard for this leg of the voyage volunteers for scare-booby duty. Stationed on the bow, he fights off repeated raids, trusting that the boobies lack night landing capability and dusk will bring relief. Sometimes, while other birds are mounting a diversion, one slips under his elbow and manages to gain a foothold on the pulpit until it's dislodged with a tail-flip. The persistence of the boobies is successfully resisted until the cover of darkness provides protection from their attentions.

ISLA GENOVESE

A dolphin circus team performing aerial acrobatics welcomes us into Ecuadorian water. Our landfall is an outer island, a long way from the tourist boat mêlée around the central area. At anchor in the huge caldera of an old volcano amid teeming bird-life, there's no sign of humanity. There's a little beach in the corner where I step ashore among several sea lions that don't move. Most stones on the beach are occupied by swallow-tail gulls. They don't move either. Nor do the frigate birds, perched in the fringing bushes along with numbers of red-legged and masked boobies. It's the same with the legion of red and orange crabs and the marine iguanas on the rocks. A sea lion pup a couple of feet long swims through my legs, frolicking on its back and inspecting everything earnestly. When it tires and flops to sleep on a rock, its parents continue the game with us in a little lagoon, a sea lion swimming pool.

A short scramble through some mangroves reveals a colony of frigate birds, the males trying desperately to attract ladies with extraordinary displays of their inflated throat pouches, balloons of bright scarlet. Each bush holds another one. Some have gotten lucky, but the majority look as if they will have to be patient for days yet, waiting to perform a symbolic task: Once a male frigate bird thinks he has an arrangement with a lady, he goes off to gather a twig, which he presents formally to her. She gets the message, and if she consents she sets to building a nest. The frigates, however, are of a larcenous nature, and find it easier to steal the twig from another flying frigate. Terrific aerial battles ensue to secure the baton.

Magnificent frigate displaying

Mockingbirds, grebe-like lava herons, Darwin's finches, gulls, terns and petrels, all are entirely unafraid. Acceptance as just another animal, one that's not scary, conveys an extraordinary sense of peace, of belonging together in a world where aggression and dispute have unaccountably been banished.

Overnight we are joined by Sergey Shcherbakov in a tatty little ketch called *Siberia*. His is a remarkable voyage, surely the only sailor to start a circumnavigation from Omsk in Siberia, 1,700 miles from a sea that is, in any case, the Arctic Ocean, frozen solid most of the year. He gratefully accepts a few vodkas while explaining how he navigated his little boat across the top of Russia. To prove how far north this is, he grabs our inflatable globe to point to Cape Horn, which is less than two thirds of the way from the equator to the South Pole and more than 2,000 miles from it. He spins the globe to show how, to get round the northern point of Siberia, he was within 700 miles of the North Pole. It's something hard to imagine here, in the heat of the equator.

He and his crew are short of funds. "For voyage to be circumnavigation," he says, "boat must cross equator. We were rolled over near Alaska, all masts and rigging broken. Wonderful Americans there mended boat for us, but we used money and have no money for Panama Canal and no time now to sail round Horn, so we cross equator here in Galápagos and will cross back again after one hour. Then we see if we find sponsor to send money for Panama Canal."

We donate the remains of the vodka and hug him *bon voyage*. I hear much later that Sergey and *Siberia* successfully made it back home. They deserved the sort of welcome accorded Ellen McArthur.

A climb to the top of the island as the sun starts its ascent reveals a flock of tame petrels, stormy and otherwise. Brilliant-white masked boobies return our stare, sitting proudly on their ground nests, each brooding two eggs. These birds are raising a curiosity: fratricidal chicks. Nature has ordained that only one of the two

Reach for Paradise

will ever make it and arranged natural selection in a very direct manner. Darwin never, apparently, used the expression "survival of the fittest," but this is its simplest illustration. Having terminated its sibling, the prevailing chick grows into a big soft toy, retaining its baby down until it's a waddling fluff ball the size of its mother.

On another stretch of island, the weird seduction ritual of blue-foot boobies is in progress. This seems to me nature's square dance:

You got these feet of a cerulean blue
To a sexy booby baby that's a most attractive hue
If she wants to get to heaven, make her nest in the Big Dipper
Show that booby lady you've the finest flying flipper

Left foot, right foot, lift 'em high
Make her believe these are feet for which to die
Raise your feet again, march on the spot
Prove the truest bluest feet is what you got

Got her interest now? Strut your stuff
Show that bird that you're real tough
Head held high, and raise your thighs
Those flirty flirty feet will win the booby prize

Stretch out your neck, beak pointed to the sky
Persuade that lady that you can really fly
Spread your wings and whistle your tune
To a booby baby lady that's the way to croon

Now act shy, now act haughty
Make her think you're nice but can be naughty
You may have your evil day if you display
And you cock your tail in a captivating way

If she won't come upstairs yet, you do it all again
She can play darn hard to get, that pretty booby hen
Left foot, right foot, lift 'em high
Make her believe these are feet for which to die

There seems no fear of predators here, though the short-eared owls must eat something. Red-tailed tropic birds trail their elegant paradise tails over us as we ride around in the dinghy. None of the bigger caste of seals, sea lions, sharks and manta rays seem to notice us. An unembarrassed loving sea lion couple can't keep their flippers off each other.

We weigh anchor as dusk is falling over the enchanted island, picking our way out over the reef that nearly closes the entrance to the flooded caldera, and set sail across the equator to Isla Santa Cruz, the civilization hub of the Galápagos. Early morning brings the rousing sight of a tribe of sea lions off to their feeding grounds, checking us out on their way northeast. Half a dozen pass close under the transom, apparently racing, pounding past like galloping horses in a tight field.

ISLA SANTA CRUZ

The connection with Charles Darwin, reports of wildlife that is not wild and their remote grandeur endow the Galápagos Islands with an aura of enchantment. Success in finding the spell of the place, however, depends how a visitor manages his visit. It is easy to get in the hands of a bad tour company, spend too much, or be limited to much-trampled visitor sites. The two towns must be treated with particular caution, for rip-off merchants abound. Among the collection of small shops, administrative offices and eating places forming Puerto Ayora in Academy Bay, misleading information is frustrating as we try to arrange a trip on a local vessel. To travel around on our own boat with a hired guide is possible only at prohibitive cost. We book a tour, but there is a last minute hassle.

The operator informs us with desolated gestures, "Ah, Señor, I am so sorry. The *Cruz del Sur* has been canceled. There is something wrong with the engines. All passengers are being found other vessels."

We perforce transfer our booking to a scruffy-sounding larger craft called *Tropic Sun*. When we join the "first class vessel," which has some fifty cramped berths, the *Cruz del Sur*, the "canceled" boat, is moored nearby. We watch in wrath as it loads up and sails off with a full complement of passengers.

The Darwin Research Institute provides a haven for a few of the giant tortoises that gave the Galápagos their name. Like Darwin's finches, a different species of tortoise once evolved on each island, and, where it could obtain specimens, the Institute has been breeding them for release back to the originating islands. Two are at work fulfilling this purpose, an amorous process that appears to continue for days. Many species are gone, however, extinguished in past centuries by pirates and whalers stopping at the Galápagos to stock up. The islands were a wild frontier place where passing crews collected the gentle reptiles by the hundred and stacked them upside-down in ships' holds, alive, to provide easy meat for the voyage ahead. "The land-turtle are here so numerous that 5 or 600 men might subsist on them alone for several months without any other sort of provision: they are extraordinary large and fat; and so sweet that no pullet eats more pleasantly," wrote William Dampier of his visit on a pirate ship in 1684.

Some sailors jumped ship and stayed for years. One Creole soldier somehow obtained a deed from Peru to one of the islands and set himself up as its king, recorded with heavy irony in Herman Melville's stories, *Las Encantadas*, published 1854 when the episode was still current:

> Safely debarked at last, the company under direction of their lord and patron forthwith proceed to build their capital city. They make considerable advance in the way of walls of clinkers and lava floors, nicely sanded with cinders. On the least barren hills they pasture their cattle, while the goats, adventurers by nature, explore the far inland solitudes for a scanty livelihood of lofty herbage.

Galápagos fauna and flora are seriously endangered by introduced species that prey on them or destroy their habitat. Goats, cats, pigs and dogs have gone wild. Rats, mice and insects have wrought havoc. Diseases and alien plants have gained solid footholds. The Darwin Institute has the task of eradicating the interlopers, challenging when, for instance, there have been more than 50,000 feral goats on a single island. The fragile ecology is also threatened by illegal fishing and population growth set to double in less than twelve years, much of it immigration from the mainland of Ecuador, attracted by the money of the 100,000 tourists who arrive each year.

On a bank of lava boulders, about a hundred sea lions and their offspring are sunning themselves. We play with them in the water, the most charming and friendly beasts imaginable. The colony on the rocks ignores us and carries on with life, suckling, flirting, playing and talking, regularly emitting sounds that vary from a fat man's contented belch after a good lunch to the raucous lowing of an angry cow, this last apparently signaling us to go away,

Sea lion pup

though not very sincerely. When one chases me, the effort is shortly followed by a flop-out. It's all too much exertion in the heat. The cubs gallop on the sand and gallivant in the water, clearly possessed of a high level of gaming instinct.

The colony is deeply into the leisure business, and a snorkel expedition reveals the reason. The bay is teeming with vast numbers of fish that even a thousand sea lions and the tame sharks cannot much reduce. Lunch takes little effort. Below the waves, eagle rays and green turtles are happy to swim with us, and the sea lions in their element are superbly graceful. There are land iguanas here too, apparently subsisting on a form of opuntia, a tree cactus, which did not like being eaten by iguanas and has accordingly evolved to be ten feet high with smooth, unclimbable trunks. The land iguanas, thwarted by this unfair turn of events, now appreciate the naturally selected Darwin finches, which drop morsels down to them. I presume this opuntia to be the "dildoe-tree, a green prickly shrub that grows about ten or twelve feet high, without either leaf or fruit. It is as big as a man's leg, from the root to the top, and it is full of sharp prickles growing in thick rows from top to bottom," which William Dampier described here and named rather imaginatively.

The finches are drab little birds, yet the varied beaks of the thirteen species that evolved between the islands were responsible for inspiring Darwin's earth-shaking theory of natural selection after the *Beagle* spent just five weeks in these islands.

We watch in awe as a team of blue-foot boobies lines up like a fighter squadron about to attack. They wheel over and hit the water in sequence at exact intervals. A blowhole puffs spray a hundred feet into the air, sometimes complete with a misguided flying crab. The prehistoric marine iguanas, which can spend up to an hour underwater to obtain their diet of algae, pose for us with their crests erect when not engaged with lovemaking and nesting. Iguanas seem rather casual about leaving their eggs to hatch on their own. The frigate birds know this and watch carefully for an opportunity to steal them. We observe from a few feet away as a frigate, an imposing presence not much smaller than a wandering albatross, boasting the greatest wing-to-weight ratio in the avian world and possibly the only sea-bird unable to swim, steals an egg amid loud protest, and then returns for the last one and swoops off with yellow yolk dribbling from its beak and a satisfied look in its eye. A little way off, half a dozen albatrosses sit on their nests, unconcerned with us. These huge birds normally live in high latitudes, but one dissenting species has decided the equator is the place to breed.

ISLA ISABELA

Puerto Villamil is the only settlement on the island of Isabela, a little village with a tight anchorage inside some rocks. It's dominated by an impressive caldera, fully 6 miles from one side to the other. Calderas like this were formed by explosions, usually the sudden meeting of white-hot magma with underground water. Even in these days of nuclear weapons, it's near impossible to visualize the elemental force that will blow the top off a mountain 6 miles across. Yet, in Sumatra, there is a 60-mile lake called Toba thought to be excavated by an explosion 75,000 years ago that ejected more than 600 cubic miles of material, possibly wiping out most plants and animals over the face of the world and perhaps all but a few thousand of the entire proto-human race. Existence on earth is indeed fragile.

Sitting on a rock by the shore with an iguana staring me out from its perch on my foot as a bright red Sally Lightfoot crab crawls over its back and with a couple of sea lion pups scrapping in mock battle in the mangroves by my elbow, I reflect that there

Marine iguana

are few such moments of utter harmony with nature in an average life. In the anchorage are dozens of sea lions playing and fishing, squadrons of boobies and pelicans diving, magnificent frigate birds soaring overhead. A decrepit wooden boat rotting on an anchor a few yards away has a whole crew of sea lions, athletically leaping several feet out of the water to sunbathe on its deck.

There is one final show: As we weave through offshore reefs out of the bay, a hundred or more dolphins give a synchronized display, a line of them like beaters leaping six or seven feet clear of the water. It may be an organized fishing maneuver, but I think these dolphins are jumping for the sheer joy of entertaining us.

The Land of Men

MARQUESAS ISLANDS

The first shaft of the May sun, rising gloriously astern for the nineteenth time since we last saw land, illuminates a misty mountain peak, no bigger than a fingernail, still forty miles off. Great swells, nurtured by thousands of uninterrupted sea miles caressed by the southeast trade winds, rock us gently onward as the crags and buttresses of Fatu Hiva heave slowly from the sea. We know our position on the vast blue expanse to the nearest few feet, thanks to the Pentagon's generosity with its global positioning system; yet it's a spellbinding moment, after many days at sea, to sight this reputed piece of paradise.

To my crew of three, all sailing deep blue waters for the first time, it seems a near miracle as seabirds at last signal the proximity of islands and those first pinnacles of Polynesia prick the western horizon. A greater expanse of the planet's surface than the total of all its lands is taken up by the Pacific Ocean, and we are in the middle of it. There's a feeling of abandoning civilization and heading for the moon, so remote are the continental masses of the world. Behind us is Mexico, about three thousand miles away; to our left South America, three and a half thousand. Ahead, Australia is more than four and a half thousand miles off; and to our right, Japan six thousand miles away. The specks of land ahead are part of a huge territory. From these Marquesas in the east to

Maupihaa in the west, and from the Society Islands to the southern Tuamotus and the Australs, French Polynesia covers about three million square miles. That's half the size of China. Islands of every sort await within this area, widely varied though sharing a century and a half of Frenchification and a Polynesian kinship among their peoples and languages.

FATU HIVA

That the Marquesas are spectacular is well known; yet I am not prepared for the towering mountains of Fatu Hiva rising directly from the deep sea, looming high to the heavens as we near them. Green slopes and rugged crags are capped by summits more than half a mile high that look steep even for goats. This is tropical alpine scenery of savage beauty, a landscape that would seem improbable as a stage set for *South Pacific* itself.

We round the bottom of the island, and, now sheltered from the force of the trade winds that have safely blown us across thousands of miles of empty ocean, continue up the west coast seeking Hanavave, a little village that will be our haven for a few days. The sea calms in the lee of the island, and the downwind rolling that has cradled us in a rock-a-bye-baby fashion for three weeks ceases at last. We anchor in a cleft in this high country, a small beach at its apex and hills rising sharply to a thousand feet all around except for the narrow valley running inland for half a mile before it lifts to the higher mountain above.

Hanavave is a cluster of dwellings in the *Baie des Vierges*, the Bay of the Virgins, according to French charts. Pacific missionaries objected to the original French name, *Baie des Verges,* and doctored it. *Verges* mean dicks, phalli, and are entirely appropriate for this place. On the nearest slopes rise fantastical rocks, pinnacles one or two hundred feet high, in weird shapes from which a little imagination can also make figures, or *tupapau*, the fearsome ghosts of these islands, which keep the populace indoors at night. "Their realm is in the heart of the mountain, which the forest surrounds with eternal shadows. There it swarms with them, and without cease their legions are increased by the spirits of those who have died," Paul Gauguin's girlfriend, Tehura, had related to him.

Everything is green and lush, with coconut palms clinging to precipitous ledges all about. In the valley stands a little church and a scattering of single story houses half hidden in luxuriant gardens, in the lane are welcoming Marquesans and laughing children. The people are tall and handsome, their glowing sienna skin shades hinting of Polynesian forbears tempered with blood of whalers and missionaries.

Six hundred people now live in this eight-mile long island, but it is so steep that only two small bays are habitable, and the track connecting them runs ten miles, although the beeline route is but two.

The islands' name stems from the Spanish explorer, de Mendaña, who came upon them in 1595 and tactfully immortalized the wife of his patron, the Marques Garcia de Mendoza, an early viceroy of Peru. Despite an American who named the group *Washington* and a seditious Frenchman who wanted it called *Les Isles de la Revolution,* the Spanish name stuck in its shortened form, but the real, ancient Polynesian name has also survived, Te 'Enua Enata, The Land of Men, which well expresses the fortitude of the people who covered vast distances in canoes to colonize these islands about two thousand years ago. The Polynesians who first found and peopled the Hawaiian chain came in their canoes from Te 'Enua Enata, another almost unbelievable uninterrupted voyage of discovery of two-and-a-half-thousand miles to the northwest, across the windless belt of the equator.

Álvaro de Mendaña, 1542– 1595

A handful of small boats sporting a variety of flags ride at anchor in the little bay. For each it's a special landfall after the achievement of three thousand or even five thousand miles at sea, so in excellent spirits we join other crews in Rosa's house to dine on taro and pickled shark in coconut-cream sauce.

Fatu Hiva seems magical, a sort of Narnia in summer. We run up the valleys under the coconut and breadfruit trees, flowering plants everywhere. A tall waterfall an hour's rocky climb up a goat track through old forest provides a shower and a shampoo. A boulder pool in the streambed serves as a first bath for weeks. The valley appears to have been cultivated from time to time since nature reclaimed it after nearly two thousand years of man, though no great effort is now made to gather fallen coconuts for copra. The hedges round a few paddocks are of hibiscus, grown for rope woven from its bark. The Fatu-Hivans pick for us lemons, bananas and *pamplemousses,* pomelo relations of grapefruit, perhaps the world's most delicious citrus. The owner of the single tiny store

The Land of Men

Nereus, Baie des Verges, Fatu Hiva

asks for cartridges as barter for a chicken. Some shotgun cartridges mysteriously came with the boat—perhaps the previous Swiss owner used to pot seagulls from the poop—and I worried that some customs agent might chance upon them and take the boat to pieces looking for a nonexistent undeclared gun. There is no gun aboard, though the decision was close in view of the pirates along our route that everybody wanted to warn me about.

The owner of the chicken has a rifle, so no deal. Elsewhere a hand mirror acquires some eggs, and there's a welcome baker whose open-air oven manages half a dozen loaves at a time. Rosa's little house doubles as the restaurant, if one orders a few hours beforehand to give her time to dispatch hunters and gatherers for ingredients.

HIVA OA

Reluctantly leaving magnificent Fatu Hiva with its wild horses and goats dotting the high meadows, we stop for the night in a deserted bay off a white crescent beach backed by palms spreading up the hills. Opalescent clouds pour off the heights of the island; the wavelets lapping the silvery sand are lit by the full moon shining through one gap and then another. The Southern Cross seems to have arranged a hole in the clouds all to itself.

The morning is spent spearfishing for the table. A large manta ray and a couple of five-foot sharks swim by. Like most, I was conditioned to dread sharks long before Steven Spielberg terrified the world with *Jaws*. Failure to overcome a shark phobia would, however, condemn one to stay out of the tropical waters of the Pacific, for they abound everywhere far enough from Asia and its suppliers to avoid the disastrous slaughter and "finning" for soup for the Chinese. In practice, it is very rare that sharks prove a real hazard close inshore, for they have no need to change their menu from the plentiful fish. They are certainly curious, but not usually aggressive toward swimmers, and any change of intention is well signaled. Nevertheless the lifetime propaganda against these fish has me combating the immediate adrenaline rush each time we share a reef by reminding me that the chance of becoming shark bait is far less than being struck by lightning. Annually, worldwide, there are fewer than sixty recorded shark attacks. While humans slaughter more than sixty million sharks a year, sharks kill only five or six humans. These University of Florida findings stress how extraordinarily a minor hazard can be exaggerated by hysterical media hype. Most sharks we meet are in any case white-tips, black-tips and reef sharks, which have passably good reputations, though a Marquesan boy with a chunk missing from his thigh tells me ruefully, "I was hand-feeding a black-tip, and it got upset when I started stroking its nose."

Hiva Oa, one of the two larger Marquesas Islands, has a gendarmerie that deals with the formalities of arrival in French Polynesia. Off its capital village, Atuona, dolphins give a spectacular leaping display, something that seems to be getting rarer. Whaling and the devastating drift nets of the fishing fleets, specially the purse seiners, are to blame, for not long ago these waters were alive with cetaceans. Having a drink on a large catamaran a few days later, I tax the Japanese *catelaine* with this.

"No, no," she insists. "The Japanese never eat dolphins anymore."

A gentle mention that the slaughter is often the incidental result of dragging massive walls of nets across the ocean after other prey, that dolphin meat is usually labeled whale, and that just one Japanese village, Taiji, kills tens of thousands of dolphins annually, draws a blank look.

To most sailors, dolphins are almost pets. We talk to them as they roll in our bow wave. We swim with them. They delight in showing us their exquisite skills. We believe they converse among themselves and feel genuinely friendly toward us. In another

Marquesans — Paul Gauguin

ocean, dolphins helped rescue the ship's cat, which had fallen overboard, shepherding it back to the ladder. Killing a dolphin for food would feel like eating one's labrador.

Atuona has a harbor sheltered by a breakwater, half a dozen stores, a post office and a tiny bank with an ATM. The scene is faultless. The village nestling behind a beach at the top of a horseshoe bay is surrounded by green mountains dropping straight to the sea. An islet covered in luxuriant growth shelters the bay from the ocean, and flowering trees and plants bust out of the gardens. Up a short steep hill, a little cemetery containing the grave of Paul Gauguin commands the finest view over the water. "After the disease of civilization, life in this new world is a return to health," Gauguin wrote before he died in this, his final attempt, to find his own version of paradise.

My bike, lashed to *Nereus*' rail for thousands of ocean miles, is rusty. After an infusion of oil, it is able to manage the dirt road to the southwest of the island where a narrow valley leads to a ruined city tucked under Mount Temetiu, the vertical green monster glowering over Atuona beneath a permanent hat of thick cloud. There's no one around all day except the odd Marquesan working in a desultory fashion on the roads, an occupation paid by Brussels, which seems to provide more than half the employment in the outer islands of French Polynesia. The partly cleared jungle site holds huge stone platforms, impressive ceremonial concourses and a great mass of organized stonework, which must have been living quarters for the *arii*, the priestly semi-royal caste charged with the religious and civil management of Polynesian society, the whole occupying perhaps ten to twenty acres. The fallen grandeur bears eloquent witness to the great days of the Land of Men, before the sails of the white men hoved over the horizon, bringing destruction.

Living off the land, drinking from streams and immersing myself in one when it gets hot, I lunch off too many wild mangoes for the good of my gastric juices. Though they surely belonged to a family, the mangoes, limes, papayas and all the other untended fruit trees were abandoned once the tribes of the valley were obliterated by the White Men's Curse of imported disease. It rains steadily all morning, except when it rains hard. The jungle is alive with birdsong, led by the raucous crowing of feral fowl, the progeny of chickens that did a successful chicken run long ago. It is dangerous too, with the fruit of huge trees heavy with rain crashing to the ground without warning all around. Besides coconuts, there are some that look like enormous onions, and others like giant acorns with clusters of yellow fruit like apricots making machine-gun bursts as they hit the ground. Any one of the fruits bombing down from the canopy would brain an unfortunate target. A pervasive pungent smell, which I at first suspect to be fermenting guava or mango windfalls, on closer inspection emanates from big yellow fruits that come from huge trees with ash-like fronds well over a hundred feet up. These remind me of the Marula trees of Africa, which, to elephants' delight, drop already fermenting fruits. For a week or so each year there is a giant party, elephants staggering all over the place, followed by a serious hangover in the bush. Here in the Pacific, there are no native mammals save bats to appreciate the manna.

At the eastern end of the island, Puamau is home to some rare surviving big *tikis*. We are taken by a descendant of the king of that part of the island—so Pépérou claims—who has deep feelings for his Polynesian tradition and an unconcealed disdain of the French colonists.

"In the year 1842, a French naval ship sailed in to Traitors' Bay," Pépérou relates in French, referring to our present anchorage. "Wading ashore with carbines loaded, the marines from the ship intimidated and mistreated the people of the village. The king was captured, and humiliated for days. The French soldiers laid him down and made the women of the village walk on his head. They had discovered that his hair was sacred, considered so sacrosanct that anyone who touched it was immediately put to death. His warriors wanted to rise up against the invaders who defiled their

king thus, but he wisely advised them to take no defensive action, as without guns the Hiva Oans would be slaughtered.

"Some of the warriors secretly decided to disobey. They prepared a big party on the beach and invited the French, telling them this was traditional. At first the French were cautious, but a few bolder officers investigated and reported back that all was well. Eventually the captain himself arrived to partake of the great feast, which was laid out on banana leaves on the sand. The food was piled high, every sort of fish, vegetable and fruit, but the captain observed that there was no meat. He inquired what sort of meat would be furnished. The warriors replied, 'You are the meat,' and set upon the French whom they killed to a man, before going to release the king and restore his dignity. The French were casseroled and eaten."

I idly wonder whether this story was known to Noël Coward. When watching the 1953 coronation parade in London, he was asked who might be the small man in a bowler hat seated beside the statuesque Queen Salote of Tonga who was passing by in a magnificent state carriage. "Lunch," he muttered, after considering the matter.

The trail through the rich vegetation across the mountains and ravines of the island reveals dramatic views at every turn. Pépérou points out rosewood trees used by the Marquesans for their superb carving, named for a delicate aroma of roses that emanates from freshly cut bark, a palm whose powder-puff flowers are surrounded by the little leaves that provide the Marquesans with scent, flamboyants with crowns overwhelmed in scarlet flowers. Sometimes, quite carried away with the delights of his land, both Pépérou's hands weave his words in the air rather than clutching the steering wheel, making me distinctly nervous on the most precipitous dirt road I have traveled anywhere. It often falls away vertically to the raging sea. The *Kon-Tiki* sailor, Thor Heyerdahl, wrote of traveling this road in 1932:

The art of Marquesan tattooing

> Suddenly the trail turned sharply to the left through a short pass which brought us out on the other side of the ridge and we faced a new precipice. Here too the air currents roared up from below. Another bay with white surf lay below us, with a drop as terrifying as the one we had just left on our other side. Then the rock wall opened up again. There was a mountain peak in front, and another behind. Between them passed an edge so sharp that the trail filled it completely. On either side our stirrups dangled above slopes that ran into nothing except the bands of surf far below.

High up a valley at Puamau is an ancient site, the sacred meeting place of seven tribes. On stone platforms, a number of *tikis*, the wondrously stylized Polynesian statues of their gods with hugely exaggerated features, have somehow survived onslaught by missionaries. The tallest, maybe 1,600 years old, is eight feet high, apparently the largest *tiki* outside Easter Island. Sitting in its shadow, Pépérou talks of the old customs, of tattooing and the tribal initiation of the adolescents:

Ancient tikis of Puamau

"A lady would be chosen to test the boy's manhood in front of all the people. If she remained unsatisfied the tattoos would not be made. But if she was successful in showing that he was truly now a man, he was immediately taken to be circumcised. A priest would do this, using two hot stones and a sharpened bamboo. Then the high priest, amid much feasting, would start the tattooing of the lucky lad, a process which might last for days...."

The tattoos reflected the warrior status of men, and would cover most of the body after many valiant deeds. Killjoy missionaries naturally banned tattooing along with other pleasures, but now, once again, the Marquesans are proudly patterned, their skin works of art covered in intricate geometrical representations of traditional design, applied over long and painful hours with wooden needles and hammer.

Despite surroundings as lovely as anything the world has to offer, there's a pervading sadness in these islands. For nothing substantial remains of their rich inheritance except the land. The Marquesans were annihilated by a dreadful concurrence of Peruvian blackbirders, French soldiers who sometimes slaughtered Polynesians for practice, Christian missionaries competing for souls, Americans providing guns, whalers running amok, and a gallimaufry of irresistible diseases. This hellish brew reduced the pre-missionary population by more than 96 percent. I have to work the reciprocal of the number to understand its impact. A typical town of 2,500 Polynesians was reduced to 100. Each survivor had to bury 24. Every son or mother was stripped of family and friends. The social structures and balances established over two thousand years were shattered. The plagues of Europe and the Black Death were never such grand instruments of extermination. Into this desolate void, missionaries scattered evangelical seeds where they could corrupt a chief. Following the successful example of Queen Pomare in Tahiti, many doubtless explained the holocaust overtaking the islands as just retribution for the many sins of the ignorant heathen. Perhaps they claimed that God moved in mysterious ways when a sufficient explanation for a dreadful death from measles proved difficult, TB claimed an entire family or the suffering from syphilis became tricky to justify. The native population, at one time well below 2,000, is now barely back above 10 percent of its pre-contact peak of about 80,000 people.

The *tikis* were overthrown, the children of the chiefs forcibly removed for education, the old ways deliberately eradicated and the ancient culture dismembered, leaving nothing except stories handed down by the few fathers lucky enough to have a grandson or nephew alive, piles of anonymous stones and a few sad damaged stone figures of the old gods. That the persuasion of the missionaries was successful is witnessed by ubiquitous churches and their near 100 percent attendance. One Marquesan pithily tells me, "How curious it is that the people who destroyed our ancient culture now appear to pay their religion very little attention."

A Londoner for much of my adult life, I feel a wave of embarrassment that the first of these damaging spiritual invaders was a group from the London Missionary Society, no doubt courageous and well meaning, who sailed in 1797 for Polynesia on a ship named *The Duff*.

The missionaries were followed by the whalers, often from New Bedford and Nantucket, whose heyday was the first half of the nineteenth century. Wild sailors ashore after long, tough periods at sea, glad of the safe days, good food and available women, brought further lethal doses of disease. The crew of the *Essex* under Lieutenant Porter was recorded as devastating Hiva Oa in 1812 and Nuku Hiva in 1813. This American naval frigate coincidentally shared a name with the old whaleship *Essex* sunk by a great whale near the Galápagos Islands a few years later, the incident that inspired Melville's *Moby Dick*.

In one respect it took a while for the old ways to yield to missionary zeal. Cannibalism survived until almost the end of Queen Victoria's reign, and the last known Marquesan cannibal was still alive in the middle of the twentieth century. This reluctant evolution of eating habits may have been connected with a bizarre symbiosis between missionaries and cannibals. To the indigenous peoples, missionaries were not only impertinent interlopers and food, but helped to foster an incipient sense of nationhood against the invading foreigners; while, for the missionary societies, cannibal stories were top-rate fundraising material, excellent grist for the collection-plate mill back home. That cannibalism eventually faded away may have been due to the destruction of the Marquesan population and their proud culture as much as any missionary edification.

Pépérou, uniformed incongruously in white socks and tennis shorts as he tells of ancestral customs, comes up with another nugget from his lore store: "When there was a quarrel between neighboring tribes, the chiefs had to fight. The warriors of each chief would sit in silence as the battle progressed. When one chief prevailed, he forced his opponent to his knees, and, once in this position, he cut off his head. He had to be kneeling, for if this was done to a standing foe his *mana*, the supernatural power with which chiefs and priests are endowed, would remain with the fellow. The warriors of both winning and vanquished chiefs remained silent and still as the cooks then prepared the head, boiling it in a great pot. Once done to a turn, it was presented with due ceremony to the conquering chief. He first ate the mouth of his foe, thus to gain his authority. Next came his eyes, thereby adopting his knowledge. The skull was thereupon split open so the brains of the loser could be consumed, which had the effect of conferring his *mana* and wisdom on his vanquisher. These tidbits (*"bonnes bouches"*) so empowered the chief that the loyalty of the warriors of the loser as well as his lands transferred to him, and thus his army grew large."

We weigh anchor at first light to sail the seventy-five miles to Ua Pou, but there's no wind blowing outside the bay. I therefore put *Nereus* into a lonely inlet on the northwest coast of Hiva Oa to wait for better sailing weather, anchoring in a deserted valley enclosed by high, rugged hills. A walk reveals an astonishing abandoned civilization, overgrown and forgotten. Great platforms, walls and many acres of dwellings have been swallowed up by plant life. No archaeologist or restorer has mucked around with it, and we share it only with wild horses. I presume Hanamenu, as the bay is labeled on my chart, thrived for a thousand years or more, but with the near-annihilation of the Polynesian population, was abandoned in the nineteenth century. This is the remains of a stone-age culture that had no writing, and made no stone monuments except *tikis*. Any *tikis* that survived the missionaries and European collectors are gone, buried for safety or stolen long ago. Very little is known about these remains.

Wondering where else in the world can anyone but an archaeologist feel the undisturbed spirit of such ancient works, I pick my way along a raised, boulder-paved, ceremonial way running from the beach up the center of the valley. I hear a tinkle of falling water. Wielding a bush-knife to clear a path through encroaching undergrowth toward the sound, I come upon a waterfall tumbling into a small crystal pool under a spreading breadfruit tree. It's surrounded by hibiscus and bananas, and a sweet-scented white flower grows on a shrub beside it. The scene is a Pre-Raphaelite fantasy, a film set for nymphs. Bathing naked in the pool and drinking draughts of cool water from the cascade emerging from an underground source in the mountainside, I need but a girl and a snake for this to be the Garden of Eden—though I could dispense with the snake.

The island bush even lacks any aggressive vegetation that pricks or stings, apart from little beach-burrs, so shoes are never needed. In practice biting insects—mosquitoes, no-see-ums, nonos—break the spell, but these seem to have been imported with the arrival of sailing boats from the 1800s onwards, so one day this spot may have been an insect-free veritable paradise, the preserve of a king, pampered in his pool by his harem of beautiful girls and served by his court of *arii*.

We're content to stay longer in this place when wind fails the next day too. We can find no surviving access overland, just horse and pig paths within the thickets. At least six great stone ceremonial platforms lie among the overgrown, tumbled remains of walls, roads and culverts. Most structures would have been built of wood and leaf, long ago reverted to dust, but the stone clues imply that a substantial city once occupied this hidden valley. And these were no mean buildings. One had walls four feet thick and now five feet high, but I cannot tell what further height lies buried under the accumulations of soil. Another measures 100 x 200 feet with no internal divisions. I guess that the walls were once surmounted by poles on which a roof of nipa thatch was laid, and the whole

Hanamenu, once a great city...

supported by a range of internal wooden columns; it must have been a splendid edifice.

Right by this building grows an ancient banyan tree of huge proportions. Banyans are murderers, of the *ficus* family, that lodge upon an innocent tree and drop aerial roots. Once these touch the ground and start to take nourishment, the banyan grows around its host and strangles it. Eventually the original host tree is asphyxiated, leaving its assassin the field. This particular tree has a five-foot space in the middle where its foster-parent once stood, and its multiple trunks have a spread of about forty feet. Banyans were sacred. Their convoluted torsos and high branches were the resting place of the bones of kings and chiefs, who thereby kept watch over tribal affairs long after they were gone. It is sometimes possible to locate the ruins of an old village by its great banyan tree.

Though this city of Hanamenu was surely a magnificent place in its heyday, none of our Polynesian guides or pilot books has anything to say about it.

I swim once more in the limpid Narcissus fountain, and wash my hair and a bucket of clothes under the cascade. There are guavas, limes and pamplemousses to be gathered by the spring, which has been messed up by wild pigs in the night.

The best things usually have a catch. Next day I'm covered in thousands of bites. Eden's itch. Like a poxy rash, it irritates dreadfully for five days before fading. The miniscule nono culprits are truly no-see-ums. I had no idea I was being eaten up as I dreamt by the idyllic pool.

UA POU

The anchor's raised at three o'clock in the morning, so we can make the sixty-two miles to Ua Pou in the likely light airs. Sheeting showers blot out the craggy coast as we sail into its small haven alongside *Aranui*, the vessel that has the monthly job of carting Marquesas supplies plus a few adventurous passengers from Tahiti. Peeking into the stack of red containers unloaded onto the quayside, I'm distressed to see that this island group of endlessly beautiful running water is importing caseloads of Volvic mineral water from France along with all the cola, lemonade and so on without which people seem unable to manage in even the most faraway places. Every test seems to demonstrate that even filtered municipal water is better than bottled mineral water, yet the crazy spread of the notion that anything worthwhile must be packaged seems unstoppable, even here.

The harbor town of Hakehau on Ua Pou nestles in the shadow of spectacular *aiguilles*, thin spikes of rock thrusting vertically through the horizon to a height of four thousand feet. Happily there's a clinic by the church, for my right leg is swollen like a sausage, a staphylococcus infection from a mosquito bite weeks ago. Rain thundering on the tin roof of the clinic drowns out my explanation at the desk, so I sit back and observe. There's a lovely woman with a tattooed ankle wearing a tiare over an ear. It's above her left ear unfortunately, which indicates she is spoken for. Everyone over about thirty is overweight; the men with substantial bellies. They remind me of Paul Theroux's rather caustic assertion, in his book researched when canoeing in the South Pacific, that Polynesian men and women over this sort of age become progressively indistinguishable. The clinic is clean, efficient and free, and dispenses me powerful oral antibiotics and children's anti-inflammatories, as they've run out of adult doses along with all topical antibiotic treatments. After half an hour and an inch or two, the rain stops abruptly and the sun emerges, gleaming on the drenched mango leaves outside. A vivid rainbow arcs over the village, framing the soaring *aiguilles*.

NUKU HIVA

I have to turn down a musical passenger, a Marquesan from the *Ballet Orchestre de Paris* asking for a ride to Tahiti, as we are making for Nuku Hiva, the biggest of the Marquesas Islands. It's a pity, as two crew have flown home, leaving me with only Sam until my son joins us in the Tuamotos. Sam is a slender, blond Englishman whose chief accomplishment at twenty-one years of age is a Don Juan record of conquests. He seems to be able to scent a boat with an unattached female on board from a great distance. His father dispatched Sam to me with a request to make a sailor of him, a task I'm finding elusive.

The Baie du Controleur proves to be a magnificent haven at the top of a long, three-fingered inlet, deserted except for the *Aranui*, with which we have again caught up. Now by longboat it is supplying a scattering of huts behind the beach. Sam demonstrates a second talent, concocting banana daiquiris from an aging rack of bananas with the help of fresh limes, Colombian rum and a Mediterranean liqueur found at the bottom of a locker. We celebrate a sublimely quiet anchorage, the first for many weeks.

The novelist Herman Melville arrived as crew of a whaler and jumped ship in the Marquesas, where his life with the Polynesians in this valley formed the basis for his 1846 bestseller, *Typee*. Sam and I walk inland to look for traces of Melville's tale. His hopes raised by Melville's seductive description of his sexy heroine Fayaway, Sam is disappointed when we find the Taipivai valley near deserted. For a few miles, semi-cultivated fields dotted with a few farm shacks are bordered by ridges clothed heavily in vine-clad trees, but there are no indications of the clans of thousands who once thrived here. Then an old taro farmer with bent back and wispy beard points us through some ragged gardens toward an imperceptible path up the side of the mountain. As it leaves cultivation and enters the forest, the muddy track becomes boulder-lined, and it's possible to make out that once, long ago, this was an important road. It climbs through the forest, winding steadily upward until eventually it debouches into a small clearing on a high shelf of the mountainside. Overarched by the branches of great trees, two *me'ae*, dressed stone platforms, stand out from the undergrowth. Each is still guarded by a number of *tikis* that have somehow survived destruction and theft to remain on duty, presiding over memories. Melville may have climbed up to this place, for he wrote this in *Typee:*

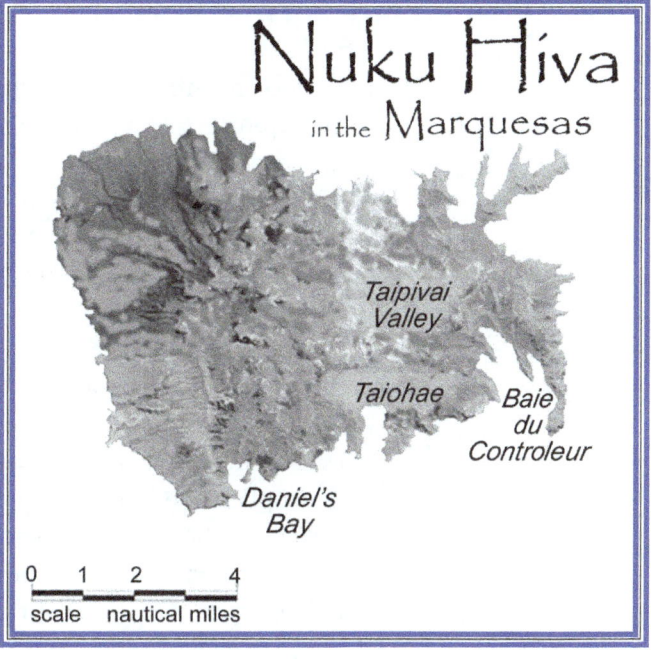

> Our journey was soon at an end; for scaling a sudden height, we came abruptly upon the place of our destination. Here were situated the taboo groves of the valley–the scene of many a prolonged feast, of many a horrid rite. Beneath the dark shadows of the consecrated bread-fruit trees there reigned a solemn twilight—a cathedral-like gloom. The frightful genius of pagan worship seemed to brood in silence over the place, breathing its spell upon every object around. Here and there, in the depths of these awful shades, half screened from sight by masses of overhanging foliage, rose the idolatrous altars of the savages, built of enormous blocks of black and polished stone, placed one upon the other, without cement, to the height of twelve or fifteen feet, and surmounted by a rustic open temple, enclosed with a low picket of canes, within which might be seen, in various stages of decay, offerings of bread-fruit and cocoanuts, and the putrefying relics of some recent sacrifice. In the midst of the wood was the hallowed "hoolah hoolah" ground—set apart for the celebration of the fantastic religious ritual of these people—comprising an extensive oblong pi-pi, terminating at either end in a lofty terraced altar, guarded by ranks of hideous wooden idols.

The wooden idols are long gone, but the stone *tikis* endure, antique, weathered and amputated. Each has only a stump where its erect manhood was chopped off by offended missionaries. With luck they will be allowed to remain in this remote spot, as Polynesians consider that *tikis* get angry if moved. The *tikis* must have been unruffled about the violent loss of their organs, though, if the missionaries were permitted to thrive.

At the end of the day we sail on to Taiohae, the scattered principal town in Nuku Hiva. A bakery is turning out excellent baguettes, croissants and brioches, which is the rule in all French territories, but there is no butcher. Meat comes from hunting your own wild *chèvre* or *sanglier*. Taiohae is another majestic bay, a mile-deep thumb of water wrapped within the towering remains of three quarters of a volcano, " in whimsically contorted shapes," as the French writer Pierre Loti saw it, weathered into sharp ridges, peaks and spires, all clothed in multilayered greenery.

All was not always so peaceful, as the local missionary Rev. Robert Thomson recorded in *The Marquesas Islands* published 1841:

> A few weeks ago a sacrifice was offered here to propitiate the deity, that he would cause rain to descend and breadfruit to grow. The victim on this occasion was a boy, seized upon the island of Hiva Oa. The head was severed from the body, which was taken to a tabued place and hung upon a tree. A smaller cooked pig was hung up with the body that the spirit of the boy might in the world of spirits live upon the spirits of the pig and the breadfruit. It is now hanging upon the tree, about ten minutes walk from our dwelling.

Loti, a pseudonymous French naval officer who wrote the classic *Le Mariage de Loti*, met Vaekehu, the last queen of Nuku Hiva, here in 1872. He recorded that she was formerly something of a cannibal, and wondered at the fundamental transition taking place: "The thoughts that contort the strange face of the Queen remain a mystery to all… Does she mourn for her independence, and the savagery which is disappearing, and her people who are degenerating and becoming estranged from her?…This deposed queen, with her great shock of coarse hair and her silent pride, still retains a certain grandeur."

An underworked clerk in the *mairie*, which stands on the site of Queen Vaekehu's little palace, introduces us to Patrice, who keeps a few horses in the mountains. From neighboring boats, a Dutch girl and a Welshman, who travels everywhere with a huge red flag bearing a Welsh dragon, join Sam and me at dawn to take a car that winds up the vertical mountainside, the only road out of Taiohea, to a small lean-to in a clearing, where we brush the mud off some horses and climb on.

A horse or perhaps a bicycle is the best method to feel a new country. Walking is too slow, and mechanical transport gives little chance of chatting with passersby, listening to birds and smelling the flowers. This turns out to be a magnificent *ballade à cheval*, a ride penetrating country inaccessible any other way. Our path leads first along the knife-edge ridges capping the rim of the double volcano crater in which Taiohea lies. We ride along crests as if on clouds—huge drops on either side—no more than a rabbit track for the horses to follow, edged by near-vertical cliffs, a toy *Nereus* at anchor far below. Sometimes the trail dips into the forest on the side of the mountain and we're enveloped in green lushness as we follow a path a few inches wide, clinging to a seventy-degree slope. The horses have to be led in places even more hair-raising than most. Patrice precedes us, his swinging machete slashing a way through where the forest presses in on the paths that *les anciens* cut to link the valleys centuries before. These mountains form formidable barriers between the valleys; there can have been only a handful of connecting trails, none more than a small goat track and often near vertical. One rides on a long rein, trusting the horses to place their feet safely a couple of inches in from the edge, for a moment's equine inattention would send both horse and rider tumbling to destruction far down the mountainside. These are wild-born horses, caught and broken in by Patrice whenever he needs to increase his stock. We enjoy a lunch of baguettes, pâté and cheese by a rushing river of sweet water, and meet only more wild horses and three piratical hunters with ponies, skinning a goat they'd chased down. The descent from the high country zigzags steeply down through forest and small plantations of pepper, coffee and herbs before we slide saddlesore off the horses in the gathering twilight, clutching booty of limes and pawpaws gathered along the way.

Our last Marquesas anchorage, Hakatea, is usually called Daniel's Bay for the old chief who lives there alone. This is another enclosed circlet of unsettling beauty, tall green hills rising on one side and seven-hundred-foot precipices towering over the other. Manta rays stir the surface, their extraordinary mouths sucking like combine harvesters, sieving up a breakfast of plankton. I nearly drop the anchor on one. With the dinghy tethered to a palm tree in a small lagoon behind the beach, it's a four-mile walk up the valley to a twelve-hundred-foot waterfall, that cascades into a pool at the top of a blind canyon, massive cliffs on all sides. There are only a couple of wild horses for company. It's scenery too huge for any photographic justice that I can do it. The pool is deliciously cool for a swim, and, by clambering round some big rocks, carefully ducking under webs ruled by enormous spiders, we can take the ultimate power shower under the falls, Polynesia's highest. Stone ruins are scattered throughout the fertile valley. The long-disused road of the ancient people, who thrived for perhaps fifteen centuries in the valley until the advent of the European guns, diseases and slaving wiped them out, is raised on blocks from the valley bottom or rebated into the mountainside. It is three warriors wide and edged throughout with great flat-topped boulders. It's the equal of any ancient Roman road; yet, unlike the Romans, the Polynesians who built it had no metal tools.

Daniel, gray and bent with age, courteously invites us to cut a stem of green bananas from his forest, and gives us drinking coconuts to succor us on our voyage to the Tuamotus, five hundred miles south. That we are received everywhere in a generous spirit of friendship seems increasingly surprising as I learn, and feel, the blood-guilt of the white tribe's Pacific record.

At sea once again, rippling through the Pacific on a broad reach toward the Southern Cross, a new moon setting and the Great Bear aft, Mars rising in the east, Jupiter sparkling to the west, and a great, unpolluted, twinkling dome spanning the heavens between, it's easy to forget the threats of the sea, the trials and the crises that will test *Nereus* and her crew over the thousands of miles ahead. The ocean is a beautiful tiger shark, gently dozing, not hungry tonight.

The Great Ocean

THE RAPACITY OF THE COLONIAL POWERS over the last two hundred years left the survival of much in the Pacific largely a matter of luck. Only Tonga escaped the greed for new territories, metals and minerals, strategic advantage and competitive prestige. Much has changed since colonial times; however, and the rare peace of the truly remote is widely restored.

As places qualifying for the paradise stakes had to be insulated from the excesses of today's urban civilization, I'd drawn a circle in the ocean, leaving New Zealand and Japan outside, along with the island chains to its northeast. Hawai'i was excluded too. The Philippines and the large island of New Guinea are more Asian than true Pacific territories, so they, too, were beyond my perimeter.

Well over 10,000 islands remained within the circle, an impossible number, which had to be winnowed down by reading. I looked for the classic books, but despite the extent of the Pacific, its representation in Western art is thin. Robert Louis Stevenson, Pierre Loti and Herman Melville romanticized it; Jack London and James Michener popularized it; novelists Louis Becke, Dean Frisbie, Charles Nordoff and James Hall reflected it; Paul Gauguin painted it; and Richard Rodgers put it to music; but there are only a handful of enduring significance. The islanders themselves, of course, produce indigenous art of all sorts, though most of their important historical artifacts were hauled off to museums in Europe and North America at much the same time as the people were being wiped out. The carving in ebony and kerosin wood, particularly in Marovo and Kiriwina, is world class, canoes are often works of art, and the hand-weaving is everywhere superb. But, dry scholarly tomes apart, there is a paucity of written work.

At my circle's borders, New Zealand was altogether too tempting to the white man, who did not take long to dispossess the indigenous peoples and swamp the culture of the Maoris, comparative newcomers themselves. The remnants of the proud Aboriginal peoples who had developed highly sophisticated societies during perhaps forty-five thousand years of undisturbed sway over the continent of Australia have been reduced after years of repression to little more than a conscience-bothering footnote in modern Oz. In the Hawaiian chain, despite the attraction a Polynesian identity has for tourists, American power and Asian immigration has left scant room for the customary ways, and nineteenth century American missionary families somehow ended up owning much of the land. Most people of old Guam and the Marianas did not survive the long Spanish occupation. Nevertheless parts of the French Pacific empire, the islands that are part of the British Commonwealth, those which were briefly under the sway of a short-lived German bid for southern colonies, as well as the many that were too small and harborless to prove of much interest to anyone, have to a remarkable extent clung to their ancient traditions, resisting the modern world.

Migrated populations from outside the area are few. Besides the considerable number of French in the Polynesian Islands and New Caledonia, the Americans and the sugar barons' Asian imports in Hawai'i, and the U.S. presence in Guam and Samoa, not forgetting ubiquitous Chinese business people, there is only Fiji, where nearly half of the people are of Indian descent following a misbegotten nineteenth century British policy of shipping Indians in to work the sugar cane plantations. There is a light scattering of Americans, Australians, Japanese and New Zealanders in islands that fall or fell under their care in one way or another. Otherwise, except for a few people whose islands were dug out from under them to meet demand for phosphates, the land has largely remained in the hands of the direct descendants of the intrepid voyagers who made impossible journeys to discover them between three thousand and one thousand years ago.

Now formed into thirteen independent states and rather more adjuncts of Pacific rim countries, as well as France and Britain (the latter represented today only by the fifty inhabitants of tiny

Pitcairn), there is nothing standard about the nations and islands of the Pacific. Customs, habits, topography and flora vary widely. Those on the Pacific's Ring of Fire have live volcanoes, islands that come and go, earthquakes and the occasional tsunami. There are high islands where volcanoes sputtered out long ago as they inched away from their hot spot in the earth's crust, raised coral islands thrust up by tectonic action, and low atolls formed over millennia by miniscule coral polyps as their host land sank beneath the waves. Some are protected by barrier reefs. Some such as the Tuamotus are themselves barrier reefs surrounding a lagoon. A few fall straight to the deep ocean floor. Grande Terre of New Caledonia is a chunk of an old landmass, peeled away from the Australian continent eons ago, just as the d'Entrecasteaux group was ripped from New Guinea.

This organization of islands into states, let alone appendages of distant countries, is recent. Even within a modest sized island there may have been no political agreement between villages before the colonists arrived.

To start to understand the real essence, the old *mana*, I sought reports from past voyagers. The Pacific Ocean was virtually untouched when the captains of the late eighteenth century set out on their voyages of exploration. It was, after all, less than five hundred years ago that Vasco Nuñez de Balboa skirmished his way across the Panama isthmus, climbed a hill and gazed upon the Southern Ocean, unknown thus far to European eyes. Balboa, who had been Governor General of Darien for two years, was accompanied by his faithful Leoncico, on full pay as a soldier of the Spanish Crown despite being a dog. He found a route down through the jungle, and, arriving on the shoreline on 29 September 1513, in ringing tones of great pomp claimed the seas and all the lands from the Arctic to the Antarctic in the name of King Ferdinand of Spain. This record landgrab didn't do Balboa a great deal of good, for during his five months' absence an unpleasant character named Davila was appointed in his place. Among other things, Davila professed himself unhappy with the dog's salary. On his return, Balboa's head was removed from his shoulders and ungratefully stuck on a pole. Yet, his discovery set the course of history, and to this day all the lands he claimed to the south and those to the U.S. border to the north (and increasingly beyond) are Spanish speaking.

Balboa's report was received by headquarters back in Seville with great excitement. Further expeditions of investigation across the neck of land connecting North and South America were rapidly commissioned. Only six years after he first set foot on the sands of the Southern Ocean, the Spaniards assembled a fleet charged with sailing south down the Atlantic to discover if it were possible to reach it by sea and thence to voyage west to the Spice Islands, the new source of Iberia's fabulous wealth and the scene of a confrontation with Portugal following the Treaty of Tordesillas, twenty-five years earlier, that carved up the unknown world between the two maritime powers of the day. They hired as captain-general the foreigner they called Ferdinando de Magallanes, just as they had employed the Italian Christoforo Colombo in 1492, and fitted out five ships for him. Right up to his end, Columbus believed he had found the westward route to the Indies, hence the historic misnaming of the West Indies and all "Indians" outside India. Now, thirteen years after Columbus's death, Magellan knew better, though he was still under a near fatal misapprehension about the magnitude of his task: He was satisfied that the world was round, but he was unaware of its size.

Magellan set off in 1519, survived a violent mutiny and, though it took him more than a month, managed to short-circuit Cape Horn with his remaining rickety little fleet of three unsuitable ships, none exceeding eighty feet in length. From Rio de Janeiro onwards, he was navigating hitherto unknown waters. Lucky with the weather at the southern tip of South America, he made the perilous passage from ocean to ocean unscathed and, perhaps more in hope than expectation, on emerging from the strait that now bears his name on a particularly placid day, he christened the great calm ocean before him *El Pacifico*.

Or he may have done so, for Magellan's words are unrecorded. His Venetian diarist, Pigafetta, who had imaginatively named the forbidding three-hundred-mile passage through which they reached the Pacific "The Strait of Eleven Thousand Virgins," wrote, "We issued forth from the strait, and were at last in the Pacific Sea."

Magellan had been convinced by a charlatan that this new ocean was not much wider than the Mediterranean and, hopelessly under-provisioned, he saw almost nothing on his desperate dash across. He did find Guam before meeting his inglorious end in the Philippines at the hands of Chief Lapulapu. Perhaps coincidentally Guam is now one of the most changed small islands. The indigenous Chamorros are virtually extinct, and it is home to an American fleet with its thousands of crew and support staff.

Only the *Vittoria* of Magellan's original fleet of five ships made it back to Spain, with just 18 of the original complement of 237 men. The captain who assumed command after Magellan's death, the first, largely unsung, man to bring a ship home from a circumnavigation of the world, the sailor who blazed the trail we were now to follow, was called Juan Sebastian d'Elcano. Trying for a second niche in history, d'Elcano set off round the world again with a Portuguese expedition in 1525, but died en route.

The Spanish were soon running an annual galleon stuffed with stolen treasure from Mexico to Manila, but in the two-and-a-half centuries after this first crossing of the Pacific, barely a dozen expeditions set forth from Europe. No one stayed long or learned much about the islanders they encountered. The most entertaining of these pioneer tales was a seventeenth century bestseller written by the sometime pirate William Dampier from Somerset in southern England. Dampier took twelve years to hitchhike around the world on a succession of buccaneer vessels in the 1680s. He was the first Englishman to make a circumnavigation since Sir Francis Drake and Sir Thomas Cavendish one hundred years earlier, and then went around two more times. The eyewitness accounts of the more careful observers starting with Byron, Wallis, Carteret, Bougainville, and Cook in the 1760s therefore reflect the native societies of the islands, their traditions and their products unaffected by the arrival of outsiders. As well as the lucid journals of Cook himself, I prize the observations of the twenty-six-year-old Joseph Banks who sailed with Cook on his first voyage, and the pronouncements of the stiff German professor, Johann Reinhold Forster, who replaced Banks as naturalist on Cook's second voyage; of William Bligh, who completed one of history's extraordinary journeys after he was thrown off HMS *Bounty* by Fletcher Christian; and of William Mariner, marooned for years alone among "savages" on Tonga at the age of twelve.

Joseph Banks, painted 1773 by Sir Joshua Reynolds

The islands that have moved farthest from their precontact innocence are those now under the direct influence of the developed world. Besides the Hawaiian chain, a state of the USA since 1959 but effectively part of the United States for the last hundred and twenty years; the

The Great Ocean

PACIFIC ISLAND COUNTRIES AND TERRITORIES

A CAUTION: Population figures may be very rough or out of date. My island count is equally indicative, reflecting the difficulty and inconsistency of defining an island. The total of Pacific islands of all sorts is suggested variously as between 10,000 and 25,000.

		POPULATION ('000)	MAIN ISLANDS
Independent states			
Fiji		881	844
Solomon Islands		524	980
Vanuatu		203	84
Samoa		177	10
Tonga		110	169
Federated States of Micronesia		108	607
Kiribati		101	33
Marshall Islands		58	32
Palau		20	300
Cook Islands		14	15
Nauru		13	1
Tuvalu		11	9
Niue		1	1
Dependencies			
French Polynesia	France	220	118
New Caledonia	France	200	30
Guam, Midway, Wake	USA	168	3
Northern Mariana Islands	USA	80	14
American Samoa	USA	50	7
Wallis and Futuna	France	15	23
Tokelau	New Zealand	2	4
Pitcairn	Britain	–	1
Provinces			
Admiralties	PNG	565	57
Bougainville	PNG	175	15
Trobriands	PNG	12	25
Louisiades	PNG	?	?
D'Entrecasteaux	PNG	?	24
Galápagos	Ecuador	30	19
Rapa Nui (Easter Island)	Chile	4	1
Juan Fernández	Chile	1	6
Norfolk Island	Australia	2	4

Reach for Paradise

USA holds sway over a number of islands, including Guam, the Northern Marianas and part of Samoa among the more important, and is an influential protective treaty power in others like Federated States of Micronesia and Palau. The French empire continues to extend over the Society Islands, the Marquesas, the Tuamotus, New Caledonia and a few smaller groups. Noumea, Pago Pago and Papeete are already western outposts. Easter Island is part of Chile, and the Galápagos belong to Ecuador. New Zealand and Australia feel their hand is needed to help economically or politically in some independent countries like Papua New Guinea (PNG), the Solomons, the Cook Islands, Tokelau, Tuvalu and Niue.

Nevertheless, vast tracts of ocean, whether Polynesia, Micronesia or Melanesia, contain island populations that remain outside the modern world. They know about it, they may have traveled to it, they appreciate artifacts and medical help from it, but they live their daily lives much as hundreds of generations of ancestors before them, without money, electricity, phones, TV or manufactured food. Their gardens supply their fruit and vegetable needs. Pigs, fowl and fishing furnish their meat. Good water is seldom in short supply, and the few clothes required in a tropical climate can be traded from occasional passing boats. Schools are one departure from the old days, usually available, sometimes free. The outboard motor is another, the universal Yamaha, which has enabled villages to market their ocean and garden produce and exploit their *bêche-de-mer* or trochus fisheries. And medical help is on hand, though it may be a few days' journey away.

All the peoples of the Pacific, as of most places, were invaders once. The general direction of migration over the last five thousand years has been from China and Taiwan through the large island groups that now form Malaysia, the Philippines, Papua New Guinea and Indonesia, and thence east and southeast. This was long after the Aborigines arrived in Australia—perhaps walking there from Asia when, according to geologists, Tasmania, Australia and New Guinea formed one land mass. A number of distinct population groups have survived as current inhabitants. Though few in number, the most widespread are the Polynesians who made voyages that dwarf the accomplishments of European explorers to colonize eastwards to the Marquesas, then north to Hawai'i and east again to Rapa Nui and back southwest to Aotearoa. Abel Tasman had not troubled to inquire this land's name when he called it Neu Zeeland and claimed it for The Netherlands.

Some damage was done by these peoples, though insignificant when set against what came later. In New Zealand the Maori ate the last moa around the fifteenth century, and the rats they unwittingly introduced did the birds no good, for, in the absence of predatory reptiles and mammals, the native birds had no need to go to the trouble of building nests in trees. The hogs and dogs that accompanied the Polynesians for food over vast ocean crossings in their double canoes were no doubt ecologically unsound, and would have been excluded by quarantine officials nowadays, but are benign compared to the domestic cats and invasive plants that arrived later. I have seen no evidence that the root and fruit canoe crops that Polynesians brought with them spread uncontrolled or damaged native species, but I've not discovered who should be consigned to purgatory for the spread of ants, termites, mosquitoes, no-see-ums and sand flies.

The glaring exception is the devastation of Rapa Nui, as this isolated scrap of land was known before the Dutch explorer Jacob Roggeveen found it in 1722 and named it for the day he saw it, Easter. The descendants of Hotu Matu'a, the Polynesian navigator who colonized Rapa Nui around 900 AD, took six hundred years to destroy the forests. The island, which probably once supported 20,000 people, became a wreck: no wood for canoes, the birds eaten, the land eroded and impoverished. Tribal society crumbled, the three hundred *ahu* were pulled apart and close to a thousand grotesque *moai* were abandoned or toppled. This self-inflicted eco-suicide, its end dispassionately recorded by Captain Cook, was then compounded by the impact of Europeans so that, by 1872, just 111 Easter Islanders were left to be counted.

Probably the direst of the problems now, bad governance and the threat of rising sea-levels apart, is the opposite; exploding population threatens many islands, for intensive land use is often incompatible with the health of the soil, which, usually a thin covering over coral or young igneous rock, requires rotation and time to recover from cropping.

Though a handful of European navigators crossed the Pacific in the two and a half centuries following Magellan, western traffic had no real impact until the great voyages of discovery from 1770 onwards. These adventurers, Cook especially, opened the way for the whalers, traders and blackbirders who infested the ocean over the following century. Then came the colonists: the military, the planters, the shopkeepers and officials. Doomsayers, using words like "rape" and "rip-off" in relation to the strategic and commercial incursions of the West, are justified on many levels. The introduction of alien species, including missionaries, wiped out unique flora and tradition developed over thousands of years of oceanic isolation; foreign logging companies stripped the islands of the ancient cover of tropical rainforests and sandalwood; fishing rights have been granted for derisory prices, often threatening disastrous depletion of fish stocks; mineral extraction has taken a toll; and nuclear testing by the Americans, British and French has left radioactive waste and shattered atolls.

The fabric and culture of societies in island after island was destroyed as the critical mass of populations dropped below 10 or 15 percent of the precontact number. In most of the islands between 90 percent and 95 percent of the people eventually fell victim—plagues of measles, smallpox, TB, cholera, and venereal diseases registered on a miserable catalogue of horrors to which they had no immunity. And the traded iron spearheads, knives and guns that displaced traditional hardwood clubs radically increased the already lively internecine killing rate.

Of course, the annihilation of native populations as the old world adventured into the new was not peculiar to the Pacific. It seems to have happened wherever Western advances were made. The 20 million Mexicans alive when the Spaniards arrived were down to 1.6 million a century later, huge numbers dying of smallpox. The curse of the old world was at its most extreme in Hispaniola, the island shared by Haiti and the Dominican Republic. When Columbus arrived in 1492, the population may have been around one million. By 1535, the time of the conquistador Pizarro, there were virtually no people left at all.

The violent arrival of hundreds of thousands of Japanese and all their war hardware and establishments in 1942 caused cataclysmic disruption in the western Pacific, with more to follow as the Allies forced them back north again. Aid, the Mormons and the Peace Corps, replete with alien demands and concepts, have probably been equally disturbing in practice. Climate change, pollution and rising sea levels now threaten coastal communities, low-lying atolls and fragile reef systems.

That independence has led some countries down the path of bad and corrupt government is often blamed on the colonial power granting their freedom, as if it could have resisted the tide of history flowing strongly in the thirty years following the defeat of the

Japanese. The Tongans have a problem in this respect; they have no outsiders to grouse at.

Since the days of Cook and Bligh, the most significant invasion of the South Seas has, however, been the coming of the missionaries, bent on extinguishing the old ways. The predations of governments, sailors and adventurers may have passed through like a strong wind, but the effects of Christian missionaries did not. Mendaña had deposited a boatload of Franciscan friars in 1567, but they seem to have made no impression. But when the London Missionary Society determined to export earnest evangelists in bulk at the end of the eighteenth century, things started to change. That they pacified the villages, finally achieved the abolition of headhunting and cannibalism, introduced schooling and systematized the languages is to their credit, but the cost was dire. They succeeded in destroying much of the ancient culture, they introduced a plethora of Christian sects competing for souls at heavy cost to the local population, and they and the sailors brought diseases that wiped out most of the intended flock. From the Americas to Southeast Asia, however, the seeds planted by the missionaries have thrived and the churches rule. Populations have more or less recovered and life is peaceful. What political violence there is, in Suva, Bougainville and Honiara to name recent trouble spots, is localized. With the exception of Port Moresby in Papua New Guinea, violent crime is rare.

Mortal threats are largely gone now, though filariasis, hepatitis and AIDS have arrived as killers to replace syphilis, measles, cholera and TB. Malaria and dengue fever are common. More local problems include ciguatera, the poorly understood toxicity affecting larger reef fish well up the food chain in various places throughout the tropics. This may have always been endemic (Cook probably got it), though several Society Islanders tell me that it results from the French atomic testing at Moruroa Atoll.

Whaling by the Japanese continues under the risible excuse of scientific research, and the South Koreans catch two minke whales a week "by accident." Longline fishing and the use of massive drift nets by the Taiwanese and other Pacific rim countries devastates fish stocks and kills seabirds, which are getting rare in many places. The rapidly growing population of richer Chinese pay silly money for shark fins for their soup, which has led to a disastrous massacre of shark populations, and now manta rays, whose gills are unaccountably regarded as medicinal, are also murdered. And the swiftlets, whose homebuilding efforts provide the raw material for bird's nest soup, are in decline. It is largely Chinese demand, too, that drives the logging of remaining rainforests, often by Malaysian corporations.

Most menacing of the twenty-first century influences is the osmotic insinuation of Western culture powered by modern electronics, which everywhere tends to appeal to the young and to drive out traditional things. Growing towns have largely discarded their island traditions, and some places, like Niue, are being abandoned, emptied by the draw of Auckland.

Existence in the villages seems timeless, however, an Arcadia where life is simple and easy, good food is plentiful and earned by only a little work, and cares seem few. The landscape is beautiful; the people, lovely; the climate, benign; and the ocean, full of marvels. The sober captain Louis-Antoine de Bougainville wrote, two hundred forty years ago, that paradise was here. If not for its own people, perhaps it still is for urban drifters, singed by worldly disillusion.

A Dangerous Archipelago

THE TUAMOTU ISLANDS

Single-hander sailors enduring weeks of solitude on this vast sea seldom admit to loneliness. Perhaps the need for constant vigilance leaves no space for boredom, while many prefer their own company to the foibles and cares of fellow beings.

Nereus can carry up to six; with a crew adapted to the communal living in a confined space that ocean sailing demands, loneliness is no problem. Temporary crew and native islanders are often soon friends enough to share the doubts and passions of the voyage. Yet, as the months go by, the certainties of a settled existence seem long ago and far away. My necessarily transient relationships gradually fall short of a replacement for the home and hearth, which, in any case, have vanished along with my marriage. Occasional family and friends who can manage the time and complicated logistics to become part of *Nereus*' voyage are thus invaluable. The distance is now too great for my hardworking children easily to join me, so it's inspiriting when an e-mail from my elder son brings news of his plan to join us from London. Our five-hundred-mile passage from the Marquesas must take no more than four days to rendezvous with a puddle-jumper ferrying Rupert the last hop from Tahiti to a Tuamotu atoll.

At dawn on the third morning out, under a steady procession of trade wind cloudlets shading through a range of pinks as the sun

The sharks were quicker...

erupts from the eastern horizon, a fish takes the lure on the starboard line. Busy with a log entry, I fail to notice the jerk of the bungy cord and increased tension of the nylon. Fishing for the pot, we don't fool with light lines; it takes a quarter of a ton to break one, which has happened only a couple of times. When I pull it in, all that the sharks have left us, the crumbs from their table, is the truncated head of a fifty-pound tuna, maybe a yellowfin. The sad remnant prompts an odd vision of me as Ernest Hemingway's Old Man, afloat in his little skiff on a limitless sea with bloodied hands and nothing but the skeleton of the greatest fish of his life. The scraps around this fine fish's gills are something the Old Man could have used in his agony, though, enough to yield a couple of meals. The feeling of metaphor fades as Sam hollers merrily and reels in a thirty-pound wahoo on the port line.

Another day on, a low blur on the horizon focuses into a line of coconut trees in the golden rays of another sparkling June dawn: Makemo. This is our first coral atoll, part of the Tuamotu chain, which covers thousands of square miles of ocean broadly to the east of Tahiti. These atolls perch on the rims of ancient volcanoes, rising thousands of feet straight from the ocean floor, yet none pokes more than a few feet above sea level, or looks from the air like anything more than an etiolated donut. Each atoll encloses a lagoon, a shallowish stretch of water studded with reefs and coral heads; the atoll band, from a few to a few hundred feet in width, can be dry land or reef just below the surface. Their size varies, the largest being fifty miles long and half as wide. Occasional motus seem to float on the quiet lagoon surface, palm-shaded islets that have developed where the coral was lifted a little to accumulate some soil. A few lagoons are inaccessible from the ocean, but most of the atolls are pierced by one or two narrow passes scoured by the tide flowing in and out with great force. Navigation in the Tuamotus, known since Captain Cook's time as The Dangerous Archipelago, involves careful timing and management of these passes, as well as a wary eye on the coral heads that tower up without warning within the lagoons.

MAKEMO

A small village near the pass with five churches of different denominations and a "cathedral" feels under spiritual attack. To the southeast, at the limit of the tropics, there is another, grander island cathedral on Mangareva in the little Gambier archipelago, close enough to the site of the French atmospheric nuclear testing of the 1970s to be equipped with a fallout shelter into which the population was herded when a big bang was imminent. This was paradise of a particular sort for a fundamentalist French priest called Father Honoré Laval. For the glory of his God, Laval had his flock build the 1,200-seat cathedral together with another two dozen churches, towers and assorted edifices, including a convent in which the unmarried girls were immured. The cathedral was, of course, sited right on the most sacred Polynesian site, the main *marae*. Priestly efforts and diseases succeeded in reducing the number of inhabitants of Mangareva from about five thousand to less than five hundred by 1887 before Laval was hauled off to Papeete, tried and declared insane.

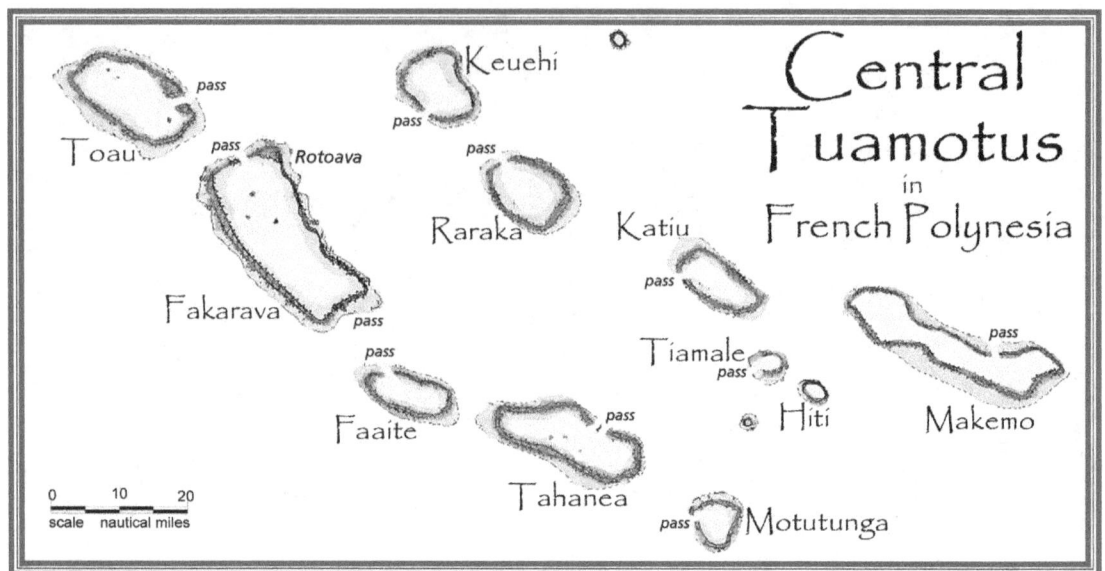

A shabby hut advertises *steak-frites*, burgers and hot dogs—I don't dare inquire "steak of what?" in case the answer is dobermann, pekinese or plain yellow mongrel, for islanders are partial to mutt. Not a place to risk a hot dog, so we dine aboard.

The morning is overcast as I hitch in the baker's pickup truck to meet Rupert at the airstrip a few miles out of the village, only to pass him coming the other way on the back of the Gendarme's truck, his fair hair streaming in the wind as he inhales his first gloriously unpolluted mid-ocean air after a day and a half's tedious travel from Europe. Suffering paternal Polynesian hugs, embarrassingly unfamiliar to a young Brit at first but a necessary introduction to Pacific ways, he is installed on board. Disentangling the anchor from the coral rubble, we sail a few miles across the lagoon, dodging numerous heads rising like giant baroque pillars rooted on the bottom a hundred feet below, their tops riotous coral gardens hovering just under the rippled surface, swirls of color like a Rothco palette. The hook is let drop in crystal water in the lee of the upwind side of the atoll, a long white beach interrupted by a couple of motus fronting the narrow reef that protects us from the crashing surf of the deep Pacific. There we can snorkel on the coral, beachcomb the reef, make a fire to cook fresh fish on a motu, and Rupert and I can catch up after a long separation while enjoying an outrageously beautiful place.

"Coming from a city to this scene is like entering a theatre while the show's on," he tells me. "It's an instantaneous transposition to make-belief."

The clams for supper are up to a foot across their wavy mouths, each embedded in coral into which they rebated themselves while the enveloping coral grew around them. Only their wide lips are exposed, mantles ranging over remarkable patterns in hues of yellows, greens, turquoise, blue, brown. The coral is alive with them, sometimes a dozen nested in a rock no bigger than a stool.

Giant clams

TAHANEA

Planning a voyage in the Tuamotus is like moving around a Clue board. You have to get through the door into the next atoll on your throw, which is the time available between daylight tides. You can only leave for another if the leg is short enough, or long enough to exit one door and arrive at the next at the right state of tide and light. Each accessible atoll, which typically measures fifty to a hundred miles around the outside, has one or two doors and may be more or less navigable inside its lagoon. There are seventy-seven of them.

The little village on Makemo is suffering an outbreak of dengue fever. It's best to move on before an aedes mosquito vector nibbles one of us. After minimal restocking at the unaffordable prices prevalent in French Polynesia, we sail overnight to Tahanea, which, though forty miles by fifteen, is uninhabited. The turquoise water sparkles around us, the only souls on the atoll with three hundred square miles of lagoon to ourselves. Snorkeling reveals polo-ball-size smooth clams, which we gather and cook for dinner

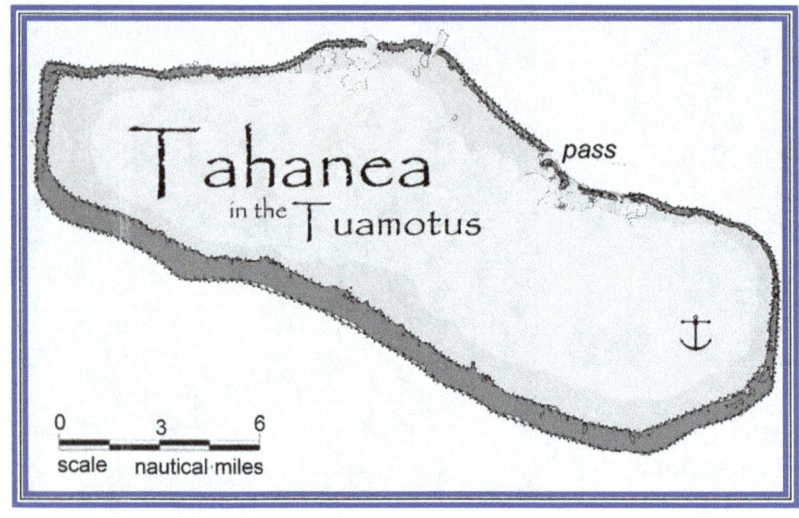

on a fire on the motu. A couple of the abundant young palms yield heart of palm for a salad.

After some dreamy paradisaical days, we travel back down the lagoon to its single pass and dive down a wall of sharks. Hundreds of fish species, of amazing shape, pattern and color hang in the inflowing current amidst an impossibly polychrome coral seascape. No design scheme has been overlooked by mother nature when it comes to tropical fish; in no other department except perhaps insects has she been so ebulliently prolific. Because of the great tidal flow of water carrying the nutrients that kick off the food chain, the coral, sponge and fish life is at its most exuberant in the passes, which, in turn, attracts sharks and moray eels. They are always the liveliest places to dive.

"You said you'd teach me about the muddy waters of business life when I left school," Rupert says as we wash the salty taste of diving out of our mouths with beakers of red wine, "but I never thought I'd actually meet sharks by the hundred."

FAKARAVA

Fakarava is a larger atoll to the west. Having negotiated another narrow swirling pass, we sail across its calm lagoon, dodging oyster lines for thirty miles, to the little village of Rotoava, which promises a meal ashore, the first in a month for Sam and me. The industry of the Tuamotus is the culturing of black pearls, largely a Japanese affair, hence the oysters. Our table under a coconut trees outside a tiny Rotoava pension is shared with a trio of holidaying French chefs, which stimulates an effort at serious Gallic gastronomy by the proprietor.

These atolls are as different from the grand Marquesas as islands could be, a pattern of variety to be repeated across the Pacific.

At the northwestern end of the Tuamotu chain, Rangiroa boasts luxurious hotels on its beaches. At the opposite extreme, eight hundred miles southeast of Tahiti, where until 1996 the French were defying their furious Pacific neighbors by continuing to test nuclear weapons, we would be chased away by the French navy. Over thirty years, 181 nuclear bombs were exploded at Moruroa and Fongataufa, bequeathing an enduring legacy of radioactive problems.

As we leave the Dangerous Archipelago on a southwesterly course for the bottom end of Tahiti, two hundred thirty miles away, the blow from the southeast increases. Heavy with horizontal rain mingled with sheets of stinging spray, the squally wind is sweeping us at great speed through the murk when a loud, metallic crack is quickly echoed by a yell: "Dad, get up here!"

I rush on deck.

A glance through the whipping, saturated air is enough. Our main boom has broken.

The boom is a Danish invention into which the mainsail rolls, a good design vitiated by flimsy construction destined to give continual problems until we eventually junk it in New Zealand. Strapped into harnesses and clipped to the jackstay, Rupert and I struggle to get the flogging sail under control as Sam fights at the helm to reduce the rolling that flings the spar from side to side like a bludgeon. Heavy, wet Dacron thunders at our heads as the mast swings through an arc of a hundred degrees. The deck bucks and rolls beneath our feet, while the now detached boom threatens to sweep us overboard. With plenty of oaths lost against the howling wind, wet through, bruised and slapped raw, we battle to get the sail down and the boom tamed and lashed tight. The stitching is destroyed, and the leech of the sail is shredded where it has whipped into the shrouds, both boom and mainsail unusable. The gale strengthens, shrieking fury, firing solid rods of rain in storm-force gusts at our faces as we secure the final ties and lash the boom.

We get under way again under a patch of reefed jib and mizzen, soon creaming along at nine knots, butting steep seas that threaten to consume *Nereus* in curtains of green water. At this speed, landfall is much earlier than planned, which is awkward, for the weather is too strong for a safe night entrance to one of the lagoons within Tahiti's surrounding reefs. The prospect of heaving to in such a sea is still less appealing. So, toward a moonless midnight, relying largely on instruments and encouraged by the knowledge that Captain Cook once put into the same place without even a chart, we gingerly feel our way in, riding great waves through an unlit pass with the crash and hiss of raw ocean smashing furiously on reefs on either hand.

6

The Society Islands

TAHITI

A gray dawn finds us close under the high green hills of Tahiti, protected from an angry sea by the wicked reefs negotiated last night. Only now does it occur to me that Cook entered in daylight, following his longboat crew who rowed ahead casting a lead line.

"Wow! Perhaps we were a little bold," Sam says to Rupert, looking at the maelstrom still boiling in the reef pass when he thinks I'm not listening.

The mountains rising steeply behind the coast road spew grand waterfalls every few hundred yards. The shoreline is covered in fleshy plants with white flower clumps, the scurvy grass that served to keep many a crewman healthy until, well into the nineteenth century, it was finally proven that regular vegetables and citrus would keep the dreaded mariners' malady of scurvy at bay. Unenlightened captains regularly lost more than half their crew to this disease. Cook, ahead of his time as usual, dosed his men with a noxious concoction known as portable soup, and gathered fruit and greens for his crew here and wherever he could. This is Tahiti Iti, the smaller of the two mountain masses in the shape of a figure eight, largely surrounded by navigable lagoon, which make up Tahiti.

Keen on calmer water, we head for Papeete via the lagoon up the west side of Tahiti Nui. The wind has abated to twenty-five knots,

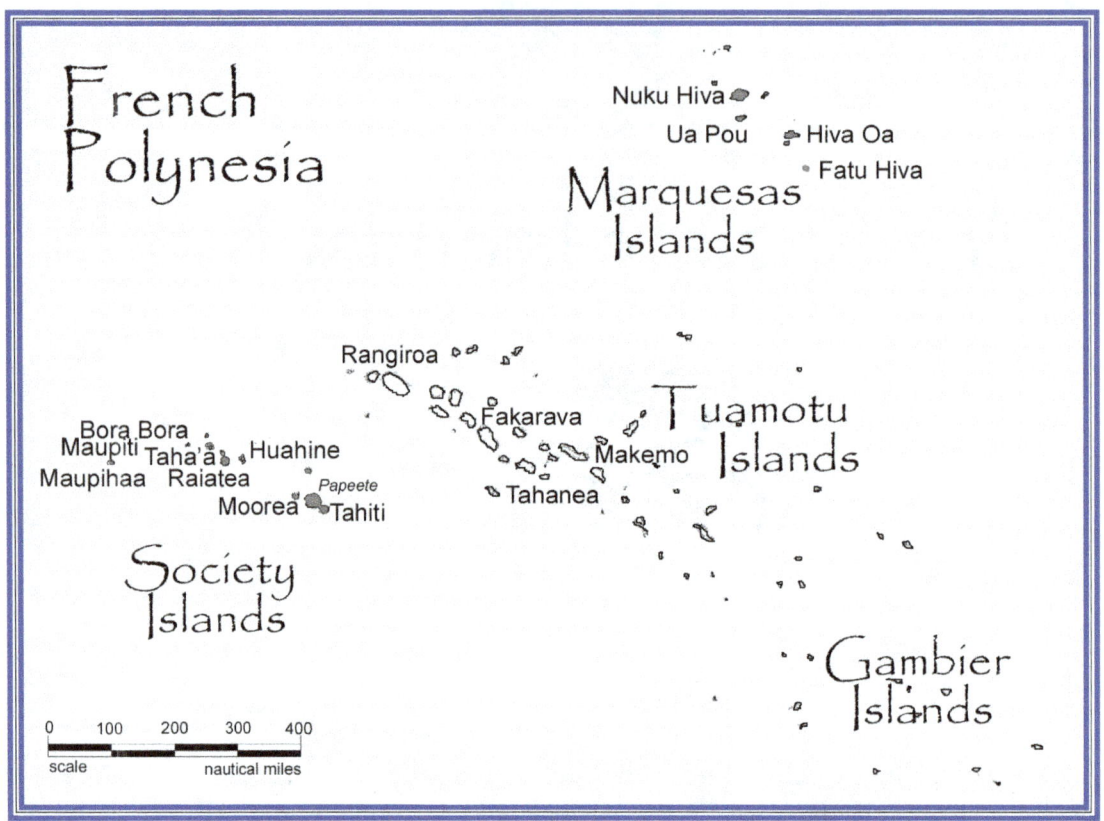

but, after two days of storm, fifteen-foot waves still crash over the lagoon walls. Amid the seething surf and lashing rain it's hard to find a break in the reef. When we do, plenty of adrenaline is needed to surf through to gain the comparatively calm lagoon. The rain remains unrelenting. Navigation through the opaque lagoon water is tricky. *Nereus* grounds with a horrible crunch on one reef. We're fortunate to get her off under her own power. Arcing waterfalls spout from high on the mountainsides like a giant's colander under pressure. The few steep valleys leading inland disappear into heavy, gray cloud.

With *Nereus* at last secure on a marina slip, the three of us ride *Le Truck*, Tahiti's idiosyncratic homemade bus service, into Papeete to feast in the *roulottes*, gastronomic vans parked on the quayside, serving all sorts of delicious things from *crêpes, galettes* and *gaufrettes* to *steak-frites* and many varieties of *poisson cru,* the pickled raw fish that we often make on board to extend the life of a catch. American tourists are overheard slandering these gourmets' delights with the soubriquet "roach coaches."

Sam loses no time disappearing into Papeete's narrow back streets in search of old-fashioned compensation for weeks in lonely places, while Rupert steers me into a bar apparently populated by beautifully dressed and good looking girls. Getting rather excited, we order drinks and consider who to chat to. He spots the catch first, and pokes me in the ribs with a surprised giggle. "Dad, you know something?" he says. "These women are all men!"

I'm slower, or perhaps more optimistic. "Are you sure?"

The disappointment is confirmed. We've stumbled into a transvestite bar. Having no idea how to cope with men-girls, we down the drinks fast and retreat, only later discovering that transvestism is a phenomenon common to many South Seas islands. Here called *mahu*, they are usually the offspring of Polynesian families whose tradition it is to raise a son as a girl if they have no daughter. The *mahu* are held in high esteem—unless, that is, they become *rae rae*. It is a bunch of *rae rae*, transvestite prostitutes, we have stumbled among.

These graceful, willowy *mahu* are the antithesis of Polynesians once they have passed the beauty of youth. One cannot but be impressed by the startling general obesity. Heaps of starchy roots, responsible for keeping weight in line with prestige in the past, are nowadays supplemented by spam and shiploads of junk food. The polywaddle merits registration at John Cleese's Department of Funny Walks, the gait of those whose thighs are so inflated that one foot can only pass the other at a considerable distance, generating a duck-like rolling movement. Local airlines flying Polynesians around don't worry much about their luggage, but do weigh the passengers. The serious, sad side of this is the island incidence of diabetes, many times that of Australia and New Zealand.

After two centuries of stories about Tahiti's downward slide, I don't expect too much. I am therefore not disappointed. The topography is startling, eternally lovely. But the ancient culture was wrecked long ago. Caroline Alexander, in her 2003 book, *The Bounty: The True Story of the Mutiny on the Bounty,* underscores the deterioration that happened even between the *Bounty*'s visit in 1789 and Bligh's return in 1792 to redeem himself by trying once more to transport breadfruit saplings to the Caribbean:

> Canoes soon appeared, and in one a native man was seen by Bligh's quick eyes to be wearing a European shirt. This seemingly trivial detail proved to be a harbinger of great and tragic changes wrought

in this paradise of the world. Few European ships—the Pandora, Vancouver's Discovery and Chatham—along with a crew of a shipwrecked whaler, had touched at Tahiti since the departure of the Bounty, but already European contact had left more than venereal disease, which was rampant as before, and Bligh observed a new fondness amongst the islanders for liquor. A small arsenal of firearms, gleaned from various ships, was a proud and closely guarded treasure. While Bligh's company remained in Tahiti, they were witness to the flares of regional strife that had always undermined island life, but these were deadlier now than ever before, thanks to the European guns and, as a result of such strife, Matavai was a deserted village. The handsome Tahitians were dressed in sailors' ragged cast-offs and it was difficult to find, as Bligh noted with sadness, the gleaming white bark cloth that they had worn with much elegance.

Paul Gauguin arrived here a hundred years later after "a sixty-three day voyage of fervent anticipation," heavily influenced by Pierre Loti's tale of his idyll with Rarahu, a fifteen-year-old Tahitian girl, and seemingly unaware of the ravages a century of missionary zeal and colonial interference had inflicted. Those hundred years, as in the Marquesas, witnessed the annihilation of ninety-six out of each one hundred inhabitants.

His expectations of finding in Tahiti an earthly paradise had been raised to great heights by European exaggerations, but it took only a short while for disillusion to set in: "This was Europe—the Europe which I wanted to slough off...the colonial snobbery, the imitation, grotesque to the point of caricature, of our customs, fashions, vices, and idiocies of civilization. Had I traveled this far only to suffer the very things from which I fled?"

Gauguin stayed twelve years in all, relocating to a simple village far from Papeete where he attempted and failed to re-create his idealized Tahiti. In a memoir, *Noa Noa*, he caustically illustrated his disillusion: "In the society of the *Arii*, prostitution was a sacred duty. We have changed that. Prostitution has not ceased in Tahiti since we have heaped upon it the benevolences of our civilization. On the contrary, it prospers. It is neither obligatory nor sacred. It is simply inexcusable, and without grandeur."

Finally fed up, he abandoned his young women and returned to France. But the vision of his paradise remained strong. Permitting hope to triumph over experience, he sailed once again for the

Gauguin's Tahitian studio

South Seas where, on his second attempt, he ended up in his final resting place in the Marquesas Islands.

Tahiti had been corrupted by Western adventurers remarkably quickly. De Bougainville named the island *La Nouvelle Cythère*, celebrating the home of a Greek goddess of love. Both Joseph Banks and Johann Reinhold Forster, who took Banks' place as botanist on Cook's second voyage after Cook and Banks had fallen out over the latter's enormous retinue and the unseaworthy additions he had made to the ship, thought Tahiti the epitome of South Seas civilization:

> Otaheitee and the neighboring Society isles are in this point nearer to happiness than any other nations we met with. They have a greater variety of food and in greater abundance than any of the other nations. Their habitations are clean and roomy. They have ideas of many things which never occurred to other nations of the South Seas, their intellectual facilities enlarged by instruction and exercise, are capable of comprehending, retaining, reproducing and combining ideas; and what is still more happy, the simple but rational education, the happiest organization and the mildness of their climate concur in forming their minds for benevolence, and in filling their hearts with soft and tender feelings, and a charitable disposition.
>
> ...Their hearts are capable of the most tender connexions, of which in our mixed and degenerating societies we have very few instances, perhaps none at all, where such a disinterested, generous love, or such an enthusiasm of passion forms the basis of the tender connexion.

This was Forster writing in 1773. Though everyone apparently hated him—"a deceitful and undeserving man," wrote Cook later—he seemed respected as an observer and a scientist. Beaglehole, the New Zealander whose edition of Cook's journals is the seminal work of scholarship, labeled him "dogmatic, humorless, suspicious, censorious, pretentious, contentious, demanding." Not exactly the companion to choose for a long voyage, and a reminder of my good fortune in having, among the fifty crew who sailed the Pacific with me at different times, only one person I was happy not to see again.

Banks, who was to lead a long and distinguished life as Sir Joseph, president of the Royal Society, provided the first report of surfing in 1769:

> It was a place where the shore was not guarded by a reef as is usualy the case, consequently a high surf fell upon the shore, a more dreadful one I have not often seen. I think no European who had by any means got into it could possibly have saved his life. In the midst of these breakers 10 or 12 Indians were swimming who whenever a surf broke near them dived under it with infinite ease, rising up on the other side; but their chief amusement was carried on by the stern of an old canoe, with this before them they swam out as far as the outermost breach, then one or two would get into it and opposing the blunt end to the breaking wave were hurried in with incredible swiftness. We stood admiring this wonderful scene for fully half an hour.

To anyone who might still feel the faint pulse-beat of ancient Polynesia, all that was evocative about Tahiti is long gone. "A forlorn and disgusting town," Alain Gerbault, author of *A Paradise Is Dead*, called Papeete in the 1930s, and that was before Tahiti's eighty miles of roads became as crowded as Paris, stimulating a proposal for the construction of a commuter railroad. A bit strong, perhaps, for if the idyllic visions of the past are forgotten, Papeete is an agreeable town and Tahiti might still be magic if seen through hungry eyes.

Rupert Brooke, aged twenty-seven, passed three months in Tahiti just before the outbreak of the Great War, finding a period of paradise for himself with a Tahitian girl, Mamua, for whom he composed a poem beautifully expressing the spell that Polynesia could cast:

Mamua, when our laughter ends,
And hearts and bodies, brown as white,
Are dust about the doors of friends,
Or scent ablowing down the night,
Then, oh! then, the wise agree,
Comes our immortality.

Mamua, there waits a land
Hard for us to understand.
Out of time, beyond the sun,
All are one in Paradise,
You and Pupure are one,
And Taü, and the ungainly wise.

There the Eternals are, and there
The Good, the Lovely, and the True,
And Types, whose earthly copies were
The foolish broken things we knew;
There is the Face, whose ghosts we are;
The real, the never-setting Star;

And the Flower, of which we love
Faint and fading shadows here;
Never a tear, but only Grief;
Dance, but not the limbs that move;
Songs in Song shall disappear;
Instead of lovers, Love shall be;
For hearts, Immutability;
And there, on the Ideal Reef,
Thunders the Everlasting Sea!

And my laughter, and my pain,
Shall home to the Eternal Brain.
And all lovely things, they say,
Meet in Loveliness again;

Miri's laugh, Teipo's feet,
And the hands of Matua,
Stars and sunlight there shall meet
Coral's hues and rainbows there,
And Teüra's braided hair;
And with the starred tiare's white,
And white birds in the dark ravine,
And flamboyants ablaze at night,

And jewels, and evening's after-green,
And dawns of pearl and gold and red,
Mamua, your lovelier head!
And there'll no more be one who dreams
Under the ferns, of crumbling stuff,
Eyes of illusion, mouth that seems,
All time-entangled human love.

And you'll no longer swing and sway
Divinely down the scented shade,
Where feet to Ambulation fade,
And moons are lost in endless Day.
How shall we wind these wreaths of ours,
Where there are neither heads nor flowers?

Oh, Heaven's Heaven!—but we'll be missing
The palms, and sunlight, and the south;
And there's an end, I think, of kissing,
When our mouths are one with Mouth.

Taü here, Mamua,
Crown the hair, and come away!
Hear the calling of the moon,
And the whispering scents that stray
About the idle warm lagoon.
Hasten, hand in human hand,
Down the dark, the flowered way,
Along the whiteness of the sand,
And in the water's soft caress,
Wash the mind of foolishness,
Mamua, until the day.

Spend the glittering moonlight there
Pursuing down the soundless deep
Limbs that gleam and shadowy hair,
Or floating lazy, half-asleep.

Dive and double and follow after,
Snare in flowers, and kiss, and call,
With lips that fade, and human laughter
And faces individual,
Well this side of Paradise!
… There's little comfort in the wise.

Society Islands

Brooke died the following year on his way to fight in Turkey. Shortly beforehand, he received a letter from Matua that well conveys the love that early explorers encountered:

> Sweetheart you know I always thinking about you that time when you left me I been sorry for long time. We have good time when you was here I always remember about you forget me all ready oh! mon cher bien aime je t'aimerai toujours...je me rappeler toujours votre petite etroite figure et la petite bouche que me baise bien tu m'a perce a mon coeur et j'aime toujours ne m'oubli pas mon cher...I send you my kiss to you darling—mille kiss.

The white man has infected Tahiti with one last, recent horror: the introduction of invasive species. Just miconia, a pretty houseplant normally seen decorating suburban windowsills, has now displaced about 70 percent of Tahiti's indigenous forest.

MOOREA

James Michener, in *Return to Paradise*, wrote this: "Nothing on Tahiti is so majestic as what faces it across the bay, for there lies the island of Moorea. To describe it is impossible. It is a monument to the prodigal beauty of nature." Nevertheless, I shall describe it as a heart, but with two deep indentations in the top where the traditional heart carved into a tree would have but one. Cook's Bay is to the east and Opunoha Bay, to the west.

We shy away from a block of high-rise apartments floating in Cook's Bay, a brutalist cruise ship out of Papeete, preferring the unoccupied Opunoha Bay, a deep, beautiful, empty inlet. This, perversely, was the bay in which James Cook based his ships. Opunoha means stonefish, and indeed the bay holds a thriving population of these wonderfully repulsive, toxic bottom dwellers.

Diving on Opunoha's outer reef, far enough from a noisy hotel strip three miles away, we find the corals undamaged and fish abundant. How did natural selection come up with a fish divided precisely vertically into two portions, the front half black and the back half white? Of all the wonders in this ocean, the fish astonish me most. It's a wild guess that I have met between two thousand and five thousand different sorts, so extraordinarily varied that description is impossible outside a set of huge tomes with acres of

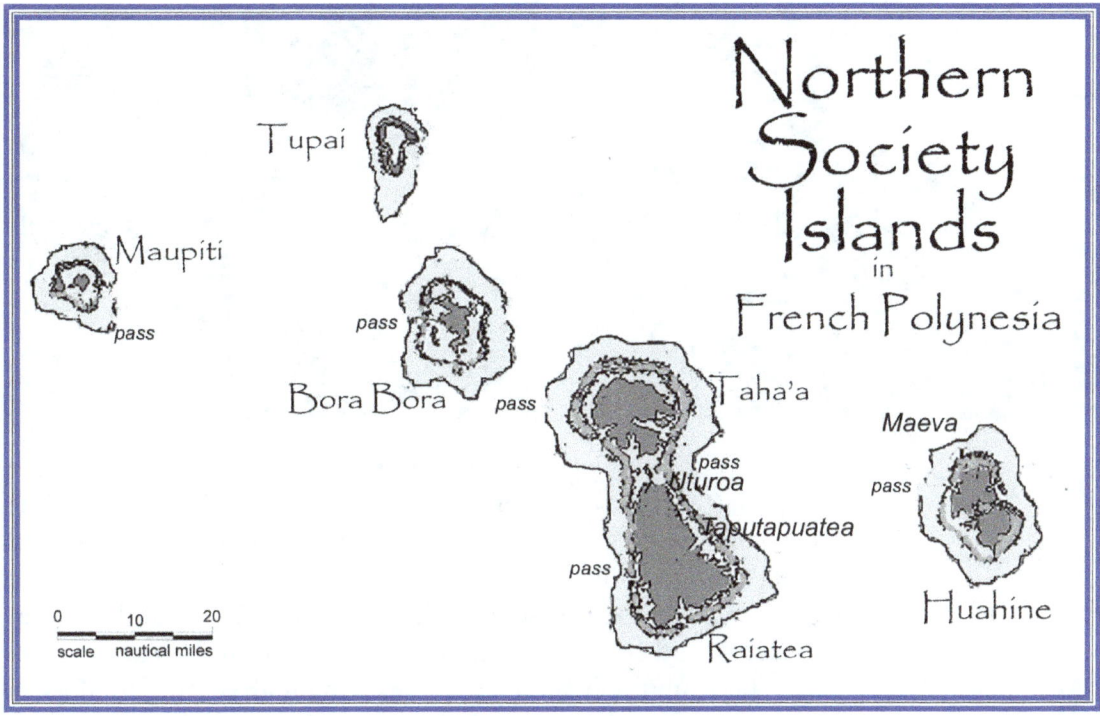

color plates. On each dive we meet old friends and are enchanted by new curiosities. The diversity of shape, pattern and color scheme seems limitless. If a creative team of commercial draftsmen, CAD experts, and art departments of advertising agencies were locked in a room for a month with hordes of schoolchildren with paint boxes and instructed to design fish, they might come up with half of the world's tropical fish. But would the team be able to invent a new one capable of surviving? One that does not already exist somewhere? Unlikely. I have learned to recognize a few, often by genus rather than species, for the varieties within each genus are prodigious. There are more than 100 sorts of butterfly fish; 60, of angel fish; 180, of wrasse; and 200, of damsel fish. Many have evocative names: the humpnose unicornfish, honey-headed damsel waltz with dusky sweetlips, and moustache triggerfish. My Polynesian favorites include the regal angel fish—brightly striped in green yellow and blue from head to tail—and one of the four varieties of Picasso triggerfish—a solitary sandy bottom dweller of subtle rainbow designs on a creamy skin.

Inland from Opunoha Bay, craggy mountains enclose an unspoiled bowl where a *lycée agricole* teaches pupils from all over the Society Islands about the cultivation of tropical fruits and vegetables. I bicycle along for a *dégustation de confitures*, tasting pots

Picasso triggerfish

of varied jams and jellies emerging from an effort to sell direct the somewhat experimental produce of the lycée. After touring the groves of strange cultivars and hybrid fruits propagated here and tasting enough jellies to cause sugar overload, I wobble back to the boat with a backpack loaded with banana, cinnamon and starfruit confitures, and several pineapples swinging from the handlebars.

Not far from the *lycée*, a few stones lying high on the shoulder of a hill mark the site of a long-abandoned village, noted by archaeologists for the remains of an archery range. Sweating rivers from the steep ride up but a sucker for traces of ancient culture, I ponder a riddle of this place, which proves that Polynesians long possessed the technology of bows and arrows. Yet, according to all scholarly researches, the islanders, whose way of life was as warlike and murderous as any, never got beyond considering archery a sporting activity for officers. Before the arrival of gunpowder from China changed war for ever, the outcome of Old World battles frequently turned on the skill and number of archers in each army. That Polynesians ignored the lethal potential of arrows is odd.

Rupert and Sam have now been replaced by new crew. A big, white smile surrounded by an incipient effort at a black beard is Pablo, who's introduced himself on e-mail through a cruising website. He is seeking an adventure before his working life in Spain kicks off. And my old friends David and Eminé have interrupted their life of corporate communications and growing olives to fly from Istanbul for a few weeks.

We anchor *Nereus* off a little jetty in the mud at the top of Opunoha Bay, where Marimari Kellum has invited us to visit.

"My father sailed into the bay in 1920 in an American four-masted, one hundred fifty-foot brig at just the right moment to buy the whole valley," Marimari relates. "It had been confiscated from a German trading company after the Great War. But, ten years later, the family fortune vanished in the crash of 1929, and we, in turn, lost it."

Marimari endures in the old house, cocooned among luxuriant Polynesian plants under a canopy of magnificent trees, occasionally looking wistfully across to the family paradise, now state owned. A graceful lady sitting amidst her collection of photos and memories, she's a font of prewar stories of the idle planters, crooked traders, cruel blackbirders and drunken captains who once infested the South Seas. On the corner of her lawn stands an iron missionary cooking pot, the size to stew a batch of three missionaries. I know it's a missionary pot, having studied hundreds of cannibal cartoons, though she prosaically calls it a try pot, a whale-blubber reducing vessel.

Missionary pot

HUAHINE

Marimari joins us for dinner on board, bringing a horse-bucket full of avocados and pamplemousses. As the last red glow of a magnificent sunset fades from the western sky, we run her ashore, and then head out through the pass for an overnight sail to Huahine, eighty-five miles northwest.

In 1773, Tobias Furneaux, James Cook's number two captain on his second voyage, sailed the *Adventure* this same route. He came away from Huahine with a trophy that would intrigue Georgian London right up to the king himself. The prize was a young man named Omai, the first native of the South Seas to be seen in Europe. He was entertained in palaces and great houses the length and breadth of England. A splendid, full-length portrait by Sir Joshua Reynolds (Omai was attired in utterly incongruous Arab robes) was recently sold by Christie's for $15 million, the first society portrait of a brown man ever painted. Omai was eventually returned to his homeland on Cook's third and last voyage in 1778, loaded with a curious choice of gifts, including bottles of port, an organ and a suit of armor. Perhaps puffed up with his own importance and lacking the protection of the high birth that he'd

Society Islands

Omai, Sir Joshua Reynolds

claimed among the foreigners, he could not reintegrate. His folk showed little interest in the wonders he had seen, and he was shunned as a sort of outcast, condemned to eke out a miserable existence in an unimportant village until his untimely death less than three years later.

My voyage bears no similarity to Cook's. Yet a parallel niggles at the edge of my conscience—the notion of taking away something of the exotic spirituality of the Pacific, and, later setting it before people who I fondly hope may relate to things I try to describe. When travelers to strange shores gather together, we grumble that the attention of home audiences for our tales of adventure is ephemeral once past routine questions about storms, freak waves, favorite islands and pirates. Omai, too, proved a nine-day wonder, losing the attention of a fickle public well before his two years in England were over.

We anchor off the capital village, a two-store metropolis standing where Furneaux received Omai on board after much negotiation and Cook returned him, and set off on bikes. In the north of Huahine lie the ruins of old Maeva, a remarkable spread of *marae*, stone platforms lining the shore with an *ahu*, a raised ceremonial area, at the seaward end of each, flanked by tall slabs of coral set on end. These would have been at their grandest in Cook's time. The place is a silent witness to past rituals, celebrations, magic—a cathedral of the polytheistic era. Was it serendipity that some ancient peoples invented writing and others ignored the potential of recorded signs and the written word? The reason was not the lack of materials in Polynesia, for tapa is surely the equal of papyrus. Without writing, very little is known of the history and habits of the hundred generations who developed a highly complex society centered on *marae* like these.

As Eminé leads the way along a vanilla-bordered trail, she suddenly hesitates. Two enormous women block the path, brandishing machetes. They tower over Eminé, who is by Turkish standards of more than average height, but that makes her no match for these Amazons appearing in the jungle. Trees of equivalent girth were logged and carted away for ship-of-the-line masts long ago. They

Crew at Maeva, Huahine

smile delightfully, murmur *bonjour* and continue with the task of tending vanilla vines. I can feel stories being mentally composed, for Eminé comes from a Turkish newspaper family and David was a BBC correspondent. We traverse the great stone blocks of a large forest *marae*, shaded by an immense banyan tree, and emerge at an open *marae* on the hillside above the forest. This ancient platform, which without doubt witnessed many alarming rites before missionaries chased out the Polynesian pantheon of gods of stone, wind, fire and sea, enjoys a glorious view over islands, lagoons and ocean. The delicate scent of vanilla pervades an incomparable scene.

Nearby stands a Sofitel with a "coral garden," inferior to most of the coral away from habitation but with a splendid plantation of Christmas tree worms. These create a shell with a little door, around which growing coral gives them protection. Two perfectly shaped Christmas trees reside in each shell. When retreat is indicated, they go inside and shut the door. Otherwise from each door issues the double Christmas tree, up to an inch high, of an astounding range and combination of colors. Debating whether this could be a particularly harmonious couple, we conclude that the double Christmas tree living in each house may be the twin ends of the same worm sticking out.

After returning the rented bikes, we sail down the lagoon to a lovely bay containing little but two expensive hostelries. Everything has proved expensive in French Polynesia, which enjoys an exaggerated exchange rate. Despite great debate, we get it wrong, selecting one run by a transvestite *mahu* who dislikes customers. Requesting a coffee to wind up dinner, we are firmly told the place is *fermé*, though it is but 8:15 P.M. The other more congenial shack plies us with coffees and cognacs till late.

TAHA'A

Taha'a is an easy twenty-five miles west of Huahine. With *Nereus* at anchor in calm, pale blue water beside a pass where two little palm-sprouting motus mark the ends of the encircling reef, I go diving for shells. In a deep hole lurks a giant, a huge moray eel that I fail to spot until it is within a couple of feet of my mask. Face to face with the nastiest set of teeth in the ocean, I'm momentarily mesmerized by its terrifyingly overstocked maw, slowly gaping open and closing again as it eyes me up. Recoiling with reflex fear that makes my scalp go taut even under water, I find to my horror three more monster moray eels undulating around me. Each is eight or more feet long and as thick as a football thigh. Morays have a sinister way of threatening passing traffic, scowling with a slowly yawning jaw, slithering menacingly a few inches in and out of their lairs. The bite of even a thin, two-foot moray can take a finger off, and once bitten by its backward-slanting teeth, it is hard to get its jaws open to recover whatever mangled body part the creature has chomped on. My companions are the giants of the species, truly fearsome monsters. Though it's claimed that they are really very friendly (by the sort of people who get on well with crocodiles, I suspect), that the yawn serves only to push water through their gills, and that they can be tamed, I prefer sharks. Retreat is indicated, at high speed to the surface, to safety aboard and a restoring beaker of whisky.

Another couple of miles in from the reef, we moor outside a shack with "Hotel" just discernible in faded lettering on its corrugated iron roof. By its jetty are enclosures containing a small bronze whaler and several turtles. Its owner has a passion for rescuing turtles from the fishermen, who would otherwise eat them and sell the carapace. Once any damage is repaired, he releases them back into the ocean. His contribution to conservation is no cheap indulgence, for he pays the fishermen around $80 for each uneaten turtle.

Hibiscus dinner comes with entertainment. Dancers part and make way for Déta, a fine figure of a three-hundred-pound

Polynesian Bacchus clad in nothing but a short pareu and a wreath of bougainvillea in his hair, blessed with a face the features of which—forehead, nose, moustache, bottom lip and chin—are a perfect straight line. Déta's instrument is the one-string bin, a large black plastic trashcan, upended, with a small hole in the bottom. A string is inserted through this hole and knotted, the other end being secured to the tip of a three-foot stick. The stick is held on top of the trashcan so that the string is tightened when it is canted a little away; the note is obtained by tensioning the string thus and holding it against the stick while being plucked with the other hand. It's a modern mutation of perhaps the most ancient string instrument of all.

Déta follows his solo with a coconut-opening demonstration, instructive to those of us who, like Tom Hanks in *Castaway*, find a hundred strokes with a machete to be necessary to gain entry to a coconut. Accompanied by a dozen musicians banging and tapping carved wooden percussion instruments, the coconut is de-husked with three mighty blows on a sharp upright stick, cracked with three light taps of a machete, and then finely grated in a minute flat on another pointed stick projecting from his stool. This lesson will be put to good use later.

Deta and the one-string trashcan

Society Islands

As the sun sinks in a blaze of gold over the craggy outline of Bora Bora, the turquoise water lapping at our hull, bright coral and lovely fish just under the keel, music wafting and cold drink in hand, I feel for the hundredth time on this voyage how remarkably fortunate we are, at least on the borders of elysium. Though we're in daily touch with civilization by e-mail, the real world is far distant, turned off. Or is this the real world, not just the flavor of paradise?

RAIATEA

Across a narrow strait at Uturoa, capital of Raiatea, the *Hawaikinui* is expected at midday to bear Eminé and David away to Papeete for their plane back to Istanbul, so we sneak in to the commercial dock to await her. She chugs alongside in a cloud of smoke three hours late and is turned around by a swarm of buzzing Caterpillar forklifts in an hour. The *Aremiti* is equally late bringing Lulu from Spain to join the crew, fortunate for her as she has to bully her way aboard the overbooked steamer in Papeete at the last minute by waving a press card and claiming to be a famous TV journalist.

Hawaikinui is a reminder that, here in Raiatea, we are in the wellspring of Polynesian culture. Whenever the *vaka*, the great ocean sailing canoes of the ancestors, came upon new lands to be settled, the most important island in a group was named after the Polynesians' time-shrouded origin, Hawaiki. Raiatea is the old Hawaiki of these islands, the hallowed home. Here was the doubly sacred *marae* of Taputapuatea, honored among Polynesians for the dedication of *vaka* and crew before setting forth on brave expeditions across the ocean, including Pa'ao's thirteenth century invasion of Hawai'i. Though little of the *marae* has survived, it has at least been spared the indignity of a Christian church being plonked on it. The temple of ancient standing stones frowning upon the wide sea remains an eerie spiritual place, where, once daytime tourists are gone, the old gods still rule.

The crew for the next few hundred miles is completed by a recently qualified lawyer flying from England. On the evidence of a couple of short passages among the Society Islands, however, he judges that life on the ocean is terrifying and bows out. After a circuit of Raiatea we sail the twenty-five miles to the single entrance pass through Bora Bora's surrounding reef. Strange that we always seem to be the only sailors putting to sea on a Friday the thirteenth.

BORA BORA

Bora Bora was once written Pora Pora, as Polynesian languages are ambivalent about *b*'s and *p*'s, as they are about *k*'s and *t*'s, and *r*'s and *l*'s. "Cook was changed into Toote," Forster noted. There are few consonants in Polynesian languages, only seven in Hawaiian, for instance, and they are used sparingly. Rules dictate that each vowel is pronounced separately, and consonants must be separated by one or more vowels. A marriage between Polynesian and Polish might produce a balance of vowels and consonants seeming sensible to an English speaker. A Polynesian goddess, who resides on the top of the Bora Bora mountain, has the name Oaaoa. We run an A-list competition, won by Lulu, who trumps Faa'a, the airport suburb of Papeete, with a village on Taha'a called Faaaha.

The Polynesian languages of New Zealand, Hawai'i and the scattered islands of the South Pacific sound similar to the European ear and have much in common, something that Captain Cook noted with surprise as he considered the vast distances separating the island groups and the seeming impossibility of anyone crossing such expanses of ocean in canoes. We know now that they stem from the same roots through the ocean migrations of the last three thousand years. They have supplied English with few words; *tatu* (tattoo) and *tapu* (tabu, which means "sacred" as well as "forbidden") are the usual examples. Two other suspicious words I come across are *pusi* (cat) and *puke* (ill), though they could have traveled either way.

Bora Bora is grand. The nearly unbroken outer reef forms a protective ring of crashing surf enclosing the main island as well several smaller islands, with 2,400-foot Mount Onemanu looming craggily in the center. The globally-distributed travel posters do not lie; the broad lagoon is every sort of blue and just deep enough to sail all round the central island, except for a mile or so at the south end where some of the seriously expensive hotels are clustered. I avoid spending much time in popular places, but Bora Bora is a worthy exception.

We are in time for the *Quattorze Juillet* festivities, which cap two weeks of parades, contests and dancing, celebrating the fall of the Bastille all over the French world just as every 14 of July is celebrated in metropolitan France, though camouflaged here under the guise of a Polynesian fête. The festival, which kicks off at eight in the morning with bike and banana races in the square, is

Society Islands

Bora Bora sunrise

a competitive island affair, more dogs than tourists about and not a Frenchman in sight. There are bands from Bora Bora's five districts, each with their leading dancers. The girls are clad in intricate confections of grass, flowers and leaves, oiled skin sparkling and pelvises vibrating at impossible frequency to the tamure beat. The men's knee-shaking is hypnotically manic, the music pure, compelling percussion as the musicians bang, tap and saw away on a weird assortment of wooden boxes and drums.

It's music, too, that draws us to church. Christianity is new enough in the islands to have a near universal grip. Perhaps this will erode with the passing of another century or two, fading into a social routine or an obsolete set of beliefs as for many in the Western world. For the present, it is Christianity that sets the scene and pastors who set the agenda. A traveler who ignores this misses the heart of Oceania.

The *Temple Protestant de Vaitape* is dedicated to Ebene Ezere, perhaps an allusion to the stone that Samuel erected to commemorate some divine assistance in slaughtering Philistines and named Ebenezer. Sunday morning service is conducted by two pastors in Tahitian, with a lesson from St. Luke, the Good Samaritan, read in English for our benefit. Our expectations of the singing are not upset. Without any accompaniment, sections of the congregation leap to their feet and burst into song, seemingly unprompted, lovely songs with complicated internal harmonies. Some of the old hens sound like roosters greeting the dawn, but in their flowery frocks and magnificent millinery—prolifically decorated hats of palm fronds, hibiscus and pandanus—they deserve to be forgiven the occasional shrill note. The lilting hymns seem to me to express not so much Christian fervor as an unbroken thread of island spirituality.

It seems curious that protestant prelates justify their existence in paradise by preaching damnation and propounding visions of hell. We are eventually driven forth when, after one pastor with the demeanor of a stage version of Mephistopheles has delivered an interminable fire-and-brimstone sermon, another launches into his stride. This seems to be the cross-denominational Pacific custom; at a Methodist service in Fiji we were to suffer five officiants, all women, taking turns to preach competitively at a cowering congregation.

Lifted by the singing, I climb a long way up the mountain that gives Bora Bora its distinctive outline, a steep root-hanger of a faint trail in the deep shade of big trees. I always feel a pull to climb to the top of high islands, perhaps hazy whether I am a hillman or a seaman at heart. My childhood Devonshire home stood on a wooded hill looking across Lyme Bay, and I have spent many weeks in the high Alps. Rudyard Kipling, a family friend and my sister's godfather, well expressed an equivalence in resounding verse:

Who hath desired the Sea?—the sight of salt water unbounded–
The heave and the halt and the hurl and the crash of the comber wind-hounded?
The sleek barrelled swell before storm, grey, foamless, enormous, and growing–
Stark calm on the lap of the Line or the crazy-eyed hurricane blowing–
His Sea in no showing the same—his Sea and the same 'neath each showing–
His Sea as she slackens or thrills?
So and no otherwise—so and no otherwise hillmen desire their Hills!

Who hath desired the Sea?—the immense and contemptuous surges?
The shudder, the stumble, the swerve, as the star-stabbing bowsprit emerges?
The orderly clouds of the Trades, and the ridged, roaring sapphire thereunder–
Unheralded cliff-haunting flaws and the headsail's low-volleying thunder–
His Sea in no wonder the same—his Sea and the same through each wonder:
His Sea as she rages or stills?
So and no otherwise—so and no otherwise hillmen desire their Hills!

We sail round the island through some narrow and shallow dogleg passes to the end of navigable waters, anchoring for lunch with pure white sand two feet under the keel. Then we bump along the bottom through the constricted entrance to the once beautiful

Baie Maitira, now lined by expensive hostelries. Fortunately, the hotels in Bora Bora have been built in the comparatively unobtrusive cow-pie bungalow style, often over the water so guests can appreciate marine life through coffee tables while sipping pina coladas. In relation to Bora Bora's worldwide fame, there are surprisingly few hotel beds, though supplemented regularly for a day or two by a cruise ship.

There is a spot where locals hand-feed the fish; it's easy to fool them with a small piece of antler coral that they are being tempted with something delicious. I'm quickly enveloped in a piscatorial cloud, jostling and queuing for a taste of my bit of coral, nibbling my fingers, giving a close-up view of innumerable species. From the front, like this, one can observe normally unseen detail. For instance, a fairly nondescript reddish fish has its upper lip camouflaged to appear to be two huge, light blue buck teeth. If a Bugs Bunny fish exists, this would have to be it. Parrotfish, squirrel fish, all sorts of striped wrasses, angel fish, endless variations of butterfly fish, and a thousand others nose up to my mask in a magical mêlée of flashing fins.

Even here in Bora Bora, a destination that has stimulated more acres of purple prose than most in the Pacific, the tat and hype of tourism can be easily avoided. Bloody Mary's bar with its roll of famous visitors escapes our attention, as do the hotels; the celebrations we join seem entirely local affairs. Perhaps hotel guests are not encouraged to venture beyond the cocoons of in-hotel entertainment and organized excursions in the lagoon. When we thumb a lift into town for more great dancing in the square, dogs outnumber the tourists watching.

MAUPITI

The books disclose that Maupiti's lagoon is accessible only through a difficult pass. Selfishly, I bless the guides for their excessive caution, for we have glorious places to ourselves where the few passing cruising boats are discouraged. The western high island of French Polynesia proves to be another fragment of paradise, my favorite island of the Societies.

The entrance pass is indeed interesting: narrow and crooked, with rough reefs all about. Once through its hungry jaws, the passage winds in among pretty motus and then along a channel beaconed through coral for two miles across to Maupiti itself.

It's not large, about ten miles around with a population under a thousand. A lagoon of turquoise water sleeps in the evening shadow of the high Gibraltar-shaped volcano-plug that created the island a million years ago, sheltered to seaward by a ring of motus. It's Sunday morning as we park *Nereus* opposite the church standing at the water's edge. Unaccompanied melodies come drifting across the water. Luscious scents too, for even in this quiet byway, a boulangerie is turning out delectable croissants and *pains-au-chocolat*.

Climbing the steep, jungly mountainside above the village is like using an inclined treadmill, for the drifts of ancient coconuts underfoot roll back with each step. Most high Pacific islands lack tracks up through the steep forests, for islanders seldom go to the top without a good food reason. Tracing vestiges of an ancient *piste* overrun by the thick foliage, we nearly make the top but the route for the last hundred feet eludes us. Rather than climb a cliff face, we retreat, plastered with sharp burrs and sustained by the hearts of a couple of palm trees dismembered with the ship's shackle knife. From around a thousand feet, Maupiti is a gem nestling in this lake of every blue, edged with forested motus, each skirted by a shimmering beach. Eagle rays can be seen here and there, snuffling around the coral outcrops that color the shallow, crystal waters.

While their father, a jovial fellow with a full set of teeth except all the front ones, fetches three heavy stems of bananas in his canoe from a far motu, little Teruia and her pretty big sister, improbably named Gladys, bring bracelets and necklaces of sea urchin and shell, and then sail with us to a tiny beachside pension on a motu by the pass for a meal of parrotfish *cru* and roasted breadfruit under an old purao tree festooned with bananas and rusting spearguns. The proprietor, retired captain of one

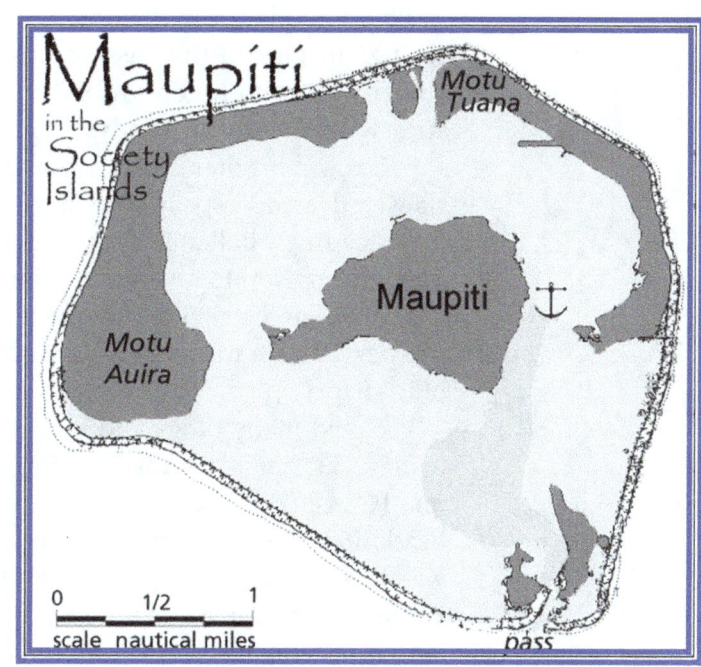

Maupiti

of the little Society Island supply ships, plays ukulele and sings island songs for us under a tree pendulous with at least a hundred threatening coconuts as the crescent moon sets over *Nereus*, rocking quietly on the stream bracketed between palm-covered motus.

This is a place for dreams, so we stay a while, snorkeling the strong currents of the pass and eating with island people ashore. Fabien comes to lunch on board, a chic young man whose dalliance with the lovely Gladys has made him the father of a small son. His kid brother offers a kebab of the ugliest things in the sea skewered on his spear: two moray eels and a stonefish, the latter a leading challenge to gourmets. Its ventral spines deliver a powerful poison to anyone unlucky enough to tread on it, yet bits are considered delicious. By contrast, ribbon eels are among the prettiest. The startling eels here are cadmium yellow with electric blue stripes.

I've read many blogs and books by voyagers, but no one seems to have as much trouble leaving beautiful, hospitable places as me. It's another wrench as we squeeze out through the pass and head into the setting sun once more, as we must. By the graveyard watch, little Maupihaa is abeam, the western outpost of French Polynesia and the francophone area. From here on it will be local languages and English until Nouvelle Calédonie, another part of the sprawling French Pacific empire lying two thousand five hundred miles farther west. With the mizzen boom groaning from the weight of three mighty racks of bananas swinging aft, a quota is imposed: All crew members must consume at least four bananas for breakfast, under penalty of doing the day's dishes.

Pablo with Maupiti ladies on board

Paradise Past

THOR HEYERDAHL developed a theory that Polynesians came initially from South America, spreading thence westwards across the Pacific. He had the courage to set out from Peru in 1947 on his fragile *Kon-Tiki* balsa raft to test this idea by following what he surmised was the same route. He made it to the Tuamotus, where *Kon-Tiki* came to a grinding halt on a reef. His theory has fared even less well. The mystery of the ocean migrations of the Polynesians has become better understood with examination of the clues, the traces left by the pigs, dogs, chickens and rats they took with them, the spread of taro, breadfruit, yam, coconut and bananas, DNA and linguistic analysis, and occasional Lapita pottery, first found in New Caledonia. Anthropologists now seem unanimous that the islanders sprang originally from Southeast Asia. The Lapita People were on the Solomon Islands by 1300 BC and got as far as Fiji and Samoa before fading from history. Their successors colonized Polynesia, reaching the Marquesas at the time of Christ and thence settled Easter Island and Hawai'i over the following few hundred years, and New Zealand (where they became the Maoris) about 1000 AD. The final habitable Pacific island, Chatham, which lies four hundred miles east of New Zealand, was colonized by Polynesians only a hundred years before Europeans turned up. Chicken studies indicate that Polynesians even reached South America.

Open water distances they covered were thus vast. The people who traveled for weeks out of sight of land in primitive craft may have been the finest navigators the world has ever seen. They had no metal, no instruments, no compasses, no paper charts. They wrote nothing down, for they had no writing. It has, however, become clear that this was no haphazard venturing into the unknown, and that their navigation was a considerable science, built upon by successive generations. The knowledge of navigators was treated as reverently as that of the gods, and navigators ranked with the highest in the hierarchical systems of the Polynesian and Micronesian islands.

The invention of outrigger canoes made the voyages possible. The hulls of small canoes were usually shaped from a single log with a stone adz, but the great double canoes were built of planks lashed together with natural fibers and caulked with local materials. "Canoe" may have come to sound a misleading term, for oceangoing *vaka* were up to a hundred feet in length, and records show them carrying fifty to a hundred people and more.

The navigators understood how to read the presence of land from wave patterns at great distances, and from cloud reflections, birds' flights and flotsam. Once islands were discovered and populated, the challenge was reliable navigation from one to another over hundreds of miles of empty ocean in changeable winds and currents, and often overcast conditions. The master navigators taught their favored heirs how to use the sailing instruments. Their methods used star-paths at night, the sun when close to the horizon, wind and current patterns learned over generations, and—most complex of all—the underlying ocean swells. Despite there seldom being less than three different swells present, all overlaid with wave patterns from local winds, the navigators could distinguish the characteristics of each swell and deduce a heading for the canoe. The systems they developed were accurate enough to support considerable traffic. The professional navigators were so confident in their abilities that, when the magnetic compass was eventually available, they used it as a backup if at all.

Western contact eventually spelled the end of regular traditional navigation along with so much else. To control their islands, the Germans banned voyaging altogether. By the twentieth century, there was no remaining master navigator in Polynesia.

Among the few daring to follow Ferdinand Magellan on Pacific voyages of discovery or pillage were Drake, Mendaña, Quirós, and the Dutchmen Le Maire and Roggeveen. But little was discovered for two hundred years, and little changed until the voyages of the late eighteenth century. Cartographers filled the blank spaces on maps of the Pacific with monsters and guesses at a presumed "southern continent."

Then, led in 1765 by Admiral John Byron, the poet's grandfather, a handful of adventurous captains found thousands of South Seas islands within a few years.

Their reports inflamed European visions of a far-off Eden. Byron chanced on some of the Tuamotus before sailing on to the East Indies, Philip Carteret saw Pitcairn Island in 1767 and continued to the fabled Solomon Islands, and Samuel Wallis found Tahiti. Less than a year after Wallis, the French soldier, explorer, seaman and mathematician Louis-Antoine de Bougainville arrived in Tahiti. It was his log that, when published in Paris, set Europe alight with tales of sex in the Pacific, a basis of folklore that has persisted ever since:

De Bougainville
1729–1811

> The boats were full of females who, for agreeable features, are not inferior to most European women, and who, in point of beauty of the body might, with much reason, vie with them all. Most of these fair females were naked...
>
> The Tahitians pressed us to choose a woman and come on shore with her, and their gestures, which were not ambiguous, denoted in what manner we should form an acquaintance with her...
>
> I felt I had been transported into the Garden of Eden.

Samuel Wallis had sailed from Plymouth in August 1766 in the *Dolphin*, furnished with instructions to reinforce tenuous British claims to recently mapped bits of the Pacific, and to find new ones. The following June, Wallis "discovered" Tahiti, which he named George III Island for the reigning monarch, ignoring the existence of any established local name in the imperial fashion of the day. He reported that he was met by three hundred canoes, some loaded with provisions, some with warriors who pelted the *Dolphin* with stones, but many with women apparently offering all sorts of favors. Once the warriors had been cowed by a couple of salvoes, friendly relations were established. The Tahitians went mad for the metal objects the sailors showed them, the first they had seen, and nails, pots and implements commanded many pigs, fruits and fowls in exchange. The sailors quickly discovered that a metal present would secure the most delightful experiences with the local ladies, and quietly raided the ship for objects to be traded thus. One nail might be exchanged—so it was soon established—for one screw.

Once all easily accessible metal had been converted, the sailors started in on the *Dolphin's* fastenings, removing any nails they could access. It all came to a head when able seaman Pinckney was caught taking the large nails fixing the cleats to which the mainsheet was belayed, and, after drawing the spikes, throwing the cleats overboard. Instead of the trade he had been expecting to make, he was whipped three times round the deck, though "most of the crew being equally criminal with himself, he was handled so tenderly, that others were rather encouraged to repeat the offence than deterred by the fear of punishment," as Wallis recorded in his log.

By this time the sailors were sleeping on the deck, having traded all the fastenings to which their hammocks were attached. Wallis had to leave Tahiti swiftly to save his ship.

Capt. Wallis arrives in Tahiti, From Hawkesworth, pub 1773

Captain James Cook voyaged the Pacific three times between 1769 and his death in Hawai'i in 1779, charting more new lands for the Europeans than any man before or since. He passed three months in Tahiti in 1769 and returned on both his subsequent voyages. Mindful of the *Dolphin*'s near destruction at the hands of its own crew, he carried plenty of spare nails.

Apart from the excursions of a Spaniard, Don Domingo de Boenechea from Peru, between 1772 and 1777 with boatloads of missionaries who proved thoroughly unsuccessful in converting Polynesians and a fleeting visit in 1787 by the first ship to carry English convicts to the terrible settlement at Botany Bay in New Holland (soon to be renamed Australia by Matthew Flinders), no one else appeared in Tahiti before the famous Captain Bligh in the year of the French Revolution, 1789. Cook's log, like the others, celebrates the discovery of paradise, though in more measured terms than the Frenchman's. Two of Cook's crewmen actually attempted to desert to stay with their girls. He quickly thwarted their escape and departed the siren island in good shape. It was the *Bounty*'s crew who were first to be entirely bewitched.

Capt. James Cook 1728–1779

Captain Bligh had been ordered to collect breadfruit saplings and transport them back around Cape Horn and up the Atlantic to the West Indies, thereby to experiment with feeding slaves more economically. The information on which he was to base the enterprise must have been worse than sketchy, the reports of Cook and the few others. This project broke new ground in numerous respects, and can only have been given a modest chance of success. HMS *Bounty* was unable to weather Cape Horn, sailed around the world the other way and arrived in the wrong season, arboriculturally. She had to hang out in Tahiti for six months waiting for what was believed to be the correct time for transplanting the breadfruit, a delay that provided time for temptation beyond the men's endurance.

Led by first officer Fletcher Christian, the crew formed deep attachments to the Polynesian ladies and tasted a paradise unimaginable to ill-nourished men cramped in filthy, stinking quarters subject to iron discipline for months on end on a dangerous

Paradise Past

Cook's Resolution

cockleshell. As they were passing through Tonga, three weeks after the *Bounty* finally sailed out of Tahiti with her cargo of young trees in April 1790, they mutinied. This has often been presented as the reasonable revolt of a crew against a tyrannical captain, but though the trigger may have been Bligh's inflexible view of his duty, it was in truth the pull of paradise. These men had seen heaven, experienced it, and though the retribution of the British navy was inevitable, a few months of bliss seemed worth any penalty.

Bligh was bundled with eighteen companions into the longboat and shoved off. In the next forty-one days, he completed one of the world's most remarkable survival voyages, navigating utterly unknown waters and arriving exactly where he aimed for in Timor, four thousand miles away. It would have been beyond the imagination of that starved and half-dead crew that the British National Maritime Museum recently paid $250,000 for Bligh's coconut drinking shell and his horn mug, together with the silver bullet he used to weigh out an ounce or so of daily food for each man.

Twenty-four-year-old Christian, now in command of the *Bounty*, had the crew heave all the breadfruit saplings into the sea and headed back east where they lingered once more in Tahitian heaven and the *Bounty* was doubtless plundered for the remainder of its nails. Knowing the Navy would be along to deal with the mutineers, Christian at last set sail with eight of his crew plus twelve Polynesian women and six Polynesian men, abandoning a further sixteen English crew who even then remained unwilling to leave their paradise in Tahiti (the British navy did indeed round them up a year later), and sailed off to find a refuge. Having tried a number of islands, he recalled Carteret's brief report of Pitcairn more than twenty years earlier. Despite its remoteness, a thousand miles upwind from Tahiti, and the almost total absence of information (Carteret had called it "scarce better than a large rock in the ocean") Christian hunted for it and after quartering the ocean for many days found it. The ship was burnt and a little settlement on Pitcairn established. He and the others may have initially seen this as their final paradise, safe from the fury of the Sea Lords in

London, but it was not to be. They quickly fell out. Within ten years, aided by the hooch they managed to brew, all the men had killed each other or themselves—except one. John Adams was discovered years later by the British navy. Converted to The Lord and, with the aid of the *Bounty*'s salvaged Bible, Adams was preaching in a little chapel. He was left in peace with his ten remaining women, and survived a further thirty years. With his newfound devotion to God, his female flock, and the children of the mutineers to bring up, his memories of an impoverished childhood in city slums and the miserable life of a sailor, and no one save God to tell him what to do, the two-and-one-half-square-mile island may have been as close to paradise for John Adams as any man has experienced. Pitcairn is now solely populated by the descendants of those children, about fifty of them.

Admiral William Bligh
1754–1817

This familiar story spawned five feature films, with Christian played as some sort of hero by Wilson Power, Errol Flynn, Clark Gable, Marlon Brando and Mel Gibson. Like most of the audience, I thought of the Pacific of the time as a well traveled sea, unaware of Bligh's remarkable fortitude and skill at a time when instruments were rudimentary, only a handful of European vessels had sailed the vast Pacific, and the chances of the previously reported position of an island being correct to within fifty or a hundred miles were slight.

It was tempting to sail to Pitcairn, but, like Easter Island, it has no harbor and poor shelter. Many, even the majority, of the few sailors who get there find they cannot spend time ashore before they have to head for the open ocean again in the face of grim weather.

Paradise Past

The One-Family Island

PALMERSTON

"*NEREUS, NEREUS*, welcome to Palmerston."

Getting a response to a radio call is unique in the islands, and it's from one of the farthest of all, an island with a population of just fifty-one souls.

"You sail round the north of the island," the voice says. "We will meet you on the west side and show you where to put the anchor."

"Roger, Mr. Marsters," I say. "See you shortly."

I can address the voice on the other end of the airwave by name for a remarkable reason: For one hundred forty years, everyone on Palmerston has been part of a single family—the Marsters.

We do as bidden. Now partially sheltered from the near gale, we follow the surf three miles down the western, leeward side where an open boat is waiting to shepherd us to the only possible spot to lodge the anchor on a small coral shelf a few feet square, forty feet down the outside of Palmerston's encircling reef.

Our four days at sea, plowing a lonely furrow through the center of the Pacific to reach Palmerston, are repaid in gold. This speck of land, a distant outlier of the Cook Islands two hundred miles from its nearest tiny neighbor, is close to the perfect tropical island of the imagination, the stuff of fantasy. For a boy like me growing up in post-war European austerity, years when an orange or banana was a luxury and an avocado unheard of, stories of exotic desert

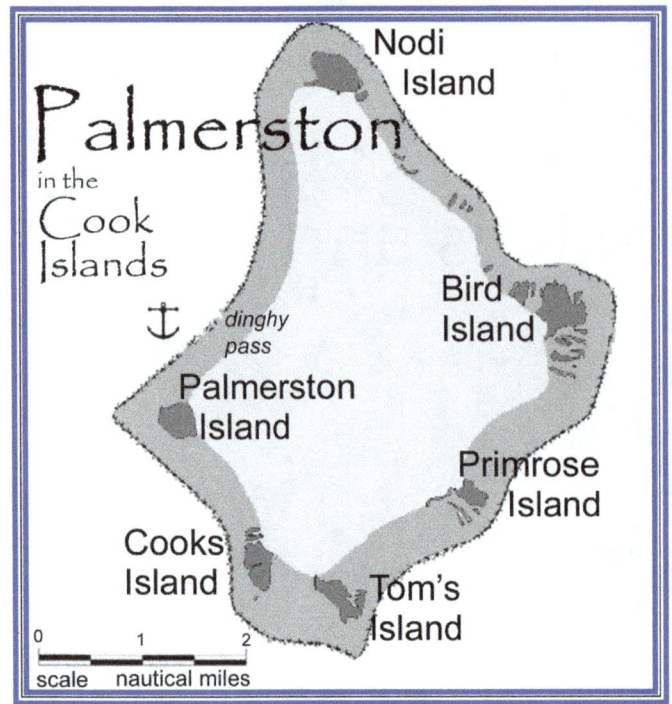

islands were serious escapism and stirred wanderlust. Though the wispy memory of the Swiss Family Robinson, Robinson Crusoe and Treasure Island have grown faint with time, nothing could come closer to the south seas paradise of imagination, the blues and greens of ultimate natural beauty.

We are soon visited by a boat bearing four men, two of whom are designated health and agriculture officers. All, of course, are named Marsters.

The following morning a radio call brings Simon Marsters out at the tiller of a thin boat. He's a handsome man with latte coloring, the bearing of an Englishman, and the Polynesian features somewhere between Indian and Caucasian, that prompted early anthropologists to believe that Polynesians must have somehow sprung from European stock. "Jump in and hang on!" he commands.

We get a roller-coaster ride through a narrow, crooked, three-foot-deep gash in the reef against a strong outgoing tide, and thence across a shallow lagoon to a sheltered beach. This main island of the atoll ring is shaded by coconut palms interspersed with fruit trees and frangipani. Well inland stand groves of mature mahogany, planted by the ancestors. Pandanus fringes the fine white beach girdling the island. Inside the ten-mile-long encircling reef, which drops sheer to the ocean bed fourteen thousand feet below, the lagoon runs from the palest aquamarine to every blue in the paint box, speckled with isolated growths of coral showing clearly through transparent water. Around the outside, a chain of lush green motus edged with white sand protects the calm water within from all but the fiercest moods of the ocean. Even the main harvest of the sea, the parrotfish, are multicolored iridescent marvels. The air is crystal, for the only pollution that reaches this far is occasional volcanic dust.

William Marsters, an English seaman, arrived in Palmerston in 1863 to start a coconut plantation. He found it unoccupied, as had

Captain Cook a century earlier. After a gypsy life in the central Pacific, perhaps he was fleeing rules and monogamy. He'd recruited three Polynesian ladies from Penryn, a small island a few hundred miles to the northeast, each of whom bore him a family. His wives were not sisters, as Pacific lore sometimes has it, though two were first cousins. He found time to spare from growing coconuts to acquire a fourth wife and raise twenty-three children. The island, leased for an unaffordable and unpaid £50 a year from the British Crown and now reputedly his through a personal gift from Queen Victoria, (finally regularized in 1954 when the family ownership was confirmed) was at his death in 1899 divided among the three families. By the fifth generation there were more than a thousand descendants.

Parrot fish

There's no suggestion of interbreeding on the island, for William's will contained strict instructions governing intermarriage as well as the allocation of land. Over the years, most of his descendants have emigrated to Rarotonga, the capital of the Cook Islands, to New Zealand and elsewhere, producing a diaspora of Marsters in the southern hemisphere. But representatives of each family have followed William's constitution and survived on the island to enjoy their Palmerston inheritance. Aside from the greatly diluted admixture of the patriarch's British genes, the people are Polynesian.

Like many a Pacific island, Palmerston was first spotted by Captain Cook. He returned to gather fodder for his shipboard animals on his third and final voyage, plotting its position so accurately (just nine miles out, after months at sea only a 36-second error on Harrison's recently invented chronometer) that it was 1969 before anyone bothered to correct his data. Like most of the charts we use, the hydrographic information for the area is based on nineteenth century surveys, but I am glad to find in this case that the adjustment has been incorporated. An atoll can't be seen from a small boat's deck further than this.

"You will have lunch with us," Simon tells us. "But first you have to see about the paper." Once Melbourne Marsters has reluctantly

The One-Family Island

completed pages of immigration formalities, which Rarotonga has just incongruously imposed on this far-flung dot on the chart as a contribution to the world's meaningless bureaucracy, a fine meal of mahimahi, barracuda, and honey taro pancakes with Simon's family of eight is followed by coffee with Goodly Marsters and a game of volleyball. The music of the trade wind in the coconut trees accompanies lilting songs by Mamma and the older ladies, rehearsing for Cook Islands Independence Day celebrations. At dusk, Simon loads us with fillets of parrotfish for supper and a loaf of bread his wife has baked, and returns us to *Nereus*, rocking in the ocean swell just off the reef. He chuckles at my anxiety about his finding his way back in through the turbulent, crooked alleyway pass in the dark after several large gin-and-fresh-limes on board. Sailors have this great advantage over land travelers to rare destinations: hospitality can be two-way.

The land populated by the families of William Marsters, now in their fifth to seventh generation, has no harbor, lagoon entrance or airstrip. Everybody lives together on one island of about half a square mile, which together with the ten uninhabited islands scattered widely round the reef total three hundred fifty acres of land, is equitably divided between the three families as laid down by the founding forefather. Coconut palms are everywhere, added to by an island tradition each time a child is born on the island.

"The placenta is buried and two coconut trees planted on the spot; these become the property of the child," Edward tells us as he shows us his island. "Few of the coconuts are picked up now as copra prices are depressed and transport expensive, so we gather only what we can use ourselves."

Being a coral atoll, little useful vegetation grows naturally other than palms, arrowroot and pandanus, for which the old sailors' name "screwpine" is still in use. The islanders have nevertheless made the barren earth produce abundant fruit and vegetables.

"We made swamps by excavating the coral sand down to the bedrock," Edward says, "then collecting the fallen leaves from island trees. You can see the spoil piled around the edges."

The protective banks are five feet high, which doesn't sound like much, but it doubles the height of the island above sea level and has served as a refuge to the people when cyclone-driven seas have swept across the reef and through the houses.

As we sit drinking coconuts one evening, Melbourne Marsters relates how a cyclone, still remembered as The Big Blow, tore through Palmerston in 1926, destroying everything except William

Palmerston main street

Marsters' own house, constructed of massive timbers from an 1865 shipwreck and standing to this day. "The church was recovered two hundred yards from its foundations, dragged back and secured with heavy piles. This was also built from salvaged ships timbers. The approach to the pulpit is the gangway from the *Tour d'Auverne*, which was wrecked on Palmerston in 1913 with a cargo of coal, wine and rum."

The islanders acquired rights to the lot for £30, probably never paid. There's no record of the party that followed. The tiny church's ceiling was once the captain's cabin wall.

Each member of the Marsters family evidently recognizes how special Palmerston is, despite the familiarity of living there, the inevitable problems of being so few and so remote, and lacking virtually everything others take for granted. Water must be caught when it rains, fuel for generators and boats has to be shipped in at great cost, connection to the Cook Islands capital and the outside world is limited to a single short-wave radio. Yet the islanders defied the Cook Islands government in voting down the offer of an airstrip.

Edward explains, "We only get supplied by a boat from Rarotonga about three times a year. It's very uncertain when they come, but you see we have everything we need, and passing boats like you fill some of the gaps and sometimes carry mail."

The One-Family Island

Clearly, there are some who would appreciate the money to be gained from a bit of tourism, but they remain a minority. The cash earnings of Palmerston were estimated by an old New Zealand study at £1,500 for the period between 1925 and 1950—the total for the twenty-five years, that is, equating to about $5 per person per year. Even in a tropical subsidence paradise this proved a tad inadequate, and a decision was taken voluntarily to limit the population to around the present fifty.

Nevertheless these are no primitives. All adults have spent time in New Zealand or Rarotonga, some further afield where one islander even acquired a Marsters degree. They understand well the context in which they are trying to preserve the unique, halcyon lifestyle of Palmerston.

Each day we negotiate the pass with Simon, loaded with gifts for the school and our hosts. The family insists on doing our washing. We give talks to the children at the school about anything we think might interest them, and then they sing to us and ask us to join their games. Darling Marsters is the oldest at thirteen, and shyly asks for my address. I tell them about high mountains and snow, and explain horses, while Lulu and Pablo speak of cities, office hours, trains, and television. They listen wide-eyed to these marvels. After a generous lunch of parrotfish cakes and coconut trimmings, we return to free-dive the drop-off under the boat among friendly fifty-pound groupers, several species of big parrotfish, huge sting rays and half a dozen sharks.

Our last day, we are bidden to eat with Mamma Marsters and her family at three in the afternoon, after she has taken Lulu to gather clams. Without telling us, the women of the family have been preparing a feast for us since before dawn, cooked in their *umu*, the ground oven traditional throughout Polynesia. First comes coconut-fed chicken, and then coconut jelly with arrowroot. For the main course, bosunbird is served.

"On a set day each month," Simon relates as he dishes the birds up, "the families collect young bosunbirds from the other islands in the lagoon, and those captured are shared out between all the people on the island that day."

Deemed the greatest of Palmerston's delicacies, a bosunbird banquet is a privilege, the Palmerston equivalent of the fatted calf. Though fish-eaters, they are surprisingly good. They seem to be a variety of tropic-bird, white and black with a long, thin streamer of a tail, which consists of just two bright red feathers.

Then it's time for a round of the island for tearful good-byes and embraces and promises to keep in touch. The Marsters load us with gifts, shell necklaces, coconut fans, coconut-fed chicken, bread for our journey and fresh drinking coconuts from Simon's tree, prepared on his spear. Little David, the island's cheeky imp, comes back to the boat with Simon so Lulu can dress some nasty sores on his lips. After putting some doggerel disguised as a poem into Simon's guestbook, we disengage the anchor from its coral knob and, exchanging repeated farewells over the VHF until we are out of range, head over the horizon.

SAMOA

The Cook Islands are few, scattered over an immensity of ocean. Aitutaki, the second largest, is the beautiful home of the best dancers in the entire Pacific, but entry to its moderate anchorage is limited to boats drawing five and a half feet or less. We need seven and a half feet of water, so we carry on to an intriguing, very small country called Niue, a route that costs us the chance of visiting Samoa, which is to our north.

Samoa is cut into two countries, the western half independent and the smaller eastern part under the governance of the United States, a political division that dates back to the colonial expansion of the nineteenth century when the Western powers sometimes met head-to-head as they vied for whatever they wanted in these lands, which were utterly defenseless in the face of a frigate. One day in 1889, seven warships lay at anchor in Apia Bay, representing three powerful nations. As the diplomats of the USA, Britain and Germany squabbled over the rights of their respective countries to the goodies to be obtained in Samoa, particularly use of its excellent harbor (so they thought), a greater power took a hand in matters. A mighty storm blew in and wrecked them all bar the British ship, the *Calliope*. There must have been much crowing about superior British seamanship, though they could not foresee the metaphor for colonial efforts foreshadowed by the international wreckage.

Robert Louis Stevenson might have called this poetic justice. Perhaps he did. Only forty-four years old at the time, he died just five years later at his home in Samoa where he'd created his own paradise. Carried by chiefs up a path they cut through the night to his chosen spot high on Mount Vaea overlooking Apia, he lies beneath the epitaph he penned himself:

Under the wide and starry sky,
Dig the grave and let me lie.
Glad did I live and gladly die,
And I laid me down with a will.

This be the verse you grave for me:
Here lies he where he longed to be;
Home is the Sailor, home from the sea,
And the Hunter home from the hill.

There, too, live the splendid people who fed Margaret Mead mouthwatering anthropological fare when she arrived to find out all about them. To great acclaim, she published her findings in 1928: *Coming of Age in Samoa: A Psychological Study of Primitive Youth for Western Civilization.* This was a huge bestseller in many editions and several languages, pruriently telling of sexual promiscuity without guilt among the native teenage girls and boys. It remained a standard university text for years. But it was all an elaborate hoax; she had been thoroughly had by the "primitives" with whom she lived a while, and was ignominiously discredited. We found the same impish sense of humor and desire to confound earnest westerners with remarkable native customs and strange habits all around the Pacific, and we had a few laughs with the perpetrators when we could wise up to them.

Western Samoa dropped the "Western" in 1997, infuriating American Samoa, which claimed this was a cunning ploy to detract from its own samoa-ness. Pacific sailors who have been at sea for months often make hungrily for American Samoa and its superstore delights. We decide these are not a sufficient attraction to outweigh the famed pong of Pago Pago's two fish canneries working day and night, processing a high percentage of the central Pacific catch so that it can be imported into the United States free of duty. And, indeed, there is not time enough to sail around Samoa if we are to reach New Zealand before the onset of the cyclone season. Reluctantly we sail on west.

Savage Island

NIUE

Journalists catering to our nineteenth century ancestors routinely wrote about "savages" in places soon to become euphemisms like "Lesser Developed Country" and "Third World." "Savage" conjured up visions of danger and bravery, enlightening contact between the forces of progress and human residue of the dark ages, the civilizing duties of missionaries and explorers. An isolated mid-Pacific blob on an old chart bears the intriguing name Savage Island. I have to go there. It turns out to be a country, one of which no one I know has heard, unique in this globalized age.

The four-hundred-mile passage to this Savage Island takes four days in ideal gentle trade wind conditions, rippling downwind at four or five knots under spinnaker and mizzen with the mainsail furled. Making our landfall a couple of hours after night has fallen, we feel our way toward a white line of surf defining the fringing reef. In moonless dark, it's a vast chunk of black, a hole in the starry sky with a pale fringe for a skirt. With a spotlight we find a mooring buoy laid offshore this lonely country, for its shores drop steeply so there is no anchorage, nor any form of harbor.

The island has resisted the name by which Captain Cook honored it when he tried to land in 1774 and was sent packing by the "Indians," having noted that they had blood-red teeth. He saw enough to recognize that it had little succor to offer a ship and dubbed it Savage Island after a close encounter with a native spear, a title that still endures on some charts and is much resented by the people. He did not, however, linger long enough to learn that the red teeth were the result of eating their excellent red bananas rather than each other.

Niue, the Polynesian name of the country and of the island, holds two records: the largest uplifted coral atoll and, bar the Vatican, the least populated country in the world.

In an attempt to attract a dribble of tourism, Niue has adopted the sound-bite title Rock of Polynesia for its two hundred fifty square miles, which rise from a narrow fringing reef like a two-layer wedding cake. It's different from any island we've seen. It is girt by cliffs that continue down to some of the world's deepest ocean bottoms, without lagoons or beaches. Nor does Niue have rivers and streams, for the plentiful rainwater simply sinks into porous limestone. This renders the coastal waters unbelievably clear. More than a hundred feet of underwater visibility is

Cave formations, Niue

routine, the diving among the very best for the very few who get there.

It remains almost as hard to get ashore nowadays as when Captain Cook found it. A concrete jetty has been constructed on a convenient jag of reef, strong enough to be only occasionally damaged by towering storm waves that break fifty feet over it. On the jetty is a simple derrick. Choosing our moment, we attach the dinghy to a sling, leap out as a six-foot wave crest passes, hoist it up on the jetty as quick as we can, and wheel it to a parking space. There is no other landing.

Cook noted "curious rock formations" in his Niue journal, grottos, stalagmite-filled caverns and rock arches around its coast that we bike to see, finding ourselves in some remarkable places. The limestone Talava Arches line up like a vista of overhung alleyways in old Jerusalem. Another cave, reached by narrow steps descending into a nondescript burrow, contains an iridescent swimming pool, refracted rainbow colors playing on massive stalactites hanging into the water like unsupported pillars so that, in reflection, the pillars are the soaring symmetrical columns of a natural polychrome temple.

The few people of Niue love to talk story. A wrinkled fellow called Nineteen, stopping his pickup to offer to bring the boat pawpaws and coconuts, describes with the sadness the depopulation taking place. "I have six family houses to look after now," he says. "The old people have died, and the young people have gone to New Zealand, so nobody wants them." There are abandoned houses in all the villages, and there is no realtor on the island. The nicely named funeral parlor, CARMEN DAED CENTER, has little work.

A few years ago there were more than five thousand people. The attrition is the result of New Zealand passports and free entry enjoyed by Niueans, like Tokelauans and Cook Islanders, making it easy to depart for the dreams, jobs and bright lights of Auckland. There is almost no countervailing immigration, partly because of traditional land tenure systems. Land is permanent, a gift of the gods to be held by its occupants only as transients. Buying and selling land is alien to tradition. Thus land is held by families rather than individuals, more than 95 percent of whom now live in New Zealand. A land conveyance needs the consent of every adult member of that family, which can run into hundreds. Should a foreigner buy land without it, a family member can return with a challenge and legally chuck him off. The result is land paralysis, with no way outsiders can safely occupy land for business or buy a house. Despite the steady loss of population and the almost total absence of people in their twenties and thirties, Niueans don't seem to want to develop work opportunities, and land reform is not discussed, so the country is emptying. There are less than one thousand five hundred residents now.

Throughout the Great Ocean, the only real asset of islanders is usually land, protected everywhere away from foreign domination by traditional customs and laws in place to prevent its alienation to newcomers. While foreigners sometimes find it possible to circumvent these barriers through a nominee or company, they have generally proved a boon, serving to keep land in local hands and prices within reach of natives of each place, if indeed there is a market at all. In most, land is never for sale. For land is more than an asset, it is part of the island soul itself. Haoles in Hawai'i know nothing of the islands if they fail to recognize the deep pain that followed the loss of family land through past ignorance of foreigners' wiles and motives. Here in Niue, however, some sort of jolt is necessary to provide work for ambitious young people who see no future in their own country and emigration their only real option. Perhaps releasing a modest amount of land into new use on the basis of enforceable long leases might be a start.

We can dive the reef drop-off from our mooring, though there are always sharks about. These still give me an adrenaline frisson even though they don't seem to eat anyone much in the mid-Pacific. Entirely ignored by the fish, which are presumably fatalists about their chances, sharks are curious creatures and usually come over to investigate a white body in the water, carefully approaching from behind when they can. It's disconcerting to be eyed up by a huge fish that reached such a state of predatory perfection a few million years ago that no further evolution has taken place, a creature with a reputedly voracious appetite for other creatures, like me. I meet my first unicorn-fish, which besides the single protrusion on its head is equipped with razor-sharp, colored knives sticking out either side in front of its tail. Best not to mess with these either.

We're invited one evening to the only resort hotel. Operated with New Zealand government money, it is near empty as Niue has failed to overcome its problem of remoteness in attracting tourists. The smart little airport, which doubles as a golf course, is now down to handling all of two aircraft a week, each with twenty-one passenger seats. Thin traffic for an entire country.

Niue has one internet café, which is free. The ex-Peace Corps American who runs it explains how this is possible. "The internet link by satellite is so expensive that there's no point charging small fees for using it," he says. "So we finance it through sale of Niue domains." These end in the apparently desirable suffix ".nu." Websites called things like brand.nu, something.really.nu, and what.she.nu outnumber the population many times. The suffix has special attraction for French speakers, for whom *nu* translates as "naked."

As we return to the mooring in the dark, a whale surfaces with a sigh near us. It stirs a sparkling lake of phosphorescence and makes the dinghy feel very fragile.

From Niue we sail west, Tonga bound, over some of the world's deepest water. The bottom of the trench to the east of Tonga drops away more than six miles—about the cruising height of jet planes. Swimming above this void when there's a windless patch is strangely unnerving, as if all the monsters lurking on the edges of old maps of the known world are somehow gathered in the blackness beneath. The sea floor has been stretched and compressed by tectonic movement into very rugged territory—at one point close to the trench it rises to within eight hundred feet of the surface—and it remains active. As Tonga drifts east on its plate at an inch a year, outlying islands on the rumples of the earth's crust appear and disappear beneath the waves again. Sailors have to treat their charts with more than the usual caution in these waters.

With this abyss below, we sail across the International Date Line, which kinks nearly five hundred miles east from its normal 180° line of longitude to embrace Tonga in with the lands to the west, Fiji, Australia and New Zealand, its main cultural connections and trading partners. We thus pass straight from Thursday to Saturday. It feels peculiar to lose a complete day of one's life, rousing some sympathy for the rioters in September 1752 who suspected the belated switch from Julius Caesar's calendar to Pope Gregory's was a cunning plot to steal eleven days of their lives and increase the rent. In the good company of Magellan, Drake and Phileas Fogg, I find it tricky to work out where the day has gone.

Basket weaving, Niue

Savage Island

103

I wish that my daughter could be on board, for the mislaid day is her birthday and she might have spent another genuine year as age twenty-nine. On reflection, half the missing day has been returned already, added hour by hour to other days as we were regularly changing time zones while sailing toward the sunset. We've enjoyed twelve twenty-five hour days since leaving the Greenwich meridian, and we will claw back the other twelve hours as we circle the rest of the world.

In the later watches of the night, I am steering on a back-bearing on Jupiter, which is in a neat little row with Saturn and Venus in the constellation of Taurus, my zodiacal sign. The astrological idiocracy would surely divine something significant from this.

10

Where Time Starts

TONGA

The cliffs of Vava'u rear rugged from white socks of crashing surf as we make a Tongan landfall in early dawn light and coast twenty miles around to Neiafu's entrance. I have no chart at this point, but a sketch in *The Lonely Planet* serves to guide us to the Port of Refuge, a sheltered stretch of water aptly named by a Spanish captain who came upon Vava'u in 1781. Cook, for once, had missed it, after the Tongans deliberately misled him that Vava'u had no harbor.

Since Queen Salote stole the show at Queen Elizabeth's coronation in 1953, in the popular conscience Tonga has conjured up the very essence of South Seas paradise. We planned to bypass the main island, Tongatapu, in favor of the central and northern parts of the extensive group, which seemed to have more on offer to paradise pilgrims than the capital, Nuku'alofa. Even further north lies Niuatoputapu, known to sailors as New Potatoes, but though this is an enticing island with but a handful of boats and two uncertain flights a month connecting it to anywhere, we are headed for the wonderful patchwork of islands lying within a sheltering reef system that make up Vava'u.

They came into being when the powerful god Tangaloa was fishing one day and felt his line snagged on debris. He gave a mighty heave and up came this sparkling archipelago, dozens of islands and islets set on a wedge of shallow water running from high limestone cliffs in the north to a few low rocks and reefs in the south. Wherever you look is a protected seascape dotted with islands, large and small, high and low, cliffs and beaches, crashing reefs and placid bays. A few of the islands have small villages on them, and expatriate escapees have established a dozen tucked-away restaurants. It is a magnificent place for a boat.

Tangaloa was also the creator of men, though the Polynesian tradition is less appealing than the tale of Adam and Eve in the Garden of Eden. The god went about it by planting a seed in a log. When the log rotted, a white worm emerged, wriggled around a bit and then broke into three segments. Each piece became a man, the three forbears of all Tongans.

North Tonga has happily resisted regular overtures of hotel developers, and only a few ropy old aircraft and boats ferry small numbers of people among its scattered isles. Though Paul Theroux saw this somewhat acerbically ("Tongan snobbery, offensiveness, incivility and rampant xenophobia had kept the great glorious archipelago of Vava'u one of the least spoiled places in the Pacific"), I feel this to be the serendipity of insularity and delightful inefficiency rather than a considered policy.

All white guys are *palangi* or *papalangi* in Tonga, much as *gringos* to Mexicans or *haoles* in Hawai'i, though it is a term of wonder rather than abuse. Before the first Europeans arrived, headed by the Dutchman Abel Tasman in 1643, it was considered that Tonga and its neighbors were surrounded by an impassable ocean stream. Tongan mythology seemed to have forgotten the stories of the great migrations that brought canoes of brave people from Southeast Asia to the islands of the Pacific, first reaching Tonga four or five thousand years ago. The word *langi* means "sky" or "heaven," so *palangi* conveys something like sky-traveler, because the only way for the newcomers to have gotten to Tonga was from the sky.

VAVA'U

We await with some trepidation the arrival of customs and quarantine officials after their weekend off. It's wise to be generous with the quarantine department, which has a reputation for removing anything that takes their fancy. All is well when we part with a bag of yams plus a bottle of rum and a "fee" for three huge men who crowd into the saloon. It probably serves as their pay for the week.

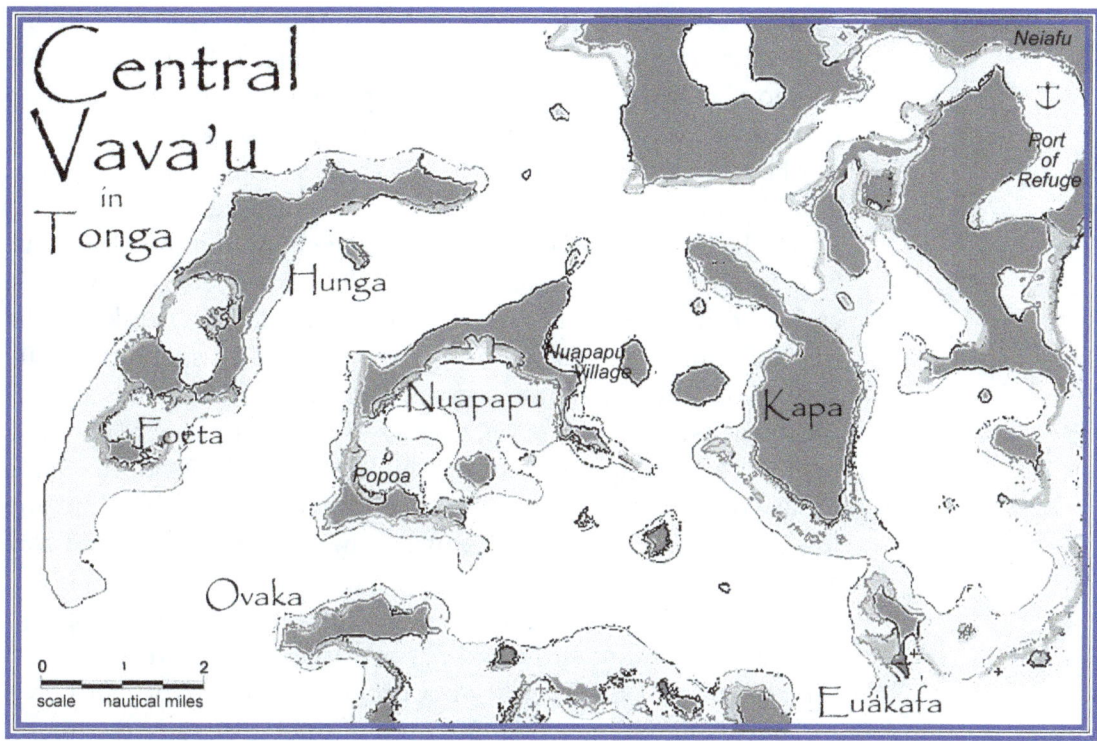

Together with "overtime" for the immigration officer, we shell out $70, a pile of money by local standards.

A scooter proves a genial introduction to the main island of Vava'u. Most of the highways are unpaved, so steering around the potholes while avoiding coconuts, horses, dogs, hogs and hoglets all over the roads takes concentration. On one muddy corner I lose it and bounce through the remnants of a chain-link fence, careering into a village graveyard and sliding to a halt in gooey mud with the scooter on top of me. As well as the fading flowers and flaking figurines lovingly supplied to keep the departed company, Tongan graves have big, colorful blankets hung about them that soften the landing of errant scooter riders flying in over the hedge. I unwind a couple of flowery blankets in which I'm swaddled and pin them up again, apparently unobserved, before threading the scooter between the graves, seeking a way out and wondering about the constituents of the mud plastered all over me.

The land, unlike our previous unkempt Pacific islands, is all under cultivation, neat crops of yams, manioc and taro under the shade of mango, breadfruit and coconut trees. The road passes through half a dozen villages, bristling with churches of different denominations, for the pastors have put down deep roots in

Tonga. Here it is customary in many churches to read out the list of contributions of parishioners in order of size. "Can it be Christian to shame the flock into putting money, perhaps more than they can afford, into the collection box?" Pablo asks.

About ten Christian churches have been established in Tonga. The Wesleyans, who number the king among adherents, have split into at least three factions and are being chased by the Mormons, who wear dark coats and ties and trade schools, English lessons, and volleyball pitches for souls who may not smoke, drink, or take tea and coffee. The Salvation Army is dressed in sparkling white shirts with military epaulettes over Tongan skirts and mats around their waists. Every so often a new wave of missionaries arrives, inspired by God to travel to the idyllic islands of the South Pacific to save the heathen. They seem surprised when they can't find any left to save, but they entice some from another church and stay anyway.

A tide of missionaries followed the London Missionary Society's expedition to Tahiti at the end of the eighteenth century. "By 1850 the conquest of the Pacific was complete," wrote Norman Lewis in *The Missionaries*, a condemnation of the terror and destruction wrought. The vivid description of a shipload of starched Boston Calvinists sent out in the 1820s penned by James Michener in his novel *Hawai'i* has stayed with me, along with the oft-repeated but generally accurate quip: "They came to do good, and they did right well." There's a famous aphorism attributed, probably mistakenly, to Jomo Kenyatta:

> When the missionaries came, we had the land and they brought the bibles.
> "Let us pray," said the missionaries.
> When we opened our eyes, we had the bibles and they had the land.

A Californian girl, Patricia Ledyard, was hired in 1949 by the Wesleyan Mission to run its girls' school here in Vava'u. She stayed on and made her home in a village across the water from our mooring, where she died not so long ago at a great age. She knew the stream of missionaries arriving in Tonga, and remarked in her book *My Tongan Home*:

> I had been prepared for them to be, in their religious views, narrow, but I had expected them to be also the most sincere of people, fired

by a love of human-kind and desiring to call all men "brother." Mr Pauson and his staff had brought speedy disillusion. It seemed they knew nothing of love and that the last thing in the world they would do would be to consider a Tongan as a brother. Lest it seem that I arrived too quickly at my judgement, I feel compelled to say that twenty additional years of observing missionaries and listening to their talk has reinforced rather than altered my original opinion.

There is, of course, another view. Writing in 1839 on a whaling ship, a young New Englander, Francis Olmsted, observed:

Many persons visiting places where missionaries have been established go away with less favorable opinions of what has been accomplished by these devoted men than they ought to entertain, but it arises from a want of a comprehensive view of the past… It is almost impossible for one from our own favored country to conceive of the depth of degradation and pollution and the revolting cruelty that pervaded the character of the Polynesian Islanders in every aspect of life, before they were visited by the heralds of salvation.

Riding a scooter round the countryside, I can stop and talk to Tongans everywhere, glad that, thanks initially to these missionaries, the days of cannibalism and hostility to *palangi* are over, for the large men all tote large bush-knives. Rugby balls, pursued by large boys, often bounce across the road. It's rugby that gives Tonga an international sporting presence, and the Tongan diaspora is a fertile source of players for the All Blacks of New Zealand.

There are extensive shallow seawater lagoons where the ubiquitous pigs have taken to the sea to root around on shallow reefs. French gastronomes value *agneau pré salé*, lamb raised on the salt marshes of Normandy, and I wonder whether organic salt pork comes into the same category. On a wide reef, Kerela is carefully rinsing pandanus leaves and setting them out to dry on the rocks where they will remain for a month or so before a final indoor drying to prepare them for weaving into baskets and mats. In her bright headdress and red *kofu*, she looks like a solitary foreshore flower.

Old men are washing pandanus baskets of kava root in the sea, chewing it all the while. Kava is a mainstay of culture in Tonga as in other the island groups. Tongan occasions, whether marriages, conferences, the reception of guests or the cementing of alliances, are always marked by the ceremonial quaffing of kava. Strangers

Salt pork, Vava'u

are expected to present a bunch of kava root to the chief on arrival in a village, and it is an honor for an outsider to be invited to join a kava circle. Tongan kava is a mild narcotic, which induces feelings of numbness and general well-being, and, in quantity, becomes a moderately soporific drug. Later, in Melanesia, it proves much stronger medicine. The brew is made from the roots of a particular sort of pepper plant. Required to drink the stuff many times to be sociable and fall in with tradition, I thank heaven that preparation has changed from the time the roots had to be chewed by the women of the village. Once thoroughly masticated, they would spit the juice into a communal bowl and then filter it through coconut fibers to make it ready for the men. Now, it is usually pounded and ground, though old hands complain it's a travesty to prepare it this way. A numbness of the lips and tongue is first felt and then a happy state is said to take over—if, that is, you can sink enough to float a boat and stomach the taste, which is like last week's laundry water, lightly seasoned. But anyone who wants to sit cross-legged discussing politics with the elders or to join the young men for a binge evening must expect to consume many shells of the potion.

There are dogs everywhere, often fitting Forster's note on Cook's second voyage:

> The dogs are of a singular race; they most resemble the common cur, but have a prodigious large head, remarkably little eyes, prick ears, long hair, and a short bushy tail. They are chiefly fed with fruit...they are exceedingly stupid, and seldom or never bark, have the sense of smelling in very low degree and are lazy beyond measure. They are kept by the natives chiefly for their flesh, of which they are very fond, preferring it to pork.

These dogs, middle sized and usually yellow, are the direct descendants of the canoe dogs that traveled with early Pacific voyagers. Mutts were taken along not for company but as food for the astounding brave forays into the unknown that these early people made. Through the dogs' subsequent isolation, the strain is one of the oldest and purest on earth, and largely vegetarian.

Washing kava roots

Here in Tonga there are also ubiquitous pigs. Parent pigs wander freely all around the towns and villages with families of squeaking piglets, ever in danger of becoming pressed ham on the roads. The owner of Neiafu's best restaurant says that they are only eatable as sucklings, and he imports his pork chops from New Zealand. This is just as well, as dogs still get eaten in Tonga and there may be confusion in the kitchen. According to the extraordinary account of William Mariner who, as a teenager, was a marooned captive in Tonga from 1806 to 1810, dog was always called pork so as not to offend visitors from other islands. The pigs are given the freedom of a town or village; a village is often entirely fenced in, allowing the pigs to roam as they please, but not escape to the bush. The consumption of pork is central to Tongan feasting; no ceremonial meal is complete without it.

Mariner's story, pieced together by a London doctor and published in 1815, is one of the most remarkable descriptions of life in a place wholly unaffected by the world's colonizing powers. He described preparations for an important feast thus:

> Four poles, about eighteen feet long, were fixed upright in the ground, to the depth of a few feet, at about four feet distance from each other in a quadrangular form, the spaces between them all the way to the top being crossed by smaller poles about six inches distant from each other, and lashed on by the bark of the foa, a species

of the Hibiscus. The interior of this erection was filled up as they proceeded with yams. Afterward other upright poles were lashed onto the top with cross pieces, still piling up the yams; then a third set of poles, etc. till the column of yams was about fifty or sixty feet high, and on the top of all was placed a baked pig. Four such columns were erected, one at each corner of the malai (ceremonial platform), the day before the ceremony, and three or four hundred hogs were killed and half baked. The following day the hogs were carried to the king's malai, about a quarter of a mile off, and placed upon the ground before the house, as well as four or five wooden cars or sledges full of yams, each holding about five hundred.

Thirty years earlier, Captain Cook had been presented with such a pile of yams topped by two baked pigs and a live one. He noted in his journal: "It would have taken the ship's carpenters several days to make a similar structure, and they would have demanded all sorts of things which the Tongan carpenters could do without."

This was not the end of the hogs' function. Mariner again:

The company being at length all arrived and seated, the king gave notice that the ceremony was about to begin. The young chiefs and warriors, and those who prided themselves in their strength, then got up singly and endeavoured to carry off the largest hog. When one failed another tried; then a third, and so on, till everyone that chose had made a trial of his strength. To carry one of the largest hogs is not an easy thing to be done, on account of its greasiness as well as its weight; but it affords a considerable share of diversion to see a man embracing a large fat baked hog, and endeavouring to raise it on his shoulder. As the hog was too heavy for one man's strength, it was carried away by two, whilst a third followed with its liver...

Mariner provided a cannibal recipe too, learned as an eyewitness:

Some of the younger chiefs, who had contracted the Fiji habits, proposed to kill the prisoners, lest they should make their escape, and then to roast and eat them. Some of the prisoners were soon dispatched; their flesh cut up into small portions, washed with sea water, wrapped up in plantain leaves, and roasted under hot stones; two or three were disembowelled, and baked whole same as a pig.

It's disappointing to find the music at Neiafu's high school ball influenced by imported ideas, but at least the dress at a formal occasion remains traditional. The most Tongan form of garb is the *ta'ovala*, a mat woven from pandanus and worn as a heavy overskirt by both men and women on all important occasions, or simply to be chic. It's obligatory when in mourning. Though it may appear to be the superannuated attic carpet that has been recycled to mulch a flowerbed, the older the mat, the more gravitas is accorded the wearer.

Dipping deeper into the cultural pot next evening, we're given tickets for Miss Cosmos, a beauty queen competition. A large hall on the waterfront is crammed with Tongan families. Each contestant must perform a ten-minute dance and then another, and at the end the winner is chosen from such as Miss Harbor View, Miss Hula Hula, Miss Vava'u Netball Team and Miss Hot'n Spicy Curryhouse. The audience goes wild as each beauty dances, and they fall about at the antics of the jolly Hot'n Spicy, who is splendidly fat. Miss Beluga is the eventual winner, a tall and willowy lovely thoroughly worthy of the title. The peculiar thing about the competition, though, is that all the girls are blokes. These men are in drag not for the evening but for life; like the *mahu* of Tahiti, they have been raised as girls and live as women in their families, respected citizens of the community. They are cheered on by many more *fakaleiti*, semi-women, in the audience.

Everywhere in the Pacific, they dance. Each group of islands has developed distinctive traditions; children are taught from an early age while many men are competent on ukelele, guitar and percussion. In Hawai'i it's the swaying *hula*, in Tahiti the *tamure*, which appears to demand an extra joint in men's knees and girls' pelvises and a fast eccentric motor to power them. The Samoan *siva* and Cook Island dancing resembles Tahiti's, but is subtler. Much of Micronesia's dancing is under Spanish or missionary influence. In Melanesia there are powerful traces of ancient dances of dedication and of war. Tonga's dances are less familiar—the lakalaka, the ma'ulu'ulu, the kailao war dance. All are sinuous ballets of the hands, arms and bodies, telling stories woven in the air, sung to haunting melodies. The ma'ulu'ulu is performed sitting in rows. Costumes are constructed with enormous care from shells, leaves, seeds and flowers sewn to hibiscus fiber, tapa cloth or pandanus mats. The girls' bodies, fragrant with scented monoi oils, glisten in the torchlight as they writhe slowly and sensuously to the lilting music.

Lulu has to fly home, to be replaced by a British friend, Miles, for a few days. But his connecting plane from Nuku'alofa breaks

Winning men, Miss Cosmos

down. It's the last flight on Saturday, so he has to kick his heels in the rundown capital for two days as absolutely nothing moves or opens in Tonga on Sunday, which commences on Saturday. This seems an apt illustration of Tonga's motto, "The Land Where Time Starts," reflecting the extra twenty-four minutes that moving the International Date Line east of 180 degrees gained the country (though, since outreached in 1994 by Kiribati and in 2011 by Samoa, it's wrong).

Sailing among Vava'u's islands, we leave lonely footprints on the fine white sand of virgin beaches on deserted islands and penetrate quiet forests of fruit trees and tropical greenery. We snorkel on undamaged reefs, sup in the little eating houses, make friends with locals and civilization's fugitives, stare at stars bright enough to illuminate the landscape when there is no moon, and meet whales as we are wafted about the pattern of islands by fresh breezes.

After one lunch on a deserted, travel-poster-white crescent beach, we head for the night into the large lagoon of Nuapapu. As we're passing the spherical island of Kulo (which being a fanny in his language causes our Spanish crewman, Pablo, a fit of giggles), Miles, who is relaxing in the pulpit at the sharp end of the boat, suddenly gives a great yell. His cry, "Thar she blows!" which he knows to be the correct form of salutation since he's reading the boat copy of *Moby Dick*, hails a whale lolloping along, spouting from time to time. We follow her until she slowly raises her vast fluke high in the air and sounds. Ten minutes later the cry is heard again as she surfaces near us with her suckling calf. It is hard to estimate the length of an adult whale, as you only see a bit at a time unless it breaches, but the humpback calf is about the size of an elephant. The magnificent beasts stay close to us as we sail in a circle. They seem to take no notice of us. Australian sailors later ask us about the color of the antifouling on our bottom. "You're lucky it's blue, mate," one says. "I knew a boat with its rudder attacked by a whale. It had teeth marks right through it. The bottom was black, and the whale thought it was another whale and got pissed off when it wasn't."

Others tell us to start the engine or generator so the whale can work out that we are not a possible object of desire. On the quayside I find an Australian lady waving an arm around in a great state of excitement. "See this arm," she says. "I was snorkeling with this whale when she opened her enormous mouth and I was half sucked in along with all the plankton… This arm was right inside her mouth…She was feeding her calf…Then everything went white. I couldn't see a thing. I was swimming in a sea of her breast milk…rubbing against the barnacles all over her…I'm raw…"

Vava'u is one of few places to swim with whales, so we go out with a local boat. A pod of eight whales is in the middle of the channel with their calves. To join so many might be foolish, so over by an island we make for a mother and calf where there's someone in the water from another small boat. "Awesome," floats across the waves in truly awed US tones as we cut the motor and don masks. The power and grace of a leviathan at close quarters is shattering. Her pectoral fin alone is three times as long as me. She knows I'm here, cruising alongside a bit of her head like a wee pilot fish, and somehow I feel welcomed, perhaps as a toy for the calf that is sporting along at her side. The lady humpbacks are larger than the males, up to fifty feet in length and some forty-five tons in weight, though this depends on when you see them. For half the year, on their long winter voyage from the krill-rich waters of the Antarctic to calve in Vava'u, they eat nothing as they cover perhaps five thousand miles, never sleep, and on arrival deliver a one-ton, twelve-foot baby demanding thirty daily gallons of milk. Suckled on milk containing ten times the fat and twice the protein of cows' milk, the calves put on about fifty pounds a day. No one seems sure what proportion of the mother's body weight this selfless program of activity uses up, but some marine biologists reckon about one third.

When Pablo and Miles depart to fly home, I post an ad for crew in a bar at the water's edge and go off for a sparkling single-handed sail to Foeata, the remote island location of the Blue Lagoon restaurant, said to produce good food. After dropping the sails and drifting awhile with some whales, I stop short of the narrow, twisty passage into the small lagoon. It appears the sort of place one would not wish to leave single-handed in the middle of the night if the weather blows up, and I chicken out. A yachtie tells me later that this was a good decision. "The place is like inside a washing machine," he says. "The tide goes out one way and slops in another way and you would have been up all night."

Aborting Foeata, the idea of a good dinner at Popao pops up, so I sail along the south coast of Vaka'eitu and into the large lagoon of Pablo's butt island, Kulo. Popao, a simple guesthouse just opened by an Austrian, stands hidden by forest high on a ridge, alone on its lovely island, as stunning a remote island hideaway as could be wished. Around the corner there is the finest reef in Tonga. Clambering out to the seaward side at low tide in the morning, I snorkel over coral that would put any botanic garden to shame for its variety, its kaleidoscopic colors, its intricate beauty. A vivid blue kingfisher sings above my head on the branch of an ironwood tree as I sit on the beach taking off my flippers. I'm full of the wonder of nature's subsea splurge. It is a curiosity of Polynesia that nature has endowed its underwater fauna with the gaudiest garb, while drabness rules above ground. The kingfisher is one of few birds with any color about it at all. It's partly the result of human intervention, the brightest birds having been hunted and trapped for their plumage. Red feathers formerly had enormous value for ceremonial regalia, the gold of a metal-less society, and even served as money. Now, only abundant Tongan butterflies help to restore the balance.

EUAKAFA

An ancient coal barge converted to a sailing vessel with two masts and a polyglot crew of twenty adventurers is anchored in the bay below Popao, and the captain's Swiss girlfriend wants to bolt. Valerie is headed for Fiji, so I sign her on.

A few miles away is Euakafa Island, where we land on a beach and walk up through steep, thick forest to search for the tomb of Princess Talafaiva who, in the Tongan folk tale of The Fo'ui Tree, lived with her court on the island shore some five centuries ago and was beaten to death for lingering with a "handsome man." The fo'ui tree's spreading branches had allowed the libidinous fellow to climb over the palace wall. In Tongan folklore the "handsome man" is a Don Juan sort of character, quite irresistible to women, so he had his wicked way with the defenseless maiden. Her grieving husband, the king of Euakafa, laid her in a fine tomb on the topmost point of the island.

If ever the island held a royal court or a princess's tomb, no stones remain.

Dozing off toward midnight as the moon illuminates the deserted island, I hear strange and lovely music resonating through our steel hull. I have never heard the song of whales but this has to be the cetacean concerto, a baleen ballet, and we leap up on deck. Drifting a few yards from the boat in the gentle ripple of the sheltered water are two humpbacks, one singing to his lady and spouting from time to time. It is claimed that humpback whale song can be heard through the water fifty miles away. Their repertoire of clicking, humming and grunting apparently extends over a seven octave range, sounds that are unique to each whale like a human voice, songs that are composed anew each year as a variation of what went before. Having inspected us, the whales slip slowly on, an ancient, evocative memory in the powerful beam of an unveiled full moon.

FOEATA

One afternoon we sail into the lagoon at Foeata Island, the washing-machine anchorage off which I have been warned. It is in truth a wonderful place, though our entry involves striking a shoal charted in a slightly different spot. Valerie, reef-spotting up in the pulpit, fails to see the coral as we are sailing into the evening sun, a basic error when visibility is at its worst with the western glare on the water.

Once untangled, we anchor in transparent water over white sand, surrounded by three islands within lines of reef. The only habitation is a small cluster of *fale*, traditional Tongan huts built of bush materials, forming the Blue Lagoon restaurant, run by Friedl, a cantankerous German with his Tongan wife. As ex-chef of Vava'u's only passable hotel, he has a reputation as the best cook in Tonga, so we park the dinghy on his beach and go to seek supper. Friedl, a large, ginger-hairy man, inspects us through pebble lenses the size of dimes and interviews us in the accents of the Kaiser. Apparently satisfied with our custom, he cooks a superb dinner. The following morning, ashore again to inspect his three immaculate bedroom *fales*, we encounter an irascible version of the chef and get thrown off the island for no obvious crime.

Swimming to the beach of a deserted island of about half a square mile on the other side of the little lagoon, I wander all around, marveling at a perfect place. One is permitted flights of fancy in paradise. Here I can build a sublime dwelling in which to live an idyllic life. The chosen spot lies in a grove of casuarinas on a small headland between two bays, fringed with white, powdery beaches. A drop of a few feet to a protecting reef gives access to fishing and diving in coral wonderland while, behind, the ground rises gently to a hill some hundred feet high and clad in pandanus, mango, coconut trees and green jungly things of many unidentified sorts. Yam, taro, banana, sweet potatoes and pineapples will grow here with nut trees and citrus. A small family of wild goats is already in residence, but pigs and chickens will join the domestic menagerie, and all sorts of fruit trees will quickly be established—breadfruit, lime, soursop, jackfruit, guava, pawpaw, avocado, pamplemousse. The cliffs and hill lend themselves to gathering plentiful rainwater to be stored in silos out of sight, and for power an array of solar panels can be set up in a clearing invisible from the surrounding sea. All the materials for construction of a traditional house are present, and it would be simple to lay a strong mooring for *Nereus* in the bright waters of the sheltered lagoon. There appears to be nothing unpleasant on the island, whether animals, bugs, plants or of human origin. A short-wave radio or satellite phone will provide all the necessary intercourse with the outside world, although it might only be used occasionally to exchange the odd e-mails with family and friends. And, close at hand, is Friedl and his kitchen.

But a Garden of Eden needs a woman. It's been said that sailing is an affair between the captain and the boat, but that doesn't seem adequate. Who might I share it with, now that my marriage days are over, out here in the islands where kindred spirits of the opposite sex are as common as mermaids? From the early days, most westerners solved this dilemma by taking up with and sometimes marrying a south seas beauty, but I feel the limits imposed by the lack of any common background and culture. And I still have thousands of miles to sail. I have no intimation that, this very year, I may happen upon an ideal companion on a tiny island.

Or that, within months, all the trees on my perfect island will be flattened by a devastating cyclone, fantasia blown over the rainbow.

Back in Neiafu, my notice in the bar bears fruit. A tapping on the hull announces two applicants for crew positions to Fiji: Peter, a young German backpacker, and Raphael, a chip designer from Switzerland sporting the beginnings of an imperial beard. They are without sailing experience, but they look strong and competent and interesting, and I sign them on. This makes the crew up to four once more.

We eat pretty well on board, often experimenting with half-understood recipes and strange roots or their topknot of greenery. We try all sorts of fish, freshwater shrimp and mussels, and crayfish the colors of the rainbow. As well as delicious fruits there are enticing cutnuts and ai nuts, crinkly things with a kernel like an almond but tasting like a pine nut. Eating fresh fish and taro-tops the first evening with the new crew while at anchor in the Nuapapu Lagoon, I complain of a fishbone stuck in my throat.

"I've got a bone in my throat also," adds Raphael.

"Me too," squeals Valerie.

"And there is one down my throat," gurgles Peter.

We reach for the usual lump of bread to deal with the problem, but it just gets worse as though everyone's gullet is inflicted with several fishbones. It takes a while to get it; it's the taro leaves. They came from the market, but unlike millions of sensible taro-eaters in the Pacific, I'd not ensured they were young and tender, an amateurish error exacerbated by insufficient cooking and too little coconut milk, which would have gotten rid of tiny crystals of calcium oxalate that cause the intense throat irritation. It takes a scratchy day for the fishbone feeling to fade.

NUAPAPU

Early next morning a soft voice carries through a porthole. There's a dugout canoe alongside containing two young boys and paddled by their father. "Hallo, hallo. Can you help us?" the father calls. "My son have bad foot."

Pacific painted lobster

The boy has an ugly, suppurating wound where he's trodden on a nail. In answer to a VHF call, a lady doctor from Scotland on the only other boat in the island comes over to fix it up. The father introduces himself as Anitelu, Tongan for Andrew, he says when I tell him my name, and he wonders if I can mend his broken generator. Several men on the beach are carving a new church bell out of a thick log, a six-foot version of the *lala*, the wooden, box-like percussion instrument used widely by Polynesian musicians. Played with a wooden club, I guess it's similar to the Pacific jungle drums, which, as every schoolboy knows, presaged the arrival of the cannibals.

We find we've dropped our anchor by a village that has few visitors. Prize *palangi*, we are conducted around in a bevy of children and instructed on the subsistence economy of a very poor tropical village: *kumala* (sweet potato), manioc, yams and taro crops for roots, various green leafy things for vegetables, a field of kava to make their brew, chickens, pigs and horses for meat. Though the village fronts a beach bisected by the cyclone-damaged remains of a coral jetty, it possesses no boat for fishing. The three hundred people carry the usual load of competitive imported religion; a New Wesleyan church, the Mormons, two other Wesleyan churches of splinter sects, and a Pentecostal chapel are set among the scattering of houses. The gardens, enclosed against pigs are shaded by mango and breadfruit trees and some leafless trees with fruit like emaciated avocados, but fluffy. "These we use to make pillows, and the seeds make a medicine against infections," Anitelu tells me. Inside are seeds protected by soft fibers like raw cotton. "It's kapok," he says.

There's much drying and weaving of pandanus, which with tapa appears to be the sole source of cash income. Valeti sells me a basket, and then produces a tapa cloth that is unrolled…and unrolled…and unrolled into a magnificent *gnatu* sixteen-feet wide and about one-hundred-twenty-feet long, decorated from one end to the other with panels of Tongan scenes and symbols. To manufacture a length of material of these proportions from the inch-wide pieces of bark of the little withy-like paper mulberry tree is extraordinarily laborious—a process involving removal of the bark in long thin strips, soaking, and then skillful pounding against a hollow log with big wooden mallets faced with progressively reduced patterns of stripes. This is necessary to flatten the bark to the correct, uniform thinness. A manioc (tapioca) paste is then added to amalgamate the fibers of the separate bits. After more pounding, the whole thing is dried and decorated. She offers to cut off a piece for me, but I decline responsibility for dismembering her work of many months, promising to try to persuade one of the local restaurants to buy the tapa for a wallhanging.

Valeti's tapa, Nuapapu

Next morning, Anitelu paddles out to invite us to dinner with his family, promising a pig cooked in his *umu* and explaining this involves stuffing the pig with banana leaves and hot coral, covering it with yams and any other vegetables going, and cooking it underground for several hours.

There is no one to greet us on the beach at twilight, but there are welcoming lamps in the house as we knock at the doorway. A curtain is pulled back and the door swings open to reveal a great feast laid out, and a throng of people. Piles of food are neatly spread on a narrow, foot-high table, and our host and his family await in a semicircle, full of welcomes. Once introduced all around, we are seated on mats on one side of the table. On the other side, amidst a gaggle of children, sits Anitelu's mother, Lauhingoa, and his father. Behind them, a group of family musicians sings a song of welcome. As they play softly on, Anitelu serves us, detailing each dish: "This is breadfruit in the banana leaf, cooked in coconut cream. Here is the pig, which has been cooked in the *umu*, and here is chicken also from the *umu*. This

Anitelu, Nuapapu

purple one is yam, and the yellow one with it is taro and these are two more ways we make taro. The taro leaves here are mixed with corned beef. And this is raw fish I made myself."

Everything except the corned beef is home grown. My drink is a coconut warmed on the stones of the *umu*. Gentle music accompanies our eating, which according to tradition is accomplished in silence. Once finished, the men and boys in the room come to the table to eat what we have left. This causes consternation, for we thought to show our appreciation by eating heartily, and my two young men have healthy appetites.

After a while Anitelu shushes everybody and stands for a speech. "We welcome you to our poor home and into our hearts. This is the first time our house has been honored by receiving a visit from people like you, and it is something very special for us..."

I stand to respond and give Lauhingoa a birthday envelope of cash with a photo of *Nereus* signed by us all.

When the debris of the feast is removed, Anitelu leans over to whisper, "I am the best in the islands."

"What do you mean, what at?"

"At guitar," he says.

"So do, please, play for us," I beg, for it is polite to await a request from his guest before taking up his instrument.

He does, beautifully, accompanied by three or four guitars and a curious four-string instrument. Together they play and sing old Tongan songs and songs written by Anitelu himself, haunting melodies that carry the mood and beauty of ocean islands.

When I go ashore in the morning to bring more presents for Anitelu's family, a weary man is squatting on the ground under a tree, patiently waiting to ask softly for help for his child. Two-year-old Fifita has upset a cooking pot, causing fearful blisters around her waist and bottom. The boat medical kit produces burn dressings and cream, and an "all-stations" call on the radio gleans some advice from an American doctor. I've learned one can find specialists in almost anything among the cruising community of yachts. Back ashore, I tell Fifita's mother to keep the burnt skin clean and aired,

Drying pandanus for weaving

gently stopping her smearing the antiseptic cream on the dressing with a very grubby finger.

"I think it would be wise to take Fifita to the clinic so that the wounds will be dressed professionally," I suggest before leaving.

"We have no boat," she replies. "I don't know when a boat come."

"Is there no nurse in the village?"

"No."

"What about in Matakake?"

"Nobody there either."

"It is hard here," Anitelu confirms. "There is no one on our island with medical training, and we have no boat in our village to take sick people to the hospital." The nearest hospital is eight miles away in Neiafu, so in effect this community is without access to emergency treatment.

"You have six churches in your village, with six ministers, and yet you have no nurse or doctor," I cannot resist saying. "Something is surely wrong with this."

He nods, but the hold of the church is too strong for explicit criticism.

Anitelu has prepared an exhibition of shells in his home, and is anxious I should buy a curious shell containing two integral pearls. The act of buying the shell is such that Anitelu insists on giving me a second one, a reminder of the delicate and lovely relationship between buying, bartering and giving. I get rewarded for the birthday present for Lauhingoa the previous evening too

"My mother wants you to have this tapa, which she has finished this morning for you," he says softly, unfolding a large tapa cloth painted with intricate designs.

Where Time Starts

Then he brings out a battered wooden club, black with age. "This is the war club of my great grandfather," he says, running his fingers over the startling ugly gods deeply carved into both sides of the two-foot club. Worried that it is a gift I should refuse, but will not be allowed to, I am relieved that he only wants to show it to me. Such an antique war club was surely used to shatter skulls, the invariable method of dispatching enemies in old Tonga.

The Friendly Isles

HA'APAI

The idyllic weeks in Vava'u draw to a close as we wind our way out through the southern islands in the glow of a glorious sunrise. After sixty miles close-reaching to the south in a strong breeze, entertained by a whale that appears to be standing on its nose waving its huge fluke in the air and slapping the water with explosive splashes, a mysterious activity I discover later is known as "lobtailing," we anchor late afternoon off a lonely reef in the Ha'apai Islands of central Tonga. Few cruising yachts venture to these islands beset by a mess of reefs offering no shelter from westerly winds, so we will be on our own until we reach a Fijian port.

We quickly meet Pangai's *palangi* community of eight white men married to Tongan women. Clarence, a lanky, born-again Canadian Christian, and his wife Langi are at war with the Mormons, whom they consider the great Antichrist. With liberal provision of schools and basketball pitches funded with American dollars, the Mormon churches have proved widely persuasive in the South Pacific context.

"Did you know that the Mormons believe that Mary the mother of Jesus was impregnated by Adam?" Clarence enquires.

I confess I didn't.

Clarence and Langi dig up their garden to present us with armfuls of vegetables and papayas, and we share an improbable green passion fruit the size of a football. They are generous and interesting, but we find he is known in the island as Crazy Clarence and shunned by Tongans and *palangis* alike. A sad culmination to dreams of paradise after six years on a tiny South Seas island.

There are no restaurants, but in a bar cooking up occasional food, the small community gathers in the evening with the few tourists who occasionally penetrate here. Roland, who has a little dive boat, is holding forth about coral.

"Zey recently interviewed fife hunderd people in Fiji and Tonga and asked zem from what coral was made. No one of zem knew it was an animal. Zey haff no idea how to look after it, but zis is lucky zat zere is no pollution from oil. You know vy? Because ze Tongans never change ze oil in zeir enchines." Roland tells us he was an East German Olympic athlete, a runner. Amid his disillusion with paradise he sounds as if he still has speed drugs in his bloodstream.

Coral reefs occupy in total less than one tenth of one percent of the world's oceans, say about the area of New Mexico, which doesn't seem an important enough ratio for the amount of present NGO concern for their health. In practice, huge numbers of people indirectly depend on the delicate coral ecosystems, which provide the greatest diversity of habitat and species on this planet. All corals—some five hundred different sorts are classified—are very sensitive, surviving in closely defined depths and temperatures, easily damaged by pollution and contact with nets or people. And now, like all other sea creatures with shells, subject to the added threat of acidification of the oceans if the take-up of carbon increases.

Corals multiply by division, but they also spawn. This is one of nature's miracles. One night a few days after a particular full moon in the early summer, an extraordinary message circulates among the corals, every colony of every type, that the moment has arrived to release eggs and sperm. The water over the whole reef turns milky with zillions of miniscule spermatozoa seeking eggs of their own kind. Their clever plan is that, by force of numbers, a few will survive the massive predation awaiting this moment. More amazing still, research indicates that the union can only be consummated by a sperm and an egg from different colonies, but of precisely the same type of coral, thus guarding against inbreeding

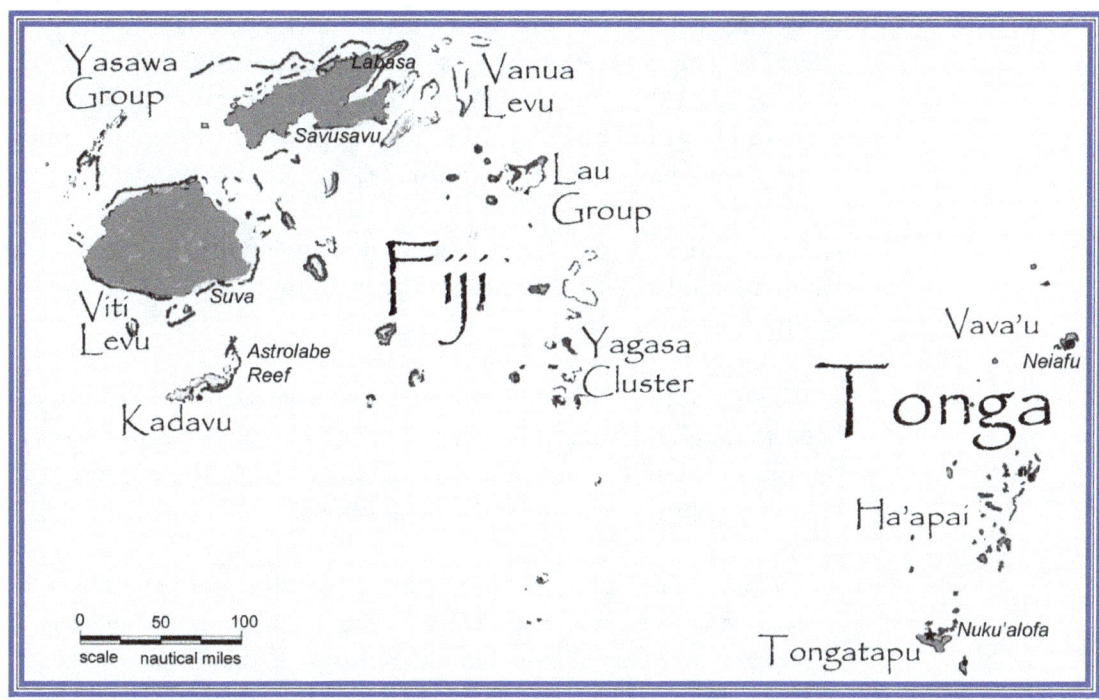

while providing a nucleus to be carried by the tide to a location for a new colony—where most coral will grow very slowly indeed, though the staghorn can put on six inches a year. The reefs built by these miniscule polyps over millennia reach thousands of feet thick, hundreds high and many miles long. In 1998, worldwide coral devastation following the raised sea temperatures stemming from a greater than usual South Pacific Oscillation—the El Niño/La Niña phenomenon—provided a stark warning of the effect of a more general global warming. This is only one of the many coral killers around the tropical world, which include silt from land where the vegetation has been burnt or hacked away, pollution, dynamite and poison reef-fishing, and cyclones.

We have seen evidence of widespread damage, and we once spent a morning with scuba bottles, gloves and poles clearing a reef of hundreds of crown-of-thorns starfish. These poisonously spiky decorations have developed particularly idle table manners, for they prefer to feed by extruding their stomachs over living coral and slurping it in. They are often cast as the villains of the coral saga, but seem to me more probably a cyclical, self-regulating phenomenon unless sustained by fertilizer run-off as seems to be happening on Queensland's Great Barrier Reef. Though an infestation can put a particular reef back several years, it may be less damaging than the effects of temperature change, poison, dynamite and dirt.

It is noticeable that Tonga has few birds, whether land or sea varieties, large or small. Again Roland supplies an emphatic explanation: "Zey haff eaten zem all up. Zey eat effryzing."

Captain James Cook felt so generously welcomed here in the Ha'apai Islands that he named the group The Friendly Isles before sailing off again.

He never knew how mistaken he was.

When young William Mariner was rescued in 1810 and got back to England after four years stranded in Ha'apai and Vava'u, he told a different story. This he had heard from those present at Cook's reception, and from the king himself:

> The other chiefs proposed to invite the captain [Cook] and his officers to a grand bomee [a dance by torchlight] and at a signal to massacre him, his officers and all the marines. But Finow, the late king's father, objected to this, as the darkness of the night would be unfavorable to their operations in taking the two vessels, and proposed rather that it should be done by day, and that they should seize the opportunity of making the attack on the occasion of a grand entertainment which was already to be given to him in honor of his arrival, and after they were all destroyed, the men, who would naturally come in search of him, were to be conducted to the further part of the island under pretence that he was there, and they were then to be destroyed in like manner. Thus the two ships, their crews being so weakened, might be taken (as they supposed) with ease.
>
> It happened, however, a little before the appointed time when the signal was to be given, that most of the chiefs still expressed their opinion that the night time would have been better than the day, and Finow, finding that the majority were of this opinion, was much vexed, and forbade it to be done at all. Thus, no signal being given, the amusements went on without interruption, and Captain Cook and his officers were much pleased with their entertainment, acknowledging it to be far better than any other that they had received at the Friendly Isles.

Cook remained unaware of this plot, writing innocently about the welcome: "I had not been long seated, before near a hundred of the natives appeared in sight, and advanced, laden with yams, bread-fruit, plantains, cocoa-nuts, and sugar-canes... Soon after, arrived a number of others from the right, bearing the same kind of articles; which were collected into two piles upon that side. To these were tied two pigs, and six fowls; and to those, upon the left, six pigs, and two turtles...." Wrestling and boxing followed, including women's contests, as Cook sat watching among a throng, which he estimated as three thousand.

He was fortunate that the Tongans' intentions were short-lived, as he wandered all over the islands, often unescorted, making many friends among the people. Though entirely appropriate now, it is a nice irony that the name he bestowed on the archipelago has stuck.

We pick our way out of Uoleva through a reef-strewn twenty miles of sea with the aid of a mid-scale 1896-based chart, the only one available. With my crew still pretty raw, I have to see to most of the sailing work and go aft to hoist the mizzen myself as we negotiate the first few shoals.

Glimpse through a Tongan doorway

"Would you hand me the chart," I ask Raphael, returning to the cockpit as coral passes close by on both sides.

Blank looks. We search everywhere, but it is gone, perhaps carried overboard by a gust. We are chartless in a treacherous place. At moments like this I console myself by remembering that the early sailors had no aids bar the sextant, compass and lead line—no charts, engine, depth sounder, radar or GPS—and they were sailing square riggers, which were far harder to maneuver than a modern yacht and would go upwind only with difficulty. So everybody acts as lookouts as we thread our wake through a maze of shoals. We are safely through to the open water in a couple of hours.

TOFUA AND KAO

Forty miles to the west of Ha'apai, a pair of mighty volcanoes rise directly from the ocean floor, the higher one towering three thousand feet above sea level. Kao is a perfect cone volcano, while, a mile away, Tofua's top was blown off at some distant time. It now

The Friendly Isles

contains a freshwater lake, though vents on the edge of the lake remain active, spewing flames that illuminate the night. There is no known anchorage and even dinghy landing is reputed to be tough, but, living in hope as ever, we sail between this Scylla and Charybdis and seek shallow water on the more sheltered, western side. The day is overcast with light rain. Thick cloud clings to both volcanoes. A growing swell from the northeast presages a freshening wind. We are now on the track of the overcrowded launch of Captain Bligh just after Fletcher Christian had thrown him off the *Bounty*, for the mutiny took place in April 1789 near this place. Bligh already knew Ha'apai; twelve years previously, as Master of the *Resolution*, Cook's flagship on his third voyage, he'd sailed through this narrow strait.

He now made for Tofua. He searched in vain for an adequate landing spot on the forbidding volcanic coast, and eventually had his men scale the cliffs. This was their only stop on the four thousand-mile voyage in the *Bounty*'s twenty-one-foot longboat, for they were attacked and driven off by the Tofuans, who killed the quartermaster as he tried heroically to release a beach anchor. Bligh wrote that the Tofuans started to clash stones together that afternoon, "as rhythmic and foreboding as war drums." He knew what this portended. Ten years before, he had witnessed the same ominous build-up on a Hawaiian beach, the day Captain Cook was killed.

Five shilling stamp depicting the Bounty mutiny near Tofua and Kao

Just as Cook and Bligh failed to find a decent landing place, the conditions defeat us. There is nowhere safe in the shelter of the black, undercut cliffs. We reluctantly abandon the grim towers and turn the bow toward Fiji, four hundred miles on.

About halfway, we pass through the Lau Group, small islands and reefs scattered over a huge area to the east of Fiji. A sailing guide asserts that the three most beautiful places in the entire area are here, but we have no permits, which are almost impossible to obtain in advance from the Fijian government. Cruiser gossip indicates that an unauthorized lurk would be direly punished on arrival at a Fijian port of entry, with little credence given to excuses of mechanical breakdown or dangerous weather.

Fiji And The Astrolabe

"YOU GO TO AMERICA, cross the continent to San Francisco, and then it's the second turning on the left."

This instruction to find Fiji was quoted by Mark Twain (*Following The Equator*) from a letter Robert Louis Stevenson sent to J. M. Barrie and Sir Arthur Conan Doyle. After this world-class name-dropping, he might have added that you can't miss the mess of islands, some eight hundred in all, which constitute the country.

RABI

More than one hundred Fijian islands are inhabited, but only three have ports of entry. We have to sail the Sea of Koro to Savusavu to check in, and then travel back overland to get to Taveuni. Now in a little open ferry, clucking with chickens and piled high with the parcels that accompany the Indians in vivid saris who cram every corner, we chug past Rabi, part of Fiji but not of it.

Rabi's recent history may be a useful precedent if the earth is in one of its warming cycles, whether human caused or not. Toward the end of the nineteenth century, an amateur geologist in Sydney, Australia, noticed an interesting bit of rock in use as an office doorstop. It turned out to be pure phosphate and was traced back to Ocean Island in what is now Kiribati (pronounced, for arcane reasons, *Kiribass*). The British Phosphate Commission was quickly established to exploit the deposit, and a rent of £50 a year agreed. What the islanders initially failed to realize was that their land was largely made of phosphate, one of three such islands in the Pacific; and once it was dug up and exported by miners, what little remained would be wrecked. As the island shrunk and became barren, it grew obvious that the population would have to be relocated. The decision was preempted when Japan invaded in 1941 and promptly shipped everybody to the Caroline Islands as slaves. At the end of the war, the liberated Ocean Islanders were set up on Rabi, where five thousand or so now reside, a nation within a nation. Should Pacific sea levels rise, the populations of numerous atolls, Kiribati included, will need a new home. Rabi may prove the case study.

TAVEUNI

In Somosomo on Taveuni, Fiji's third largest island, we are bidden to drink kava with an old man named Lekram, who subsists on the income of a tiny fruit stand in front of his two-room house. His younger friend, Washu, is not drinking kava. It being against his Hindu tenets, along with eating animals and fish or using animal products, tobacco and liquor. He explains this at high speed while expounding the principles of Hare Krishna. Then we talk astrophysics. Squatting on the dirt floor of a simple house in a small village on a distant island, we find ourselves with a quantum physicist who works with the Hubble telescope. That the islands constantly yield unexpected experiences is one of their rich pleasures.

Talk soon turns from physics and philosophy to Fijian politics, dear to every Fijian, with the two major communities at loggerheads about everything. The large Indian population results from the need for cane labor in the nineteenth century, work that the native Fijians didn't want to do.

"The Indians now make up about 45 percent of the population," Washu says. "But we are not allowed to own the land. We used to work most of the cane-growing land, which we leased from the government. But then the leases started running out and the government refused to renew them. This threw lots of Indians out of work and left the land uncultivated, for the Fijians do not want to work the cane farms."

I hear the same on a bus traveling across Taveuni. "The Fijians and the government own the land," an Indian says. "But they misuse it.

Fiji is fertile. The country could be rich, but Fijians only grow what they need for themselves and let the rest of the land go to waste."

The bus casts some obscurity on Fijian priorities: Having loaded up with passengers in Somosomo, it sets off the wrong way. Three-quarters of an hour later it trundles back into Somosomo and heads out in the correct direction. No one gets off or on. Does Fijian logic dictate that by riding around in a circle you get more bus for your buck, or is this the wise way to be sure of a seat when you are on island time? It remains a mystery.

VANUA LEVU

It's evident in every town and village that virtually all Fijian business activity, from shop-keeping to manufacturing, from farming to taxi-driving, is the province of ethnic Indians. The only Fijian business I find in Savusavu is a delightful girl who crenellates my hair with electric horse-clippers. Perhaps Fijian hairdressers cut only the curly-to-frizzy Melanesian heads and leave straight Indian hair to Indians.

The problem of the two communities in Fiji seems intractable. Fijian nationalist George Speight once invaded the parliament with an armed group and held the recently elected Indian prime minister and other members captive for fifty-seven days. Speight himself was nevertheless elected to parliament while in jail awaiting a death sentence. Military coups, international disapproval and sanctions have followed.

The obduracy of the ethnic Fijians, who see the Indians as useful visitors rather than Fijians and their land as an unalienable part of their being, and the blocking of the aspirations of the Indians, who consider the Fijians terminally idle and incompetent, is a recipe for continuing trouble in years to come in this compartment of paradise.

We are deep in cannibal country here. Jack London recorded the nineteenth century appetite of Ra Undreundre, a sort of Gargantua figure who lived at Takiriki:

> He kept a register of his gustatory exploits. A row of stones outside his house marked the bodies he had eaten. This row was two hundred and thirty paces long, and the stones in it numbered eight hundred and seventy two. Each stone represented a body. The row

of stones might have been longer, had not Ra Undreundre unfortunately received a spear in the small of his back and been served up on the table of Naungavuli, whose mediocre string of stones numbered only forty-eight.

William Mariner was present at a victory party about 1808 in the Fijian island of Pau:

> The chief, elated by these victories, resolved now to have an extraordinary feast.... The cooks advanced two by two, each couple bearing on their shoulders a basket in which was the body of a man barbecued like a hog. The bodies were placed before the chief who was seated at the head of his company. When these victims were placed on the ground, hogs were brought in like manner; afterward baskets of yams, on each of which was placed a baked fowl. These being all deposited, the number of dishes was counted, and announced aloud to the chief, when there appeared to be two hundred human bodies, two hundred hogs, two hundred baskets of yams, and a like number of fowls.

The hundred-mile stretch between Fiji's two biggest islands is more reef-beset than any we've yet encountered. Two centuries before us, a strange sight appeared in these treacherous waters. HMS *Bounty*'s longboat, rowed by eighteen hungry and frightened men, a scrap of sail on its stubby mast, with William Bligh in tattered uniform at the tiller, was creeping westward on its epic journey. No Europeans had ever been through Fiji. Though they knew nothing of Ra Undreundre's appetite as they passed Takiriki, the exhausted sailors were terrified when Fijians chased them in war canoes. Water and food were desperately short, but Bligh dared not attempt a landing. The little boat evaded the pursuers and continued on through the reef-strewn waters and out, once more, into the unknown ocean.

I have a German map of 1832, which still called Fiji "Blighs Inseln," or Bligh's Islands.

THE YASAWAS

Fate is starting to take a hand in my loneliness. Off Naviti Island in Fiji's Yasawa group, we stop to meet manta rays, reputed to like feeding toward the top of the tide as it floods through a narrow passage. Our previous attempts to swim close up with these gentle giants have been unsuccessful, so sitting in the dinghy secured to a lump of coral a few feet under the middle of the little strait, we lie in wait, snorkeling gear at the ready.

After a while, something sinister-seeming glides toward us. We slip into the water, swimming hard against a strong current. The shadow coalesces into a kite shape, a dark triangle with curved leading edges and undulating wings. A little eye watches me. I am happily tolerated as the huge fish continues to swim easily against the tidal flow, while I flipper hard alongside. There are half a dozen mantas around me, cruising just below the surface. I work hard to stay abreast of one for several minutes, slipstreaming under its seven-foot wing and peering down its barrel throat, which is stretched open to sieve up the plentiful plankton in the pass. They're beautiful, manta rays. Aquatic equivalence with Concorde or the sleek sports cars of the 1930s flashes through my mind, though nature invariably outclasses even the most graceful human artifacts.

Sitting in the dinghy in this distant place, I have been seen by an unsuspected watcher. Next day our paths converge, but we do not speak. When, at last, weeks later, she tells me haltingly of the encounter, she explains that I looked unearthly, illuminated in the glow of a mysterious light as I sat waiting in the dinghy. It scared her.

Underwater is where we finally meet. My second son, Alexi, is on leave from his London Public Relations business and flies in to Nadi with a friend, David, to take over from the Vava'u crew. We are diving with Manny of the Octopus Resort. Though we have our own gear and a compressor on board, a local dive master knows the good places. As beginners, Alexi and David use up their bottles of air quickly, especially after Manny slaps an octopus on Alexi's chest at fifty feet, causing him shock horror, and me to laugh until my regulator leaks. When they bubble up toward the surface I am left buddying with a female figure in a pink wetsuit with a pink scuba tank. We swim together through caves lined with sea-whips, sponges and pink gorgonian fans. We stroke a pink puffer fish till it puffs up like a pink party balloon. The dive over, my pink lady disappears. Her figure was nice. I wonder what she looks like out of rubber and mask.

VITI LEVU

Back in Vitu Levu, the main island of Fiji, to deliver the crew to the airport, I find the pink lady's boat tied up close by. She's called Robin. From Connecticut. She's of part Italian descent, medium height, with shining black hair and big, brown intriguing eyes. I invite her to sail to New Zealand with me.

"No," she says without hesitation. "No way."

A definite recoil is evident.

She is sailing with a Kiwi couple. Last month in Tonga they rescued her from a catamaran whose owner was unstable and threatening, they say, and she is not going to risk another marooning with a strange man.

Denied exciting female company, I track Raphael down to rejoin the crew. That a Swiss working in the higher reaches of information technology in a city as far from the sea as it is possible to get in Europe wants to be a hand on a small ship in the middle of the ocean betrays a deep sense of adventure, belied by his quiet manner and now neatly clipped imperial. After rescuing a disabled British yacht about to be washed onto the reef, we sail eastward along the coast of Viti Levu to Yanuca Island, uninhabited except for a shack behind the beach cobbled up by surf zealots to exploit a world-class reef-break nearby.

A tapping on the hull in the early morning proves to be a couple of Californian surfers paddling by on their boards. "Hey there!" A sand-blond head pops over the gunwhale, followed by a well-muscled, bronzed torso. "You goin' to New Zealand?"

His name is Andy and I tell him that, if he gets himself to Suva by the weekend, I'll take him to Auckland. It's only twelve hundred miles.

Customs knocks off for the weekend at midday Friday, and Immigration officers have gone missing, so we have to hang in till Monday to clear out. Suva, Fiji's capital and the largest town in the South Pacific islands, is a curious mixture. An Indian cab from O'Reilly's bar takes us up Gordon and McGregor streets to a Chinese restaurant. Nothing much is ethnic Fijian about Suva's commerce. Nor, sadly, is there much about Suva to take one out of one's way, though it provides my first movie in a year and houses a fine Melanesian museum.

Against my expectations, Andy turns up. I sign him on for the passage to New Zealand, little suspecting he's caught the dreaded dengue fever in Fiji. This is the only case of dengue on board despite its widening impact throughout the Pacific. He's fit, an international water-polo player. While the crew tries to avoid transmission by aedine mosquitoes bed-hopping, he shrugs off the fever in a few days.

As we climb aboard the dinghy to depart from the Suva Yacht Club, pretty little black-and-white sea snakes are writhing around the supporting posts of the dinghy dock. These are sea kraits, their fangs loaded with sacs of venom three times more virulent than the cobra's. One drop is enough, so they say, to kill three adults, and a snake no thicker than a finger can eject seven or eight drops in a single bite. However, so they say, the kraits only use their poison for immobilizing their lunch, and it has not occurred to them to bring it to bear as an aggressive or even defensive weapon. So they say. No one is swimming just there.

THE ASTROLABE

Fifty miles to the south of Viti Levu lies a huge reef ring, looping up from the smaller island of Kadavu. Its name, the Great Astrolabe, was supplied by the boat of French explorer Dumont d'Urville, which was all but wrecked on the reef in 1827. D'Urville lived dangerously. The previous month he had spent an entire week holding the *Astrolabe* off a Tongan reef, a few feet from wreckage. He survived these and other close calls in the Southern Ocean, eventually meeting his end in another form of transport, an 1842 train crash in Versailles when taking his family for a Sunday picnic. Among the claims of this adventurous character was that he saw the Venus de Milo with her arms attached to her shoulders. He was unable to prevent her dismembering during a scuffle with some Turks over ownership, and her arms have not been seen since. D'Urville's place in history is owed, however, not to archaeology or navigation but to anthropology. It was he who first described and delineated the three groupings of Pacific islands: the many islands of Polynesia, the tiny islands of Micronesia and the black islands of Melanesia.

For reasons connected with Fijian bureaucracy, the Astrolabe reefs are seldom visited by yachts, so *Nereus* is once again at anchor

Dumont d'Urville 1790–1842…and the *Astrolabe* on a later adventure

quite alone. This time, though, it's different. There's no land in sight.

The northern section, the Little Astrolabe, is a saucer of coral enclosing a lagoon some five miles across, without islands, motus or coral heads. None of the surrounding reef is above water level. It is a strangely beautiful experience to be rocking gently in calm water in the light of a full moon while the ocean thunders on an unseen barrier all around, the horizon unbroken save by the line of white breakers and drifting spray. We have passed close to two other offshore lagoon systems like this. In the days before GPS, isolated reefs were shunned by vessels as fearfully dangerous, but now that a boat can be navigated in all weathers to within a few feet of any place on the face of the ocean, they attract more traffic. The Beveridge Reef, a hundred miles east of Tonga, had half a dozen yachts in it when we passed by, and the Minerva reef contained several vessels praying for a fine-weather window for the fraught passage south to New Zealand. Minerva was the location in 1972 of an attempt to create a new libertarian nation by a real estate millionaire adventurer named Oliver from Las Vegas. Sand was brought from Australia to raise the level high enough for a flagpole, and Minerva dollars were minted. The King of Tonga, deciding this would not do, sent the wonderfully improbable combination of a band of musicians and a gang of convicts to shoo the interlopers off, and then claimed it for himself.

But we have the Little Astrolabe to ourselves, and that makes the difference.

At five in the morning, a small fishing skiff from the mainland swaps me some trevally for hot coffee and sugar. We stay for an idyllic day, swimming in underwater gardens, diving a pristine reef among sharks and big fish, gathering strength for testing weather conditions as we leave the tropics to head down to New Zealand. This day is as perfect as days on a boat can get, the Astrolabe a watery paradise.

Crackling out of the pass and on south through flat waters at six or seven knots, sheltered by the line of coral just to port, we fizz into the next reef system through an unseen narrow pass with transits—the navigational alignments of any beacons or useful bits of land—of the little islands dotting its calm waters to guide us. We drop the anchor on the lee side of a huddle of islands in uncharted water off the shell-strewn beach of an untouched island. There is no one for many miles as I scramble up a ridge through thick old flora, for once uneaten by goats. Toward dusk, the sky darkens as flying foxes take to the air, loudly squeaking whatever messages a fruit bat needs to communicate. It's Halloween, an appropriate evening to spend among a cloud of enormous bats. We look again for the elusive green flash as the last segment of sun sinks into the western ocean. Though Andy swears he's experienced it three times in California and it's a proven optical phenomenon, I stay skeptical.

KADAVU

More perfect sailing inside the Astrolabe brings us to Kavala Bay on the main island of Kadavu, where *Nereus* comes to rest between mangroves in placid upper waters near a village named Solotavui. A handsome young man, Kubha, introduces himself. Having briefed us about the village he conducts us to the Chief to present our *sevusevu*, our gift of kava, and drink a few shells with him and some elders. We are invited to a feast, eaten sitting cross legged on the floor, fingers serving for cutlery. A cat and a puppy vie for the food on my plate, and a multicolored Kadavu musk parrot perches on my hand as I munch a supper of fried parrotfish, dalo and plantain.

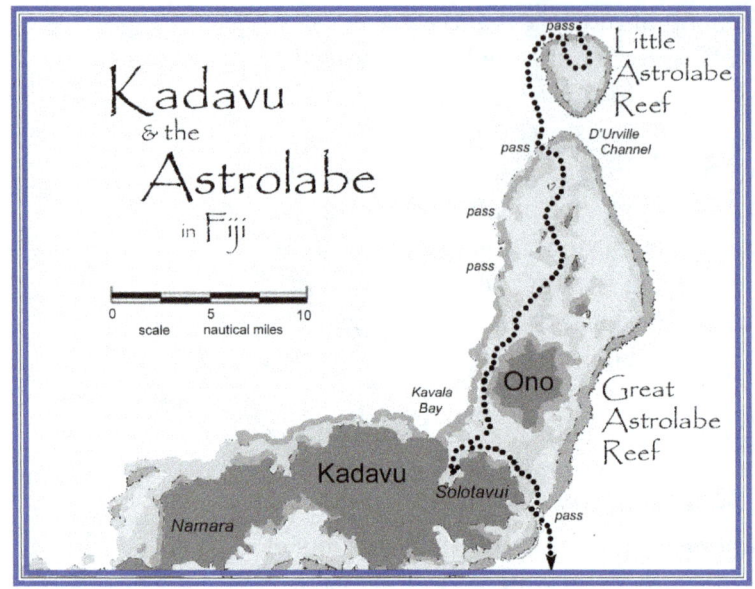

Kubha comes with us next morning in the dinghy, puttering up a winding, overhung mangrove lane to his home in an isolated clearing under the hills at the head of the bay. After crossing his uncle's palm with our remaining Fijian silver in return for formal chiefly consent to penetrate inland, we walk a narrow track through tall forest to a waterfall that tumbles into a dark round pool. Here we swim in sweet water, climbing the black and slippery rockface to dive out through the cascading stream into a rainbow. The forests echo with the sound of birdsong–honeyeaters, musk parrots and fruit doves. Unlike most of Fiji, the alien mongooses and hopping yellow-billed Indian myna birds have not made it here to decimate the indigenous populations. The forest is old, primary growth spared by the loggers of long ago because of the high costs of extraction and the ferocity of the Kadavuans.

We return through the mangroves, which I have learned are more an idea than a tree. The term covers upwards of a hundred varieties of vegetation, some unrelated to others, with the common factor seeming to be the ability to exist with its feet partly in salt water, partly in fresh. With a few expert strokes of his machete, Kubha prepares drinking and jelly coconuts for our voyage then shakes down a shower of fruit from his tamarind tree.

"Only strangers eat tamarinds, but they only eat them once," Mark Twain remarked in *Roughing It*. Nonetheless, it's satisfyingly thirst-quenching to suck them.

Kubha is philosophical about the village life. "We have nothing. It's very difficult to get money in a village. Village people can live without money, until they marry, for then one must have a whale tooth to give to the girl's family. Without a whale tooth they will not consent to let her come. It is expensive to buy a whale tooth, and one cannot find them on the beach anymore. So I must go to the city to get some money."

Chief ready to receive sevusevu and some silver, Kadavu

Kubha, Kadavu

"Why a whale's tooth?" I ask.

"The whale tooth is very important part in our customs. I don't know why. But if someone give a whale tooth, and I accept it, then I must do what he ask. If I worry that I may not want to do what he want, I must refuse the tooth."

Returning to the theme of the comparative poverty of the ethnic Fijians compared with the Indians, I ask, "Why are there no Fijian businesses? You, for example, you are a strong and clever fellow. Why do you not start your own business?"

"We Fijians are no good at business. It is not our way to make money."

Fiji and the Astrolabe

13

Kanaky–New Caledonia

SAILORS' PLANS have to stay flexible. When at last we reach our next South Seas group, a year has passed in New Zealand, an unintended year. To avoid hurricanes, cautious cruisers spend the summer cyclone season outside the tropics, so I planned to use the months to maintain *Nereus,* and then carry on. Things worked out otherwise.

Especially Robin.

A few years earlier Robin had mothballed her architectural practice to sail south from New England with her husband. She dreamed of sailing the Pacific, but the strains of the sea proved too much for the marriage and her husband abandoned ship. Eventually she set out across the Great Ocean with a new companion. He was not a lucky choice, and as his true character emerged she'd become very anxious, trapped in the claustrophobic confines of the small boat and anticipating growing violence. Then she did have a stroke of luck in the shape of kind New Zealanders who, concerned about her safety, snatched her away so she could complete her Pacific crossing safely under sail.

I determined to assail her with invitations as soon as *Nereus* reached New Zealand. Drawing deeply on what skills a lifetime of appreciating the company of women had taught me, I succeeded with difficulty in inveigling her to Whangerei, North Island, once *Nereus* was berthed several miles up a river. One look into her big, brown eyes and I knew; I'd have to try to keep her. We set off to

Robin

travel around South Island together, and then she consented to sail with *Nereus*, and we became part of each other's lives.

Much later she told me diffidently, as if it were something I could not be expected to believe and she was only half sure of herself, how she had spied me before we happened to dive together with Manny. "I saw a person, sitting in a dinghy out in the middle of the strait between the two islands where the mantas were feeding," she said. "He was a long way off, but in spite of the distance, I could see he was illuminated, glowing in some way. A sort of aura surrounded him. I was certain no one else could see it. That person turned out to be you! It frightened me. I was convinced I should have nothing to do with you."

Robin's routine mammogram indicated a problem, and a biopsy confirmed a malignancy. Treatment was necessary, with all the trauma this engenders. We thus missed our departure from New Zealand in the southern autumn. At the same time I discovered that *Nereus* had developed a sort of metallic cancer. The purchase survey of the hull, done at high cost by an English surveyor in Italy, proved useless. So while Robin was under doctor's orders, I had many weeks of unexpected boat work, learning new skills of metal cutting and grinding, swathed in protective mask, earmuffs, goggles and gloves, getting acquainted with most of Auckland's marine trades, commissioning metal fabrication, filthy from morning to dusk, cleaning, preparing and coating.

Nereus' teak deck was in poor shape too. "Get rid of it," Robin urged. "It can't be replaced without spending a fortune and it can't be properly repaired. Anyway, all the boat owners I know in the United States think a teak deck is so much trouble it reduces the value of a boat. They never last, 'specially laid over steel."

I came to understand she was usually right. Four men from the yard, Robin and I worked flat out. She was magnificent, a paragon of technical knowledge, hard work, fun and beauty. She dealt with the cancer scare by reading every published paper and researching every treatment until she knew almost as much as the oncologist and felt secure in refusing a standard drug whose side effects were more threatening than the chance of benefit. Eight weeks later the wood was gone except for the teak cap rail, the surface faired and coated with many layers of two-part primers, base coats and top coats. The sparkling white deck looked fantastic. Ever since, a complete convert, I have been boring reluctant sailors to get rid of their teak decks as soon as possible.

"I've been nursing an idea a while," Robin told me after we moved *Nereus* to an Auckland marina. "I'm going to do some sculpture in glass."

"But you need a furnace for glass."

"No, I shall use flat glass, and assemble it with something like the old Tiffany method."

I had no idea what she was talking about, but we found a shed she could use. As she produced her first work, it was clear that she had invented a new and stunning art form. The pieces she made were intriguing and saleable. But a boat is an imperfect environment for working with glass and gas burners; sculpting had to be shelved when at last the cyclone season was over, we provisioned up, said many good-byes and quit Auckland.

On the new deck with the bikes are two new toys, plastic kayaks for landing on difficult beaches, playing in the surf and penetrating shallow waters. At the helm as we sail north is my new companion. Our partnership will be tested under conditions that would shatter most.

We pass close to the Cavalli Islands, the last resting place of the *Rainbow Warrior,* which French commandos blew up, together with an unfortunate journalist, to stop Greenpeace sailing into waters where the French government was testing nuclear bombs. She was towed out and sunk where she makes a fine artificial reef for divers. The French have not been forgiven in New Zealand.

In these waters a few years back, a family yacht was rammed and sunk by a South Korean bulk carrier, generating a sharp cautionary tale for ocean wanderers in small boats. Judith Sleavin from San Diego was sailing the forty-seven-foot sloop *Melinda Lee* from Tonga to the Bay of Islands. She was run down by a huge vessel in the night. Her boat sank, her husband and her two children died. She saw the crew of the freighter watching them from the rail, but it did not stop to help. Her back broken, she somehow managed to launch a life raft and crawl into it. She survived, to be washed ashore on North Island many hours later. Despite proof of the identity of the Korean vessel, no one was prosecuted and only derisory compensation received. Several reminders flowed from this tragedy: We must never rely on ships conforming to lighting and watch-keeping conventions; move over if anything bigger than you is coming, whatever the international rules say; and have no delusion you will be able to bring maritime villains to justice under international law. Little boats on a big ocean are on their own; freedom cuts both ways.

As New Zealand sinks below the horizon, the wind on our quarter rises to force seven. For several days it blows from the same direction, working up powerful seas rearing to the upper limit of the meteorological classification "very rough." Like the majority of sailors, Robin suffers nausea when first at sea, a problem seventy thousand sea miles never cures, but she insists on standing every minute of her watches. Breaking wave crests regularly crash over the deck in a welter of spray. The express-train roar of one particular monster alerts me to glance over my shoulder. A precipice of white water towers over the boat from the height of the mizzen spreader, curling down on me, spitting elemental rage. It seems to hesitate in anticipation before triumphantly falling upon us in thunderous glee. I shrink as far as I can under the doghouse as it strikes and fills the cockpit to the coamings with foaming turbulence. Though the hatches and companionway door are tightly closed, water finds its way whither it will into the saloon and the engine room and the aft cabin. Robin wakes abruptly to find her bunk drenched; she rushes up, enquiring if we're sinking. Once I've emptied out my oilskins and checked around, I can reassure her that, but for a wetting, there is no damage. *Nereus* can handle worse than this. It takes the self-draining cockpit just a few minutes to deal with three tons of ocean. Soon Robin's asleep again in a dry bunk, our boisterous northward course hardly interrupted.

The white water fizzing past the hull against the black of the deep ocean gives a weird impression of great speed reinforced by a cacophony of sounds—the crashing of the hull on the waves, the roar of the seas, the slapping, clanking and creaking of the bones and sinews of the boat, and the moan of the wind in the rigging—though in truth eight knots is no more than a modest running pace on land. The strong winds have remained on our stern since we sailed away from New Zealand four days ago, time to pile up a considerable sea. Helming is a continuous battle with the wheel as mountains of water tower over the counter and power past, each distinct from its predecessors. Sometimes the stern rears up, the bow dips and we surf the slope down to the trough in a bath of foam. More often, the wave catches the boat under the quarter, pushing us around in a corkscrew motion. It takes only a moment's inattention to twist our little craft through fifty degrees or more, a moment that threatens dire consequences. If we are spun too far toward the wind, there is risk of a broach as the wind comes abeam; the torque exerted by the waves on the sails and hull can exceed the effect of full opposite rudder. If we are turned downwind, the danger is a jibe. Jibing in such seas can destroy the rig.

The sea is a living thing, and in turn it imparts vigorous life to a small boat. Driving in these conditions is not unlike riding an unruly thoroughbred, your fate concentrated in the strength and knowledge of your hands. Sometimes the ship is returned to her course by the wave with no correction needed. More often the effect is compounded and only violent reaction keeps her pointing downwind. Between times one's hands are in permanent motion, stroking the helm this way and that, guided by increasing experience to ride the waves smoothly while maintaining the angle of the wind on the sails.

At four o'clock in the morning I have just climbed blearily out of my cozy bunk to come on watch, leaving it warm for Robin. Hotbunking is called for in the southern chill, though with four hundred miles sailed from New Zealand, we are over halfway to the Tropic of Capricorn now, passing a tiny speck of Australia called Norfolk Island, way out in the Coral Sea. I read that Norfolk has a population of about one thousand eight hundred, two-thirds of whom are directly descended from Fletcher Christian and the handful of *Bounty* mutineers who made it to Pitcairn Island in

1790. They were moved to Norfolk in the nineteenth century when Pitcairn got too crowded, taking over the abandoned buildings of a savage penal colony, and all stayed except a brave band who insisted on going home to Pitcairn after a few years. The Norfolk pine hails from there, its other claim to notice unless you are a birdwatcher, for whom it offers rare joys.

Our motion is too fierce for an autopilot, so I am hand-steering on Antares, the major star in Scorpio. This is the only constellation that looks something like its name without great effort of creative thinking. The Greeks and Arabs who ordered the stars into groups named for animals, birds and mythical beasts, possessed imagination that even a regular stargazer like me finds hard to follow as the procession of dogs, bears, dragons, hydras and so on wheels above in its eternal cycle. Lining Antares up with a mizzen shroud enables me to keep on course while comfortable on the cockpit seat beside the wheel, leaping to the helm from time to time to wrench the boat back to 330 degrees after a particularly vicious fishtailing.

"I must down to the seas again, to the lonely sea and the sky, and all I ask is a tall ship, and a star to steer her by..." I had thought John Masefield's poetic imperitive redundant with the advent of gyros and GPS. Not so. A star is still the perfect point of steering reference, so long as one sleepily adjusts for its stately progress across the heavens from time to time. At night, even fluffy clouds loom darkly menacing as they heap up on the horizon and race across the sky to take out my steering star. The threat is sometimes real, and the cumulus cloaks a wind cell that increases the windspeed from thirty to forty knots in seconds, bending its direction and bringing stinging rain into the doghouse and the saloon unless I get the companionway door closed in time. The squall lasts only half an hour or so, and then the sky clears abruptly and moonlight turns the foaming sea to silver. The tail of the Southern Cross is high in the sky aft, serving to distinguish the true Cross from two similar pretenders.

We have acquired a pair of passengers, a little migrating bird clinging to the rail in a miniscule huddle of downy feathers, and a large seabird that insists on climbing down into the saloon to travel cabin-class. I'm severely pecked for my suggestion that the proper place is the deck, and the bird is comfortably installed under the galley step. Perhaps it's a burrowing mutton-bird. Venus appears before the sky starts paling for the morning, a good pointer at 90 degrees to our course and sufficiently radiant to remain

New Caledonia at sunrise

visible through the thinner cloud. She is the harbinger of dawn, a slow lightening of the eastern sky until the golden sunrise grows strong enough to dim her out and illuminate our chaotic green and white world.

We are traveling fast, likely to finish the nine-hundred-mile passage in five days as against the seven or eight expected. Then, in the black depths of another night, disaster strikes. With a crash, the foresail, which was well reefed on its furler, blows out, ripped in a second from top to bottom. The lower half trails in the sea from the lee rail, snaking the length of the gunwhale as raging waves charge past. As if a last despairing shout, the sad remnants aloft crack from the forestay like ghost whips against the black of the night, flogging and thundering against the rigging. It takes an hour or two to control the shredded Dacron and haul the remaining rags on board, time that is measured not by a watch but by energy tailing into exhaustion. Our speed is much reduced as we set sail again for New Caledonia under reefed main and a tough little staysail.

The genoa was destroyed by the last gasp of strong wind; a rising sun finds us motoring the final fifty miles in a calm.

And my newfound companion is proved up, magnificent; calm under the stress of hard sailing and hairy moments, careful, stubborn, knowledgeable and fun. Sailing with Robin on board is going to change things. I have fallen in love with her, though I remain a suspect man needing plenty more testing.

Kanaky

Cook pines, Isle de Pins

Our early arrival in Grande Terre, New Caledonia's main island, allows time to repair the sails after the rather energetic passage, before cleaning up for the arrival of Gonzalo and Pablo, an old Spanish friend and his son flying in from Madrid. After a day in Noumea, a nickel-rich sunburnt French city of more than one hundred thousand inhabitants, we sail sixty-five miles across New Caledonia's enormous southern lagoon—the world's largest, they claim, dodging isolated reefs far offshore.

ÎLE DE PINS

New Caledonia's barrier reef is second in length only to the Great Barrier Reef off Queensland. The Île de Pins, touted by guidebooks to be the South Pacific's most beautiful island even though used by Napoleon III as another Devil's Island to incarcerate French convicts of a political nature, lies within extensive reefs at the lagoon's eastern boundary. Like all the islands raped by loggers and sandalwood traders of the nineteenth century, its forests are gone, though a scattering of pines remains to illustrate its name. Hidden within is the landlocked lagoon of Upi, several square miles of pristine water broken only by coral mushroom islands dotted here and there and a single pirogue with rickety outrigger and ancient pointy sail to riffle the surface. Perched on ironwood roots for a picnic under the shade of a pandanus canopy on a lonely sandspit, it's hard to imagine this place as arduous incarceration. The prison ruins are picturesquely draped with lianas, the beaches white talcum sand, the clear water full of fishes. "Did the prisoners thank God or the Emperor for punishment in paradise?" Gonzalo muses.

Captain Cook was intrigued by the pines on his second voyage. Though trapped in a maze of shoals all night, tacking to and fro, he was not deterred: "I was now almost tired of a Coast I could no longer explore but at the risk of loosing the ship and ruining the whole voyage, but I was determined not to leave it till I was satisfied what sort of trees those were which had been the subject of our speculation."

He bestowed the name Isle of Pines once he had inspected the columnaris trees guarding the shoreline, 150 feet high with stubby little branches bristling only a few feet at right angles to their trunks. These are known now as Cook Pines.

After a day's perfect downwind sail across the calm waters of the lagoon to get fresh provisions in Noumea and replace some booze depletion with the inferior wine that seems to get shipped to France's distant dependencies, we depart, thankful we stocked *Nereus* up to the gunwales in New Zealand. Prices are high, as in French Polynesia. I do not find the town particularly interesting, being the province of *Les Caloches*, the French colonists, to the virtual exclusion of the indigenous Kanaks. Attrition of the Melanesian population and immigration have ensured that Kanaks (a hundred years and more ago, white sailors indiscriminately called all Pacific islanders Kanaks) are, like Maoris and Aborigines, now a minority in their own country. Their country is Kanaky, but for everyone else Cook's name, echoing a brief Scottish excursion he made on the far side of the world, has stuck.

Clearing out with the usual excessive, pointless formalities (four identical forms to uplift fuel duty free, no carbons allowed, and many more), we set off around the bottom of Grande Terre, staying within the lagoon that fringes virtually its entire 700-mile coastline until wind arrives to carry us north. It increases as we sail a smart reach toward the Loyalty Islands where we duck in to Ouvéa to await gentler breezes. The wind was enough to make the crossing at an average nine knots, a passage record. Pablo is ecstatic when he hooks a big wahoo, which Robin dishes up as *poisson cru*, a ceviche lightly pickled in lemon juice, onion and coconut cream.

OUVÉA

Surging through the southernmost entrance of Ouvéa's lagoon, the sea calms abruptly as we pass a few feet outside the line of angry surf pounding the point's fringing reef. Waves that seconds before were thrice the height of the hull are no more than ripples in its lee, and *Nereus* holds the speed we've been traveling for the last forty miles as we bring her bow up close to the wind and turn toward a gleaming beach curving away to the horizon. The anchor splashes down in pale blue water, the new kayaks are shoved over the side, and minutes later Gonzalo and his son are running on the pristine sand, inspecting shells, flopping.

Once Pablo has caught an early morning ferry back to Noumea, we move to better holding a few miles down the coast, near an uplifted coral massif called the Cliffs of Lekine. There Robin and I pop the kayaks in the water again, but, as we paddle toward the beach, I spot a problem. "Turn back, there is a gendarmerie Land Rover parked behind the bush," I call softly.

Though international convention allows sailors to take shelter if weather or mechanical problems make it necessary, technically we are illegal in the island. We had to sign a declaration in Noumea that we would proceed directly out of the territory without stopping in any of the offlying islands. Being a New England lady of a thoroughly determined nature, Robin paddles onward. As her canoe grounds on the beach, a pair of uniformed *flics* emerge from the scrub. I scoot nonchalantly back to *Nereus* where Gonzalo and I surreptitiously watch the arrest process through binoculars. The interview continues on the beach for half an hour before the *flics* depart, leaving Robin to paddle back with a summons to present our papers at the police post in a nearby village. I am aware that there was a bloody incident in this far corner of the French empire only a few years back. A Kanak insurrection climaxed in an attack on the Ouvéa gendarmerie. Some policemen were killed and others held hostage in a cave behind our beach. The rebellion was put down with great ferocity at President Chirac's command. Every single Kanak concerned was slaughtered.

We consider flight, but Robin seems convinced she has charmed the nice gendarmes. Reluctantly, she's allowed to collect up all our passports and the boat papers and head off for the police post. Promises that we'll come to bail her out are pitched at her receding back. She prevails, though. They chat her up, ply her with good

French coffee and accept our claimed need under maritime custom for shelter from the roaring winds and threatening seas. They entirely agree we should stay a few days awaiting better weather. A woman aboard to deal with male officials is a clear advantage, another plus that is to prove very valuable.

The wind still howls out of the southeast and huge waves pound the ocean coast of the atoll. On our side, we are anchored off a perfect beach. The pearly sand, speckled with exotic shells under its fringe of ironwood and coconut trees, is lapped by little ripples. We enjoy four more days under our license-to-loiter in Ouvéa, riding the bicycles through the jungle among painted butterflies, giant spiders and paradise birds, and then move on one dawn across fourteen miles of calm lagoon waters. Clear of the little motus, which protect the atoll's northern pass, with the wind still blowing hard, we set a course for Vanuatu, 200 miles to the northeast.

The Pandemonium– Vanuatu

TANNA

The island of Tanna is home to a supremely materialistic vision of paradise, of which we would be part. *Cargo,* in local lingo, means goods from industrial countries, stuff from corned beef and fine clothes to radios, candy, cars and guns. Tribes with no experience of manufactured goods saw, saucer-eyed, the possessions and accoutrements with which US forces were equipped when they appeared in the islands to face Japanese invaders. It was rumored that one day great cargo would arrive, enough to solve all problems and supply all needs for ever, and the name of the bringer would be Jon Frum. The idea flourished and became a cult, a cargo cult, a faith, rather as certain Christian sects await the Second Coming with confidence. Whether Jon Frum resides in the active volcano that dominates the area or far away in the USA is uncertain, a matter for much debate.

Sailing in from unknown places, we will be carefully inspected, for who is to say whether I am Jon Frum or not? He is expected on some fifteenth day of February, which is accordingly an important festival, but the Frummers are ready any day. They first laid down a rough runway for Jon Frum to land his plane, and a ramshackle jetty in case he came by sea, and it's a sure sign he's imminent that their village Lenakel now has a little airport and a fine new wharf, constructed with Japanese aid.

The Frummers' symbol is a red cross, for GI medical tents were particularly well equipped. It is easy to suppose that the name derives from a quartermaster introducing himself with words such as "Hi fella, I'm John frum Alabam'…" as he unloaded lavish supplies under the eyes of astonished clansmen.

When Christians look skeptical on being told of the Frummers' belief, they may be answered: "Yes, we expect him seventy years now. But have you not waited two thousand years for your god to return?"

Tanna's reputation is assured, though. Throughout Vanuatu, when we ask about some antique custom or strange manifestation, the universal answer is, "Not here. But maybe in Tanna…"

To our dismay, the stiff wind fails to cooperate in blowing us to Tanna; we cannot achieve the necessary wind angle in the rough seas. We have to put the helm down and make north for Efate instead.

An albatross appears while I'm checking the fishing lines, beadily interested in the pink squiddle trailing in our wake. This giant glider from the cold regions of the south, riding the air currents of the world's oceans for months at a time, is a fine sight, depressingly rare. Its wingspan of up to ten feet, the largest of any bird, enables it to glide without flapping its wings for hours on end. Thankfully, it doesn't dive on our lure, though longline fishermen, trailing perhaps five or fifty miles of wire studded with hooks from their deep-sea vessels, are responsible for serious depletion of their numbers. The squiddle attracts a nice albacore tuna before we enter the sheltered waters of Port Vila on the island of Efate, enough for several meals for the three of us.

EFATE

Port Vila is named in a guidebook as the most beautiful capital city in the Pacific, outrageous hyperbole for an average scruffy island town sporting some government buildings, three small supermarkets, a little French gloss, and half a dozen places to eat, albeit nestling amidst an impressionist riot of flowering shrubs and trees. However, there is just one place in all Vanuatu where a boat can plug in to electricity, a rare luxury for a Pacific yacht not to be repeated until we reach Australia months ahead, enabling us to dispense with the clattering generator for a while. Tied stern to the wall, we languish in the foulest weather yet experienced in the tropics, incessant rain culminating after a week in hour after hour of shattering thunderstorm. Our washing machine can use the juice, but nothing will dry.

The weather is unusual, caused by the fringe of cyclone Gina, which formed in North Vanuatu, generating winds over one hundred knots as it approaches. The cyclone season is over, so Gina is a nasty surprise. For decades there has been no cyclone as late as June in Vanuatu—and Ida in June 1972 was only a modest sixty-knot affair. Cyclone areas and seasons are well delineated, but an El Niño or a little meteorological aberration sometimes stretches the limits. Boat owners' precautions involve finding the best hurricane-hole with the least fetch, and then securing with multiple heavy lines to moorings, tree roots, anchors, whatever is available. Boats suffer more cyclone damage from storm-driven debris and other craft breaking loose than anything else, so rivers are not advisable. Best is to snuggle in among mangroves, though this is hard for a keelboat. Vila harbor is doubly sheltered behind islands, but that's not shelter enough if Gina comes this way.

In the event, Gina narrowly misses Port Vila. Crossing her track later we see the devastation of islands in her trajectory and thank our sea-gods that we were not sailing to our initial schedule in Gina's path of destruction. Robin's description of personal encounters

Kava preparation, Vanuata

RR Acrylic on canvas

with two West Indies hurricanes encourages me to avoid the same experience at all costs.

A sister Nordia, belonging to Franz from Vienna, is moored next door with its original teak deck in place, looking very tatty. As Robin is lecturing Franz about the joys of getting rid of it as we did, a big smile beaming from a coal-black face emerges from the companionway, followed by the large man owning it. He introduces himself as Chief Sandi and takes us to his house to tell us the story of kava, illustrated with lashings of his own brew. A complete circlet of pig's tooth nestles in the centre of his broad bare chest, while an already imposing presence is heightened by a crown of exotic feathers upon his head. His ample stomach, girdled by a red cummerbund holding a fresh skirt of pandanus leaves in place, secures his rank in the ancient hierarchy. The outfit has been well honed for tourists, and is none the worse for it. By now an old kava hand, I select the largest coconut, and then, to prove I'm no passing yachting wimp, another shell. Robin tells me afterward I swayed a while, fell over, and then seemed to find it hard to get up off the floor. Compared with the milkteeth stuff in Fiji and Tonga, Vanuatu kava packs a mighty punch.

Once assured that Gina has lost her power, thoroughly drenched and still unable to distinguish a DVD soundtrack over the explosions of thunderbolts and the hammering of torrential rain, Robin and I reach the end of our patience and cast off our wall.

A thing comfortable to do in rain is swim, so we anchor in the shelter of nearby Mele Island and jump overboard. Immediately below, an octopus is in possession of a chunk of reef, looking as old as the rocks amongst which he camouflages himself, changing his shades of color as subtly as a chameleon as he squiggles slowly through the coral landscape. The sinuous manner of octopus locomotion is bewitching. His body is the size of a football, and his eye, fixing me through his slithering coils, unblinking.

The wet weather finally clears as we continue north to Nguna Island through the landlocked Havannah Harbor, in fact an eight-mile deepwater lagoon, which once held up to two hundred vessels of the US Navy retreating for rest and repairs in the Pacific war. A scattering of dwellings and a school are all that replace the echo of war now.

While raising the mainsail, the boltrope jams solid in its slot running up the mast. To fix it we sail back into Havannah under jib'n'jigger, as Robin calls the rig of foresail and mizzen. The new in-boom furling equipment we installed in New Zealand has proved excellent—but my misgivings about powered winches have been borne out by the force with which any snags gets compounded. I try every strong-arm approach I can think of short of damaging the canvas, but it's solid.

"I'll have a go at it," says Robin.

"If I can't fix it, what's a delicate creature like you going to do?"

Ignoring the edge of sarcasm that creeps, uninvited, into my voice, she disappears below and returns with a steaming pan of water, a chunk of wood and a clamp. "You get the big hammer while I fix the clamp," she commands.

When I return, she's got the track heated to expand it and the sail clamped round the baulk. "Now hit it," she says.

Obediently I strike the baulk a mighty blow, and the jam drops obediently out of the track.

Until Robin came aboard, my crews were charming but devoid of much sailing knowledge. They were useful enough, standing watches, handling sheets and halyards, cooking and keeping the captain happy, but never before had I sailed with someone who knew boats well enough to share the technical challenges. Though her background as ballet dancer, architect and painter was not obviously compatible with the ocean and her big brown eyes spoke to me more of the bedroom than the engine room, Robin has sailed thousands of miles, done more diving than me, mended more breakages and solved more problems.

Paradise research needs a partner for more than all this, though. As well as the companionship and help and love and sympathy and encouragement and the other myriad things that two people can add for each other, there's appreciation. It's lonely to marvel alone. Nothing is so wonderful that its wonders are not heightened by having someone to share it, to reflect it, to confirm and boost one's awe. This is something missing from the great travel literature written by solitary globe-trotters and the journals of single-handing sailors. With Robin aboard, one plus one equals at least five in this ocean of delights.

Gonzalo gets a lift into Vila, vanishing in a cloud of dust to fly to Madrid by way of Noumea, Tokyo and Paris. As I return to *Nereus*, a dugong sticks her nose out of the water close by. In the morning two of these curious beasts are snuffling around our anchorage. Along with its close cousin, the Florida manatee, the dugong is the only vegetarian marine mammal. Hairless, pinkish walrus-shaped creatures up to about half a ton and ten feet long, they also go by the name of sea cow. The ni-Vanuatu tell us they taste like beef too, which may explain why they are getting rare. When one sticks her snout out of the water to take a breath, she looks sort of human, at least to a sailor on a regular ration of rum; thus she is thought to have inspired stories of mermaids, at least in the febrile minds of sailors deprived of female company for months.

I'm clearing the forward cabin of sheets and hauling the mattresses on deck to air when Robin hears me cry "Eureka!" She comes running to see that I've discovered a sizeable locker below the lower bunk. It's full of liquor loaded in Spain, 15,000 miles and three years back, its existence quite forgotten.

The common language here is Pijin, locally known as Bislama. A phrasebook entitled *Evri samting yu wantem save long Bislama be yu fraet tumas blong askem* helps. With an estimated 105 languages among the 200,000 ni-Vanuatu, a common tongue was a necessity, so they adopted the strange form of Pijin English that developed in the late nineteenth century among the islanders collected by piratical "blackbirders" to work on sugar plantations. Between 1863 and 1914, some 90,000 Pacific Islanders were taken to Queensland and Fiji and a few to New Caledonia and Samoa. On the other side of the Pacific, Spaniards stole over half the population of Easter Island to man their American colonies with slaves. A few went willingly for the money and the experience of leaving their island, but most were kidnapped or tricked by the blackbirders. Among documented deceptions used were ropes hung from the ship's sides as people were invited alongside to trade. The crew then dropped stones through the bottoms of the canoes clustered round. The canoes sank, the islanders climbed up the ropes and the ship sailed off. Some blackbirders pretended they were missionaries. Others piled trade goods as gifts on the beach and rounded up people when they went to collect them. One blackbirding captain had a tank welded to his bilge. He asked the village to send their best men to move it, and once they were in the hold, the hatches were slammed shut and off they sailed.

The conditions on the sugar plantations were usually appalling, exacerbated by dreadful attrition from European diseases. Half the islanders would be dead in ten years. These people spoke hundreds of different languages, and Pijin morphed into the language of their communication, drawing on all the local languages as well as English and French. Returning laborers brought the new language back home together with information of the world outside the horizon of each island group, and many useful things besides. Manufactured goods, pawpaws and better varieties of bananas, kumara, pineapples, tobacco plants, and pumpkins are among the present-day staples introduced by the few stolen people fortunate enough to regain their villages.

As the sun drops over Moso Island, a small outrigger canoe appears from nowhere, sailing under a coconut frond, then another and another, until the dense wall of mangroves around us seems to exude canoes and the bay looks like a flooded plantation of young palms. Each carries families who paddled across in the morning to tend their gardens on the big island, a spot conveniently placed so that the evening breeze will blow them home to Moso once they have gathered a sail for the crossing, to be used on arrival for firewood for cooking. The canoes are of a construction unchanged for a thousand years or more, a dug-out log around ten feet long, with two or three poles fixed across it connecting to tripods lashed to a single outrigger log. They shout a cheery hello as they pass or stop by to chat, to ask for help mending something, or to bring us bananas and island cabbage. The gibbous moon easily illuminates the flock of diminishing dots surmounted by their little fronds until they are home in their village tucked in behind the mangroves on the point across the water.

Havannah, homeward bound

The Pandemonium

EPI

We are now among a double string of tropical islands set as I imagine the pattern of a sea horse, none too far apart for a day's sailing, a thousand miles from top to bottom, high, rough and beautiful. The night sky is lit by the glow of several active volcanoes, their fire reflected in the sea. There are few Europeans outside the two small towns, and rarely a western vessel to be seen. Occasionally a dirt road, more often a walking track connects villages, but most rely only on boat communication. The waters are full of fish. Fruit grows profusely. A welcome is assured in Vanuatu villages. The beef is among the world's best—at least the Japanese think so and make off with most of it. It adds up to one of the world's finest cruising areas.

At Epi, we carefully drop our anchor on a sand patch in Lamen Bay to avoid mowing the seagrass. A roneo'd flier seen in Vila warned us this is where Epi's resident dugongs graze. An enormous mahimahi reeled in on the way proved too big to lift on board and eventually got away, but a twenty-two-pound wahoo provides enough to trade for a beef dinner in the leaf-clad eating hut on the beach. Franz the Austrian is here, wearing an AIR FRANZ T-shirt, which betrays his profession, pilot to the Islands.

A village on Epi
RR Acrylic on canvas

He's flown a Cessna into the coral airstrip with an Australian client, the beef for our dinner, and a warning about an island a hundred miles north: "A Swiss yachtsman, another Fritz like me, was told he shouldn't swim in Utapua because of the crocodiles," he says, "but he thought it would be okay to spend a few minutes in the water checking the anchor. A crocodile got him. They buried what they could recover on the island, and I was sent to collect his wife, who couldn't handle the boat."

This story was corroborated later. There are saltwater crocodiles on a number of Melanesian islands; heaven knows how they got there across hundreds of miles of ocean from Australia or Southeast Asia. The slow migration of marine growths, seeds, even land birds across trackless ocean is understandable, but breeding pairs of crocs? Somebody claimed they had been deliberately introduced by a bishop.

MALEKULA

Next morning a dugong is hanging around the boat as the anchor is lifted from a sandy bottom alive with turtles and rays. A short sail takes us to the Maskelyn Islands, which occupy the southeastern corner of Malekula, escorted for part of the way by large dolphins jumping above the boat's rail to take a look at us.

Malekula is renowned for the last stand of the penis sheath. On the island live the remnants of two tribes known as Big Nambas and Little Nambas, the word "namba" denoting a decorous wrapping applied to that portion of anatomy. That this was once a widespread mode of apparel in Melanesia was borne out by a journal note written in New Caledonia by Charles Clerke, who sailed with Cook on two of his voyages:

> They were totally naked to the penis, which was wrapped in leaves... I gave one of them a stocking—and he very deliberately pulled it on there—I then gave him a string of beads; with it he tied the stocking up—I then presented him with a medal which he immediately hung to it—in short let that noble part be well decorated and fine, they're totally indifferent about the state of all the rest of the body.

We're prevented from traveling inland to meet the Nambas, large or small, by another massive thunderstorm and its soggy aftermath; hours of deafening lightning persuade us to disconnect as much electronic equipment as we can. I suspect from anecdotal evidence that the cost of repairing lightning damage to boats' electronics exceeds that caused by storms and wrecks.

"Now, put the computers in the ovens," orders Robin, on the principle that a metal box carries an electrical surge around an object.

I'd assumed that, being a steel vessel with a stout web of stainless steel standing rigging, we were in effect protected by a large metal box, but when I read of lightning "having a potential of up to 100 million volts, multiple current surges of up to 175,000 amps, with temperatures running as high as 60,000°F," I realize induced currents can be uncontainable. Thunderstorms are not so rare in any event; at any given moment there are some two thousand in progress worldwide. So, feeling a little silly, I do as I'm told and into the oven the computers go.

AMBRYM

It rains a foot overnight. Dawn reveals water opaque with runoff from the surrounding hills, no chance of penetrating inland and no visibility for diving in the intricate reef systems around the dozen or so delightful Maskelyns. We hang around, waiting for the trough producing this weather to move on, using the dinghy full of rainwater to do the washing, then wind our way out through twisty coral channels. Several whales breach nearby, hitting the water with splashes visible for miles as we cross to Ambrym to anchor in the lee of some high and active volcanoes off a black sand beach by the little village of Ranvetlam. As *Nereus* is squared off, a fleet of canoes puts out, offering fruits and vegetables.

"You wan' pawpaw, pumpkin?" asks a striking fellow called Jeffrey. "Or mebbee island cabbage, coconuts, avocados?"

Robin shows interest and inquires, "What would you like from us?"

"We need almost everything," he replies, though after little thought he crystallizes his requirements to some Captain Morgan.

We work out too late that Jeffrey is the village alcoholic, and he makes off with a half bottle of rum in exchange for a pumpkin and the sincere promise to return with an agreed list of other fruit and veggies. He doesn't, and belatedly we resolve for the future to deny the existence of any boozeable trade goods on board.

Joseph Bong and Ray come alongside. "You wan' talk about walking up the volcano?"

We do.

"You come to the village. We arrange a guide. Maybe Ray here be your guide. Weather maybe okay."

As the top half of the 4,000-foot Mount Marum volcano is shrouded in heavy smoke and cloud laced with threads of lightning like a neon spider's web, the weather is going to be important. At least my chart shows it as 1,270 meters, but a very faded French map—the sole item in a small leaf-hut labeled "information house"—marks it as 870 meters. To frustrate German efforts to gain territory in the Pacific, France and Britain agreed in 1906 to share the governance of Vanuatu. This odd arrangement, called The Condominium, inevitably led to disputes about everything and parallel systems of administration, measures, and total confusion. The Condominium was soon known as "The Pandemonium."

One matter unsuitable for duplicate rules was driving. To resolve the problem as to which side of the road to use, in a rare fit of agreement it was decided over sundowners one evening to conform to the next vehicle to be shipped to Vanuatu, whatever it might be. In the event, a Rosbif assumes cunningly organized by the Frogs, it was a car ordered by a French priest, so the driving is on the right. This is a mistake, as the cheapest cars available are shiploads of used imports from Japan, which drives on the left. The Pandemonium flourished in glorious chaos until independence in 1980.

The difference of opinion about the height of the mountain that we are to climb is nevertheless surprising. Maybe it grew between one survey and the next, not as improbable as it sounds on the Pacific Ring of Fire where entire islands can come and go.

Samuel paddles up, his paddle a longboat oar from some ancient wreck. "Would you be able to help the community," he asks. "Our boat has a hole in it and we haven't anything to mend it?"

"We have epoxy," I tell him, "but no fiberglass. We should be able to fix it somehow, though."

To the villages, yachts like us represent Modern Technology, however incompetent we actually are. Samuel's boat turns out to be the fruit of an application to the UN Development Corps, which failed to provide materials to repair it when, inevitably, it got damaged, and now it has been washed onto a reef in a storm and several panels stove in.

Once we've fixed it, a more bizarre request in this primitive place comes from Robert. "You help me?" he says. "My lawn mower broken."

There are no trucks, no roads, no wheeled vehicles, barrows or carts, no generator, not even horses, yet Robert possesses a lawn mower. We find a new spark plug for him.

This community of a few hundred people in some ten villages on the northern corner of Ambrym is connected with the other end of the island and the outside world by only the occasional boat or small aircraft. Widely feared as the most effective magicians of the islands, they are also the finest carvers in all Vanuatu. Everyone wants to show us carvings in rosewood, breadfruit wood and stone. Asking prices are quite high, and, unusually, it is impolite to bargain. With thousands of miles of carving territory still ahead, including the two areas of supreme skills in the Solomon Islands and Papua New Guinea, we have to try to keep our powder dry.

Snuggled among the plantations are some coral-built copra drying furnaces. Once there were only a few coconut trees in island villages, sufficient for family needs. When whale oil prices rose, coconut hegemony spread as trading companies acquired all the tropical land they could, coconuts were planted far and wide, and a huge network was established to collect, process and ship the final product. Copra became the main, often the only, source of island income. When demand for coconut oil's major uses in cooking, lighting and soap faded, competition from efficient plantations in Australia and huge new palm-oil plantations in south Asia seemed to condemn the far-flung plantations on Pacific islands, their only widespread cash crop, to rot. Though the price rocketed over $1,000 a ton in 2008 and again in 2011, it has languished most of the last twenty years in the $200-$600 range, not much for a crop that has to be collected, husked, cooked over a wood fire for at least two days, and humped a few miles without mechanical help or even wheels. There's some light on the far horizon from inflating world oil prices. Bio-fuel can be made from coconuts, and where the cost of getting diesel to remote places is high, it may be competitive without the sort of sticks and carrots endemic in the Western eco-stampede. I would like to think that a revival of coconut plantations in the islands is a possibility. Ranvetlam is representative of island villages. Apart from a dribble of money from passing yachts for carvings and volcano guide fees, copra appears the only hope of useful income.

Sailing from New Zealand to Vanuatu and the Solomons, we are traveling a section of the Pacific's Ring of Fire, the unstable boundary where the Australasian plate meets the Pacific plate, the largest tectonic slab of the earth's surface. As we are about to climb a very active volcano and look upon one of the world's only lakes of living molten lava, it seems wise to do some research. About 550 volcanoes have erupted within recorded history, and a further 1,000 are considered live. Of this total of 1,550 potentially active mountains, a thousand constitute the Ring of Fire in the Pacific, varying from apparent dormancy for centuries to occasional cataclysmic eruptions. In between, some like the one we are about to ascend rumble with constant background activity. History is little guide to the future, for of the last 16 volcanoes that blasted off mega-eruptions, 12 had not misbehaved since the annals started. The potential is mind-blowing. When Tambora on Sumbawa, an island to the east of Bali, exploded in 1815, the Governor, Sir Stamford Raffles, reported that Java, five hundred miles to the west, was in total darkness. Large rocks fell seven miles away. Buildings were crushed by the weight of several feet of gray ash. Ships couldn't move through the pumice in the sea. Just 36 of the 12,000 local inhabitants survived, and another 82,000 nearby islanders died within a year in the aftermath of that eruption. For those closer to an eruption, a pyroclastic flow consisting of superheated gases and ash at 800°C can travel at 60 mph. Its cousin, the lahar, a torrent of mud and volcanic debris, may do even more damage.

From our seaborne point of view, to be feared are tsunamis created by a landslide or the collapse of a mountain above or below sea level. When Krakatoa, a small island in the Sunda strait between Java and Sumatra, Indonesia, erupted in 1883 after three months of violent rumblings, a series of huge explosions blasted a fountain of ash fifteen miles into the air, raining destruction on houses for miles around. Then, one dawn, the volcano blew up. The bang was recorded two thousand miles away in both directions, possibly the loudest noise ever heard by man on earth. The evacuated magma chamber below the volcano had collapsed, allowing the sea in. The shores dried up as the water disappeared into the gigantic void, but a few minutes later it was back in the form of waves 150 feet high. "Like a high mountain, the monstrous wave precipitated its journey to the land. Immediately afterward another three waves of colossal size appeared. And before our eyes this terrifying upheaval of the sea, in a sweeping transit, consumed in one instant the ruin of the town," reported a rare survivor, the engineer of the Dutch ship *Loudon*.

The day after Christmas 2004, there was catastrophic evidence of the destructive potential of a tsunami. Just off the northern point of Sumatra, south of the Bay of Bengal, there is an important meeting of tectonic plates where pressures accumulating for many years without relief caused a big movement and an earthquake of nearly Richter 9. The heave in the seabed set off three tsunamis, which spread outwards in tiny ripples, accelerating to about 500 mph as they crossed the Bay of Bengal and the Indian Ocean. As each felt shallow water, it slowed and grew, until, crashing in on thousands of miles of shoreline as a thick, heavy series of waves about 20 feet high, they destroyed hundreds of towns and villages in ten countries and killed over a quarter of a million people. There had been no major tsunami in this area since 1830, and this was a small one.

"I'm not at all sure I want to go there," Robin mutters, staring up at the smoldering volcano, rather pale.

Shortly before lunchtime, we peer into hell.

A curtain of cloud billows and shreds to reveal glimpses of a seething mass of boiling rock, explosively emitting great jets of burning lava. The primeval roar is of storms at sea, express trains and unimaginable monsters; choking gases issue from unseen vents, not sulphurous steam smelling of rotten eggs but a cocktail of stinking chemicals from the bowels of the earth. Breathing is impossible until a wayward finger of wind wafts the wraith of noxious fumes away.

Perched precariously on the crumbling rim of the caldera, we look down upon a truly awesome scene. The ground falls away near vertically for a thousand black feet into the base of the volcano. In a cup at the bottom seethes a lava lake, a wild cauldron spewing forth fiery red serpents of molten rock, reproducing in microcosm the violent formation of a planet, a vision of astrophysics not a million light years away through a telescope but here, at our feet, raging with raw geological ferocity.

It wasn't easy to get here. Ray told us to be ashore at 5:00 A.M. After two hours of steep climbing through thick greenery, we reached the rim of a flat delta where millennia of ash eruptions have been flattened by rain into a plain. This took another hour of fast walking to cross, with breaks as Ray cut palm-heart or climbed a tree to throw down drinking coconuts. The route across the delta

Lava lake, Marum volcano

was a very odd geographical feature, a gravel boulevard, black, level and bare of vegetation, snaking through thick bush for miles. Black side roads led off from time to time where the heaviest rains had created tributaries of volcanic emissions. Flowering trees and rare orchids brightened the borders of the forbidding landscape.

Once across the delta, an hour's scramble up a craggy streambed brought us to the vegetation line and welcome pools of clear water from which we drank deeply, seemingly free of unpleasant chemicals from the center of the earth. From there, feeling like Frodo in the last of Tolkien's trilogy entering alien terrain for hobbit or man, with a final effort, we reached the crest of the bare, black, wind-scoured ribs of the upper mountain. This is a somber, raven territory.

We cannot remain long in the noxious atmosphere on the crater's lip. Starting back down the eight miles of mountain, breathing freely once more, I console Robin with the thought that, in this search for bits of Arcady, it's as well to glimpse the fires of purgatory for contrast. "What does he know of heaven, who only heaven knows?" I misquote.

Ray's village is small and well tended and, with a hundred cows, well off.

"What are the cows used for?" I ask once we are safely down.

"For meat, for milk and for marry," he replies.

The Pandemonium

Palm heart snack on the river of ash

"You are married? How many cows your woman cost?"

"I am married to a girl from Ambae. She cost two cows, which I have to give to her father in Ambae."

This sounded challenging, as the island of Ambae is sixty miles of open ocean away, and I visualize the two fattened cows out at sea in a canoe. Pigs might have been easier, and I wonder aloud about the rate of exchange.

"About ten pigs is equal to one cow," he says. "But not special pigs with circle tusks, which cost many cows."

He then explains how male pigs are carefully nurtured to yield the best tusks. Their upper canine teeth are removed to allow the tusk to grow unimpeded and without grinding. The pigs are fed by hand to avoid the chance of breaking the tusk, while the pig's owner works on making it grow round in a circle or even a double circle. Experts can sometimes achieve as much as three circles. Though the process takes several years of care, it's rewarded by great value, for pigs continue to play a central part in Vanuatu's traditions.

The path to the village from the black-sand beach off which we are anchored winds for a mile through magnificent groves of banyan trees, towering up to leafy vaults like the fluted columns of a gothic cathedral. On our way to meet Ray in the early morning, the children of the village were off to school in the neighboring village, each carrying a neat laplap parcel wrapped in a leaf to be cooked for lunch on the hot stones of the school fire. I encounter them again on the way home, but this time I am suddenly surrounded by bouncing children screeching, "Lolly, lolly, lolly." It seems that news of the lollipops we handed out to a couple of children too young to be at school has percolated the four miles to the next village. There's not enough candy for all of them, so a difficult allocation problem arises.

Forlornly I ask, "How you going to decide if two of you children have to go without?"

The answer is silence and twenty-four hungry sheeps' eyes. It is a moment to chicken out, so I choose Bellane who appears to be the oldest, hand her the packet and make them all promise to agree to whatever fair allocation method she proposes. They all nod eager agreement and there are a few moments of quiet as I retreat fast behind the next banyan tree. Then mayhem breaks out, and poor Bellane is jumped upon and scragged.

As we get ready to sail off, Joseph paddles up at speed, breathless. "Have you any rope for me?" he asks. "My cow, the only one I have, has broken loose. I cannot find its rope and it is damaging the village."

He produces a pamplemousse in exchange for a few feet of old warp and hurries back to catch the beast.

PENTECOST

Continuing north up the sea-horse's back, the next island, Pentecost, was the home of bungy jumping long before it was adopted by the Dangerous Sports Club in the 1970s. Once, long ago, a beautiful Pentecost girl named Melo married Tamalie. Though she cared for him a great deal and looked after him as a good wife should, Tamalie was a bad type, and he beat her often, especially when he drank kava. One day she told him that though she loved him very much she would leave him if he beat her anymore. He grew very angry and went to get his stick to beat her. She ran from the house and out into the forest. When she paused she could hear Tamalie coming after her. Terrified, she ran on deep into the forest until she could run no more. Tamalie's pounding steps were close behind. With her last strength she pulled herself up into a great banyan tree and hid among the thick branches. She could see Tamalie's furious face below as he searched for her. In her fright she knocked down a nut. He looked up, saw her and started to climb. She climbed higher, keeping just ahead of the enraged husband, until she could go no further. Desperate, she tied a vine to her ankle, and just as Tamalie reached out for her, she jumped. Tamalie leapt to grab her and fell like a stone to the ground below where he was quite dead. Melo bounced back from the ground upon her vine and was unharmed. Though she grieved for Tamalie like a dutiful wife should, she was not very sorry.

Ever since, so it is said, the islanders of Pentecost have celebrated Melo's jump, though in true Pacific fashion the women of the village are not permitted to jump or even approach the jumping tower nowadays. The success of the yam harvest may depend

Nanghol tower with two jumpers

upon the dedication of the jumpers each May, so the business of jumping is taken most seriously.

A delicate tower up to one hundred feet high, constructed of hundreds of pieces of rickety timber secured around a growing tree with vine rope and sennit, carries the narrow platform where the young men of the village tie a liana to their ankles and hurl themselves into space. Survival depends upon exact measurement of the vines and judgment of their elasticity and that of the jumping platform and of the swaying *nangol* tower itself, so that the fall is broken gently and the jumper's head brushes the ground below, which is tilled to represent the ground to be fertilized for the next yam crop.

Chief Willie, boss of Homo Bay, relates how there was once a fatal accident. "In 1974, the Queen of England came here," he says. "Her royal yacht was anchored just out there, and there was a *nangol* tower built for her. A boy jump and was killed. We think he had not made it right with the spirits."

Tradition has it that a jumper may say anything at all before he jumps, a sort of confessional, but if he has not made his peace with the spirits he may be in trouble.

Chief Willie's heir, Luke, and his cousin Clifford take us to inspect a tower, a dinghy ride down the coast and a muddy hike up through palm-shaded cow pasture to a ridge between two bays. The rain lets up just long enough to take photos while Clifford, who is fifteen, tells us about the jumping:

"These two vines here, these mine," he explains, pulling the ends of two long lianas free of their tether at the base of the tower. "Each jumper have his vines, long so they come to his head when he stand under the *nangol* tower."

"You wear namba for jumping?" I ask.

"Yes, namba what we put."

"Nothing more?"

"No."

Perhaps this minimal uniform is why Pentecost women have to keep their distance from the tower, to be spared the sight of naked testicles descending.

The rain is unceasing and the wind considerable, so we stay put on the boat after our walk to the *nangol* tower. As we're playing backgammon in the evening, I notice that the boat is behaving strangely. "Why is she riding broadside to the wind," I mutter to Robin. "Very curious."

A trip up on deck reveals that we are adrift, propelled west into an increasing sea by a lively wind. One hundred fifty feet of anchor chain is hanging vertically from the fairlead. This is awkward as the anchor windlass has been misbehaving, and to manage with a short in the casing we have to operate it on a circuit breaker by the companionway. Once it's eventually wound in with much shouting the length of the boat, we head back for the bay against rods of stinging rain blasting out of an inky night. We feel our way toward the shore using the radar to find a patch of better holding to drop the anchor and a lot of chain, which hooks firmly this time, though the wind is still gusting over forty knots from various directions. We are luckier than the only other yacht on the coast, an Australian a few miles north of us, who is blown onto a reef.

By midnight, the weather has cleared. Marum volcano is glowing a devilish red on the skyline as we enjoy a relieved nightcap on deck.

MAEWO

It's an easy day's sail to a horseshoe bay in the neighboring island to the north, Maewo, where we anchor by a thundering waterfall, which serves perfectly as both shower and laundry. Chief Nelson welcomes us warmly and gives us the run of his village and reefs, important in Vanuatu as consent is needed to swim, dive, or go anywhere on shore. It is always forthcoming, sometimes at a price, but not to ask is to court quiet disfavor.

Ansanvari, Maewo

Nixon and David, Chief Nelson's sons, take us hunting with lights a couple of hours after sunset. Robin grabs a huge crayfish, which graces our table an hour later. David emerges with a fiddler crab and an octopus, which clamps onto the dinghy and is difficult to prize loose. The ink-black sea is full of mysteries: A galaxy of fairy lights is a shoal of little fishes; the ominous shadow blotting out the starlight, a leopard ray; the strobes and twinkles, often bioluminescence emitted by organisms too small to see when unlit. It's a different world, populated by creatures and corals that shun the daylight hours. Tonight's prize is meeting with a chambered nautilus, a beautiful ocean creature representing the last of a genus of ancient cephalopods otherwise only known as fossils.

This is the ship of pearl, which, poets feign,
Sails the unshadowed main,
The venturous bark that flings
On the sweet summer wind its purpled wings
In gulfs enchanted, where the Siren sings,
And coral reefs lie bare,
Where the cold sea-maids rise to sun their streaming hair.

Thus lauded by the nineteenth century American poet, Oliver Wendell Holmes, the nautilus is a distant relative of the octopus family, the sole one with a shell. Nautilus live below two hundred feet, so it is rare to find one near the surface. He is propelling himself rather inefficiently a few feet down while adjusting buoyancy in his remarkable system of three-dozen inner chambers, the archetypal model for all submarines. I let him go, only for Nixon to bring him back to me, offering the shell to keep and the fellow within for dinner. He is disappointed when I release him a second time to sashay off into the gloom.

Snorkeling a big coral bommie in the bay next day, Robin suddenly sticks her head out of the water with an excited shout of "Dugong, dugong!" The three of us swim along awhile together, the dugong between us looking like a sort of pointy sausage with a fin at the back, if indeed it's reasonable to compare dugongs with anything else on earth. She seems entirely happy with our company.

"What happened to the octopus? I was looking forward to eating octopus," Robin asks when an octopus-free dinner appears on the table.

"Very sorry, this dog eat it when I am not looking," apologizes Nixon, looking rueful, giving the unapologetic cur a kick. He is training to be a chef in Santo. Instead of octopus, he serves up a perfectly cooked pig for supper, to the accompaniment of songs sung by the crowd of village children who'd proudly taken us on a tour of the neat dwellings of Ansanvari beforehand.

Three men of the family are making kava out of a large root, sitting on low stools, grating, squeezing and filtering the mixture through a cloth filled with coconut fiber. Their skin is dark, their hair frizzy, the scene antique. "This is very good kava, very strong," they say.

It is. But by now, rather than getting acclimatized to kava, my stomach is starting to rebel. When a half a bottle of pinot noir doesn't erase the queaziness, I resolve it will be the last kava brew I drink.

Little disturbs the deep peace of the bay until, about midday, a pretty woman with flowers twined in her hair arrives in a canoe. It's unusual for a female to be unaccompanied on the water. She hails Robin shyly: "Would you take me to Santo?"

"We have already been asked to take Nixon and a friend," Robin says. "Are you the friend?"

"I am Vivian, Nixon's wife," says she, "and it's just me. He is not coming."

"No problem, just get someone to bring you to the boat at four tomorrow morning, as we're leaving before it's light."

Robin has great difficulty finding women of the villages who will open up to a Western woman and pines for female company. Once she invited a group of women on board, telling me to get lost for a while. I returned to the sad story that the shy guests spent the evening talking to each other in their own language, hardly addressing a word to their hostess. So she looks forward to Vivian's company on the voyage to Santo.

I'm a mite suspicious, however. "I am not quite sure about this," I mutter to Robin. "I think I'll go to the village and make sure it's okay to take her."

This intention is preempted by a "halloo," signaling Chief Nelson's arrival in a canoe so ancient that it may be an indication of seniority and status. "I come to ask you to take two people from the village to Santo with you, the baker and my son, the schoolteacher."

"Yes, of course, but Nixon said he and a friend were coming, and now Nixon's wife came to ask if she could sail with us."

"Ah, she is running away. She and Nixon are having some problem."

"We are happy to take her, but we don't want to cause any trouble," I respond weakly.

"The chief have something to do in these matters. I will see about it." I'm relieved to hear Chief Nelson take the thing in hand.

At the end of a lovely day, the sun sinks blood red over Bali Ha'i. A few miles across the sea from our bay lies the island that inspired James Michener when writing *Tales of the South Pacific*, wrought by Richard Rodgers and Oscar Hammerstein into their finest musical. Michener was among the hundreds of thousands of US troops posted to Vanuatu to thwart the Japanese swarming down through the Solomons in 1943. The island, in truth called Ambae, is a volcano towering from the seabed nearly five thousand feet.

"Did Michener actually hear someone murmur 'Bally high, ain't it,' and fasten on it as the idyllic location for Bloody Mary's brothel?" I muse to Robin. This nice thought is exploded on reading this line in Michener's *Return to Paradise*: "We stumbled into a filthy, unpleasant village bearing one of the loveliest names I'd ever heard: Bali Ha'i."

Nixon delivers the baker and the teacher at the appointed hour of 4:00 A.M. Mrs. Nixon has presumably been placated or locked in her room. "Probably tied to the bedpost," Robin mutters, disappointed and never impartial in a male-female issue.

As we sail past Bali Ha'i, which lacks an anchorage in present conditions, she calls from the galley, "Andrew, there is no water pressure. Have you turned it off?"

She sounds worried.

I swing open the heavy engine-room door to investigate. The room is half full of water. Disaster! I turn the pressure pump off and the bilge pump on, and quickly see the cause of the trouble. "Bloody hell!" I exclaim. "The boiler has burst again."

This is a copper hot water cylinder, made recently in New Zealand after our old one failed, and won't be replaceable this side of Australia, many weeks sailing ahead. The fresh water pump sensed the lack of pressure and was pumping water out of our tanks for all it was worth. The bilge pump chooses this moment to misbehave—the flexible pick-up extension has sucked itself closed. The situation is slowly resolved by a chain of buckets of oily bilge water, me scooping, handing them to the teacher in the saloon who hands them up the companionway to the baker in the cockpit to tip overboard.

ESPIRITU SANTO

The sun is setting as we approach Luganville on the island of Espiritu Santo through the infamous Scorff Passage. This was thickly mined in the war, but in May 1942 someone forgot to mention the mines to the captain of the *President Coolidge* as she steamed into Santo, packed with war materials and six thousand troops. The *Coolidge*, when launched in 1931, was the largest and most luxurious liner ever built in the United States. At the beginning of the war she was still one of the finest passenger vessels afloat. Now she struck an American mine, and then another. Though *Coolidge* was mortally damaged, the captain managed to drive her onto the fringing reef at full speed before she sank. All but two men were saved. The great ship then slid off the reef and now rests in 60 to 200 feet of water where she has an afterlife as one of the world's famed wreck dives.

After talking of many things on the way from Maewo, we drop off our passengers on the town wharf. Columbus, the baker, revealed he was the brother of Vanuatu's President, meaning brother in the tribal "wontok" sense often used among South Seas people.

Kodi, the schoolteacher, spoke contradictorily of the magic of their island. "In our village we do not believe in black magic; but villages from the north of Maewo, they have much magic. They can make the earth roll like the sea. This I have seen myself. They can make magic to kill people. You know, my two older brothers died only short time apart in the past year. This doctors say was hepatitis, but may be some magic from these people," he says darkly. "For why they die when they young and healthy?"

Like many, perhaps most, people in the remoter Melanesian islands, though they probably no longer practice magic widely, they fear it deeply. Christianity in the islands, everywhere apparently fervent, is a veneer under which an inheritance of all sorts of primal beliefs can be glimpsed.

One day I bicycle a few miles along the coast while Robin is blowing bubbles 140 feet deep in the staterooms of the *President Coolidge* nearby. I prefer more open waters, the prolific undersea ocean life to the sad remnant of some human artifact. After the Japanese surrender in 1945, the USA found itself with vast stores of materials in far-flung places and could not justify the cost of shipping redundant stuff home. It's hard to imagine, now, that the small, quiet town of Santo was once wartime Luganville, an encampment city with four big hospitals and forty-three cinemas among the range of installations demanded for the battle-efficiency and comfort of

The wreck of the President Coolidge, 1942

a hundred thousand soldiers. The United States offered the locals a deal to buy, for a small fraction of their worth, jeeps, lorries, diggers, bulldozers, construction materials and stores of many sorts. The canny French planters, suspecting the Americans had no intention of taking all these things away, planned to get them for nothing, declining to fork up even the eight cents on the dollar offered. Incensed at this parsimony, the commander had a short jetty built, running out onto the fringing reef at a spot where it drops vertically away, and drove the lot into the sea while the chagrined planters watched. The vast pile of rusting material remaining, though dissipated a little by scrap merchants and storms and the attrition of sixty years of corrosion, covers a large area of the reef and the seabed. The place is known as Million Dollar Point. The million dollars at discounted 1945 prices might be a quarter of a billion today.

We are put onto a jack-of-all-trades who insists he can weld up our hot water cylinder. I'm skeptical. He's persuasive, and he's right. His success allows us to head north again. By evening *Nereus* is tucked close inshore behind a reef in Hog Harbor where she suffers two days of violent squalls, winds from every direction, heavy rain and tropical downpours, culminating in another mammoth thunderstorm. One bolt of lightning spears the water with a deafening crack less than two hundred yards away; my rain gauge, a muesli bowl, fills up several times overnight. The anchor is laid on shallow sand dotted with bommies, and each morning we find the chain wound round coral in a fearful tangle, tracing our gyrating path in the hours of darkness.

Weather information in this area is poor. As well as trying to determine whether a low, a trough or a front is affecting us, we have to watch the convergence zones, prevalent where air masses meet in low latitudes. These behave differently from the other meteorological disturbances, often producing a confused patchwork of bad weather, continuous lightning and haphazard squalls with short-lived winds of up to gale force striking from any direction.

GAUA ISLAND

Arriving in Gaua Island, we find Lakona village at the foot of a rugged cleft running up the side of a volcano, fronted by a black sand beach where *Nereus* is greeted by three canoes carrying three chiefs. After chiefly discussion with his colleagues in the cockpit,

Water music quartet, Gaua

Jonstar, the *kastom* chief of the area in charge of educating the children in the old ways of magic, dancing, games, ritual and all such *kastom* matters, is appointed our keeper.

Despite its years of government by British and French officials, Vanuatu remains a deeply traditional country, its 190,000 inhabitants divided between thousands of villages with little communication. *Kastom*, Pijin from "custom," implies the inherited lore and tradition that affects all aspects of life. It's hopeless to try to learn much about tradition, as, like the language (over a hundred languages infers that the average number of ni-Vanuatu speaking each language hardly reaches 2,000), it's usually different in the next village. The dancing, the magic, the carving, the *laplap*, the ceremonies, even the value of women and pigs, all vary widely. In the south a bride price might be set at a few cows, or many pigs. In Santo, cows are two a vatu, whereas big pigs with proper curly tusks command tens of thousands of vatu. In the north, the clear order of *kastom* precedence is men, pigs, women and dogs.

We are entertained in family leaf houses, and Jonstar invites us into the *nakamal*, the village meeting house. Magic is performed for us by a chief who can fish up a fish on dry land, levitate a large *laplap* bowl, make fire. He makes coconut chewed by a boy come out of his ear down a fresh bamboo. Sitting on a grassy bank by

Laplap preparation, Gaua

a pool in a river, we are given an unforgettable concert of "water music"—primordial rhythmic sounds created by a team of women up to their waists in the river, using only their hands to bang and slap and drum the water's surface. We sit cross-legged on a hut floor as a chief and his sons prepare a special *laplap*, first roasting ground manioc and taro in banana leaves on hot stones, and then taking an hour to pound each into a dough that is mixed together and made into a large flat cake, garnished with cooked coconut cream. This is man's work, tabu to their women. The family invites us to share their *laplap*. It's exceedingly good.

Gaua has no road or track suitable for anything with wheels. The villages remain remote from the modern world, although it is starting to intrude in minor ways. Passing yachts, in Gaua about one a month, are reasonably regarded as floating goody-boxes, a source of gifts and perhaps some vatu. A copra boat calls occasionally, though because of a dispute it has been absent for four months. A long day's canoe journey will reach a doctor and dispensary. Yet life is close to idyllic. There is plenty to eat from the garden; wild pigs, goats and cows; a sea full of fish, shells and crustaceans; and domestic cows, pigs and horses. Existence is simple, village wars history. Villagers no longer eat interlopers either, though cannibalism persisted in these parts until the mid-twentieth century. Chief Jonstar recalls that politeness demanded, on such a feast day, that an arm or a leg was saved and presented to a friendly neighboring village. The villages have almost nothing from the outside world, perhaps an occasional transistor radio, a flashlight and mask with which to fish at night, and a manual sewing machine a few decades old. Otherwise everything is of local materials, and even these are not much exploited. There are no wheeled vehicles here, though a cart or barrow would be simple to knock together, and pig and cow hides are burnt rather than dried or tanned for leather.

VANUA LAVA

In Waterfall Bay, in the most northerly of the main island chain, Kerely, who is accustomed to looking after occasional passing yachtsmen, brings six of his family to watch a King Arthur and the Round Table DVD. "Perhaps we are in Avalon ourselves, among these islands," Robin says as the family paddles off toward a gibbous moon rising through the mango trees on the hill, and we sink into our bunks to dream chivalrous dreams.

Kerely takes us to his garden on the hills above the waterfall next day, pointing out the trees that are of use to the community. We try to memorize features of one tree, looking undistinguishedly much like a hundred others, which is poisonous even to the touch. Another—a palm locally called *nomela*—provides leaves still used to cast a tabu that may not be broken. He parts some fernlike undergrowth to show a square pattern of stones on the ground.

"This is the oven used in former times to cook men," he says softly, watching carefully for our reaction. "Here on the mountain so the people could see the smoke."

No one in cannibal country ever claims that women were eaten.

Nearby, the ridge becomes knife-edge, dropping steeply through the rainforest to a turbulent river on one side and falling sheer for three hundred feet to the coastal shelf on the other. "Here the enemy people were thrown off the cliff," he tells us, managing to look both ashamed and proud at the same time. "Many people were thrown down here." Far below, a narrow path leads to a cave in the bottom of the cliff, in which are stacked, in neat ordered rows, the bleached and moldering skulls of the victims. Their bones are sorted into racks beneath.

Back at sea level, we walk around the point to the massive waterfall that gives the name to the bay, the final shout of two rivers that combine just above it. Perhaps the world's finest coastal waterfall, it is neither possible nor necessary to get under it to wash, for the huge volume of cascading water creates its own gale, carrying the spray like a super power-shower to blast anyone standing nearby.

"We are having a festival here in September. Can you come back then?" Kerely asks.

Sadly we can't, though we want to, for in this very remote spot he is organizing three days of *kastom* activities to culminate in his grade-taking ceremony with all the traditional ritual this involves.

"There will be many people from the big villages. All the activities will be beautiful," he tempts.

"I am sorry that we cannot return then, for we must be far away. But I will tell other yachts to come to your celebration," I promise. "I will send messages to Vila, and to Santo, and to Fiji, so yachts will know about your festival."

Thanks to the miracle of SSB radio, I find a boating acquaintance sailing in Fiji who says he'll post the details in Musket Cove, and get e-mail addresses in Santo and Vila for people we've met along the way who might pass on the details. It's especially sad to miss Kerely's ceremony. In certain places, the rank of Vanuatu chief is not hereditary, but granted through an elaborate process of grade-taking whereby a man proceeds upwards through a hierarchical structure. The elements of qualification consist of *kastom* knowledge, learning, community support, and wealth, which is expressed in terms of pigs. The candidate has to prove himself by killing many valuable pigs on the day.

I hear later from a Dutch boat that saw my flier at Aore in Santo and sailed up to the Banks Islands that the three-day festival was an amazing success, full of chiefs from all the villages, every *kastom* activity, a gory pig slaughter and a lot of fun. Sixteen yachts saw the messages and made the journey, the greatest number ever seen in those waters together. Kerely was thrilled.

The capital of Banks Islands, Sola, is over the mountains on the eastern side of Vanua Lava. After sad farewells to Kerely, we sail the island's rugged southern coast in boisterous southeasterlies to check out of Vanuatu. Sola turns out to be the worst anchorage yet encountered for shelter. Strong winds gusting over the hill and cross-seas washing around the point roll us all over the place. Thankfully, the mud holding is like concrete, for we are only a hairy two hundred feet or so off a threatening lee shore. But there is little rest. Solo sailors usually learn to open an eye after every twenty or thirty minutes of sleep to check that all is well; the same thing seems to happen to me when in a perilous circumstance.

The provincial capital boasts four tiny shops, virtually empty as the island supply boat is a couple of months overdue. They are able to sell us a few presents for villages further along the way and gas for the outboards. Having been given our clearance, the most expensive yet as a daily cruising fee is charged for our time in Vanuatu waters, (perhaps not unreasonably, as this country has no income tax or any kind of personal tax so far as I could tell, being funded by aid, import duties and a peculiar tax on withdrawals from banks), we thankfully exhume the anchor from the mud and turn downwind, quickly dropping Vanua Lava behind at seven or eight knots under nothing but a reefed foresail. Well offshore, we nearly scrape an isolated reef charted some distance from the correct place, reminding me of a story told by Tristan Jones of a sailor who drove his yacht onto an uncharted reef off New Caledonia. He had to drag his boat by hand, alone, across the reef to deep water. It took him a week to save it.

All our charts in this area prove wildly out, even the electronic charts on the computer. Most are based on nineteenth century surveys, apparently not much updated. Though the shape of features is normally perfect, the coordinates are frequently more than a mile misplaced. Despite our modern gadgets, as of old safe navigation hangs on the Number One Eyeball.

UREPARAPARA

Next, we sail into a volcano.

The conical volcano island of Ureparapara is cleft down its eastern side, a two-mile gash stretching to its center from a rough, rocky exit to the sea, a deep fiord formed when a vertical slice like a segment of an orange blew out long ago. At the top of the bay by the single village, canoes shepherd us to a spot within a jagged reef where there is just enough sufficiently shallow water to anchor. Though blown about by williwaws reflected off the surrounding steep mountainsides, and suffering traces of huge seas that thunder at the fiord's entrance, we are comfortable in our little rocky circle. A yacht is already in the bay, the first cruiser we've encountered since leaving Santo. It's a Swedish yacht loaded with supplies, and it's soon apparent that these are desperately needed. The village head, Chief Nicholson, explains, "Our village was hit very hard by the cyclone last month. All the gardens were destroyed. We have had not much food. We have been going into the bush to find wild yams."

The old schoolteacher and his son, aboard later telling us village stories, gave a graphic account of the weather damage that is an occupational hazard of a mid-Pacific life, how the cyclone, the same Gina that scared us further south, devastated food supplies. "The wind it destroy all the banana trees and pawpaw trees and all the fruit. In the ground the taro is okay, but the wind it destroy the manioc and the kumala. It go rotten when the top blown off. The yam vines are broken, so the yams no good either."

I ask about supplies.

"We only receive a supply boat about once a year, and now it has not been for long time." Clearly the apparent idyllic life in Ureparapara teeters on the brink of catastrophe, dependent on the gods and the supply boat for necessities that cannot be grown or caught. To travel in the village's single, very small boat to Sola, twenty-five miles over a usually rough sea is a hazardous undertaking, and the boat can't carry much for three hundred villagers anyway.

Children's Day is in full swing next morning: kastom dancing and games with feasting and music later. "Now you do this," says Frederick, who's in charge, when the bamboo-throwing contest has been decided.

It's more difficult than it looks to make a short thin bamboo skid along the sand the length of the village square, like a grounded javelin. Mine slides ten yards before it veers off, and Robin's does little better. Little Simon, about twelve years old, can send it like an arrow more than a hundred yards straight down the track. This boys' game is followed by two teams of girls who have to knock down a pile of cans with a ball and then play a sort of tag while the other team tries to build the cans up again. Then it's time for a hard-fought boys-against-girls contest of cowrie shell tossing, the object being to dislodge other shells stuck in the sand at the far end of a twenty-foot pitch. The displaced shells become more ammunition.

Invited by Chief Nicholson to the evening's feasting, we return with an armful of presents and our remaining stock of vatu for village funds. We are bidden ashore at six o'clock, and ground the dinghy in a little stream clear of the surf breaking on the beach. *Nereus* lies some fifty yards out in her circle of reef, battered by occasional bullet gusts off the high hills and rocked by swells penetrating from the volcano entrance, but apparently holding fast.

Children's day games, Ureparapara

The orderly village of neat leaf houses huddles behind a fringe of mangroves lining the beach.

At Chief Nicholson's house the girls hang garlands around our necks, a lei of tiny delicate flowers for Robin and a necklace of red and green ginger leaves for me. A dozen small boys await us, clad in leaves with circlets of nuts on their wrists and ankles that rattle like castanets as they move. They dance in the fading light, wielding mini spears, stabbing at shadows and scowling manfully to conjure up the ferocity of warrior ancestors. The chief, with a speech of welcome, formally invites us inside his delicately woven leaf house where musicians play and sing in the gathering gloom. Gifts are presented, kava is produced, and, by the dim light of a lantern, we consume the pig we've seen killed and cleaned on the beach in the afternoon. Roasted yams, taro and manioc accompany the pig. It's all eaten with fingers.

The meal finished, we are led to the open space in the middle of the village where there is dancing. The stars shine out of a clear sky. The Southern Cross hangs over the silhouetted volcano above. The men of the village are absent, still seated around the kava bowl. The children dance, and the women dance. When we dance, they stop to watch. The sight of a man dancing with a woman or with children is unknown here. Men dance with men. But I dance with Robin under their amazed gaze, our first dance. They are still dancing late into the night as we shove off and motor out into the crater.

In morning sunshine, the chief's nephew Jimmy guides us up out of the caldera in which *Nereus* floats to the ridge above, through strange greenery studded with bright flowers. It's a couple of hours' root-hanger of a climb, rewarded by a magnificent panorama over the Banks Islands. New to us is a palm tree protecting its trunk with long, sharp needles, evolved to guard against what, in this land without mammals, is unclear. On inland walks, the prickly thought sometimes occurs to Robin and me that, not long ago, it might have been suicidal to be ashore here, unarmed, in the company of dusky men with razor-sharp bush-knives hanging from their belts. We would be unable to defend ourselves. No one knows where we are. To the village people Robin and I appear rich beyond dreams, and *Nereus* has plenty of things of value. The evidence would be long gone before anyone could come looking for us. A smiling face is no assurance, for in the old days a fulsome welcome was often the precursor to trickery and attack in both Polynesia and Melanesia. Though we think our welcome is always unstinting, genuine and generous, might ancestral habits still tempt our guides?

Jimmy discloses that Chief Nicholson is the highest of high chiefs, chief of not only the village nor only of the island but chief of the entire province of Torba, encompassing dozens of islands including the main one, Vanua Lava. We treat him with renewed respect, concerned that we may have patronized him, for it's hard

Ureparapara caldera

to know the level on which to converse with the ni-Vanuatu for whom English may be difficult.

Jimmy is twenty-one and still unmarried. Robin inquires about the cost of a wife, should he find a lovely girl.

"She cost pigs," he responds, "and a cow."

"How many pigs and cows?" We probe.

"Maybe two pigs and maybe one cow," he replies, "but that not all. I have to give kava too, and vatu."

"How many vatu?" We ask.

"Fifty thousand vatu," is the reply.

We are surprised, for this translates as more than US$500 and seems a huge sum on top of the livestock for someone from a subsistence economy with no apparent sources of cash, and stimulates the thought that the breeding of daughters could be a pecuniary affair. We give him a large dollar note toward his wife fund anyway.

Next day we sail out of the volcano, leaving its damaged, paradisaical village, quitting Vanuatu, and heading north once more. Our next destination is the fabled Solomon Islands. There have been several years of unrest in the Solomons; travelers' advisories are warning people off, and we expect to meet few cruising boats.

In the event, we see none.

The Terrible Solomons

15

SANTA CRUZ ISLANDS

The Santa Cruz Islands lie remote from the main Solomons, at the east end of a thousand-island chain stretching a thousand miles. Sailing north to the largest of them, Nende, around midnight we pass close by a frill of surf breaking on a reef. This guards the island of Vanikoro, and its secrets.

On Vanikoro a pair of French sailors were stranded for much longer than the prototype for Robinson Crusoe, Alexander Selkirk, who was marooned on Juan Fernández at the other side of the Pacific. In the year 1788, Admiral le Compte de Lapérouse was wrecked here. Some of his men were massacred by the local population. Those left took many weeks to construct a boat out of the

Admiral Compte de Laperouse, 1741–1788

189

shattered timbers of the two frigates and sailed off, never to be heard of again. (Though in Jules Verne's *20,000 Leagues Under the Sea,* Captain Nemo claimed to have found their resting place, reflecting continuing French fascination with the mystery of their destiny.) Two sailors, perhaps with a premonition of the fate of their shipmates, decided to stay, and so far as I can discover thereby earned the record for a tropical island marooning. They were still living on Vanikoro thirty years later, having remained in blissful ignorance of the French Revolution, the Terror and the entire Napoleonic period. If it could have been told, theirs must have been a story to rival William Mariner or the fictional Robinson Crusoe himself. Ten years later in 1827, when the first Western vessel, the *St. Patrick,* reached the island, Capt. Dillon found no trace of them.

Slowed by a weakening breeze, it's a couple of hours after the following nightfall when we feel our way on radar up Graciosa Bay, seeking a narrow shelf by a river—the only charted spot shallow enough to anchor. There is no moon. The sky is overcast. The bay black as octopus ink. We are unsure where we are until a powerful dawn chorus of land birds wakes us and the early light reveals shoreline forest arching halfway out to our masts from an inlet off the fateful bay in which Alvaro de Mendaña attempted to create the first Pacific island colony for the glory of God and of the Spanish King.

Pedro de Quirós, 1565–1614

Mendaña had stumbled upon the Solomons in 1567 when initiating Europe's two-hundred-year search for the Great Southern Continent. The only legacy of this contact was the labeling of a couple of islands, including Guadalcanal named for a village in Spain. The Spanish colonists in Peru had heard an Inca fable of limitless gold on a Pacific island to the west, associating it with the legendary King Solomon's mines of Ophir. Chasing the gold, Mendaña returned in 1595 with several shiploads of settlers whom he disembarked on this island, naming it Santa Cruz, the Sacred Cross. But the paradise he'd sold them was a hellish disaster. Mendaña with many others expired of fever within days and the rest soon sailed off under the command of Pedro de Quirós, who would be responsible for putting Vanuatu on the map on a later voyage. Whether Mendaña and Quirós deliberately mis-charted Santa Cruz remains a mystery. Although they were able to find the Solomons again themselves (though the longitude was a guess, they were sure of the latitude of 10° S, simple enough to find on a cross-staff or astrolabe), thereafter they were misplaced, lost to the Europeans for nearly two hundred years and only rediscovered in the great exploring era of the late eighteenth century.

Lata, the provincial capital of the Santa Cruz Province, is two miles across the bay from our inlet. A rusty little supply ship at the short wharf is loading relief provisions for the thousand inhabitants of the tiny, isolated island of Tikopia, two hundred miles to the east where another violent cyclone has just knocked down every tree and destroyed the gardens. I am unsure whether the emergency supplies are strictly necessary, having read in *Collapse* how Jared Diamond cites Tikopia as a survival case-study, marveling that its peoples learned to feed themselves on their 1.8 square mile dot and keep their population size constant over three thousand years of residence despite the devastating impact of about two cyclones a year. Against considerable odds the Tikopians, like the people of Palmerston, know how to maintain paradise.

A few women are settled on the ground under a spreading tree by the wharf, selling piles of green fruits. Village people mill around in slow motion with nothing much to do. A narrow, overgrown path leads to the village center where I find the immigration hut and address myself to a man playing a card game on an old computer.

Betel nut vendor

"May I check in here with Immigration?" I ask. "We just arrived from Vanuatu last night."

"Sorry, no one here," he says, ignoring himself and one other.

The Terrible Solomons

"But this is the port of entry to the Solomon Islands, and this is the Immigration Office, is it not?" I protest.

"Immigration Officer not here."

"When will he be here?"

"Mebbe next week."

As we intend to move on next morning, the idea of hanging around for a week or more awaiting his uncertain return is unappealing.

"So what can we do?"

"Try the Provincial Secretary's office." And to get rid of me, he points me to a scruffy huddle of prefabricated huts the other side of the crushed coral road.

Faded lettering confirms that one of the doors might indeed lead to the Provincial Secretary, who appears of some importance as he occupies the room adjoining one labeled "PREMIER" in peeling paint. I explain the problem.

"We cannot help. The Immigration Officer left no instructions," says Johnson identified by a roughly carved nameplate on his table.

He muses a little and confers with the others in the room, heavy with an atmosphere of having very little to do and not doing it. "Perhaps the Quarantine Officer can do something," he offers. "Come with me."

We travel at low speed across to the Agricultural Department hut, which has four doors. Each is locked. Johnson says he'll find someone while I look for the bank.

The bank is unable to provide any money on a bank card. Head office decrees, when I ask the clerk to call to check, that Visa is unacceptable. This condemns us to subsisting on the few Solomon Islands dollars we can obtain by changing our small store of foreign currency until we reach Honiara or Gizo, still hundreds of miles to the west.

The only notice posted in the bank reads: THANK YOU FOR NOT SMOKING OR CHEWING BETEL NUT.

This sign explains the heaps of hard green fruits that the women are selling. We have arrived in the betel nut quarter of the world—magenta gums, red splashes all over the ground, cannibal-stained teeth.

"It's like a drug," says Lionel, the Quarantine Man, when eventually we find him, chewing steadily. "It's addictive. It gives you a kick, more energy."

The town seems to exist in a lethargic miasma in any case. If he were right, nothing at all might get done without it.

Back at the Department of Agriculture, Lionel gives me two identical forms to sign, denying the carrying of live animals. "There is no way of doing immigration when immigration man not here," he tells me. "What you do is go to the immigration office in Honiara and tell them what happen here. You will have this paper to prove you tried to check in here in Lata."

Solomons girls at *Nereus*' porthole
RR Acrylic on canvas

He hands me my copy of the form confirming our claim of no livestock on board, which, though seeming a little lightweight for the formalities of arriving in a foreign country and importing a boat and its contents, is all we're going to get.

Lionel now insists on coming to inspect the boat, understandable attention to duty considering we are the third vessel to visit Lata in the seven months of the year to date. He depletes our stock of cold beers and removes some moldy bananas, for which he asks for the loan of a plastic bag.

There's constant canoe traffic across Graciosa Bay. For the first time in several thousand miles of islands, the canoes have no outriggers, resembling the Native American variety. Every few minutes faces peep over our gunwale, asking whether we want vegetables, fruit, carvings, shells. Robin is offered marijuana, the first time that's happened since the ganja-lush West Indies. While two young men are aboard watching a movie, we see four small faces pressed against the glass of a porthole, struggling to see the screen. The little girls in a canoe glued to the side of the boat are too streaming wet to invite inside.

We intended to sail to Pigeon Island to visit Diane Hepworth, a formidable British octogenarian who created her paradise on a pinprick of rock in the little Reef Islands just to the north, eulogized in a book *Faraway*. This is now a mini resort, "the most remote in the Pacific," states the *South Pacific Handbook*, which makes it seriously remote. But the family is away.

THREE SISTERS

We therefore continue west for two days to Mosquito Bay on one of the Three Sisters, little islands off Makira Island. Two hours after our dawn arrival, we're still struggling to anchor. Though the bay is sheltered, a rough reef bristling with bommies fends us well off the beach while the rocky bottom drops steeply away outside it. After grazing one of the bommies, we somehow lodge our main anchor on the underwater mountainside, take a seven-hundred-foot line to a tree root, and drop another anchor further down the slope to hold us out. Thus entwined in string and chain, we're still floating within a couple of boat lengths of the reef.

The island is wrapped around a lagoon where crocodiles live. One feels a little vulnerable crossing it in an inflatable dinghy. The village, on the site of an old Lever Brothers copra facility in the lagoon, is the first commercially prosperous community we've found on an isolated Pacific island. Rex, canoeing out to welcome us, explains why: "We have many good products, and we would do very well if we could find someone to manage us and sell the products at Honiara prices. We catch crayfish, and many tuna and big fish."

This I'd already noticed as Pastor George hailed us from his boat while we were struggling to anchor in the early morning. He returned after a few hours with about four hundred pounds of high value fish, landed on a hand line.

"Then we catch sharks and sell the fins," Rex says. "We can make coconut products, and copra now the price is getting better. And the best is bêches-de-mer."

Avoiding a dialogue about the pillage of the shark population to keep Chinese soup bowls full, I ask about the bêches-de-mer or sea slugs. Holothurioids in the echinoderm family, they are, apparently, related to starfishes. We have often seen the seabed littered with sea slugs and wondered which were the species considered delicious by the gourmets of China and Japan. I discover that this disagreeable looking marine cucumber, distinguished as one of the few creatures that has learned to respire through its anus, had a key role in politics. Together with sandalwood, bêches-de-mer formed the backbone of nineteenth century island trade with south and east Asia. The vast majority of village contact with outsiders took place in the pursuit of these two commodities, and in exchange for bêches-de-mer came clothes, fishing equipment,

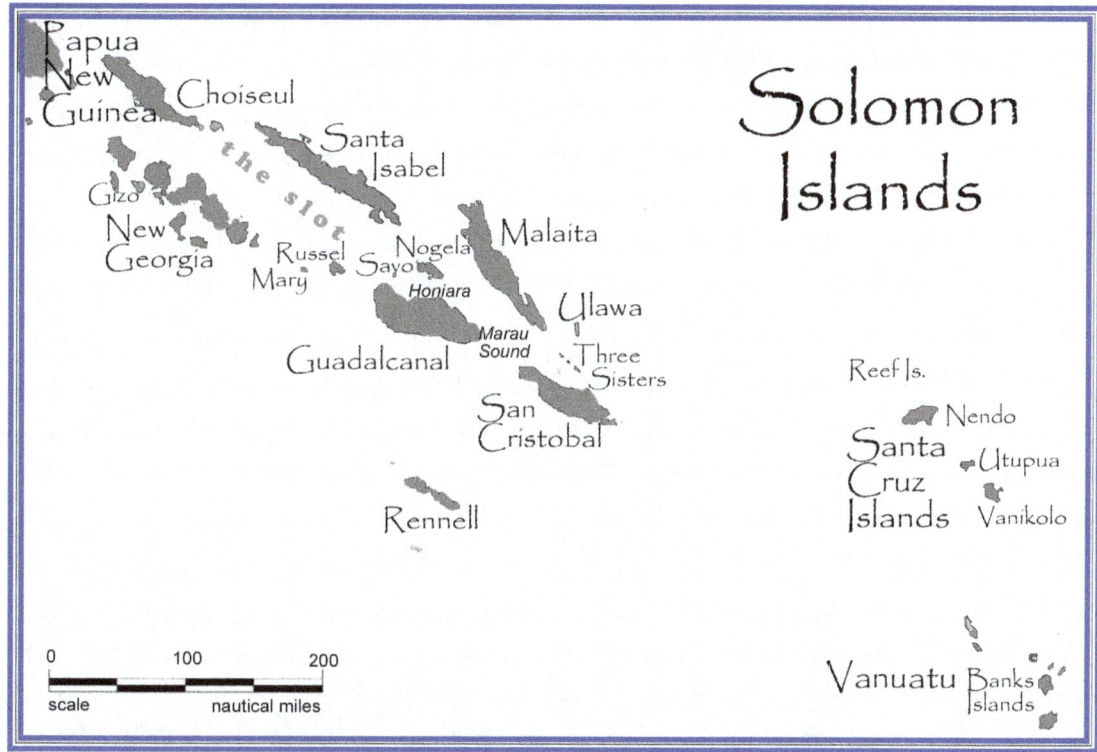

manufactured goods, and the axes, knives, iron spearheads and guns that raised the stakes in the permanent village warfare.

"No, only the white-tip bêches-de-mer are good," Rex explains. "These are very deep down, from forty to a hundred meters, so we have to get them with scuba bottles."

Sheltering in a large leaf house as it starts to rain, the divers are tallying up their harvest. Once gutted and carefully dried over a fire for two days, the bêches-de-mer look like short fat dirty parsnips, smelling faintly of the sea. The heap is counted, sorted, weighed and allotted to the various participants. Robin politely declines the offer of a small one for our supper.

A few yards from where *Nereus* swings at anchor, the reef is a coral garden with a profuse variety of sponges, none bearing a resemblance to the bathroom sort. Radial mushroom corals, strange hard discs with delicate perfect geometrical designs, lie loose among the rooted corals, some colored red and yellow and blue by the algae whose existence is symbiotically vital to them.

As we unwind our intricate anchoring arrangements, a twelve-year-old boy arrives alongside with crayfish to sustain us as we head for the central Solomon Islands. The night starts perfect for a downwind sail, but by morning we're motoring the last three hours into the Marau Sounds—a maze of islands, reefs and passages off the east end of Guadalcanal.

GUADALCANAL

The Solomon Islands have been troubled by The Tension for years. Most of the violence has been concentrated in Guadalcanal, thinly echoing the terrible battle for this island over 60 years earlier which left Guadalcanal a name written in the blood of America. After a coup, the Guadalcanal Liberation Army is causing widespread havoc for ethnic political reasons; warlord Harold Keke is terrorizing the Weather Coast in the south like a robber baron of old; and law and order around Honiara, the capital, has broken down under the strains of incompetent government, lack of police resources, corruption and tribal dispute. Tourism, always thin, has faded to nothing save a few dedicated divers and returning US veterans. We know of no other boats headed this way, and we may be venturing into a lawless place as hazardous as in the recent past. *The Lonely Planet* reminds readers: "The islanders were perhaps the world's most violent and dangerous people until the thirties. Killing, cannibalism and skull worship were central elements of traditional culture." Earlier in the century Jack London, sailing in on the *Snark*, dubbed the islands "The Terrible Solomons."

We may be lucky, though. A combined force of Australians, New Zealanders, Fijians and Tongans arrived a week before us at the invitation of the government to re-impose law and order, and though they are not fully established in Honiara and have yet to reconnoiter anywhere else, we hope their presence will provide a slightly enhanced level of security. Everyone calls their advent The Intervention.

As *Nereus* is anchoring in a horseshoe bay in Marau Sounds, a canoe paddles alongside. Elson has shells to trade.

"Have there been many yachts here this year?" I ask.

"No, you are first yacht," he replies. Since this is the only sheltered area for a long way, it means there have been no boats past at all.

Later, we wind through extensive shoals to little Tavanipupu Island, on which is located a resort agreed by our outdated guidebooks to be the loveliest in all the Solomons. Excellent food, six handsome sleeping *fales*, beautiful gardens and tall impressive leaf houses for eating and meeting, containing a fine collection of

Pacific carvings, they enthuse. With beds for up to twelve guests, it's twice the size of the usual resorts tucked away on the islands. Dennis, who created all this with a friend who since died, had to pay a bit more than the previous owner, who acquired the island for five rifles.

"The first yacht this year, certainly," Dennis say. "In fact, you are the first yacht to come in here for four years."

But Dennis declines an invitation for tea on board. "I have no one to look after the house if I go out," he says, a reflection on the uncertain times, which makes me anxious about *Nereus*, unattended and out of sight.

Dennis must have been full of energy and vision when, with enormous imagination, he created this little paradise ten years before. Now he seems defeated by The Tension, with little income for four years and daily struggles to keep the rooms clean and ready for the day when customers will come once more. The local airstrip has been closed by fighting and land disputes, and there is no road down Guadalcanal. Thus only a boat can bring guests now.

On the way back, an old fellow in a canoe fishing way out on the reef calls for a tow. With betel nut-stained teeth and two ancient hats on his head, Joseph looks like a retired pirate, but only wants a little money or a T-shirt in exchange for a nautilus shell.

"When The Tension came, we moved our village and the other villages to the shore of this lagoon where you are," Joseph says. "Last year bad people come from the big island and rob all the furniture from the resort, but it's alright now and we are living back in our own villages."

It had been worse than this, Dennis recalls. "When we were having dinner one evening, we suddenly found ourselves surrounded by armed men. They took everything they could. They came to rob us three more times after this. I stayed here all through The Tension, otherwise they would have destroyed Tavanipupu."

Among our canoe-borne visitors is Kuru, nut-brown, sun-wrinkled and merrily grinning despite a shortage of teeth, wearing little besides an ancient bilum bag tied to his waist. He extracts a small note from me for a triton shell and a larger sum in exchange for a perfect golden cowrie. He says his people came generations before from Malaita, the large island mirroring Guadalcanal the other side of "The Slot," as the channel running southeast through the Solomons came to be known in the war when the "Tokyo Express" ferried millions of tons of war materials and Japanese reinforcements to the vicious 1942 battle for the Solomons. Malaita is overpopulated and fissiparous, spilling its wars and people into neighboring islands. In Guadalcanal, The Tension is blamed on the Malaitan community, who grasp the best jobs and business opportunities and are generally tougher than the locals, who don't much like work.

"Because we were Malaitans," Kuru says, "even though we were here for many years, the GLA tried to kill us. We got guns and they went away. The Malaita Eagle Force came over from Malaita with many guns. Now the MEF gone back to Malaita, and this week we told the Australian commander has given them two weeks to give up all their guns."

The gun amnesty eventually yields more than 3,500 weapons. Most are of 1940s vintage. Enterprising villagers have been dredging up wartime ammunition and successfully reconstituting rifles deactivated and dumped by the US forces sixty years ago. But about a fifth are modern automatic weapons that these far-off, dirt-poor islanders have somehow, mysteriously, acquired thanks to the extreme reach of the global arms trade.

Several villagers ask how far the Australian helicopters /satellites/ computers can see into the ground. There is an implied subtext: How deep must they bury any guns they want to hang on to? There is a near-total faith in the power of modern technology.

Kuru's village speaks the language of the parent village in Malaita, whither he returns regularly to visit relations. "It is not long since we used to eat people," he drops into the conversation. "My grandfather, he was cannibal."

While assimilating this disquieting information, Robin, recalling stories of *mana* from Polynesia, manages to ask, "Was this for ritual purposes? Does the eater acquire the qualities of the person vanquished in battle and eaten?"

"No, no, mebbe they were hungry, and they thought it was good meat." He adds, "And you may not know that in Malaita they still eat people."

"Surely the church stopped that?" Robin says.

"This happens in the inside part of Malaita, where the missionaries never go to."

Another visitor, Joe, was recently married to a girl from the Russell Islands, a hundred miles to the northwest. He explains the deal to us. "The bride-price we have to pay is always shell money and some dollars. For a girl from the Russell Islands, we pay two shell moneys and S$400. Here we cannot easily marry someone from

Malaita, for she cost mebbe five times more." He laughs nervously at the thought.

The traditional shell money of the Solomons is minted in several places, in the east out of a type of spiny oyster. In Malaita, its manufacture is strictly limited to one village where ancient shark-worshipping customs are still strong, and men can call sharks that embody the spirit of an ancestor to come to them. Here in Marau Sounds, it seems anyone can make shell money, though it takes immense work to produce one of the money-chains used for bride-price. Each piece has ten strands; each strand is six feet long, having threaded on it about two thousand tiny shell discs—every one of which must first be laboriously shaped, polished and pierced.

I ask Joe what happens to the shell money after it's been paid over, say, if he had a marriageable daughter.

"If I get offers for a daughter, first I cook kumala, and a pig. The men who want to marry my daughter then come and I hang up the shell money of each one on a fishing line between trees. The one who bring the most shell money and dollars get the daughter, and he also get the kumala and the pig to take away. Some of the shell money I give to my father and mother, and some to my brothers. This is to reward and thank them all for helping me to raise the daughter. Most of it I keep, but if I have a son who want to marry, I give it to him."

Two foresails pull us along the coast of Guadalcanal at good speed to a dot of an island girdled with white coral sand, a mile off the north coast, barely large enough to provide shelter from wind and swell. Four years ago this island held a resort, which thrived until it was attacked by Malaitans and abandoned by its Australian owner. Swimming ashore, we find only the concrete base of its buildings; everything else, even the corrugated iron of the water cistern, has been taken for reuse. The bush has already reclaimed the ground, though some exotic plants are fighting well. There seems to be an unusual population of brightly colored birds, perhaps the escapees of the hotel aviary. Just offshore, the multicolored coral harbors a cloud of feather dusters, worms residing in short tubes that extend a cloud of feathers from the end to catch passing microscopic morsels. When disturbed, an amazing mechanism retracts the feathers in an instant, though the home tube is only a tenth as long as the feathers.

The Intervention forces are evident as we approach Honiara—busy Australian naval vessels and clattering Sea King helicopters.

Once parked in a space in the poor harbor next to the single, elderly Solomons patrol boat, we check whether the yacht club is still functioning after four years of The Tension. It's members' Lottery Night, and the club is full with a crowd of expatriates who would be at home in a Graham Greene novel—wiry and deeply lined, fat and multiple-chinned, sun-dried and skin damaged, many with a bizarre approach to facial hair arrangements. A wizened member advises that it's certainly necessary to stand watch all night to prevent theft by silent Malaitans who will steal up in canoes and cut the rigging from our mast. But on the whole they remain immersed in local gripes, insensible to a notice on the jetty that promises Overseas Sailors Welcome. Some of the members have taken up with very young locals. One, who can't be far short of eighty, complains to anyone who will listen of the difficulty he's having with his nineteen-year-old partner. The Pedophile Community Yacht Club, an Australian lieutenant wickedly calls it. The place is sad but familiar, one of the expat bars of poor countries the world over that provide a refuge for people whose version of paradise was eroded by boredom and myopia long ago and whose relationship with the "natives" is colored by servant problems, fear, and a desperate effort to retain a sense of superiority.

To mark the anniversary of the US landings in Guadalcanal in August 1942, there's a memorial service up on Skyline Ridge. Ten nations were involved in the battles for Henderson, the strategically vital airfield (now Honiara's airport), that the Japanese had started to build. The violent struggle lasted for six months as American forces first took it and then had to defend it against repeated waves of assault until the eventual Japanese withdrawal in February 1943. Nearly 40,000 men died here, and a huge number of warships were sunk and aircraft downed. This bloody battle cost the American side two aircraft carriers, eight cruisers and fourteen destroyers.

From the American Memorial we look down on Iron Bottom Sound, the graveyard of these ships and many others, more than sixty in all. Nearby is the bitterly contested Bloody Ridge, where 700 heroic marines held off 2,000 Japanese. Memorial speeches are full of extravagant praise for the coastwatchers, a motley collection of heroes hidden in the bush on islands far behind Japanese lines. At great risk to themselves, they radioed details of enemy troops, ships and aircraft movements, enabling US forces to prepare as each squadron of bombers or Tokyo Express flotilla approached down the Slot. Echoing Admiral Halsey, a speaker declares, "But for the coastwatchers, Guadalcanal would have fallen; and, but for Guadalcanal, the Pacific would have been lost."

Back in town, Customs and Immigration charge me S$350 for entering the country. I ask a yacht club member whether this will really go to the exchequer.

"No way, no way at all," he growls. "The corruption goes right through here. Your money will be in their pockets already."

Stories of corruption are everywhere, in expat and local communities alike, probably more accurate than the misleading prognostication about the course that events will take. "Next week," a middle-aged member pontificates, "a team of Australian auditors and solicitors is arriving to go through the government books for the last three years. You'll see 80 percent of the top officials fleeing the country or in jail when they've finished."

It won't happen, of course. Corrupt officials ensure that there is no one else to do the job, hanging in somehow even when found out. The Australian Federal Agent charged with the personal protection of the Prime Minister wonders aloud about the nature of his duty if his police colleagues come to arrest his charge, suspected of all sorts of misuse of public funds. In the event the P.M. is a consummate enough politician to duck and weave, and hold out somehow.

The Solomons are close to the bottom of the Pacific-failed-states-league table in terms both of embezzlement and incompetence, a tough call as most of the countries we have enjoyed so much within the tropics bear a heavy weight of corrupt elected politicians and officials. In Vanuatu, it was said that, as there were no obvious taxes, most people fail to realize that money stolen through corruption is their money. What is black and white at a senior level often becomes gray further down the line: Officials may not be paid, expected to live off direct income from the public; corrupt bosses may steal the salaries of their juniors, who are encouraged to collect whatever they can for themselves. The Australians recognize it will take years to reverse the rot that has set in.

Serious, too, is the misuse of island resources. Rubber, cotton and, surprisingly, rice failed as cash crops in the Solomons, but copra worked well until the declining price condemned the vast plantations of old coconut trees to rot. Fifty years ago, Solomon Islands exports were 80 percent copra, but by the 1990s this dropped to 10 percent, with timber and fish taking up the slack. Logging now accounts for a quarter of exports and fish products nearly half, very little from sustainable stock in either case. The rape of the forests and the fisheries is a heavy charge on future generations, paralleling the world's squandering of its hydrocarbons. The Solomons have huge potential for renewable timber, controlled fisheries and tourism, but a long way to go to exploit it.

Honiara has a large, colorful market. We are steadily learning more about tropical fruits and vegetables, but there's always something new. A large dark green thing catches Robin's eye. It's the size of a watermelon, smooth-skinned but nubbly.

"What is this?" she inquires.

"Bean."

"A bean?"

"Yes, bean."

The last giant bean we were given from a Vanuatu garden was two feet long and as thick as a fat cucumber. It was rather good. This one looks troublesome, and we pass. We do cook one some weeks later, however, in Papua New Guinea. Half a bean is more than enough for the two of us. The thing is pithy inside, with seeds like a zucchini, not bad stir-fried. We are given it in one village and pass the seeds on to the next village where they say it is unknown.

Robin then finds some strange eggs for sale, bigger than ducks' eggs and a little elongated. "And what are these eggs?" she asks.

"These megapode eggs."

We've heard of megapodes, though we have yet to meet one. Chicken-sized birds with big orange feet that live only near volcanoes, Megapodes need the thermal activity for their egg hatcheries, choosing a location where the ground temperature is precisely 33°C and burying the eggs three feet deep in the warm soil. Villagers dig up the eggs. Market produce comes from the egg fields of Savo Island, a volcano sticking up on the other side of Iron Bottom Sound. The battle of Savo Island had been responsible for much of the metal on the ocean floor when a Japanese flotilla had snuck around the back of the volcano and caught the American fleet at anchor by surprise, a major naval scandal of the war.

"How do you cook megapode eggs?" Robin asks.

"We cook them for one hour."

"In boiling water?"

"No, in earth oven."

It seems easier to purchase an already-cooked egg, neatly wrapped in a banana leaf. Robin and I breakfast on it the next morning, with fresh toast. It's 90 percent yolk, rich and good.

Another requirement is paper charts, for we don't believe in relying solely on the electronic version. We trot along to the hydrographer's department to seek some for the northwest Solomons.

"I'm very sorry," says the hydrographer with a sad shake of the head. "We don't have any charts."

"But, surely..."

He interrupts me. "We get them from the Australian Navy, and unfortunately we have not paid what we owe them. So they are not sending any more charts until we pay them."

Megapode eggs

The general breakdown in government and public services is reflected in the frequent interruptions to the power supply in Honiara and problems with fresh water. The Australians had to make an emergency loan earlier this week for a load of chlorine. People say that the treasury is empty because the government has been buying off rebel leader Harold Keke and his GLA. "Protection money" and "extortion" are words used by some of the wiser among them. At least there is no necessity for traffic police; impressive potholes limit speed to 10 mph or less, and there are no traffic lights in the country.

Paul, the hydrographer, nevertheless says he'll see what he can do, and finds me well-used old charts that just about cover the missing area.

David Stanley's *South Pacific Handbook*, without which no traveler to these parts should set forth, waxes lyrical about the Mataniko Falls, near Honiara: "One of the most amazing waterfalls in the South Pacific...a gigantic, swallow-infested, stalagmite-covered cave, with an arm of the river roaring right through. The river itself pours out of a crack in the limestone cliff just above and tumbles down into the cave through a crevice totally surrounded by white water..."

We have to see this, but on inquiry I am told no one has gone there for a long time, it's dangerous to wander outside Honiara, and the trail is overgrown. We persevere, however, and Wilson, the master of ceremonies at the Skyline Ridge memorial service, eventually says he's fixed it with the owners of the land. He takes us to the end of the road at Tuvaruhu village and yells for Pascale, who emerges from a small leaf house preceded by two pigs. He consents to guide us.

After half an hour's sharp climb to the sound of Sunday hymns drifting up on the morning air from an Anglican church, we ascend more gradually through open upland pastures studded with orchids—if elephant grass is indeed pasture. The track is barely perceptible as we pass sites of two villages attacked and abandoned during The Tension. Virtually nothing remains. Evidence of war is everywhere—lines of overgrown foxholes and bits of concrete, shells and bombs. Mount Austen rises a mile or two away across the river, with the bitterly disputed Hill 27 on its flank. Galloping Horse Ridge is over the river to the left.

As the pasture translates abruptly to jungle on the edge of a deep river defile, Pascale confesses that he hasn't been to the waterfall for years, since before The Tension started.

The sound of falling water swells as we slither and slide steeply down through thick rainforest, hanging onto vines. At last we part the final liana screen and look upon acres of magnificent living waters. The river splits at the top of the falls, part of it pouring into a cave as if through a huge bath plug and part of it falling as a curtain into a rock trench and thence being carried into another passage. These two branches emerge from a black cave below, and fall again to join the main stream. The rest of the water cascades down wide limestone terraces, which are somehow formed so that the water flows over them perfectly evenly, a quarter inch deep—a large, smooth, curved water surface, which seems an impossibility of nature. The terraces are interspersed with falls and pools, and we clamber over them for power showers and swims. Pascale relives his boyhood, climbing around the falls, jumping into pools, showering in the spray.

"Do you want to go back by the river?" urges Pascale, once we are well cooled off from the trek.

Peering down the high and narrow gorge carrying the torrent out of sight below the falls, I am uncertain whether this sounds like a good idea. "We have cameras," I say. "They would get wet."

"I will make a raft for your backpack," says Pascale, and he proceeds to chop down a tree and a banana plant with his bush knife, preempting our decision.

We climb down to the bottom of the falls on velcro limestone, so unslippery that our bare feet hold fast to a 45-degree pitch, load the backpack onto Pascale and his raft, and leap into the frothing, turbulent water.

High above is a slit of blue sky with the green walls of the gorge topped by green forest reaching out to close it off. The river runs narrow and fast at first, and we are carried along by a powerful current, bouncing off the odd timber blockage or stone outcrop. The raft has little buoyancy. Pascale starts disappearing beneath the seething waters under its weight, drowning in the attempt to keep the pack dry. Grabbing his shirt, we manage to pull him onto the bank. More trees and lianas are cut to construct a new and better raft, which floats a little higher. After another mile we find occasional shallower patches, and the flow starts to ease. We can soon wade on the bottom or scramble along the bank, though the gorge still towers above. Eventually the chasm broadens out, gardens appear on the banks, and for the last couple of miles we can walk a winding route through the cultivated valley with another dozen crossings of the river. Children play in the water, and, being a Sunday, laundry is in progress in the little creeks where seventy years ago the river ran red with blood. We are hours late for poor Wilson, patiently waiting to drive us back to Honiara.

Pascale enjoying Mataniko Falls, Guadalcanal
RR Acrylic on canvas

We rise early next day to sail on, but the windlass doesn't function when I press the button to raise the anchor. With two eighty-pound anchors and a quarter ton of chain rode, a powered windlass is close to a necessity, so we have to slow down and find a way to get this fixed. As Australian Iroquois helicopters with riflemen hanging out repeatedly buzz the harbor, we unbolt the windlass and investigate the works. A solenoid has failed. After we vainly visit eight possible sources for a replacement, the ponytailed son of a yacht club official, and the only helpful person we discover in that grizzled expatriate community, finds us a Malaysian who undertakes to rewind the coil. A couple of days later it is done, a repair that lasts until we reach Australia. We set off, pleased to be going on, happy that we have not been attacked or robbed in Honiara. Despite the presence of the Intervention forces, it has not felt a very safe place; everyone has a bad experience to relate.

RUSSELL ISLANDS

As we leave Honiara by Iron Bottom Sound, to port is the point where the last Japanese troops were cunningly evacuated one night in 1943, after months of bloody battle, abandoning Guadalcanal to the surprised and delighted Americans. Savo volcano rises to starboard, the source of our megapode egg. Paul Theroux canoed to Savo while collecting experiences for *The Happy Isles of Oceania*. He pitched his tent on its shore and was horrified to find the population coming to the beach in the morning to do their business, the men one side and the women the other. I discover, however, that this was long-standing official policy. "Instructions To District Headmen," dated 1918, brought the accumulated wisdom of the vast British Empire to bear on the sanitation problem with this recommendation: "People living in villages near the salt water cannot do better than go to the salt water below high water mark to evacuate."

The Russell Islands are split by a narrow channel. Halfway down, effectively in the middle of the islands, this canal broadens into a placid pond. While we're swimming to cool off, ladies in a canoe assure us that the local crocodiles like to bite people. We hastily haul ourselves back on deck. Other women are collecting mangrove clams, and to Robin's delight we can trade a dishful for supper. She claims these *deo* clams look just like the quahog of New England, and digs out her old clam recipes.

Deo clams

A man paddling by tells us we are the first boat this year, but last year there was one too. As the sun sinks behind the mountains, Robin says to me as she often does, "Just look." *Nereus* is quietly at anchor in a mangrove-fringed lagoon, two or three canoes are fishing a long way off, children's singing drifts over the mirror water from a distant village. We

Final touches to our croc, Russell Islands

are parked on a parrot flight path; they fly over in twos and fours, and then flocks, squawking and twittering a mighty chorus.

A couple of miles away from our tranquil pool is a village of Polynesian people famed for carvings of animal and human figures full of grace and movement—eagles catching fish and snakes or feeding the young; warriors; crocodiles; spirit trees of eels, fish and rays. John offers us a nearly finished crocodile in a fine-grained wood called kerosin, now the material of choice in islands where ebony is getting hard to find. Next morning, as we pause by the village in *Nereus*, he paddles out to deliver the croc, now sandpapered and polished and with gleaming nautilus shell inset for his hungry eyes.

The coat of arms of the Solomon Islands is supported by a shark rampant one side and a crocodile rampant the other. I wonder aloud whether the Ministry of Tourism PR team ever okayed this.

Thirty miles off is an uninhabited mid-ocean speck locally called Mary Island, an extinct volcano sticking up alone. There is no anchorage, but we know that *Bilikiki*, the Honiara live-aboard dive boat that appears to be the sole continuing tourist activity, has laid a mooring on the leeward side. We find the mooring in 160 feet of water a few yards off the rocks, and borrow it. After a swim with a shoal of bumpnose parrotfish nearly as big as us, we go exploring. The greenery is impenetrable, but it's possible to clamber around the rough coral apron girdling the island. The spot is primeval. A wall of magnificent old trees rises to 1,000 feet. Jungle birds, herons and sea-hawks swoop low over the boat. A pair of huge birds with yellow beaks and horny heads have wings so large that the air seems to vibrate when they fly. We have no notion what they are until we meet them again in the Marovo Lagoon. This is a raw, remote place, especially when we're secure in the knowledge that it's a hundred to one against *Bilikiki* turning up, wanting its mooring back.

The hum of a motor wakes us the following morning. A gray shape looming toward us in the early dawn light materializes into *Bilikiki*.

The skipper generously offers to make provision for us between their boat and a stern line ashore, as it's far too deep for an anchor. There seems some wind to move on, but it's a mistake not staying and diving with them, which we regret as *Nereus* wallows in a five-knot breeze toward our next destination. A turtle drifts past and a lone dolphin gives a spinner exhibition, jumping out of the water and doing a complete rotation by the bow, as we find a way between wooded islets into the magnificent Marovo Lagoon, our landfall in New Georgia.

MAROVO LAGOON

The best yachtsman's guide to the region is Warwick Clay's *South Pacific Anchorages*, which covers a vast area in an accurate and unfussy way. Clay often mentions visits by persistent locals in canoes with wares to sell, but only in Marovo Lagoon does he manage to convey the impression of being under siege. In one paragraph the word "pestering" occurs five times.

Our anchor has not touched the sand before the first canoe is alongside, and though it's already late afternoon, others put to sea from nearby shores and distant villages. Some continue to turn up after nightfall. We trade for produce of land and sea, but the real business is the sale of carvings.

Canoes form a line to come alongside. Fiberglass canoes with outboards, wooden dugouts, aluminum banana boats. Fleets zero in on us. All have anchors made from Second World War junk that we politely decline to take on board. We send messages that we will inspect collected carvers' wares in Mbili, a village a couple of islands away, if only they will stop arriving at the boat, but still

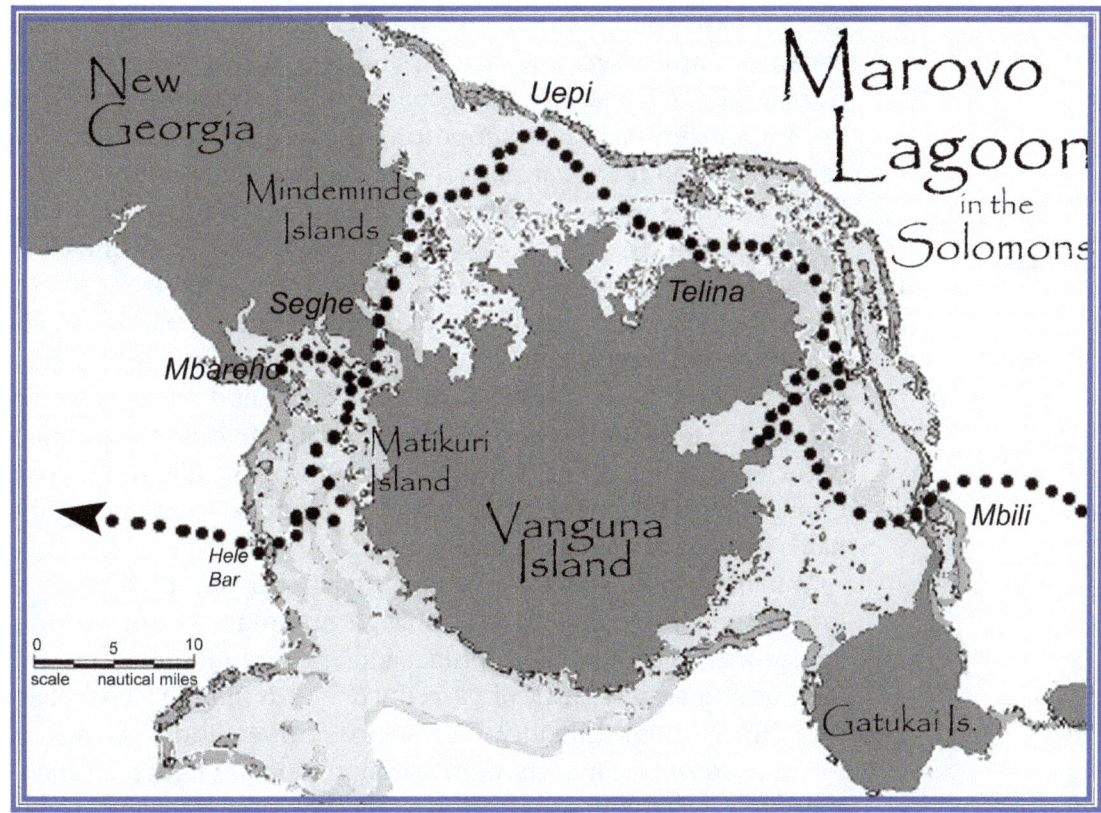

they come from near and far and tie up alongside throughout the following day. No protestations of barter fatigue succeed in diverting them. Years ago, Flanders and Swann sang a funny song about a gnu, a wildebeest by another name, containing the line "yet a gnother gnu." "Yet a c'nother c'noe" echoes in my mind as each succeeding craft pitches up.

We could have sent them packing after the first few, but it's not so easy. The standard of carving is exquisite, the people are polite, lovely and in need, and the last yacht to provide a selling opportunity left ten months ago. Soft touch, admitted, but they tell us how children's school fees have to be paid, S$85 a term, four terms a year at primary school, illnesses treated at the clinic many miles away, gas acquired for the outboards to get there, and malaria dosed with chloroquine. Even if they had some money, goods are not available as the cargo coaster has failed to restock the few scattered stores, so clothes and a hundred other things are needed. It's not difficult to welcome all of them with open arms.

Using ebony, kerosin and rosewood, the peoples of Marovo Lagoon create figures of fishes, octopi, people, turtles, and birds, kastom-based designs imbued with great individuality. There are walking canes, ewers and masks, and lots of the highly stylized warrior heads carved originally for the prow of canoes, known as *nsu-nsu*, including a dove supporting the head for a peaceful voyage and a skull for a war party. None are like the shelves of indifferent carvings vainly awaiting buyers in tourist shops, and all are quite different; these carvers would no more copy someone else's work than avoid Saturday church. Eyes are sea-snail front doors. Faces are inlaid with a profusion of nautilus. There are bowls of every shape and size in kerosin, and spirit fantasies in queen ebony. Carvers know how to bring forth the figures and fishes latent in the timber, to work the wood grain, to create life from the promise of the raw material. The plentiful coconut wood is not much used, though. Without power tools it quickly blunts a knife, though its hard, defined grain makes lovely dishes.

When we take stock, we've acquired pawpaws, a fat jack for lunch, three large crayfish, bananas, a pumpkin, unknown nuts and green vegetables, a dolphin paddle I commissioned for the dinghy, and a great stack of carved wood, too much to find boatroom for without difficulty. Our favorite carver, Tonsa, brings an intricate spirit tree incorporating twenty undersea figures in a fantasy of seaweed and coral. In exchange we've parted with a pile of Solomon dollars plus fishing gear, videos, string, crayons, lollipops, cans of food, books, magazines, matches, soap, bedsheets, towels, diving gear, sandpaper, glues, paint and paintbrushes, pencils, reading glasses, batteries, earphones, T-shirts. I've soldered a hearing aid together, too.

A couple of our visitors confess that they are *bakslidas*, not good churchmen; looking carefully both ways and dropping their voices so the words will not float across the water, they test us for gifts of forbidden tobacco and cigarettes. The villagers of Marovo were converted from their headhunting habits by the fundamentalist Christians, the Seventh-day Adventists (SdA), and are consequently denied these things as well as pig and the plentiful crustaceans on their doorsteps.

Old Chief Lucas pulls rank to cut in front of the canoe line and introduces himself without formality. "I am Lucas. I am a Chief here, and I am also the Minister of the school."

He tells us his father was a wartime coastwatcher, and he runs a tourist lodge that has had almost no guests for four years. As a good SdA, he's not permitted the tea we offer him, pork, which is the easiest meat to produce on a coral island, or the abundant crayfish. Apart from the curiosity of the continuing existence of this faith, which might have faded away at the time of The Disappointment, the double failure of the Messiah to materialize in the year 1844 to fulfill the prophecy that formed the basis of Adventism, I feel it an inappropriate set of commandments for the Pacific.

Robin shows Lucas the strange nuts we have acquired as part of a trade, which look vaguely like shelled almonds. "What are these?" she asks.

"These ngali nuts. They grow on these trees." He points to some huge trees near the shore. "The nuts are picked off the tree by the hornbill bird, which eats them whole and uses the outside skin for its food. The rest of the nut is shitted out by the hornbill, then is gathered up by village children. The children hit the nuts with rocks to break them and get the kernel. This what you see here." The hornbills' used nuts are delicious and not expensive like the only other pre-digested food I know of, the Kupi Luwak coffee beans of Indonesia, which have passed through the gut of civets and can take the price of a cup of coffee over $100.

The hornbill turns out to be the giant bird we encountered on Mary Island, Blyth's hornbill, the only one of about eighteen Southeast Asian hornbill species to have made it to the central Pacific. These impressive birds have most peculiar nesting habits: Once a pair has found a suitable hole in a tree high above the ground, they peck away together at the wood with their huge beaks to enlarge the aperture so the female can squeeze inside, but only just. Presumably with her consent, she is then imprisoned, carefully sealed in by her husband with a birdshit-and-mud mixture, leaving only a narrow slit window through which her magnificent beak can be seen protruding, as if a bizarre limb of the tree. The mother loses her feathers, which seem unnecessary when a hornbill is incarcerated thus inside a tropical tree, and hatches her brood, which are made particularly comfortable, as birds go, on the heap of feathers, while the hornbill friends of the family deliver food to the waiting beak. Once the young have fledged, the opening is breached and the young emerge ready to go, presumably thoroughly embarrassed by their admiring hornbill mother who is now utterly bald.

I know none of this as I watch half a dozen of these remarkable birds flying around our Marovo anchorage with that heavy air movement, the flap of their wings thrumming like slow helicopter blades at maximum pitch. Their long yellow necks, horny heads and spade-end beaks put me in mind of Jurassic vultures from a Disney dinosaur movie.

We motor slowly through the lagoon by eyeball navigation, avoiding widespread shoals that are only vaguely located on the chart, steering by the hundreds of wooded islets dappling the aquamarine waters. All navigation marks shown on our chart are missing. At Mbatuna, there is supposed to be a market, but we've got the time wrong. Everything is gone. As we lift the anchor to carry on, a tousled head appears at the gunwale from a motorized canoe.

"Hello, I am John Wayne," says the engaging looking fellow.

"Heavens, it's the legendary John Wayne," I call to Robin.

He grins. "Only here in Marovo."

"We know about you from our books," I tell him. "*The Lonely Planet* calls you 'Local legend John Wayne'." I think better of mentioning the Dirk Sieling pilot book that states: "Fame has drastically inflated the prices of his carvings… there are some top carvers here that easily equal John Wayne's renowned skills."

He presents us with a fat, white cucumber and, arranging to meet later, motors on with his family.

John Wayne lives at Telina whither we are bound anyway, and paddles out to invite us ashore once we are anchored. His workshop is on a spit of the big island, Vangunu, opposite the tiny island of Telina, which is all village, some of the houses built out over the shore line on stilts. John's patch of land holds a small guesthouse and a splendid garden of orchids. I get orchid fever with the camera in macro mode. There are more than two hundred varieties of natural orchid in the Solomons, which I'm sure must be the orchid capital of the world—until I find that both Borneo and the Philippines claim nine hundred varieties.

We are quickly spotted by the locals. It seems advisable to see as many artisans in the village as possible before they start laying siege to us by sea. Here, as well as a range of superb carvings in wood, there are earrings and pendants of ebony inlaid with shell, tiny carvings fashioned out of the ivory-like nut of the sago palm, and scrimshaw work on whale teeth, pig tusk, crocodile teeth and even a dugong tusk. There is much intricate basket and tray weaving, the islanders' skills honed and passed down through many generations.

Canoes piloted by little children bring soursop, eggplant, starfruit, beans, peppers and lots of unrecognized green vegetables. One paddled by two enchanting ten-year-old girls bears a tiny pikinini in the stern clasping a bunch of bright flowers. She presents it to Robin with shy giggles. Unlike Polynesians, Melanesians have frizzy hair. But one of these little girls is the granddaughter of a Japanese and has long, straight, lustrous locks that Robin braids in the cockpit, giving her a nest of combs to keep. The girls are so pleased they soon return with a bigger bunch of flowers. The trading basis develops into a steady floral supply.

Relief from the sales pressure comes only with Friday dusk when the Adventist Sabbath starts and all activity must cease.

Telina Island is rounded, like half an egg, its dwellings crowding the slopes right to the water's edge. The top of the island, though, is claimed only by a large, unfinished church, commanding the lagoon from the best position. At nine o'clock, Robin and I turn up in our Saturday best for the weekly service. We seat ourselves inconspicuously in a rear pew, but are quickly spotted and led reluctantly to the front. Hymns, the Bible and teaching material are in English, though the service is in Pijin. The pastor translates bits for us to ensure we can follow, and an old lady sits with us to identify the hymn numbers and look up the biblical references within the sermon, which we all read out in unison.

We sing at least two dozen hymns, and, as parts of the service seem to be run by different ministers, two hymns turn up twice. No one seems to mind. The church has wide, glassless windows on three sides affording views through the tops of breadfruit trees

A gift of flowers

RR Acrylic on canvas

The Terrible Solomons

and sago palms over the Marovo lagoon, islands everywhere, out to the distant ocean breaking in a narrow entrance. On the other side of the church across a shallow channel lie the forested slopes of the large island, Vangunu, rising to a cloud-topped mountain with a horseshoe bay beneath. A more beautiful location in which to daydream through a sermon is hard to imagine. Is this a place appreciated by the ministers and Adventist congregation as an Eden in which God's house is set? Or is it just a site that has absorbed much community treasure and a huge amount of unpaid work, where the rule is endless exhortation to conform to the rules?

After several opportunities to give money, the church accountant reads out contributions and cumulative family totals. A tithe system is in force; the old hymnal a kind lady lent is bookmarked throughout with tithing receipts. Though the cost of a church like this is enormous for a largely subsistence community, the existence of a single religion per village is perhaps an improvement on the Christian civil war for souls we've encountered in other Pacific islands.

Somewhat exhausted at the end of the three-hour service, we are bidden outside by the pastor and stand in a line to shake the hands of the congregation of hundreds as they file out. I feel like fraudulent royalty.

After a tour of the extensive gardens on the rich alluvial soil of the valley bottom, John takes us bush-walking up a steep hill to the foot of an inland cliff. Sitting outside a shallow cave overhung by a bulge in the mountain, he invites us to visualize life in the old days. "You have met my wife," he says. "This was the place where her people came when there was a raid on the village. They had to live here and beat off any attack from the canoe people until it was safe to go back to the sea."

A spider with a gleaming gold back runs his main hawser between us as if we are not there. The antediluvian hornbills appear, stirring the air with thrumming wings. John cuts a particular vine yielding fibers that he shows Robin how to spin into a thin yarn of great strength. Before nylon, he says, this served well for all the functions of string and cord. We pick ngali nuts, crushing the shells with heavy rocks, and kutnuts, which can be split in half with a bush-knife. The root of a reedy plant is peeled back to reveal little sacs like the inside of a passion fruit, deliciously sweet to the taste. Bright butterflies and flowers are everywhere.

Crossing a stream on the way back, we notice a pool and tell John we'll catch him up at home after a bath. Small boats and marinas have showers, never a tub; it's blissful luxuriating in murmuring water deep in the forest as sunbeams penetrate tall trees, dappling the sandy bottom with refracted ripples and occasionally highlighting a squawking cockatoo swooping above.

Back at his house, John shows us a picture of his great-grandfather sketched by an Australian trader and dated 1895. "This great-grandfather go on the last Marovo headhunting expedition in 1913." He points proudly at the picture. "They go to Isabel Island in a war canoe, but he was very disappointed when he found the people in Isabel had been converted by the Anglicans, and seemed to have a strong spirit. He returned to seek a spirit like the Isabel people found, but first when he came back he found his brother killed and he had to go find the murderers for pay-back. Then the missionaries of the SdA came from Australia just at that time and he accepted their spirit, and the village took it. That was the end of the headhunting here."

Isabel is some fifty miles away, and war canoes were powered by warriors, no sails. Other documented raids went up to three times this distance between the islands, and hundreds of miles between island groups.

"Surely the warriors arrived in Isabel exhausted after paddling to Isabel?" I remark.

"No, no," he says. "On the prow of the canoe was the *nsu-nsu*, the spirit. The spirit was strong. His eyes never closed. With the spirit in front of them the warriors stayed strong."

Across the lagoon on one of the northern barrier islands is the best of the few resorts still functioning in the Solomons, Uepi. We make for it across a testing ten-mile stretch of shoal-strewn waters—without a chart. It's not that we don't have the chart; it has never been surveyed. Proceeding gingerly, often at only a knot or two when there is less than ten feet of water under the boat, we make it without touching bottom. The Solomon Islands Pilot contains a chartlet for the last bit, which turns out to be wholly inaccurate. The threatening reefs are in quite the wrong places. I ask the Australian resort manager whether he has seen this.

"Yeah," he says laconically. "It improves the wreck diving."

Unlike the other Solomons resorts we passed, all destroyed, Uepi is open for business. There are five-foot-long monitor lizards strolling around among a few diving guests who join us the following morning to search for pigmy pink sea horses. It's unusual to be furnished with a magnifying glass before entering the water.

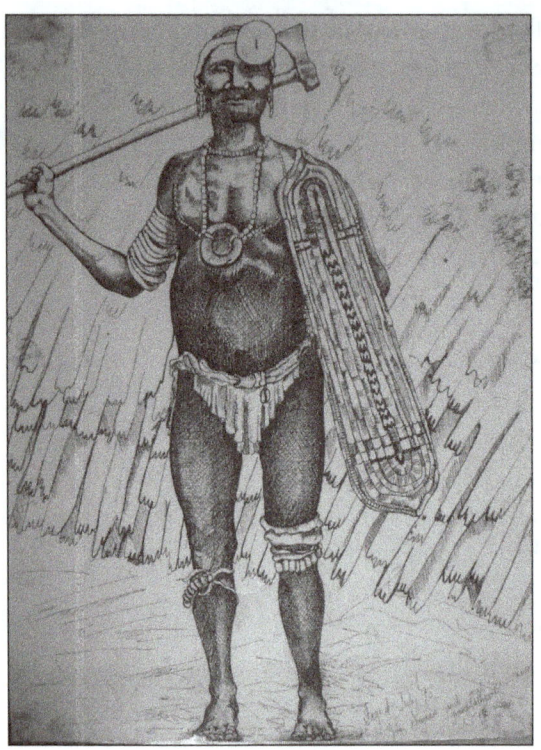

Ancestral Solomons warrior, 1895

This proves useful to look at some exquisite tiny nudibranchs, but becomes essential when, on a salmon-colored gorgonian fan at about eighty feet, we track down the sea horses, precisely the same shade as the fan and so tiny that, without the magnifying glass, I cannot see them at all.

On a gray showery morning without much color in the water to show depth, we set off again across the uncharted shallows of the island-studded Morovo lagoon. Dropping our canoes into the water near the village of Mbuinitusu, we paddle into the Mindeminde Islands.

If a hilly area has been flooded, say, by the construction of a dam, the tops of the hills become islands. The Mindeminde Islands have this appearance, though they are old. Fifty mangrove-girt islands, all uninhabited, crowd into an area of little more than one square mile. Between them clear water washes through with the tides, swirling around multicolored coral heads. Cockatoos and parrots shout in the treetops, pigeons roocoo and birds we can't name inquisitively buzz our kayaks. Frigate birds appear, their huge wingspan casting shadows like passing airplanes. Around one mangrove corner, I come upon a Melanesian gathering clams. He is as startled as Monostatos on encountering Papageno. A white man! In a bright yellow plastic canoe! Ooooooh.

Back on *Nereus*, Charlie is waiting to show us Mbuinitusu, his village crowded onto a single small island. It's quite rich, having sold its soul to Malaysian loggers busy demolishing the growth of many centuries in the hills of the adjoining big island. "My people did live deep in the bush and high up in the big islands, Vangunu and New Georgia, always frightened by raids of headhunters," Charlie says. "But when the headhunting stop, we come back to the lagoon."

Once the British put an end to most of the headhunting in the last decade of the nineteenth century, the people kept their gardens on family lands inland but emerged from the bush to build new homes on the seashore where the air was cool and the fishing was easy.

We motor through the Seghe narrows, anchoring off a decrepit jetty to go shopping—only to be told that the single store is closed down. That this jetty is still standing is remarkable, as it formed the end of a wartime runway built from scratch in the extraordinary time of nine days by the US forces fighting their way back up the Solomon chain after beating the Japanese out of Guadalcanal. Before that, Seghe had been the hidden base of Donald Kennedy, perhaps the most effective of all the coastwatchers, responsible for the rescue of many aircrew as well as reports of imminent air raids and troop reinforcements.

Another five miles of tortuous travel between islands, reefs and bommies takes us way off the beaten track to the village of Mbareho, set on two small islands toward the top of a blind arm of the lagoon. We're greeted effusively, the first visitors for three years.

Four small boys in a canoe check us out and return in an hour laden with lovely flowers, which they shyly present to Robin. Then another canoe-load of pikinini florists arrives; there are soon ten buckets of amazing flowers to find boatroom for after decorating the cockpit for a photo. When news of our rewards has spread, the girls start turning up with flowers too. At Main Street prices we are worth thousands. There are more than two dozen varieties of orchids in the extravagant bouquets of flowers and ornamental leaves. Though we ask them to bring no more, the lure of our lollipops, pens and balloons is too strong; the next canoes try limes, and then beans. A huge black crab arrives for our supper, followed by banana leaf packages of kutnuts and fresh donuts.

Another canoe brings Pita Aldio, local woodcut artist on the medium of banana paper, to invite us crocodile hunting. Our 15 hp Yamaha outboard is slung on the back of a heavy dugout canoe piloted by Pita with John, sometime crocodile guide to not a lot of passing yachties, spotting up front with the help of another ebony-black headhunter's grandson. An hour after nightfall, we head off up the lagoon by the dim light of a new moon. The canoe throws off a luminescent bow-wave, slicing through water, which is as flat as float glass as we cut the engine and paddle silently along the mangroves. The drip from the paddles is lost amidst the muffled ploshes of surfacing fish. Scents of the bush seem intensified. Treetops are sharply backlit by a distant, silent electrical storm. In the narrow arc of a flashlight, a red eye gleams for a moment as the canoe glides toward it. The eye disappears, leaving not a ripple on the surface as the crocodile moves off. It reappears some yards away glinting a warning in the beam as we creep on, our paddles dripping

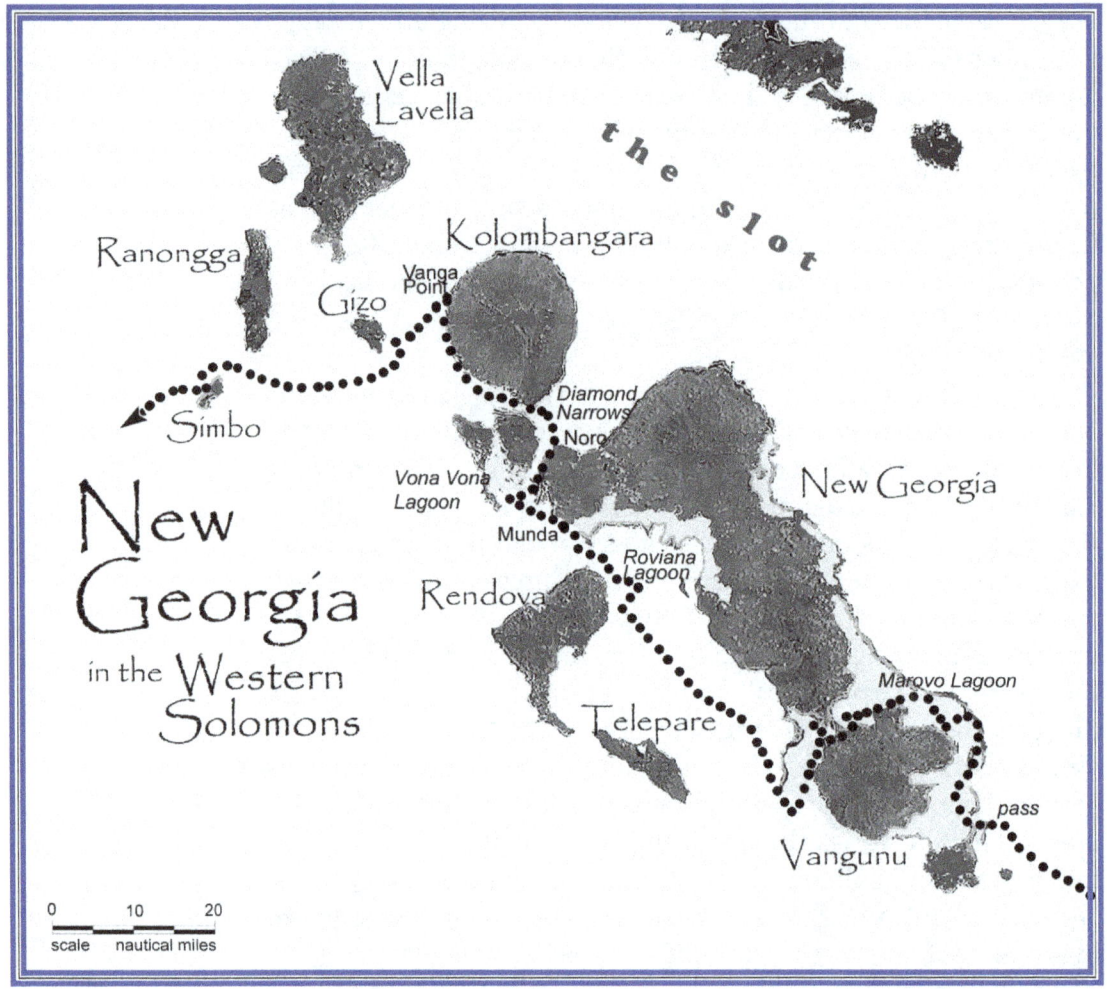

phosphorescence. And, suddenly, there is our croc, all two feet of it, looking thoroughly confused in the light. More a pet than a threat.

After finding a few more little crocodiles around the periphery of the upper lagoon, Pita explains that the village chief sold a concession for the village's land on the mainland to Malaysian loggers, busy across the water tearing the primeval forest apart. The chief pocketed the money and the loggers wiped out the crocs. Although there are frequent dissatisfied mutterings in the villages, the traditional status of the chief gives him a moral authority that seems to preclude any form of insurrection. Thus the timber, which might be the people's future lifeblood in many ways, just as on this poor soil it contains nearly all the nutrients of its piece of territory, is removed with impunity.

It reminds Robin of Bonaire, in the Dutch part of the Caribbean. Bonaire's great boat-building industry came to an abrupt end when the island was denuded of trees and left largely desertified. John tells us that his bushwalks are no longer possible: The loggers have clear-cut it all, there is no bush. Once again we mourn with the village people over lost hardwood forest, which cannot be regrown in several lifetimes, abandoned to secondary growth or rough bush where farmers scratch crops from the thin soil for a few years until that, too, erodes and is useless.

The morrow is the Sabbath, the annual Pathfinder Day service. Adventists are organized to an extent on military lines, with the Pathfinders their youth corps. A hundred children wearing yellow boy-scout neckerchiefs form up to march into the church, marking time as they line up to enter the pews. Our Pita, resplendent in a green forage cap and uniform with a broad sash, festooned with ribbons, badges, buttons and stripes, is MC. He blows a little whistle to signal the next procession or bring the Pathfinders to their feet for an oath of allegiance. The District Pastor, a bishop equivalent, makes an interminable sermon in Pijin about family duties. He has the thoroughly liberated Robin coming nicely to the boil when he asks the congregation to read together from the Epistle of Paul to the Ephesians: "Wives should obey their husbands in all things..." Luckily she can't see across to my neighbor's Bible, which reveals in the next verse that St. Paul enjoined equally that slaves should obey their masters in all things...

I remain ambivalent about the iron grip the Church has on the villages. These are people whose close ancestors went in perpetual fear of headhunter raids or were themselves headhunters and cannibals. They were uncivilized in the broadest sense, having developed almost nothing outside the adjuncts of a warring way of life. With the coming of European knives, spearheads and guns, only the young warriors were spared perpetual fear in their fastness in the bush. The missionaries put an end to all this and stopped the vendetta-like payback tradition, often getting eaten for their pains. Many of the early missionaries must undoubtedly have been brave, as fearless on behalf of their God as are Islamist extremists. Seeing the near 100 percent conversion, they must have been effective at the job too, even though their usual guiding principle seems to have been that the end justifies the means, for their object was often achieved by bribery and fear. The people are peaceable, charming, and devout. *Bakslidas* are the exception.

Movie night aboard

Yet, yet. Traditions and customs have been ruthlessly destroyed, and with them identity and pride. Brains have been washed and generations subjected to oppressive propaganda. Much of the teaching must be little better than gobbledygook, for the messages of the different sects are mutually exclusive in many respects. Communities carry the great weight of a disproportionate church overhead. Missionaries often lived well and even got rich on the backs of their flocks, and the head-office of their life is a glitzy palace presided over by wealthy evangelists a million miles removed from a little village on a remote Pacific island. Reading Norman Lewis's authoritative work, *The Missionaries,* one cannot doubt the misplaced fervor, the debatable goals, and the lack of respect and understanding that drove the missionary machine to spread its tentacles to the farthest corners of the earth.

A knocking on the hull at sunrise announces Pita's arrival to take me fishing in the canoe, still powered by our outboard. Two hours later we return empty-handed.

"You see, Solomon Taio, who has the only cannery here in the Solomons, they been taking all our fish," Pita mutters disconsolately, reflecting the inevitable dilemma of trying to create an industry in this magic place. "They been emptying the lagoon for bait to use on their tuna lines."

After breakfast, Pita pilots the canoe along a narrow cut through thick bush across the peninsular separating Marovo Lagoon from the sea. It's necessary to raise the outboard frequently and pole over shallow patches while pushing overhanging growth aside. Eventually the canoe emerges into a lake. "This place," Pita proudly relates, "was the final tuning place for my ancestors' big war canoes—up to fifty seaters—in the old days." This would have been a considerable business, for we were now close to Roviana, the fortress base of the most feared headhunters even by Solomons standards, from which they ranged far and wide on bloody pillaging expeditions. The lake is completely sheltered, glassy calm, so canoewrights could get the weighting and trim exactly right.

A further channel leads to the open sea where we snorkel under a limestone cliff at the site of an ancient battle between war canoes. "This we know was true, for when Australian divers come here we find many, many stone axes at the bottom," Pita says. "There are cave passages through the cliff, so lookouts run back to warn when raiders coming."

Pita's daughter emerges from the mangroves with a bag of clams to eat with the edible seaweed we have gathered from the place of the stone axes. While I'm jigging for squid to supplement this, Pita tells of the giant Taga-taga, who was never defeated in battle but came to a sticky end when he was bitten by an enchanted crab. "His enormous skull," he says, "big like a cooking pot. You still see at a tabu place in the hill."

In response to a request for a chicken for supper, a fine white bird arrives, strutting on the end of a lead, a miniature lei of green orchids hung around its neck. As I pluck the sacrificial bird while sitting on a stone by the water's edge, Pita talks of the hardships and traditions of Marovo life, and wants to know something of Western cities. Robin meanwhile draws plans for a new house for Pita's family and teaches Rayleen to make pancakes. Afterward the family watches *Saving Private Ryan* on board. Islanders invited aboard for a DVD always appreciate plenty of violence, whether guns, swords or martial arts. I suspect the reason is their proximity to ancestors whose life was raiding, warring, fighting—pleasures now strictly proscribed by the pastor. Having borrowed our single sideband radio to talk to his children's school, Pita gives us a letter for them that we must deliver in Buruku, forty miles on.

Crossing the lagoon to a peaceful bay of Matikuri Island in strong midday light, it's easy to avoid the crowded bommies lurking just under the placid surface. The aim is to exit Marovo Lagoon early next morning for our first open sea passage in a month, but the wind doesn't blow. Matikuri holds a rundown resort where another Pita gets a Jimmy Buffet tape in exchange for some pawpaw. He's working with three nephews in a desultory fashion to repair the leaf roofs in the hope of tourist reappearance now that The Tension might be fading. As always, our news that there are no yachts apart from us in the central Solomons is disappointing. I suspect that it will be a while before Western government travel advisories cease to discourage visitors. Even if the peace fails to hold, there seems no significant risk outside Honiara and perhaps Malaita, which leaves more than nine hundred of the world's most beautiful, unspoiled islands available.

At nightfall, Pita comes crayfish hunting with us on the windward reef, a hazardous activity in kayaks with lively surf rolling us around the living coral and only one waterproof flashlight between us. Once the last of the waxing moon has set, we have to make do with the red light of Mars, tonight at its closest and brightest in 250 years. With no more Jimmy Buffett to offer, Pita's reward includes Brahms' fourth symphony. I wonder if this might start a trend.

The early morning breeze blows fresh as we feel our way very gingerly over the Hele Bar towards the ocean once more. The charted buoy that indicates the deepest part, providing a bare five feet under the keel, is inevitably missing. Depth over sand in such clear water is impossible to judge accurately, even standing high on the pulpit rail staring through Polaroids. One can't help tensing in the trough of each swell, expecting time and again to bump the bottom until the blue shades darken into deeper water.

MUNDA

Once past high green mountains towering over the lagoon where John F. Kennedy was based when, on 1 August 1943, his ship, *PT109*, was rammed and cut in half by a Japanese destroyer called *Amagiri*, we round two sharp reef points and turn north toward the Munda Bar. We could find no chart of this area, and the buoy said to mark the deepest passage over the bar, charted at less than twice our draught, is of course missing. Hearts beating faster, we surf over the bar, large waves pushing us onward, white water breaking on both sides and the bottom clearly visible. Fortunately, we have already discovered the old pilot book to be unreliable. It gives us rough directions: turn east, make for a gap between two islands, three miles off, three course changes before then, with shoals and reefs to be dodged all the way. We travel very slowly where the level of uncertainty peaks, but make it to the gap without touching bottom with a least-depth of three feet under the keel. In the shallow water behind an island just to the north of this gap is a huge dump of US war materials. I find it hard to visualize this placid scene crawling with troops in 1943 when American forces assaulted and captured the half-built Japanese airfield.

After the gap, the route turns west again, the wind now behind us. The pilot book shows the one-mile passage as twisty and narrow, so this time I let the pressure of the wind on the hull take us with occasional prods from the engine. We flag a passing local boat in hopes of help identifying the channel. The crew wave merrily back without recognizing our need. Fortunately, Robin spots a floating coconut that turns out to be three inches of a crucial marker still showing above the low tide level, so we round this and see a thin stake a hundred yards ahead. We guess this could mark a reef, so we leave it to starboard, and then wiggle a bit around some bommies and eventually drop the anchor in front of Lambeti. Phew!

The bikes haven't been off the boat for two months and have corroded grievously from the salt of the seas. Lack of gears isn't a serious snag on the flat land around Munda, however, especially riding down the middle of the runway. This is a 747-size affair, which, while under construction for heavily laden Japanese transports of 1943, was disguised with a vast roof of suspended palm tree tops. These failed to fool the USAF who bombed it to bits anyway, invaded it and then had to mend it. If the Solomons could get their act together, this could be a perfect gateway airport to an incredible tourist area, bringing desperately needed income. But need is outweighed by land disputes and the unease of Solomons politics, which seem to make proper use of the runway unfeasible. Part of me whispers long may this last, though the country desperately needs money and tourism is its best shot.

Once I've installed new chains and gotten the brakes vaguely working, we cycle off to inspect what amounts to an open-air war museum. Rotting concrete platforms and rusting metal detritus are still visible everywhere in the bush. One village is built on a huge concrete base like a railroad concourse, itself set on hundreds of concrete-filled 40-gallon drums. In a clearing in the jungle stand a

A small selection of nudibranchs (this page and opposite page)

pair of Japanese antiaircraft guns, pointing at the sky, still clearly showing the scars of heavy cannon shells.

A tall, sun-browned New Zealander with a wicked expression is wandering along a track through six-foot high hedges of pink and white orchids. An explosives expert, he says he is, when he goes off occasionally to do some work outside the Solomons. I can't help wondering if he's a safe-breaker with a perfect retreat. He explains that New Georgia is an area of female land ownership, all property rights vesting in the daughter of the family. He shows us around a little village belonging to the local girl he married. A tidy enclosure looking more like a proper kitchen garden than the usual food plants hidden among weeds betrays the foreign influence.

The owner of Agnes Lodge and his wife, Zahi, are building a house on the tiny islet next to our anchorage. It appears that he married the lovely island along with the lovely Zahi, for, as in most Pacific places, it's impossible for a foreigner to acquire land legitimately. To have land here involves acquiring the lady proprietor. In such areas of matrilineal inheritance, this would be a problem for Western women hankering after the deeds to a patch of paradise.

Landing craft that fought their way to Munda in 1943 still rust quietly away on little islands scattered through Roviana Lagoon. Once eyesores, they have become part of the landscape. We exit the lagoon's chain of protecting islets to Mushroom Island, which rises 1,500 feet sheer from the seabed. This may be the Plum Pudding Island to which JFK swam after *PT109* had sunk. Fifty feet down the drop-off, a green turtle meanders along with me a while. We have met loggerhead, leatherback, hawksbill, and Pacific Ridley turtles by now; to swim and play with them never palls. My favorite undersea marvel is much smaller, however, sometimes almost invisible and always hard to find. I have learned to love nudibranchs. Of the panoply of undersea wonders in these tropical waters, nudibranchs are my pin-ups. Before diving Pacific waters, I'd never heard of nudibranchs. Seldom more than an inch long and lacking any form of shell, to warn off predators, nudibranchs have developed a range of exquisite patterns and colors that rival orchids. With a stunning little blue and white one crawling on my hand, a paraphrase of St. Matthew floats into my head: "Even the Solomons, in all their glory, are not arrayed like one of these."

A white, hard coral has adopted the perfect form of an urn, three feet high, hollow center, the outside a spiral construction. I find my first very own sea horse, a transparent steed only a quarter-inch high attached to a gorgonian fan, very hard to spot. These fans are enormous, ten feet across and always growing at exact right angles to the current to gain the most from passing nutrients. Some corals only extend their tiny tendrils at night, but here both hard and soft corals feed in the stream, rippling in the currents like miniscule wheat fields at harvest time. Exotic sponges in a delicate array of colors and huge tendrilled anemones with their attendant families of anemone fish dominate the prolific reef wall life.

Later on Shark Point at the seaward end of the reef, a six-foot banded sea snake, as fat as my arm with a cobra-like head, glides above gorgeous displays of fans and of sponges among straight-lipped giant clams that hang off the coral wall with a look of Sesame Street characters as they open and close their mouths. Robin tries to grab a big crayfish before it escapes into a hole in a cloud of silt. A pure white triggerfish isn't in our books, and beautifully patterned starfish litter the seabed. I talk to a green turtle sitting on a rock in the wall at sixty feet, and shake him by the flipper before he idly cruises off. Robin gets a fit of bubbly giggles when I lower a white sea-slug with pretty markings slowly in front of her mask. She avenges herself dropping a powder-box starfish the size of a cake-tin on me when I'm not looking. It is hard to say where a sub-aqua paradise might be, for there are ocean gardens of miracles all over the Pacific. Diving on these reefs comes close.

To reduce the nitrogen in our blood between dives, we must wait two hours, so I jog on the white sand of a nearby unoccupied island while Robin beachcombs for shells. Thirsty, she commands me to open a coconut for her.

"But we have no tools," I say.

She looks disappointed that her man isn't islander enough to open a coconut without tools.

The Terrible Solomons

Desperate to rescue my reputation and dimly recalling coconut technology learned in Polynesia, I meet the challenge with the aid of a giant clam shell and a sharp stick stuck in the ground, earning an admiring "Wow!"

NORO

From Munda the route leads back through the labyrinth of islets and reefs, and then up Diamond Narrows, more like the wooded upper reaches of a northern river than a passage between tropical islands. A tiny anchorage at Noro, just wide enough to swing on a short rode, is attained by squeezing *Nereus* through a small hole in a reef. The placid pool inside is bordered by trees emanating an evening chorus of frogs, insects, birds and hymns. There's a rasping noise too, interpreted by Selwyn who arrives in a canoe with some carvings, as the sound of a sleeping snake. The notion of a snoring serpent is intriguing until Selwyn explains that a brown snake known locally as a sleeping snake projects this grating sound.

Refueling on the fish quay at Noro, the only bowser for a long way, is not quite straightforward. We have to wait half a day for tired officials, charges are opaque, and the squeezer delivers a liter-a-second whoosh. The customs man agrees to let me uplift fuel duty-free, but careful inquiry elicits that there's a catch 22 in operation. The catch is that, if duty of 15 percent is deducted, then tax of 15 percent is to be added on.

VONA VONA

Vona Vona is another startling inland sea, a fifteen-mile lagoon hemmed in by islands, most of it crowded with coral banks separated by narrow channels winding around in a higgledy-piggledy fashion, a nautical version of a maze. One small resort has survived on a little island within, supported by a few traveling divers independent enough to ignore reports of Solomon Island dangers.

Robin, an inveterate spelunker, persuades me with difficulty to join the two divers in residence for a cave dive on an isolated islet. This involves dragging dive clobber ashore across rough coral rubble, and then scrambling through a tangle of mangroves to find a forbidding black pool tucked under the base of a small cliff. The stygian minipond, barely five feet across, is as inviting for a swim as a drain in the road. But it's too late to chicken out. I tog up, grab the tail end of a long string, splash in after the others and sink through the murky water straight down fifty feet. This I do not like. I can see nothing, not even my hand, despite fresh batteries in my flashlight. A storm of stirred-up silt forms an impenetrable fog. I blindly follow down a narrow pipe to a sort of U-tube bottom, the aluminum bottle on my back clanking against the rock walls and my octopus tubes catching on every unseen knobble. I can't stop thinking that getting them hooked would cut my air supply. The silt settles just enough to read the depth gauge, squinting at my wrist two inches from my mask: We are 110 feet under, inside, the island. In utter claustrophobic darkness. I clutch the thin cord tightly and wind it around my hand, so it cannot be lost. It's all there is to connect me to salvation from this wet purgatory, surely beyond Dante's imagination. At last the duct leads upward once more; dim blue light encircled by the jagged outline of a cavern's mouth opalesces slowly into sunlight filtered by 70 feet of depth and a heavy fringe of sea fans. My relief is huge as I emerge into open sea amidst the burgeoning life on the outer wall of the reef. The colors of coral and fish have never been so vivid. Being born must be like this. Even Robin seems less keen on cave diving after this one.

Pacific green turtle

A couple of miles across the lagoon in the dinghy, Nelson Boso expansively welcomes us to Madou village and conducts us to Chief Andihite, of whom permission is humbly begged to visit Madou's Island of Skulls. Ten Solomon dollars does the trick. Nelson, a graduate of the University of the South Pacific and a former member of the Solomons Parliament, is full of ideas for new enterprises, something these islands desperately need; we talk of collecting old computers for schools, indigenous nut crops, teak nurseries, tourism. It strikes me that a sophisticated person is not expected to choose to live in a leaf house in a remote village. Suppressing an unworthy notion of a politician who might find it expedient to disappear to the bush for a while, it doesn't, however, take a genius to realize that the life can be close to ideal. Food is easily provided by family gardens, chickens and fishing, clothes for the tropical climate cost little, and necessities requiring money are few. The *wantok* system makes for a better model of society than most in the West. *Wantok*, Pijin from "one talk," denotes the close tribal affiliation between villages sharing a language, and implies a high level of community identity and mutual support.

Village aspirations fired by glimpses of mainland life may of course transcend this picture of utopia; canned goods can quickly become more desirable than fresh, and videos a requirement. Yamaha powers most canoes and needs fuel. This is one reason that many Solomons communities have fallen prey to the Southeast Asian loggers, who offer easy money to buy such goodies. When the villagers replant trees, companies sometimes pay immediate money for the right to take the timber when mature, a clever ploy irresistible to cash-strapped landowners even though the price may be grossly inadequate.

Skull Island, which lies just off the end of a long thin barrier island, is tiny, forty paces or so across. Its sheltered beach is lapped by a placid blue lagoon while the roaring ocean surf grinds away at the ragged coral shelf on the outer side. We pull the dinghy up on the sand under old spreading trees and pick our way along an overgrown path to the island's center. A rough stone cairn stands in a little clearing. From a recess in the top, the chiefs' empty eyes survey their last domain. Their heads are supported by the skulls of warriors carried back in triumph from raiding expeditions. All about, in piles and hollows and even built into a wall, the skulls of defeated warriors lie in eternal obeisance. "My grandfather," Chief Andihite boasts, "he has brought many of these heads to the village."

Island of Skulls, Vona Vona

The spirits of the chiefs continue to protect this tabu place of mortal remains. As we stand in front of the crumbling skulls, lost in thoughts of the violent past, a threatening crack gives a second or two's warning and we spring

Which of you is gunning for us?

aside just in time to avoid a heavy branch falling from the tree above. There was no wind to shake it loose.

Pushing the dinghy off the beach, Robin, quite spooked from our narrow escape, wonders which of the skulls was gunning for us. Now that we have interrupted the eternal peace of their island necropolis, will we be hunted and haunted? I think she murmurs a little apology for the disturbance, just to be on the safe side.

"A kastom burial of an important person is like this," Nelson explains. "They make piles of stones round the body, who is propped up in a sitting position so that only his head shows from the top of the heap. After a suitable period the head is twisted off and interred in the stones on the island. Only the head signifies; the rest is thrown away."

As we return to *Nereus* across lagoon water of every shade of blue, shoals of tiny fish fly all about us, a storm of silver snowflakes. We call these flashing swarms "confetti-fish," and often pause to enjoy the sight of the millions of tiny bodies flying in perfect unison like a single creature, scintillating in the sunshine.

We anchor in a pool back down the lagoon so as to get to the local market early next morning. The horizon is a composition of thirty islands with occasional glimpses of the outer reef and Pacific rollers beyond, the volcanoes of Rendova and Kolombanggara bracketing our haven to the south and north. As sunset stains the sky red and purple behind the western islands, Hana paddles up, a golden youth in a painted lake, and promises to catch fish for our supper. An hour later Max, the chief's grandson, so he says, comes formally to grant us the run of this part of the lagoon, which belongs to his village. He ferrets about in the bottom of his canoe and comes up with a coconut crab, a real delicacy. The coconut crab is a different shape from other crabs, with a prominent thorax like a wasp, a land crustacean that may soon join the legions of endangered species since it grows slowly and gets eaten fast. It costs serious money when occasionally appearing on Pacific rim menus.

We assume Hana sent Max to bring us the crab instead of fish, cook it up and go to bed. Three hours later, I wake, sweating from a nightmare about the engine knocking itself to pieces because I have forgotten to put oil in. The hammering is still there, insistently echoing through the steel hull. Stumbling up into the black night, wiping deep sleep from my eyes, I find Hana's white teeth beaming over the gunwale, his canoe full of reef fish. We trade some and stuff them into the fridge, thank him generously, and sink back into our bunks.

KOLOMBANGGARA

Kolombanggara is an almost perfectly round island, some twenty miles in diameter, with a craggy old volcano rising to 3,500 feet in the middle. The wind follows the coastline around and stays nicely on *Nereus*' stern as we sail a semicircle around half of it.

In a small bay at Vanga Point is a surprise. Fields stretch up the hillside. There is a farm with cows and pigs on green pasture and parkland, hens in well-built henhouses, tilled gardens of fruit and vegetables, and carefully tended seedbeds neatly set between stands of experimental trees. These surroundings would be unremarkable in northern climates or New Zealand, but in the Pacific tropics it's like arriving in the imaginary land of Erewhon. Brother Tony is on the jetty to welcome us.

"This was once a Lever Brothers logging camp," he says as he shows us around. "With its infrastructure of hard roads, water supply, jetty and buildings, it was perfect for a vocational and agricultural college. This is one of about a hundred of the schools we, that is the Marist Brothers, have been building in the Pacific since 1836. Here, we teach about 160 young men from all over the

Coconut crab

Solomons agriculture and a range of artisan skills. We train teachers, too."

The Marist Brothers are new to me. I learn it's a French Catholic teaching order founded in 1817 by St. Marcellin Champagnat of Lyon. Brother Tony explains that they are happy to teach any Solomon islander at Vanga Point, irrespective of religion.

Unilever once owned a lease over three-quarters of the island, exporting cut logs to Australia for plywood as the timber was not of high enough quality for veneers, a sad and cheap end for the magnificent hardwood forests that clothed the slopes of the volcano. Unilever, whose logging once accounted for 15 percent of total Solomon Island exports, was eventually chased out after problems with an improbable character who wished to be known as the Holy Mama. This divine had established a church, organized his many followers on communistic lines, and called his village Paradise. A certain coconut tree, under which the Holy Mama had been visited by an important vision, was one day inadvertently felled by loggers. The Holy Mama got cross. The Unilever camp was raided, its buildings burnt and its equipment destroyed. Soon afterward, the relatively paternal Unilever ceased operations. The void was quickly filled by more ruthless logging companies from Pacific rim countries.

This splendid place has two particular advantages for us: First, Vanga Point provides the only hosed supply of good drinking water we have found in the Solomons. Needing five hundred gallons to fill our tanks, we are not enthusiastic about lugging it aboard in jerry cans. And there are bush tracks here. Most villages in Vanuatu and the Solomons lack runnable trails, so I lose no time in grabbing running shoes and disappearing up through the farm and into the bush. Stopping occasionally to drink sweet water from the frequent streams and douche myself in the rapidly heating morning air, I run through flowered jungle alive with bird calls. Huge orange bellflowers strew the ground under some trees, a carpet of crimson bottlebrush bristles under others. The hinterland bush is devoid of people. The sensitive plant with pink powder-puff flowers provides ground cover as it does throughout the tropics, and another widespread medicinal plant looking like mint with stalky flowers forms azure drifts. A lizard, a skink of sorts, is bright gold and electric blue.

The college lies in the lee of the volcano when the prevailing southeasterlies are blowing. The winds accordingly sometimes bend around it one way, sometimes the other, but at night there is a rather pleasant phenomenon: A package of cold air rolls down from the heights of the volcano, steeply reducing the pre-dawn temperature and causing us to reach for two covers. Brother Tony says that it sometimes drops to 60°F, compared with the usual fresh morning 83°F.

To help repay some of our generous welcome, Robin suggests to Jonas, the construction teacher, that she give a talk to the College, choosing as her subject tropical island architecture—in other words, planning houses constructed from forest materials (which many destructive bugs find organically delicious) for extreme conditions of sunshine, rain and wind. A bonus challenge is the changing orbit of the sun, which transits to the north in the northern summer and to the south in the northern winter, providing two midsummer days each year as it passes overhead and two sun-facing facades.

In a leaf-roofed schoolroom, open at the sides, before an audience of fifty building-and-carpentry students joined by another thirty from the English class, Jonas introduces Robin in Pijin: *"Robin hem kam prom Amerika. Hem sel prom Boston siti ist koust long USA. Insad long siti hem abaot 3 milion pipol ol keta stap. Hem wok as atitak po 20 ias. Hem spesalaes long kout haos po atitak. Long one fala prosect hem kost 100 milion dolas."*

Roughly translated: Robin, she come from America. She is from Boston city on coast of USA. In city are about 3 million people. She work as architect for twenty years. She specialize in courthouse architect. A single project it cost $100 million."

Pijin is a lesson in languages. It may lack certain finesse of expression, but without genders, cases, tenses, articles or more than two prepositions, it seems to do an excellent job. The Pijin of Vanuatu, Papua New Guinea and the Solomons, although different, is generally understood and has the remarkable consequence of uniting the speakers of about a thousand separate tongues. Its name is unconnected with birds, but comes, apparently, from a Chinese word for "business," which is why the Chinese-influenced *lingua franca* of Hawai'i is also Pidgin.

After an early Sunday morning run in the bush, we fill our tanks with sweet water at the college jetty. The slow trickle of the low-pressure hose gives an opportunity for the entire community to wander by, starting discussions on every subject and angling for invitations to see inside a Western yacht. We congratulate Brother Tony and his team on a unique effort, slip lines and head off to Gizo. No wind.

Taking on water, Kolombanggara

The Terrible Solomons

GIZO

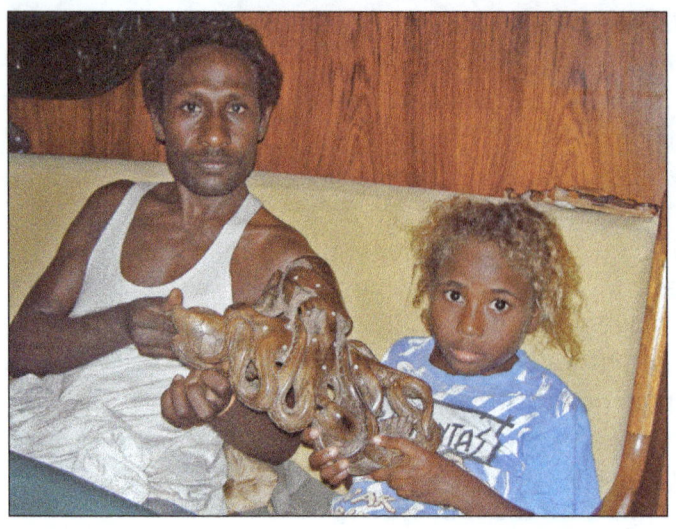

Tonsa with finished octopus

Gizo, the second city of the Solomons, proves a rundown shanty strip. The few patches of road free of uncollected rubbish are a mess of betel-juice reds, daubed like a twentieth century abstract sold for millions in New York. Japanese aid has paid for a new market, but a dispute has prevented it from opening for months. The market for garden produce is still operating in the filthy ruins of a wartime Japanese goods yard. The town is expensive as well as dirty. To change money, the bank wants a turn of 40 percent, generously offering to buy a foreign note and sell it to someone else for 40 percent more in addition to a $10 fee and some tax besides.

Tonsa, last seen leaving Mbili on an overloaded old coaster with his heavily pregnant wife for the hospital in Gizo, spots us and borrows a canoe to bring an incomplete octopus in kerosin wood. We feed him well and commission the finishing of it for Robin, who has been hankering for a fine carving of an octopus. In a dark, unsteady hut wobbling on stilts at the water's edge, we negotiate with a group of stone carvers from Ranongga, a nearby island with a fearsome headhunting reputation. The last reliably documented headhunting raid was mounted by the Ranonggans only months before the Second World War. The children of these headhunters seem to eye us up as potential specimens while they sell us a few fishes sculpted from a striated rock that looks like fossilized wood, and an enchanted figure with the body of a man and the head of a bird with an exaggerated beak like a toucan. This figure is a magic Kasko, whose task it will be to charm fish onto our lines.

SIMBO

Armed with a copy of a mud-map for Simbo, an island twenty miles south of Gizo, we duck in to anchor off a village inside its western reefs. The magic Kasko fails miserably in his first job as fish-finder, but perhaps it is he who brings us to a magic place seldom visited by outsiders nowadays. Even before the anchor is released, we're surrounded by a crowd of canoe-borne pikininis laughing, splashing and playing like dolphins around the boat.

Sampson Eli, chief of Legana village, is an imposing, bare-chested figure with the old skirt stretched around his hundred-inch waist barely meeting in the middle; "You should have come to Simbo last week," he intones in a mellifluous, deep voice. "We had very big celebration and people come from all over Solomon Islands, and from Bougainville as well."

I'm already aware that Simbo has been celebrating. The centenary of The Arrival of the Gospel in the Island was a major event that had united, temporarily, all five squabbling churches established in this island of fifteen hundred souls, and I am able to present the Chief with a copy of the *Solomon Star*, which dispatched a religious affairs reporter to cover the story and ran it on half a back page with a picture. I read the piece aloud to a large group of village people, who may be finding themselves in a newspaper for the first time. There is much exchange of profound glances, tongue clicking and muttered awe, while each scrutinizes the photograph for a long while.

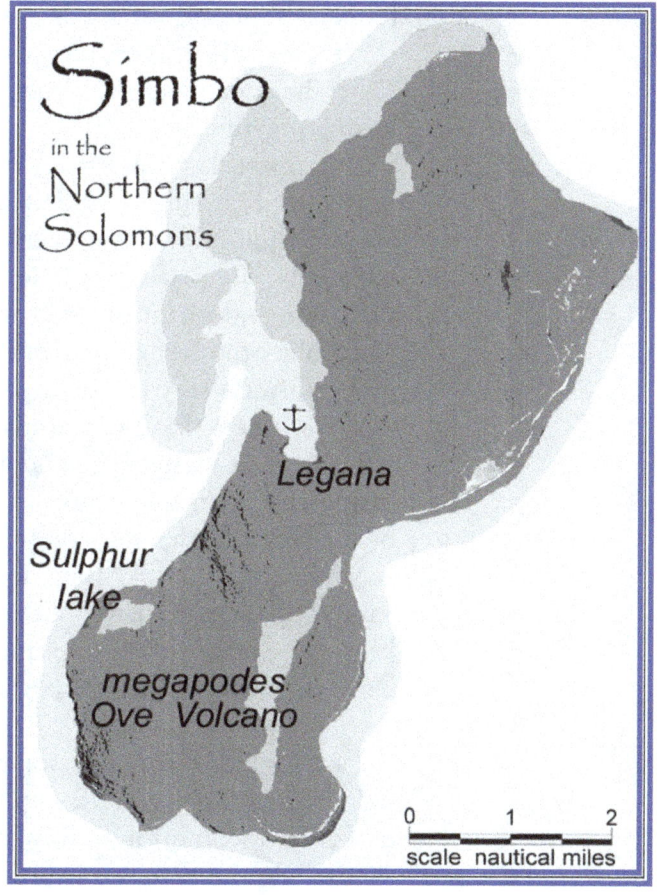

Robin and I chat our way around a picture-perfect Pacific village and return to *Nereus* towards sunset. She is anchored tight under a steep forested mountain, alive with an evening chorus of bugs and birds. From across the bay drift close harmonies from one of the churches. Four canoes arrive, bearing boys singing as they paddle. They sing for us as the sun sinks over the palms, part songs in their own language, rocking in the canoes, and having huge fun singing their hearts out. They are so delighted with their rewards—shrieking with pleasure and falling out of the canoes repeatedly—that Robin worries I am dishing out alco-lollipops.

Simbo has an extensive off-lying reef on its sheltered west side where we hitch the dinghy to some coral and reef-comb for fish and shells. A handsome young Simbonian accompanying us spears some fish as black as he is. Polo declares that he is the seventh of eleven children, and the third son. His father gave what he could to the elder brothers, which didn't include his land as this would belong only to the daughters, the custom in Simbo.

Polo goes on: "So, for me, he said, 'I will give you a special gift.' He chewed some betel nut very well and told me to open my mouth, then he shot the juice into my mouth. He said to me, 'Now this is my gift; you will be a fisherman under the water, you will always be able to catch as many fish as you want.' It is true. It was magic. I can stay under the water a long time, and I catch fish like nobody else does."

I inquire about our musical neighbors. "Last night we heard harmonious hymn singing from that little village across the bay for several hours. Who was that?"

"It is the place over there, which is just one family," he replies. "They have eighteen children, all from one mother, and they like to sing together."

Polo insists I accept a magic piece of shell that has been bleached in the peculiar sulphur lake toward the south of the island, and a kastom shell-money ring, carved from a giant clam. "This money used for bride-price here," he says. "The man have to come in to the room and put it on the ear of the girl. Then he negotiate the price with the father and brothers and they agree. The kastom money always stay in Simbo, but any Solomon dollars can go out to the brothers in other islands."

Bride price seems to be endemic in Pacific societies. But it's confusing that men must buy wives here when it was customary in northern countries not long ago for fathers to pay someone, by way of a dowry, to take their daughters away. The Pacific custom of valuing women positively seems the more civilized—a thought I keep to myself, fearing to plunge into the snakepit of debating the worth of a lady with Robin.

We are visited by a succession of islanders. Stewart, headmaster of the village school, puddles up in an ancient canoe, using only his hands for locomotion, followed by Bensley, who has been trained as nurse to the community, the nearest the island has to a doctor.

Legana village, Simbo
RR Acrylic on canvas

Neither has ever encountered a computer, and they are rendered tongue-clickingly speechless when we demonstrate some of the capabilities.

We wonder about islanders' health, and modern-day plagues. "When we do a test we find that 75 percent of the people here have malaria in their blood," Bensley says.

Malaria was endemic in the Solomons before the arrival of the Europeans, perhaps the only lethal germs going the opposite way to the mortal infections of diptheria, flu, cholera, smallpox, measles, TB, syphilis and so on that decimated all island populations. The blackbird laborers returning from Queensland and Fiji were partly, though innocently, responsible. Those were the few of the 30,000 men taken from the Solomon Islands between 1870 and 1904 who managed eventually to regain their homeland. There's evidence that some of the invaders deliberately introduced disease, sending dying men and women into villages so that they would infect others, much as some white settlers in North America brought Native Americans generous presents of blankets impregnated with smallpox spores. The arrival of trade goods caused more deaths too, as the new materials freed time from food provision for fighting, and better weapons fueled the permanent warfare between tribes. I am misusing the word "decimate" as is mostly misused, for it properly means to reduce by a tenth; in most islands it was only a tenth of the population that survived the combination of feuding with neighbors, slaughter by foreigners, blackbirding and disease.

C. M. Woodford, author of *A Naturalist Among the Headhunters*, was from 1896 the Resident in Tulaghi, the then capital of the Solomons, the first Resident appointed after the British Solomon Islands Protectorate was declared in 1893 to stymie German expansion plans. This post was equivalent to Governor of a colony, though he had few resources at his disposal in a protectorate. Seeing the annihilation around him, Woodford recorded this apocalyptic statement: "The whole population of the British Solomons will disappear...My opinion is that nothing...can prevent the eventual extinction of the Melanesian race in the Pacific. This I look upon as a fundamental fact and as certain as the rising and setting of the sun."

This bleak prophecy nearly came true. Happily, a few Melanesians proved resistant and populations gradually recovered, though huge chunks of history and tradition were lost.

Bensley politely asks if we can spare any doxycycline for use as an antibiotic against chlamydia. As Robin hooks some out together with other stuff from our medicine cabinet, Bensley goes on to ask if we can somehow help with health teaching aids, as he has nothing. It's depressing to hear that no birth control education or help is available at all in this little island where the population appears to have doubled in less than fifteen years. Families of six to sixteen children are the norm, and land to support them is very limited.

"Have you been to the top of this mountain?" Bensley asks, indicating the towering slope above us. "There is a very interesting cave there, with bats with big heads and no wings. In this cave there are two passages. When people here die, just four days after they die they go to the cave and write their name on the wall of the cave, and they say who are their loved ones they leave behind. When they finish, they go down one of the passages, and they come up in the Shortland Islands."

The Shortland Islands, whither these spirits are bound, are over the horizon, some fifty miles to the north.

Bensley tells me he would like to stay in touch, so I give him my card with an e-mail address. "Andrew Rayner, that is a very nice name," he says, reading the card. "May I have your permission to call one of my children by this name?"

I am not sure if he means one of his own future offspring, for he isn't married, but I think he is suggesting the name for a child born in his little clinic. Perhaps I will soon have a young namesake playing in the crystal waters of the lovely bay, growing up in his own paradise.

The Big Man in Simbo is Reuben Lilo, Simbo's representative in the Solomon Islands Provincial Assembly. Reuben Lilo is locally known simply as The Honorable, and it is to The Honorable that we pay a S$20 kastom fee to go on a megapode bird expedition. This turns into a most unusual picnic.

We pick up Polo in the dinghy. The crew is completed by his wife, Veronica; our cook for the day, Rono; and a freshly scrubbed white chicken.

The chicken complains loudly when Robin jumps in and lands on it.

"Of course, I forgot it's normal to go on a picnic with a live chicken," she says to no one in particular, adding an apology to the chicken.

A couple of miles south we land on a beach of polychrome boulders stained shades of orange and yellow by chemical emissions spurting from deep in the earth. Rono, who has a game leg, remains behind to prepare lunch in a fumarole and look after the dinghy, while we lead the chicken across a narrow neck of land to a lake. This is an old crater, a green sulphurous lagoon in the shadow of a volcano separated from the sea by a ribbon of rubbly land and now connected to it only by a passage too narrow for all but the smallest canoe. This is fortunate, as the lake water would surely have stewed the fabric of our dinghy. Its shore is bubbling with hot springs, nemesis for the chicken which is dunked in clear scalding water to kill it and render it easy to pluck. It contains an egg, which Polo reserves for lunch. Growing in the very hot soil by this lake, and apparently nowhere else, is a dogbane-looking shrub with pretty white flowers. To tolerate hell's garden temperature, it must be awfully rare; so I present a spray to Robin.

We set off up the side of the volcano, aptly called Ove, which is mysteriously cratered like Bloody Ridge in Guadalcanal after a week or two of Japanese shelling. Generation after generation of pits have been dug in the hot soil, some roofed over with pandanus panels, between which we have to negotiate a rough and narrow path, leaving us in constant danger of losing our footing and plunging underground. The pits serve as megapode hatcheries, since a megapode is only happy to lay an egg in sand at 33°C.

Natural cooking, Simbo
RR Acrylic on canvas

The chick is already fully fledged when it emerges and digs its way out, able to scramble to safety in the nearest hiding place. To support this extra development inside the egg, the yolk is huge and rich. The eggs are highly prized. By digging pits a few feet into the volcano, Simbo people are able to persuade the birds not to burrow a deep hole themselves, so it's easier to unearth the eggs. Megapodes flap around our heads complaining at the disturbance, but quickly return once we move on.

Polo points to one of the thatched pits. "This one used for hatching eggs when we find the number of the megapode birds is going down," he says. "Mebbe three or four hundred eggs were collected here for hatching. But before they hatch people come and steal all of them, because they very sweet when they getting ready to hatch. This was the end of the try to breed megapodes for ourselves."

Eggs containing half-developed embryos are usually thought disgusting by westerners, including us, but in Asia and the Pacific they seem a delicacy.

Someone from the World Wildlife Fund has estimated Simbo's annual megapode harvest at 140,000 eggs, providing 60 percent of the island's income. A twenty-year-old report claimed the population of megapodes had remained stable for a long while, but was now declining due to over-exploitation and feral cats. It suggested quotas, a closed season and a cat hunt as remedies, and a provincial law was promulgated. Despite these good intentions, nothing happened and numbers are still falling, Polo tells us. The traditional checks and balances serving to preserve an important resource seem to be creaking under the pressures of exploding population.

We dig up some eggs and climb back down the ridge of the volcano to the beach. Steam issues from several fissures among the boulders, stained sulphur yellow or coppery red by the cocktail of chemicals ejected from Ove. Rono has selected a fumarole for our lunchtime cooking, within which he has already baked kumala and tapioca, together with the chicken. The eggs are wrapped in green leaves and placed in a yellow plastic rice sack, which is then lowered into scalding steam roaring under pressure from the bowels of the earth.

The floating chorus of Simbo

In the evening, Polo brings over some of his family to watch a DVD. Seven pikininis, plied with coca cola and the popcorn Robin cooks up on movie nights to ensure a proper Roxy ambiance, sit tight-packed on the saloon squab, and the lights are dimmed. The TV fails to function. Nothing will persuade it to come out of standby mode. The best rescue available is to show world maps and photos on the computer, for we have no digital games. But we are left with a row of dreadfully disappointed little faces. It will be months, even years, before another opportunity for a movie comes by.

The chief asks for a picture of himself with his wife. I have a print ready when he visits the boat. He manages to maneuver his enormous girth over the side and squeezes it down the companionway and into the cabin. The Melanesian indication of wonder is a *tsk tsk* clicking of the tongue against the front teeth, the sort of sound which indicates displeasure with children elsewhere. The chief's staccato *tsk tsk*ing conveys amazement with everything.

Each day brings great gatherings of children in canoes, arriving with every kind of fruit and vegetable and shell to trade for our long thin balloons that are all the rage. Little people are invited aboard for coke or cooking or photos of themselves, while their envious friends' faces jostle at the portholes. The surround-sound chorus of young voices laughing, talking, singing is like a flock of parakeets.

Older villagers come to trade or tell a story or offer to guide us to one or another tabu place. Not much is produced in Simbo, just

The Terrible Solomons

Bensley and
ancestors, Legana
RR Acrylic on canvas

a few inferior carvings and some weaving. Despite that, we are offered a plastic tobacco pipe, not very old coins and more kastom shell-money. Polo fishes a speckled grouper for us, as good as cold water monkfish. The gnali nuts here are plentiful, delicious roasted, lightly salted. Robin creates a big pawpaw pie for a fund-raising supper for a school workshop. Like the standard fish curry and rice, it's eaten with fingers.

Stewart offers to lend me a high-school tome about the history and culture of the Solomons, written from a local angle which makes it a rarity among books we can find about Pacific Islands. When I go to collect it, he's sitting on the ground in a crowd outside Bensley's little green clinic. A sick old man who'd been brought in by boat from a village at the north of the island has died, despite Bensley's efforts. All the people of the village have gathered to show respect.

The sun crossed the equator on September 23, and is chasing us at two degrees of latitude a week. In Simbo, at about eight degrees south, the shadow of my head just reaches my toes at midday. As long as we are swinging at anchor and there is some breeze blowing through the boat, the nights are pleasant, and we sleep naked with a light sheet. On the increasing number of windless days as the season changes, it is tropical hot.

On our last evening in Simbo, I make a little speech of thanks and we walk to the landing into a chocolate-box golden sunset. From the school comes the sound of children singing. We wake early next morning to lift the anchor, but there is no wind. So we stay.

A headland a short distance away holds a skull house belonging to Bensley's village. He shows us the skull piles, the heads of chiefs and warriors killed in headhunting raids and describes the return of the village's war canoes with much ceremony and blowing of conch-shell horns. The headhunters of Simbo, like Ranongga, were feared far and wide. Skull cairns, bleached reminders of darker times not long ago, are scattered all about these islands.

Bensley then conducts us to a small village on the weather coast. The unobstructed Pacific rollers, crashing in on the reef, are full of pikininis playing like fish, somehow avoiding violent death on the jagged rock as each wave rears up and explodes on impact. His old uncle, Chief Harold, has a precious book about the headhunters of Simbo, written by a Dr. Hook in 1906, a time when he could still interview the participants. The book has gone missing, so Harold relates headhunting sagas in Pijin through wispy whiskers straggling down his weatherworn features. Bensley translates: "A special slave had to be captured and brought here from the island of Isabel, for they were the only ones who knew about these things,

Simbo goodbye

how to keep the heads and put them properly in the heap after all the meat get rotten and fall off."

Harold's hair is grizzled white against the deep black of his skin, his bloodshot eyes are sunk in deeply lined cheeks, and his age is great enough to have grown up within the old tradition. To talk of his parents' generation and their bloodthirsty activities seems to bring a nostalgic gleam to his eye.

We have a parting puzzle. Polo has looked after us well, entertaining us, guiding us and bringing chicken and fish, and we have found good presents for him and his family. On what we thought was the eve of our departure, I gave him our last precious flashlight batteries to go and hunt for crayfish. He has not turned up again. In answer our inquiries, no one knows. Whether he is in trouble or has infringed some tabu remains a mystery as we quit Simbo and the Solomons and set a course south for the two-hundred-mile passage to Papua New Guinea.

As usual, we put out the lines, and, like the last thousand miles of Solomon waters, the sea produces no fish. A lone booby and a lovely tropic bird take a careful look at our lures and fly on. I think I hear them sneer.

16

Jewels In The Ocean

BUDIBUDI

Laughlan atoll, better known by its Melanesian name of Budibudi, rises only a few feet above sea level; we are close before its treetops bulge the horizon. The radar, clagged by half a dozen shower cells, doesn't do much better than our eyes,. We have a range of possible waypoints, two drawings, a paper chart and an electronic map to help us find and enter Budibudi, all vague or mutually contradictory. So, once we have raised the atoll, we put them aside and eyeball our way around the encircling reef. A pod of pilot whales welcomes us, topped by the largest flock of seabirds since New Zealand. Over everything soars a magnificent frigate bird, majestically watching for the chance to ambush another bird and steal a meal without getting his talons wet.

"A fish!" Robin screams.

Indeed, there is something heavy on the line. I

heave in a barracuda, the first catch for a thousand miles, though not for want of trying.

Shortly thereafter, Robin yells almost hysterically, "It's another fish!"

On the other line is a skipjack. The magic Kasko is performing at last.

Budibudi is a four-mile triangle of shallow water perched on an isolated ancient volcano top rearing up from the ocean floor hundreds of fathoms below. We pick our way in through several lightly inhabited motus, pausing for a school of spinner dolphins jumping clear of the turquoise water, corkscrewing in the air. Outrigger canoes from the three small villages on the motus waste no time in sailing out to inspect us and asking what we have to trade. Soon we have a pan of crayfish boiling on the stove and the fresh barracuda is garnished with a lobster sauce for our supper.

Budibudi watercraft
RR Acrylic on canvas

Some megapode eggs arrive the next day. Contrary to all previous views, there is a species of megapodes here that do well without the aid of a volcano. Sun-heated sand is perfectly adequate for incubation, they feel. One of the three eggs contains a pulsating feathered embryo, ready to hatch, which though it would be prized by the islanders has Robin looking pale as she breaks it into a megapode egg and lobster omelet.

The white beach all around the nearest motu, interrupted by only a few fallen trees, makes a fine running track for early morning. We kayak across the lagoon to play with the dolphins that welcomed us in. Canoes visit, trading carved wooden spoons, coconuts and bananas, shells, or just to pass the time of day, look at photos or check what we can supply to this far-off outlier of Papua New Guinea.

Supper invitation, Budibudi

Tau and Elsie with their children, Abraham and Tansie, are our chief adopters and invite us to lunch in their hut on stilts. A chicken is killed and carefully prepared by fifteen-year-old Abraham, together with a pumpkin and rice mixture, roasted pawpaw and white yams. All this is laid out ready on the floor when we have climbed the tree-stump ramp to the doorway. Possessions of any kind are few in the islands; chairs and tables are very rare. We find some pots and pans to give the family, and Abraham is rewarded with fishing line, swivels and hooks, and a pink, stripy city shirt.

We are planning to dive on Budibudi's reef, presumably largely unexplored as it is well outside the reach of any coastal dive operation, when the wind gets up. Having suffered many calm days, we decide to grab it.

It's a fast close reach to the south-southwest until a steep wave bobbing up under the bow gets into the bottom of the genoa, which stretches and bursts with a whipcrack, torn right across the foot. I furl it as best I can, leaving a double-bedsheet-size section of canvas flying from the forestay to help stabilize us, and hank the staysail on. This combination works quite well, though our speed is reduced.

At midnight we hit a severe squall. Winds gust to gale force, and heavy rain comes in horizontal sheets. This kicks off a night of storm cells. With the wind backed nearly astern, conditions are difficult to sail.

As the gray light of morning diffuses imperceptibly across the ocean, unrelieved by any glimmer of sunrise, the fluky wind starts to die. Feeling as gray as the sea looks on my dawn watch, I am entertained by a troupe of dolphins using us as a stalking horse. Lining up in ranks, six or eight dolphins in precise line abreast overtake *Nereus* slowly from stern to bow. They come up to breathe in unison and then break and return to the stern to do it again. Meanwhile one or two of them have been dispatched to act as sheepdogs, swimming a hundred yards or so out and then leaping noisily about, clean out of the water, deliberately striking the surface on their sides with a loud smack. This coordinated maneuver rounds up the fish and delivers them to the waiting line of breakfasters.

MISIMA

We struggle on for a while, slopping about in a squall-messed sea with a light following wind until we fire up the engine close to Misima's harbor at Bwagaoia, a deeply indented finger of haven inside a narrow entrance.

Visas are necessary for Papua New Guinea, and we have been unable to get them ahead of time. When Quarantine, Customs and Immigration come on board, there is fast talking to do and cigarettes to be given away. As the offered alternative is sending our passports to Port Moresby by the airplane scheduled but not certain to leave a week hence, we settle for a five-day permit that doesn't exist to cover our three or four week stay. We expect to leave the country where it will be impossible to check out, so this seems unimportant. It comes at a high price augmented by a ruse of politely suggesting I have made a mistake with the cash and have underpaid, and moreover that "overtime" is needed for Leonard, who has timed his arrival for six minutes past four o'clock—precise official knocking-off time in PNG. He begs a pack of cigarettes and goes on to drink another boat's beer. Lennie the Lifter, as I hear him called, is young and smiles delightfully as he polishes his range of extraction ploys.

After paying off the officials we spend what is left of the kina exchanged at a tiny bank-hut on dinghy petrol and the few available supplies. An Australian gold mine three miles away employs about two hundred locals and brings in two or three planes a week. The gold, however, has been worked out and the mine is to close, which will leave Bwagaoia with its three little stores and tiny bakery a sleepy place.

THE LOUISIADES

Misima is the official entry point to the jeweled Louisiade archipelago. Like the big Bougainville Island to our north and the ubiquitous thorny climber that decorates the tropical and subtropical worlds in many colors, it is the great French navigator, Louis-Antoine de Bougainville, whose name is celebrated here—though tactfully he claimed he named the archipelago for his king, Louis XV. Bougainville's voyage was the first circumnavigation by a Frenchman, and also by a woman. A remarkable lady called Jeanne Baret was smuggled aboard *La Boudeuse* in Nantes as the botanist's valet, and only unmasked once Bougainville reached Tahiti in 1767. Amazingly, after sixteen months on board undetected by a crew of randy French sailors, it was the Tahitians who were first to see through her disguise. She was, of course, the botanist's mistress, and it was Philibert Commerçon, the botanist, who immortalized his capitaine by naming a plant he found in Brazil earlier on the voyage the *bougainvillea*.

Anyone seeking vast lagoons studded with islands, clear waters with prolific fish, traditional villages and remote tropical splendor need look no further than the Louisiades. Tourism is limited to a handful of passing yachts. Papua New Guinea's troubles are a world away. It suffers failed government, poverty and little outside support, certainly; but in subsistence-based South Seas islands, these things don't matter as they do to urban man.

The Deboyne lagoon lies within an isolated triangular atoll, about twelve miles along each side, to the west of most of the Louisiades. The mud-maps we now use for guidance, photocopied rough drawings and notes by a few cruising folk who previously passed this way, show only one far anchorage, but as it is getting late we enter a pass and turn right to seek our own. It's a fine spot, sheltered by a deserted island crowded with bird-life that we enjoy in our kayaks in the morning before continuing around the unpopulated island of Nivani to anchor on a shallow coral shelf under its lee. The tall, scattered coconut trees—all that is left of a long-abandoned plantation, their slender trunks topped by tiny bundles of leaves—give the hilly island the look of a pincushion.

"What can you give us?"

There's a shallow stretch of water between Nivani and Panapompom, in the center of the Deboyne Lagoon. In 1944, a Japanese pilot splash-landed his crippled Zero here and swam away uninjured. The airplane is still parked on the bottom, in excellent shape, one blade of the propeller bent from the impact and one wing crumpled, but otherwise intact under a light encrustation of coral and anemones. It's inhabited by a bright crowd of tropical fish, which fancy the many crannies in its powerful engine and empty fuselage a desirable home. I brave a fierce damselfish, attacking me repeatedly for invading its territory in the instrument panel, to climb into the cockpit and sit in the pilot's seat, grasping the joystick and flying this vicious antique. The damsel charges the glass of my mask repeatedly. I'm glad it's only four inches long. A German sailor later relates that he was severely bitten on the ankle by a moray eel residing in the rudder-pedal hole.

A large obstruction that catches my eye when I winch the anchor up proves to be a giant clam, clamped solid on the chain. To remove it, I continue winding. As it crunches in the jaws of the fairlead and splashes back into the water, I hear a screech from Robin, which seems to imply I've done wrong; it transpires she was already planning in the clam for lunch. Clams to a New England girl are real food, even if this was a hundred times the size of a quahog.

PANASIA

The Cormorant Passage takes us into another large lagoon, protected by a surrounding reef, itself within the hundred-mile-long Louisiade barrier reef. Its south side Panasia (in paradise it's naturally pronounced "panacea"), is a craggy, uninhabitable island, evidently the remains of half an ancient volcano. A kingfisher is perched on a branch singing a fishing song as we land on a beach coated in floating tufa rock—pumice emitted by underwater eruptions and evidence of recent seismic activity. A sailor later tells me he sailed through a sea of floating rocks not far off, fully four feet deep. Even here, ten miles from the nearest small village, a canoe paddles up with a family of seven aboard, the grandfather negotiating through his remaining rotten teeth for anything we have in exchange for a pawpaw and a few speckled bananas. As always he and his equally toothless son try a range of trade tricks on us, and as always we are overgenerous in giving out fishhooks, sugar and rice. I try to get the combination of a businesslike trade and a free gift understood, but the islanders probably come away from these encounters feeling that the *dimdims*, the white strangers, have been outsmarted again.

BAGAMAN

The Louisiades have suffered a drought for four months, and there is little in the gardens except pawpaw and tiny tomatoes. We manage to trade a few sorry vegetables and lemons on Motorina Island, and then head along the Calvados Chain, the string of pearls extending for a hundred miles to the east inside the huge encircling Louisiade reef, lunching off sushi slices of a kingfish pulled in en route.

It's dancing day at Bagaman school. Children hung about with leis of frangipani and hibiscus dance on the beaten soil to kastom rhythms drummed out by a group of *tamtam* players: fish dances, bird and snake dances, hunting and war dances. The scent of concentrated frangipani is intoxicating. Women sitting under trees at the top of the beach are manufacturing *bagi* necklaces, an extraordinarily time-consuming process reflecting a tradition only possible in a place where there is no shortage of time. Pink shells first have to be smashed into the correct-size fragments from which pieces are to be exactly shaped, ground and polished. Each tiny piece is hand drilled. The pieces are then matched and strung on a sennit cord to make a necklace or bracelet.

Bagaman is unkindly known among yachts as "Beggarman," on account of the skills of the locals and frequency of their visits to extract presents or trade a few bananas or a small pawpaw for anything they can get out of the boats. The island is on a crossroads

Dancing day at Bagaman school

in the Calvados chain, and the arrival of a few dozen yachts each year has a corrosive effect on the work ethic, which may never have been notable. For Australian yachts, Bagaman is often the first foreign village, and generosity has not yet been tempered by experience.

Joseph comes in a canoe to tell us a woman died today in a neighboring village, giving birth to her ninth child. "Please give me some petrol," he asks. "You see I must take some women of the village to the funeral."

It's significant that we and two old Australian cruising hands in the bay politely decline, feeling that it's yet another wheeze, a necroploy this time, to screw something out of us, for there is money in this village to buy fuel and we have seen village boats buzzing about. It's only an hour's walk, anyway.

We are therefore happy to escape across the lagoon to the outer reef, ten miles to the north. Passing over the Wori Wori patches and heading for the Wuri Wuri passage, Robin takes extra care helming. We come to rest in the palest blue water within a protecting

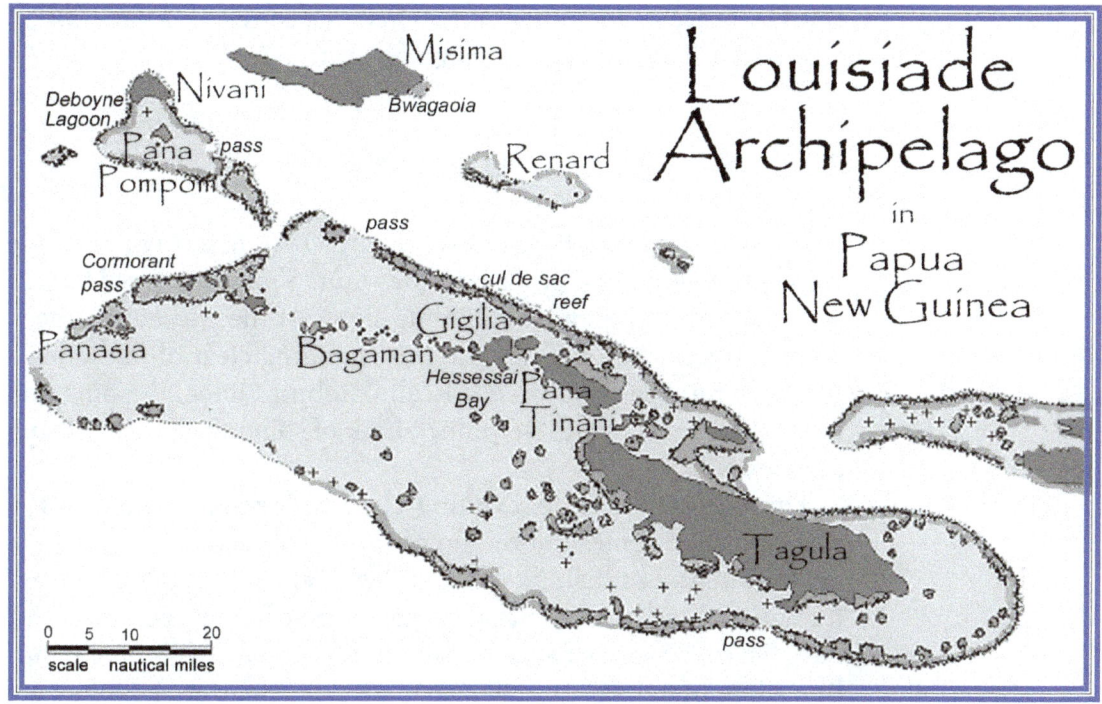

circle of coral. No village is close; only a few trees on two tiny islets break the nearby horizon.

The reef is teeming with fish of every size and shape and color, more than we have ever seen in one spot; squadrons of turtles flipper lazily by while a few sharks eye us curiously. A family of oriental sweetlips, stripy black and white with yellow polka-dotted fins and tails, make a psychedelic whirl. Robin and I are entertained for several minutes by a clown trigger-fish ballet; two of these extraordinarily patterned fishes put their tails up, their noses down, and dance in this vertical, reversed attitude around and around each other over a jag of yellow coral.

Clown triggerfish

A herd of swarthy Maori wrasse, 50 to 100 pounds each, grazes on the outer reef. At seventy feet, a huge giant giant clam is large enough to climb inside. The giant giant clam really is a subspecies of giant clam, one of nine, and this one is *huge*. According to our aged *Guinness Book of Records*, the largest, found in 1956, was under four feet

Jewels in the Ocean 253

across and weighed 730 pounds. This I measure at four-and-a-half feet, and it looks heavier. A magnificent thing.

GIGILIA

We've just caught a 21-pound yellowfin when, half way across the lagoon to Gigilia, the other line goes taut. Something very large. I start hauling and glimpse a baffling sight. At the end of the line is an indistinct mass of wings and fins, standing clear of the water.

I have no idea what it is as I call, "Robin! Quickly! Come and look what's on the line. Dolphin? Shark of some sort? Diver? Bring my gloves."

The thing dives deep, exerting close to breaking strain on the line, and then comes out on top of the water again.

"I think it's a sailfish," I shout. It has an enormous dorsal fin and it's tail-walking on the surface. I have never before seen one. Nor have we ever heard of a yacht catching a big game fish on a handline while under sail, and we have no idea if marlin or sailfish are to be found in these waters, specially in the shallows of a lagoon, albeit an enormous one sheltered by the world's fifth largest reef.

It *is* a sailfish, a magnificent creature of at least 100 pounds. It takes an hour to bring him alongside. His sail runs the length of his body and, when extended, is higher than his girth, a subtle blue-green.

This is a great fish to respect and release. But, with half a yard of sharp sword protruding from his nose and our hook well embedded in his lower jaw, this is easier decided than achieved. I can't lift his six-foot frame on board without rigging a snatch-block on a boom and using it as a gantry, risking injury and probably taking so long that the operation would kill him even if I survive. Eventually, with what help I can give him while hanging out off the steel ladder set in *Nereus'* side, he manages to work the hook out and with a powerful flip is gone.

Half an hour later, the anchor's down in the big bay of Gigilia Island as the sound of schoolchildren singing their way home along the beach drifts across the water. We trade for tiny eggs, sweet potato, bananas, pawpaw, and a peach-colored spider conch, and arrange that Noah and Monica will bring mud crabs, Joseph and Christine will look for crayfish, and John-Jeffrey invites us to visit his elementary school where he might find the first of the season's mango crop for us. In the event, no supplies arrive at all.

Though Pacific scenery is often bogglingly beautiful, it's the Pacific people that imbue in us the sense of floating through the best the world has to offer. Specially the children. So we bounce around to the windward side of the island in the dinghy next morning to accept John-Jeffrey's invitation to the miniscule elementary school where he educates forty kids. He is nursing a splitting toddy hangover, clutching his head in both hands as he shows us the schoolroom where pupils sit cross-legged on the sand floor, using for lessons old-fashioned slates and chalk donated by AusAID. We sit talking with them too long, so it's useful to have twenty or thirty children to push the dinghy, stranded by the falling tide, out through the shallows.

Late in the day a girl's face appears at a porthole. "I am Mary," she says through it, "John-Jeffrey's kid sister." As is usual and polite with people of the islands, she hesitates a while. Finally, she reaches the point. "Can you please take me back to my school?"

"Yes," I say, having asked where. "If you can be on board by eight in the morning."

"And will you give me a present? Anything?"

"No, and you shouldn't ask."

But they all do try it on, with delightful smiles, well primed by their families.

Mary arrives on the beach with three heavy sacks and some drinking coconuts for us, delicious after a couple of hours in the fridge. While we head for Hobuk primary school, three islands away on Pana Tinani, Mary chatters away in barely comprehensible English. She's a delightful passenger. Her only clothes are her mother's cast-off rags. She has no idea how old she is, and has never celebrated a birthday. Robin teaches her to clean her teeth, which are already betel-nut stained, and tries to persuade her to continue with the toothbrushes we press on her.

Finding a space among the bommies in Hessessai Bay by a plum pudding islet to park *Nereus*, we load Mary up with presents and drive her in the dinghy a couple of miles over a mess of reefs around a point to St. Joseph's, a primary school of some two hundred pupils located in its own attractive bowl between round hills running down to a wide beach.

HESSHESSAI

Mary

Mary's bags are full of bananas, coconuts and roots—her food for the next four weeks. When I've humped these ashore, she shows us the dormitories where the girls sleep on mats on the bare floor, and the eating hut in which groups mess together over tiny fires, each with three pointy stones to support a cooking pot.

When Brian, the deputy headmaster, says that Mary's school fees have not been paid, but that she is a good pupil and he is trying to keep her on at Hobuk, Robin has the germ of an idea. "How about sponsoring Mary through school," she proposes in the evening. "Brian told me how much the fees are, and as long as there is some way of getting the money to the school we might do this."

"Excellent plan," says I, more cautious. "But I bet the involvement will be greater than that. You'd not want your protégée to be without decent clothes, which will have to be sent with cruising boats from Australia. She'll need books, stationery, toothpaste and plenty of other stuff. There'll be a need to set up communications, too, for you want to know how she is getting on each term, with a report from the headmaster, and there's probably no telephone, computer, radio transmitter or post here. Then there's going to be the inevitable cry for help about something as time goes on, and you will never be quite sure how genuine it is."

We debate the idea, for Mary seems intelligent and extroverted. She is class monitor in fourth grade, and a rare Melanesian girl who is not strangled by shyness. We walk through tall grass, feathery like pampas, over to St. Joseph's to discuss the proposal with the headmaster, who arranges to come to the boat but fails to turn up. He has neglected to tell us that after only five months in the school he is leaving shortly, though the reason remains mysterious. As Brian appears likely to assume the headmastership, we put to him our offer to pay Mary's school fees for her four remaining years at Hobuk, grades five through eight. We fix Mary up as best we can: a brass hook with a yacht to hang her clothes, an airbed, pillow and pillowcases to improve sleeping arrangements on her mat; towel,

Hessessai School

shampoo, toothbrush and paste; pens and exercise books, necklace, shirts; stationery and money for stamps, and rice, balloons and lollipops. The color photo Robin prints and frames for her is the first image of herself or anything else she has ever possessed.

At the main Hesshessai village, we are gossiping with a few fishermen on the beach when a man swings past on crutches.

"What happened to his leg?" I inquire.

"It was bitten off by tiger shark last year," they say. "Max was diving for trochus shells and a tiger grabbed him. He was able to hold onto the stones of the reef while the shark was pulling him or he would be dead."

This is the first shark attack I've come across in the islands, and the villagers tell me of two others blamed on the dreaded tiger sharks on the outer reef. We shiver a moment, remembering we just dived there several times.

Fewer canoes hail us than in most bays, and we are asked for very little, perhaps because this village has a thriving business diving for bêches-de-mer and trochus shells. This has financed a couple of zoom boats with 40 hp Yamahas. They seem to have plenty of fuel. Matthew gives us a fat mud crab, which he says he tripped over on the way to his garden this morning, and I find a can of Hammerite for his canoe. Then an old man turns up with a bag of mangrove oysters, black wizened fossils enfolding a mollusk of mussel size, bonded so firmly to the mangroves that we must cook a chunk of wood with each of them. We supplement the oysters for supper with a giant frilly clam we picked up among the beautiful coral below us.

One afternoon, I climb a high hill on a small island bordering our bay. If this had been the mountain from which the devil showed Christ the earth, he would surely have been more tempted

Jewels in the Ocean

View from a hill

by the offer. A wide bay sweeps from my island around to the point where the school is located. The water is every sort of blue as it laps over the reefs and bommies. Green hills rise from the gardens and palms on the shoreline. Ribbons of bush run up the valleys. A finger of sea is visible behind the point, and then the island of Pana Wina, sea again, and in the distance Savari on the outer reef protecting the lagoon from the blue-black ocean. Behind me a shallow lagoon is fringed by a golden beach separating its pale blue water from the multiple greens of the forested hills rising beyond. At my feet stands a leaf-house village with sailing canoes drawn up on the beach in front where children are playing. For sound effects, two small girls run with me up the hill, singing in their language "Old Macdonald Had a Farm."

To their surprise, I sing it with them. It must be a rare *dim-dim* who knows one of their songs. Allowing them to survey their paradise through my binoculars causes the children huge excitement.

Village men come aboard in the evening to watch *Gladiator*. They enjoy the violent bits and gratefully bring two enormous crayfish in the morning—and a broken dive mask for Robin to weld up with a hot gas-knife. The crayfish are delicious in a sherry sauce with a stir-fry of plantain and a watermelon-size bean. We have squid too, which we are getting better at catching with a jigger off the back of the boat, though they are so pretty in their own element that I hate pulling them out.

TAGULA

A big high is at last forecast to traverse Australia, which should produce the right wind to cross the Coral Sea on a fast beam reach. As we hug Mary and say good-bye to the school after a week in Hessessai Bay, the children dance for us in traditional costumes of leaves and flowers and grass skirts, the girls bare-breasted. Then we motor past Shibumbum Island, through reefs alive with turtles to a narrow creek in the south of the Louisiades' largest island, Tagula. This is our launch pad for take-off next morning for Bundaberg in Australia, eight hundred miles south, if the wind allows. The village is small and poor. When Nancy brings us three mini eggs and six bananas in the morning, we load her up with all the trading things we have left.

The overnight weather turns to thunder and rain and then drizzle, keeping us storm-bound all day; it's irritating, as we're fretting to be under way before forecast light winds arrive. We need good visibility to pick our way through twelve miles of reefs to a little-used pass and the open ocean.

Taking advantage of a mighty deluge to scrub the decks with fresh water, wearing only a birthday suit, I am mortified when a small motor boat looms out of the lashing rain with a rash of Papuans clinging to every surface, all cheering and waving at the rare naked *dim-dim*. I salute, and they are soon swallowed up by the murk.

Graduation class at Hesshessai school

Jewels in the Ocean

Manta

The following morning is no better. A half-heard weather forecast for the Coral Sea talks of a low right over us, with a deep trough running south. The sky clears a little by lunchtime and we determine to go, despite continuing drizzle. In the poor light, we sail by mistake between the final two large bommies rather than around them as planned. Happily there is just room for us. We exit the lagoon between heaps of white water churning either side of the narrow pass, and set sail south.

Having only fresh pumpkin and the chief's pawpaw, we are anticipating having to exist on canned provisions for the journey to Bundaberg to go with Robin's home-baked bread and muffins. A kingfish and a blue-fin trevally taking our hooks at the lagoon exit are therefore most welcome. Fresh and pickled, they keep us fed for the five-day passage. I am well pleased with the magic Kasko, who has one last awesome present for us as we hit the open ocean. A manta ray or maybe a mobula jumps clear of the water on our beam, and performs a double somersault. An acrobatic fish weighing over a ton is breathtaking.

DEPARTING AUSTRALIA once the cyclone season is spent, we have a heap of things aboard for Mary. Though it's been impossible to communicate with the school to warn of our coming, we said, like MacArthur when bundled out of the Philippines, we would be back.

Fine, fast sailing over a wrinkled sea brings us at the fourth dawn to the narrow jaws in the barrier reef surrounding the Louisiades, twelve miles from the nearest island within. The trade winds, decorated with deceptively fluffy clouds but laden with moisture from thousands of uninterrupted miles of ocean convection, condense as they feel the high island of Tagula, and dump. Our Louisiade charts are unreliable, so safe navigation is by sight. But nothing can be seen through thick rain hissing and bouncing on the lagoon's surface. Standard advice is to navigate tropical lagoons only between the hours of ten and three with the sun shining high behind and a crew in the rigging to spot coral: an unattainable counsel of perfection on every count. We drop the sails and, using the current and windage of the hull to propel us with a little nudge from the motor from time to time, we sense our way through thirty miles of reefs to Hessessai Bay.

The Kasko is on duty to ensure that a fish takes each line again. After sashimiing a fillet of the yellowfin for dinner, we're in our bunks by 8:00 P.M. Countering my argument that a third crew member makes all the difference to the comfort of a passage by doubling one's off-watch time, Robin contends that the extra rest doesn't merit catering for more mouths on board and the loss of privacy in our home. I lose these debates, so we alternate four-hour watches and sink into a magnificent night's sleep once at anchor.

Refreshed and ashore in the familiar little creek, we stroll over the hill to Hobuk school. Children spot us approaching through the long grass and crane from the classroom windows in welcome: "Andrew, Robin, Mary not here," the girls shout to us. "She gone back to her home."

"When will she come back?" we ask.

"Mebbe Sunday."

"Who is now the headmaster?"

"Mr. Andrew. Mr. Hugh and Mr. Brian gone away."

A teacher who introduces herself as Pauline, the new deputy head, says, "Yes, Mary went home two days ago, and she must return this Sunday."

We resolve to wait. Pauline takes us to meet Andrew, the new head. Both the old headmaster and Brian, who had seemed a responsible schoolmaster, have apparently left under a heavy cloud. "Mr. Brian, he was chased out by the local people," Pauline says softly. "He and Mr. Hugh left even before the end of the term, nothing was done. Grade 8 students didn't get diplomas as there was nobody to write them."

Andrew has been deputed by the school board to investigate. "Maybe it was some boy-girl thing with the bigger girls in the school," is all he'll volunteer.

Pauline is very grateful for our skipjack. "How big it is. We shall never be able to eat all that." She finds us a couple of pawpaws in return.

Day after day, Mary does not turn up. This is a blow for Robin who has thought carefully about a sack of things she might appreciate. We slowly, reluctantly abandon our hopes of seeing her. I land on the little beach one last time with tools to fix the school radio and the bag of presents to climb the half-mile path through the muddy jungled valley and up over the grassy hill. The swamp life of this route is dazzling—red and gold bugs, nymphs of crimson with vermilion flashes, damsels of several yellows, bright red bluebottles, little crabs with stripy pink torsos or startling red carapaces, mudskipper fish which flipper on land, noisy flashes of red and green feathers in the trees.

After running on the beach, fine talc dividing the seven classic blues of the lagoon and a dozen shades of green on the fringing slopes behind, we give up on Mary, up-anchor and pick a route through the islands to open water and across the strait to Bwagoia in Misima Island.

Our intentions turn out impossible to realize. The writing paper and stamped envelopes addressed to the USA remain unused, and our letters to the school unanswered. Without bank details we can't send Mary's fees. Though she was instructed how to get an e-mail sent when there was a yacht in the bay, but for two lines once the Mary file remains empty.

Was this the product of the happy-go-lucky idleness of the islands, some problem of an association with *dim-dims*, or trouble from her peers? No one can say.

Homeward before the storm
RR Acrylic on canvas

Reach for Paradise

17

The Kula Ring

CHARTS FOR THE HUNDRED MILES between Misima and the nearest point of New Guinea warn vessels of a confusion of sand and shoals, islands, huge reef systems and treacherous outcrops of coral rooted in deep water. In more traveled seas, such places are buoyed in reds and greens and marked with leading lines, posts and cardinal markers in patterns agreed by international treaty. A vessel failing to carry pilot books brimming with information can be accused of negligence. Papua New Guinea, lacking the surplus resources to evolve into the nanny of its seafarers, leaves such matters in the hands of the occasional sailors venturing into its waters. Old charts—the data is all old—show an occasional lit buoy or a mark, but these are illusory. Even if part of a mark has survived, its solar panel was long ago removed to power a boom-box in someone's nearby leaf house.

Except for local canoes, no vessels have shared our sea since Australia. We expect to remain alone for the next few months of our quest to the west among the mysterious islands of Papua New Guinea, a country largely shunned by outsiders who are swayed by liability-based travel advisories and political unrest in the capital to believe that these are dangerous bits of paradise, best avoided. Similar warnings against the Solomons bully sailors to avoid some of the Pacific's loveliest islands. We fondly persuade ourselves that apprehension about outlying parts of Papua New Guinea is similarly exaggerated. In any case, we have an

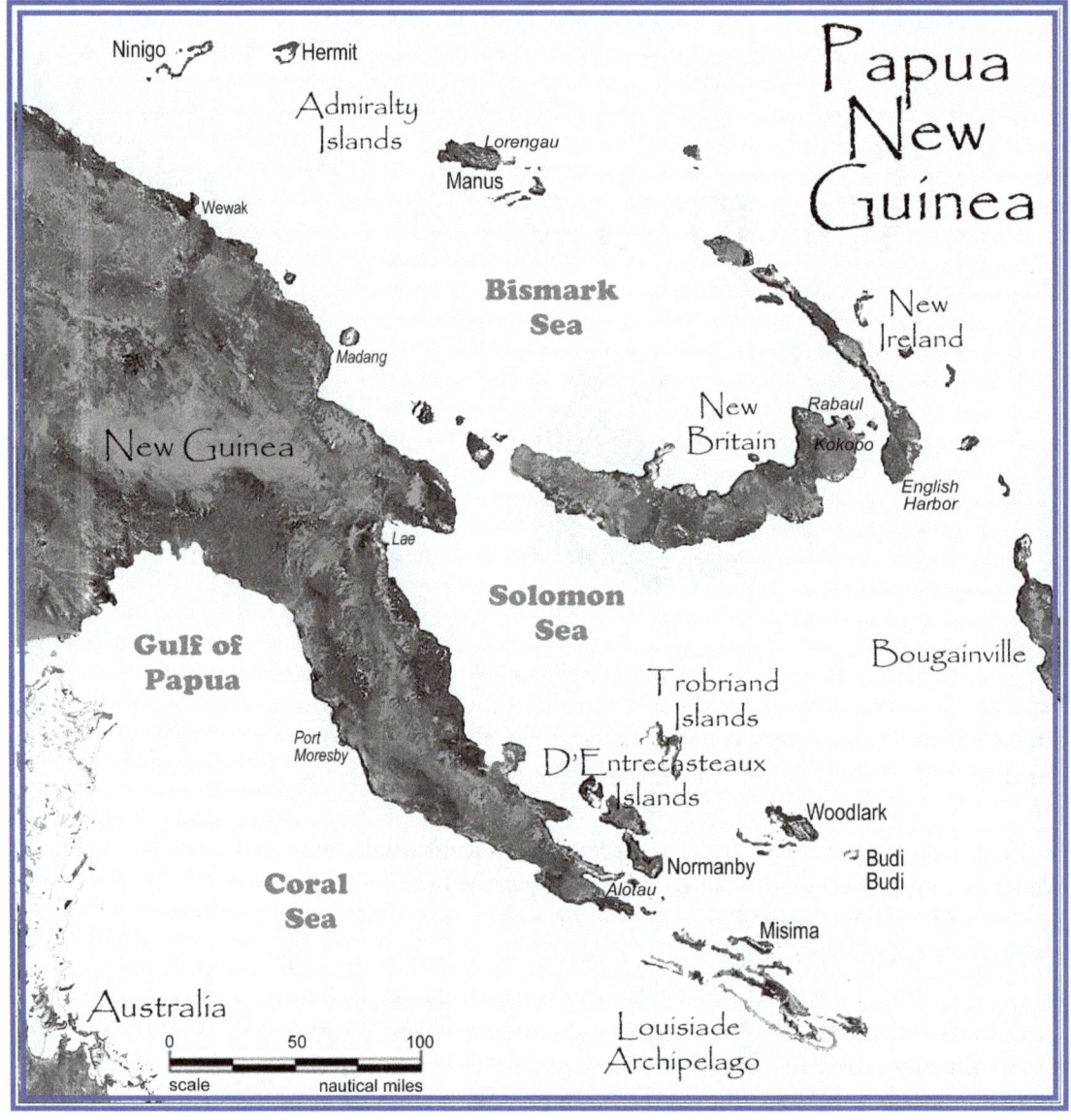

agenda. We are going to find out whether anything remains of the Kula Ring.

Only anthropologists know much of the Kula Ring. It takes some explaining, for nothing like the vast, centuries-old traditional social and economic order practiced in a hundred or so islands scattered over thousands of square miles of ocean exists elsewhere. Nobody knows how this extraordinarily complex miracle of primitive human organization and self-recognition started. No one even knows the purpose of the Kula Ring, or whether it could be significant that it exists among islands that once formed part of the great southern continent and thus were already populated when the ancestors of Aborigines reached Australia 40,000–60,000 years ago.

The island groups of the d'Entrecasteaux, the Trobriands, the Woodlarks, Misima, and the Engineers—to give them their foreign names—together with a myriad of smaller islands within this 50,000 square mile area, constitute the Ring. Canoes circulate between the islands carrying hogs and dogs, clay pots and vegetables, betel nut, clothes, and trading goods

From time to time different expeditions are organized of special canoes built to carry the two Kula items—there are but two. These are supremely the most important voyages. The arrival of a Kula canoe is announced with a great blast on a conch horn. The crew and the reception party are traditionally clad. On board the canoes are either necklaces or arm bracelets, never both. Women in the Louisiades showed us *bagi* necklets and bracelets made from spondylus shell, the principal item of island jewelry. *Soulava*, which is the name for *bagi* of Kula importance, is made of the same raw material, but is longer, perfectly matched and ornately mounted. Thousands of tiny discs of reddish shell are polished, drilled and threaded on a string, attached at one end to a gleaming gold-lip oyster shell, much decorated with whatever is considered rare and colorful, and at the other finished with bright feathers, shells, banana seeds and bush beans.

The arm bracelets, known as *mwali*, are manufactured from the central portion of a huge, white cone shell. This is suspended on a rope, hung with beans that make music as the *mwali* is shaken, and much ornamented.

Neither *soulava* nor *mwali* have economic value. They are not worn. They are not even owned, for they are passed on in an eternal succession of gifts.

Necklaces may only proceed clockwise around the ring, while armbands travel counterclockwise. Exchange is limited to recognized partners and is strictly never a barter deal. A fine necklace, however, merits a special armband in return, and if the recipient does not possess one he will have to wait to make his gift until he can match what he was given. In the meantime he may make a holding gift as a token of his obligation, and this in turn requires a reciprocal gift. The customs surrounding the preparation for a Kula expedition and the gifts' delivery are extraordinarily complex; the negotiation of the deferred exchanges involves cunning, skill and commitment of personal credibility.

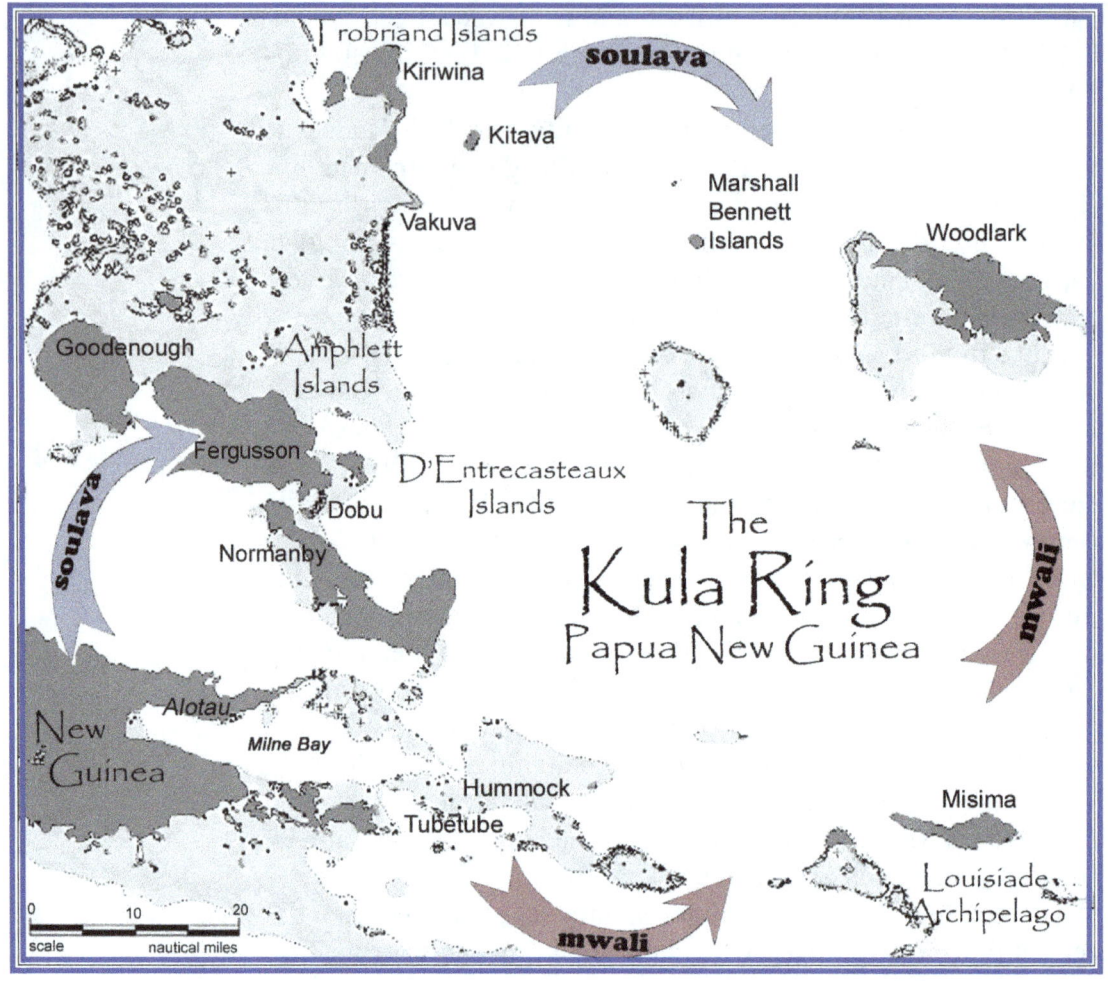

The number of Kula partners a man may have is bound up with status. Sets of obligations bind these partners together, though they may see each other only once in several years. One clear responsibility is the protection of a visiting Kula partner. Others responsibilities concern trading preferences, hospitality, wives, and the intricate webs of magic within which the system operates.

Defense from the flying witches of the south was once an important element; Leo Fortune's work, *The Sorcerers of Dobu* (1932), reveals that these were Dobuan witches. Fortune, an anthropologist from New Zealand and the husband of Margaret Mead, wrote, "The women of Dobu do actually possess...incantations which they believe enable them to fly by night to make mischief, to kill, to dance upon the graves of their former victims, to disinter their victims and in spirit hold ghoulish feasting on them. Meanwhile, the woman as 'an empty skin' stays asleep in her house." Kula endows protection, too, from the various degrees of sorcerers who may wish one harm. Poisoning, and creeping under a house to fumigate the unfortunate target to death with the smoke of toxic herbs, are specialties that may now be fading out. Hospitality remains a crucial obligation.

In 1917, a young Polish nobleman set out to understand the Kula. As a student of the ethnography of New Guinea, he committed three years to living with the natives in Kiriwina, the main island of the Trobriand group. Bronislaw Malinowski published *Argonauts of the Western Pacific* in 1922, and it is from this great anthropological study that I learned about the existence of the Ring before leaving Australia. I could discover no more recent work, nor whether anything is left of this mighty web of human relationships after a further eighty years of church activity, Western intrusion, and a world war blasting through the islands.

Quarantine officer Kingsford and Lennie the Lifter are subdued as we complete formalities in Bwagaoia, their jobs in peril due to the looming closure of Misima's gold mine. Lennie almost forgets to beg a couple of beers to take with him. After a pause to study canoe construction on Panaete, one of two islands where Kula canoes must be made, we duck in and out of the huge Deboyne and Conflict lagoons, using the lee of the many reefs and islets to make good speed with a fine quartering breeze. The night is spent sheltered behind a small island in a lagoon within a lagoon, the sole property of an osprey who demonstrates how easy island living is as he collects his dinner in our little pond, plunging feet-first to emerge with a squirming fish skewered in his talons.

Robin and I are supping on kingfish chowder under the stars when a fire springs up on the nearby beach. Its orange glow silhouettes a big canoe drawn up on the sand. A band of savages can be dimly made out preparing a large cooking pot over their fire of dry coconut shells, around which they start to dance. The fire-lit shadows flicker on the wall of black greenery behind. The beat of tamtams reverberates across the water. A rhythmic chanting rises to accompany it. There is no point in extinguishing our cockpit candles, for *Nereus* is clear in the starlight, and we cannot exit this place in the dark. Trapped, resigned to our fate, we finish supper to be well fattened up when the drumming reaches a crescendo and they come for us.

But all remains calm; in the morning the group of itinerant traders passes the time of day with us most civilly before continuing their voyage.

HUMMOCK ISLAND

After hundreds of miles of shallow water, I should by now be inured to dodging unseen hazards that lurk beneath the waves, but I'm not. The next bit of the route is extravagant, bristling with reefs everywhere, and the charts don't agree just where. Chickening out with five extra, cautiously sailed, miles to avoid a particularly evil bit of sea, eyes strained from staring into the water for indications of coral, we arrive with relief at Hummock Island, reputed to have a sheltered anchorage. It does, but our approach takes us to the wrong side, to be faced by a wide, unbroken coral shelf separating us from the calmer water.

Two men see our dilemma and paddle to our aid. Tying their canoe alongside, they climb aboard to pilot us over half a mile of shoals with scarcely a foot of water under the boat, the coral as clear as we glide over it as if the water did not exist. Solomon's hair is frizzy and graying. His weather-beaten face cracks into deep laughter lines as he tells of past shipwrecks on his reef. He promises lobsters in the morning.

A younger man, Romulus, paddles out soon after the anchor is set, his ebony frame a silhouetted shadow against the pale turquoise of the reef. "You must come to my fundraising tomorrow," he says. "I kill a pig, and the women make a big meal for all the village." His voice drops to the quiet tone the villagers use when they are about to ask for something. "Maybe you give something for each plate, a kina or something."

Ashore at the appointed hour, due to the usual lack of any real sense of island time we find it's far too early. The pig has just been killed and put in the pot with our onions, but the yams, plantains and kumara have not yet arrived from the garden. So we are introduced around the village, a neat well-constructed array of one-room houses on stilts built of palm and pandanus on a spit of fine sand.

Edward introduces himself. "I am councilor for this village," he says. I welcome you very much."

He bears himself with the sort of noble dignity Malinowski described, so after a formal response I grab the opportunity to ask, "Do you have any Kula trade things?"

"You want to see?" He indicates we should follow to his house, ducks inside and emerges after a moment with a necklace. "I have no *mwali* now, but this is a fine *soulava* necklace."

Indeed it is. A long chain of beautifully matched shell discs of about one-quarter-inch in diameter is decorated with turtleshell, black banana seeds and little glass trade beads of rainbow colors.

Edward confirms the continuing health of the Kula, and several villagers are eager to claim they take part in Kula trade, though lacking any Kula treasures at present. Kula clearly confers status. The right arm of their trade is with Woodlark, an isolated island four days' journey to the northeast, and the left is Normanby, one of the three large islands in the d'Entrecasteaux Group about fifty miles to the northwest. Arm bracelets arrive from Normanby and continue on to Woodlark, while necklaces proceed the other way.

Edward's soulava, Hummock Island

On the beach are two sailing canoes, purchased with pigs and kastom money from Panaete. "It take about fifteen good pigs in exchange for a canoe," Solomon says. This highlights the value of pigs, for seagoing canoes take plenty of skill and time to build, and the price includes the rigging and sails, cunningly crafted from rice bags.

Sitting in the shade on a mat under Romulus's house, waiting patiently for the cooks to complete their task, I am abruptly assailed by a nasty feeling in my gut. It gets rapidly worse. Tendering hurried excuses, I run for it. I'm immobilized for the rest of the afternoon. Despite an extraordinarily diverse diet as we eat our way through island provender, this is the only instance of a stomach upset in my Pacific years. We send a contribution to the fundraising, which totals more than K600, about US$200, a handsome sum for a largely cashless economy, but miss the party. This is fortunate in one way: It saves us from being entirely consumed by Hummock's no-see-ums, for we discover next day that we have been severely bitten. The people who live in a paradise marred by these pernicious sand flies seem to have developed an immunity.

The Kula Ring

Solomon once more pilots us out over the shoals; we thread between two small islands intriguingly charted as Good and Deedes and on through the lovely Engineer group to Tubetube, which I know from Malinowski to have been the hub of the southern region of the Kula, its trading partnerships fanning out to seven other islands. Yet it's a modest village, where we are taken in hand by Barbara who is tending a large flock of pikininis like a shepherdess. One is sent to fetch a *soulava* necklace for us to photograph. Before she permits us to handle it, we must first spend some time insisting that we are not trying to take it away. Though without any cash value, it is the most precious thing they will ever have.

After a squally night of dreadful itching from the no-see-um weals peppering our skin, we leave at dawn for Alotau, toward the tonsils of the deep Milne Bay which is shaped like open crocodile jaws. This will be our only landfall on the big island of PNG, the world's last land of undiscovered tribes, New Guinea. There is a line of flood water a mile or two off the coast, the navy blue waters of the deep bay threatened by an encroaching muddy green stain pregnant with old coconuts and dangerous trees washed down from mountain forests. A procession of angry, black clouds marching down the peninsula confirms it is rainy season, with little of the sun to be seen for many days.

ALOTAU

Tropical towns are not at their best under tropical rain. Some of Alotau's roads are paved, so it's almost possible to avoid large muddy puddles and flash flooding across the streets as we try to stock up at the few stores catering to the hundred thousand square miles of the Western Province of PNG, which is not connected by road with any other. People and trade travel by ship, or very occasionally by air. At the hospital on the hill, Robin asks if anyone can fix up her shoulder, painfully dislocated by an over-enthusiastic attempt to start a recalcitrant outboard. Despite shortages of most things, the hospital seems efficiently run. In return for the princely sum of two kina, less than one US dollar, a Filipino woman doctor x-rays her shoulder and then straps her up while I read notices in Pijin, like this on AIDS: NAMBA WAN TOKTRU. YUMI MAS LUKAUTIM GUT OL HUSAT I KISIM HIV PINIS (Number one fact/requirement. We must take good care of all who get HIV.)

We have come to Alotau to meet Esther and Joe Yabon, at the introduction of Gordon Steege. One of the Royal Australian Air Force's Hurricane aces in the war against the Nazis, Gordon was subsequently stationed in the western islands of PNG, fighting the invading Japanese and eventually helping to boot them out of New Guinea. After the war he'd returned to these eastern islands as an administrator.

Esther and Joe, who both work for the provincial government, arrive at the quayside after the 4:06 P.M. end of the office day. The rain overwhelms our attempt to keep the dinghy passengers dry with golf umbrellas, so we are a dripping huddle in the saloon as we present Esther with a flowery dress sent by Gordon, and a pretty dirndl for her daughter.

Joe's family is from the d'Entrecasteaux islands, where rather confusing matrilineal customs rule. In many South Seas islands, through a path of events long hidden by passing years, succession has come to be through the female line only. Joe explains that this tradition, which concerns both possessions and duties, is much more than the converse of male inheritance. The maternal uncle is the important figure to any young person. In a family of husband, wife, daughter and son, the mother and father inherit the possessions and status of the mother's maternal uncles. The children get their inheritance from their mother's brothers. In turn, the son of the family, who hopes to marry well himself, is duty bound to support his sister's family, who will eventually inherit whatever he has. The father of the family, while having if he wishes a loving relationship with his children, has only secondary responsibility for them. All duties, all hope of inheritance, the finding of the school fees, fall on the brothers of the mother.

"Gordon told me you managed to send your three eldest to university," I say, reflecting on this system. "Surely this should be the duty of Esther's brothers?"

"Yes, because I must look after my sister's children. But I am lucky that I can do this and provide something for my own children too. Esther's brothers have not been in employment, so they couldn't help much. Maybe with the present generation it is starting to fade away a bit, but now the tradition of doing things this way is still quite strong. If my nephew comes to my house, he can do whatever he wants, for everything belongs to him."

Baling a foot of rainwater out of the dinghy, I drop our laundry ashore in the morning for Esther's sister to do at the rare washing machine in the government resthouse. A Trobriand islander, Jacob,

Trobriand carver, Alotau

is waiting on the quayside with a carving that he's keen to turn into cash. "I am here with my brother as guardians of my uncle, who we have taken to the hospital, and now we have to go home to Kiriwina, all three of us."

"Why is your uncle in the hospital?" I inquire as we motor out to *Nereus* in the dinghy.

"He fell out of a coconut tree."

"But in Kiriwina it is your uncle who should be looking out for you."

"Yes, but he is only nine years old," came the reply. "I have two uncles, the other one is younger, and my mother and father have passed away."

Jacob is twenty, and now the head of the family. I don't haggle much over his superb ebony crocodile drum, and he's very happy with the price of three fares back home.

Another Jacob produces a *bagi* of good enough quality but not mounted with the beans and shells that would make it a Kula *soulava*. "I made this one myself for my auntie," he says. "It took me three months and two weeks' work. Now she give it back to me to sell so she can give something for my boy's school fee. You see, she don't have money."

When Robin's birthday comes around, the *bagi* will be her present along with a promise to have it set as a necklace once we reach the workshops of Southeast Asia, so that it will be possible to wear it proudly. Not one person in a million will recognize it as more than a primitive trinket, but we will know differently.

Pina is very disappointed that we turn down his turtle bowl on the quayside, but, not daunted, rents a seriously leaky canoe without a paddle and recruits Tom, who has long hippy hair and incessantly chews betel nut, to help him paddle out with their hands. Fortunately, Tom has to stay in the canoe, baling furiously with half a plastic coke bottle and spitting streams of red betel juice over the side like a fire hose while Pina climbs on board with his work.

"Now I bring my stonefish," he says. "It too big and heavy to take around, and I not sell it for long time. So I offer you very good price if you want to take it." He unwraps the stonefish, a five-pound chunk of polished ebony, cunningly carved, lavishly inlaid with nautilus shell and wonderfully ugly as all stonefish must be. It's not cheap. But in view of the time, skill and artistry of the carvers and their need to realize cash for hospital and school fees as well as fares for the boat home, no deal for a figure in ebony or rosewood is regretted. When we quit Alotau, we find we've spent a lot of our reserves on carvings. And we're still headed for the Trobriand Islands where they all came from.

BOIA BOIA WAGA

As we are motor-sailing thirty miles eastward along the upper jaw of Milne Bay before we can turn north, an Australian advises us on the VHF to hang a left through a channel at the end of the cape to save a few miles. He's captain of a local boat on charter to some macho gold miners fishing their way to a mine on an island a couple of hundred miles out and appears to know these waters.

An hour later we swing to port into a narrow cut separating a small island from the eastern extremity of New Guinea. The tide is running strongly against the wind, folding the sea back on itself into short, hollow surf like the roughened top of an iced cake.

Creeping cautiously along the passage, unsure of the advice and unable to see through the surface agitation, we are horrified to feel *Nereus* ground on coral. Though eyes are useful to work out what is about to happen on a boat, it's other senses that announce an emergency. A grounding vibrates right through your bones, and your soul itself shudders at the horrible crunch signaling that your universe is threatened. Fear is a taste.

Only when I've killed the motor and the ship has juddered to a halt do our eyes start to register the rough lee shore close by, and the hazy topography of the coral entrapping us. It's a maze of shallow reef wherever we look.

We don't have to tell each other there is no hope of outside help. Or that there's no time to waste.

"Check the tide," I shout to Robin as I leap over the side to inspect the bottom, both ours and the ocean's, and to see if there is a way to try to work her clear. Unlike rock or sand bottom, coral develops in a higgledy-piggledy fashion, requiring careful planning to regain deeper water. With a mask I can plot narrow corridors between the coral growths, and, a few yards to port, a marginally deeper channel leading north. Robin pops up on deck as I climb back on board. "So far as I can work it out it's around half tide, and ebbing," she says, a little shakily. "But at least there's not much tide here, about three feet maybe." Neither of us is much worried that our stalwart steel keel is damaged. Yet a falling tide threatens rapidly increasing problems. Even a couple of inches fall in the water level will leave us stuck fast, at the mercy of the remainder of the tidal drop and whatever the weather throws at us.

The narrow gut in which we're grounded connects two huge bodies of water; there's a powerful tidal current from aft pressing us into the reef. Outcrops of coral color the water in every direction, a labyrinth we must thread the keel through for a chance of floating her off.

I fire up the bowthruster to try to force *Nereus* sideways off the bommie and across the current. The small movements are not enough to prevent the tide pressing us against another big bommie to starboard. More horrid grinding sounds. "Let go the furling line!" Robin yells. With the line released the genoa is allowed to set half way. "Now back the sail," I shout back. She grabs the clew of the sail and hauls it to windward while I turn the windward sheet on to a winch. This has the effect of turning the bow a little and, more usefully, giving us a few degrees of heel. With full reverse and the bowthruster going while Robin calls directions *Nereus* judders, hold again then slides clear for a moment. "Not that way, No! Watch the red one. Back! Back!" Robin's orders to me at the helm come thick and fast. Nereus grounds again and holds fast. "Now put her in forward with the helm to starboard," she cries. With the wheel hard over the boat crabs and judders a few yards this way and that. She bounces two or three time. Then she comes free.

There's still only a few inches under the keel, and coral all around. Using the sail, engine and thruster we maneuver Nereus between the obstacles to the channel. Switching to just enough astern engine to keep her stern to the current, she's pushed by the falling tide as slowly as we can manage the remaining three hundred feet to clear water. The gut still spits us out like a cork from a bottle.

A Californian friend in New Zealand, apprised of this grounding, reassures us: "There are only 2 kinds of real cruisers: those that have hit a reef, and those that will."

Further off East Cape and its shoal waters lies uninhabited Boia Boia Waga Island. From its white girdle of fine sand, a pair of coral horns extends half a mile to the north. Between them is a calm bay where we lay the anchor on a shallow sandy bottom and reach for a restorative drink, hugging each other in huge relief. Examination of the hull amid a covey of multicolored squid reveals a modern masterwork of paint scratches, but not enough damage to warrant hauling *Nereus* before we reach Borneo, many months later.

Jogging next morning around the island beach in torrential rain, I pass a couple of men from the mainland huddled in a flimsy leaf shelter with their canoe drawn up in front. I wave—it's too wet and noisy to socialize—imagining them rubbing their eyes at the sight of a mad, near-naked *dim-dim* wafting out of nowhere on an empty island, running, and vanishing again into the curtain of rain without a word.

"You seen that *dim-dim* ghost there?"

"Gimme more betel nut, quick!"

After our near shipwreck I feel a bit like a ghost.

The channel between Boia Boia Waga and the neighboring reef is a mecca for big pelagic fish, including the world's largest, the *butanding* or whale-shark. Swimming with these leviathans is like diving on a submarine, too large to estimate the length, which can be upward of forty feet. The tail of one is half again as tall as me. The perfectly evolved creatures, unchanged for a million years, are beautiful. White spots are spread in neat rows across the black skin of their upper bodies and, underneath, their pure white hide is like 50-grit sandpaper. Before sandpaper, sharkskin

Whale shark

The Kula Ring

actually served as an abrasive. Fortunately, the largest of their favorite snacks is a shrimp, for I meet one just below the surface, up close and personal enough to feel her shagreen, stroke her four-foot-wide mouth, and be favored with the biggest kiss in the world.

NORMANBY

The light breeze is just enough to fill the sails across the calm sea to Normanby Island as the sun at last breaks through. Rounding a small islet, we gingerly feel our way into a bay where Esther has told us that we might find her father, Faiteli. Some canoes come out from the shore to advise us where to anchor, for there is coral all about. As we drift, a silver streak charges across the surface of the smooth bay. It's a long thin fish in high speed pursuit of a flying fish, bouncing as it goes. It doesn't slow down, in apparent defiance of the principles of physics.

"What on earth is that?" I ask no one in particular.

"This fish a long tom," comes a reply from below the rail.

"The yachts always anchor just here," the old man, improbably named Herod, eventually tells us, and we drop the hook on sand under fifty feet of clear water where he points.

"Yes, sailing yacht been here before. I got a photo," Israel, who visits later, says. "Last one was a blue one eight years ago."

Robin whispers a hope that the memory of our visit has such longevity.

Faiteli indeed dwells in the green groves under the tall hills together with his large family, which depending on the time of day is reported as fifteen or nineteen children. He brings his number three wife to see us the following day. His pleasantly battered face expresses experience and certainty. His eyes are alive with a strong twinkle. Our world is alien, and we are guests in his, where he is master. We feel we are Gordon's emissaries with the special task of prolonging a friendship stretching back to 1942. Robin's signature pawpaw pie is much appreciated as we talk of customs, of our travels, of Gordon. Faiteli, whose career was captaining boats in the difficult waters of PNG, is fascinated by our demonstration of electronic charts and GPS, gadgets new to him and amazing to one who has navigated some of the world's most difficult seas for fifty years without modern tools.

"We are new here," Faiteli apologizes. "So we cannot give you food from our garden, which is producing nothing yet. You see, I lived in Alotau till now, and I have just come back to my village to make a new home."

"Many canoes have come to *Nereus* bringing food," I reply, "so I thank you but we are not in need of anything. But I think you can tell us about Kula."

"Ah, yes. How long you stay? Okay, tomorrow I show you good Kula."

Underwater, the bay is a miraculous garden. Rare species abound, like the panda and white-bonnet clown anemone fish, extraordinary ghost pipefish—which disguise themselves as almost anything that grows from the bottom—multicolored feather dusters, and a solitary fire urchin like a psychedelic flying saucer sitting on the sand a hundred feet down. The polyps of a white coral, for once out and feeding by day, are a bed of a million flowers in shades of white and brown. Though fully two inches long, they slowly retract into their limestone base when disturbed, turning what was seconds before a magic carpet to solid rock. I despair of describing these things, for perhaps only those privileged to have dived in the richest tropical seas can picture the wonder of it. And we have the bonus of being in New Guinea, for here are found five times as many species as in the entire Caribbean. Many believe the Red Sea the real thing, but in east PNG's prolific waters there are more than twice as many sponges, corals, nudibranchs, fish and the rest. New creatures are discovered regularly, and it's likely we have encountered many as yet unclassified. Four hundred thirty species of coral have been identified in the Milne Bay province of PNG alone, and more than 1,100 species of fish. Lots of the fish are certainly absent from our best book, which illustrates more than 2,000. Richard Pyle, ichthyologist at Honolulu's excellent Bishop Museum, recently claimed he was discovering new species at a rate of seven per hour in these waters. Some fail to resemble fish at all, including such wonders as the leaf scorpionfish and the lacy scorpionfish, the tomato anemone fish, a shark that looks like a frilly doily called the tasseled wobbegong, and the ribbon eel, waving like bright blue seagrass from its burrow in the sand. The giant clams' mantles are astonishing, webs of every shade of blue or green, and there are all sorts of sea horses in the turtlegrass.

In the early morning, a dive boat hooks up to a tree on a point a mile out from us. Stopping by on our way to dive on an isolated outer reef, to our delight we discover that it's *Telita*, captained by Bob Halstead, author of the only book about PNG waters we have aboard and the leading expert on local seas and everything under them. He tells us he has made around eight thousand dives in these waters and signs a book of his own startling photos, taken over thirty years of Coral Sea diving. Aboard *Telita* is the Shark Lady, Dr. Eugenie Clark, American doyenne of shark experts, still relentlessly diving and researching despite being now in her eighties.

Later, Faiteli, Janie and Israel paddle out once more, handing up a well-wrapped package.

"I have brought you my Kula necklaces," Faiteli says. "These are *soulava*."

The parcel is unpacked and the contents hung from a rail, one by one.

The centerpiece, the value in a *soulava*, is the *bagi* chain. All else, the six-inch oyster-shell from which it is hung, the delicate beadwork, the feathers and red plastic disks, the ancient white cowrie shells, is icing on the cake, like the intricate setting of a great precious stone. Shell for the *bagi* comes only from two far-flung islands, each instantly recognized by an expert. Red is best. The chain of shell discs must be of even color, between three and five millimeters in diameter, less than a millimeter thick, and each disk on a chain must be precisely the same size so that the outside of the chain feels as smooth as an eel. These days it would be possible to manufacture a *bagi* replica by machine for almost nothing in a Far East workshop, and indeed if a plain one was worn in London or New York it would be thought a beach trinket, a memory of seaside holiday. The real *bagi* for *soulava*, however, takes a man (custom decrees that it is only the men who may make it) an enormous amount of fine work to produce, acquiring the shell from far away, breaking and cutting it, grinding it round and thin, polishing and drilling it, matching the pieces and threading them.

We admire Faiteli's *soulava* generously.

"How many Kula partners do you have?" I ask.

He runs through them, counting on his fingers. "Woodlark, Tubetube, Kitava, Boyowa..." They amount to more than a dozen. "One of the big ones is John Kasaipwalova on Kiriwina," he says. "You must go see him and show him the pictures you are taking of my *soulava*."

Faiteli grins wickedly at the envy this will arouse in his old friend. He reaches once more into the package and with a flourish draws out a *mwali*, the shell arm bracelet that is the counterweight to the *soulava*, the first we've seen. It is a magnificent piece too. Around the large polished arm bracelet carved out of the middle girth of a huge white cone shell is a confection of everything considered valuable. Some elderly one-inch hemp rope holds it together, jangly nuts hang from it, and tiny trade-beads are cunningly interwoven with shells and seeds.

"This is Tomanboitomanguadi," Faiteli says with obvious pride. "Maybe it is one of the highest *mwali* in the Kula; everybody knows Tomanboitomanguadi. You must show John a photo of this one. You tell him I got it and he will be very mad with me."

Faiteli's Kula collection

I am starting to appreciate that the Kula tradition remains strong, but that, since the days when it functioned as a safety network, it has evolved into a friendly and competitive sort of exclusive club. The ritual is largely maintained when a blast on a conch shell announces the approach of a Kula canoe, and hospitality is guaranteed. By skillful negotiation and careful exchange the possessor of a Kula item—it has no owner as it is forever in transit—can upgrade his participation a little at a time. The highest *soulava* and *mwali* are named and known all around the Kula Ring, their whereabouts the subject of swirling rumors or carefully planted leaks.

AR with Tomanboitomanguadi

"When I go to a Kula friend, I don't pay anything," Faiteli says. "He give me pig, *kaikai*, whatever I want. When he come to see me, same thing."

Israel unconsciously delivers a lesson in the workings of the matrilineal system. Dropping his voice to the usual confidential tone when something is wanted, he says, "Andrew, can you help me? You see I have this problem."

I have heard this opening line hundreds of times, and wait to discover what shortage we will

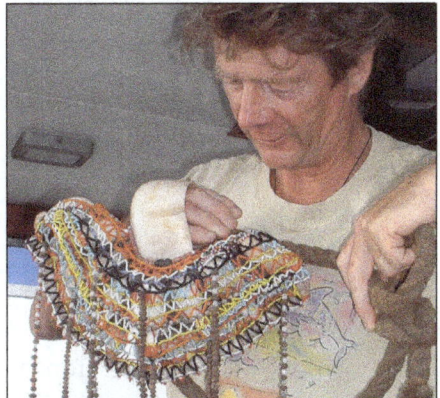

The Kula Ring

279

be asked to make good. But this is different; intellectual rather than material assistance is needed.

"I have this problem with generations, and I must provide something for the court," he says.

He unfolds a much-creased sheet of stained paper on which are listed several dozen names amid a spider's web of lines. I eventually understand that what Israel actually wants is for me to consult my computer and check his family tree for him, for he must provide evidence of his ancestry to resolve a land dispute. He expects the computer to contain all the necessary information to achieve this and is awfully disappointed when I explain that it has not yet been taught this history and is unable to help him. I do, however, extract and print a family tree for him from the paper, showing his direct descent over twelve generations from 1891. There seems a lot of generations, an average of under ten years for each, especially considering he is in his fifties, but I dutifully type up the genealogy for him. All the names on the list are women, for men have no place in the succession. Island genealogies are everywhere important and highly valued, for tradition, family, inheritance and status all hang thereon. Some genealogies penetrate deep into the mists of the past, often linking the present back to the demigods of legend.

I feel I am holding the precious secret of a Melanesian Abraham:

Lewasagi
Sineyalayala
Yasinelei
Leboiyala
Sineutea
Yasimosane
Inanilemu
Neisedi
Lemaimai
Yawani
Abemai

The explanation for the large number of names might be the succession of sisters at various points, but neither Israel nor the paper can confirm this hunch.

Before we depart Faiteli's lovely bay, we think we see Queen Alexandra's bird-wing fluttering past, the world's largest butterfly, flying like a dove. Moths around our light at night are as big as two blacksmith's hands spread out. Nearly all the world's forty varieties of birds of paradise are from New Guinea too—there is even one on the national flag—but these tend to live in the mountains and we have no time to seek them out. A variety of sea-hawks decorate the sky; the upper wing feathers of one kite are the rich russet of sunshine on autumn bracken. Over the beach at twilight flap the black shadows of the New Guinea flying fox, at more than five feet wide probably the world's largest bat.

DOBU

Dobu, the island of flying witches, is a perfect little cone volcano, apparently extinct but still exuding streams of gas from some shallow underwater vents in which one can take an ocean bubble bath, though the sulphurous fizz has an evil fragrance. Dobu commands the strait separating the two largest d'Entrecasteaux islands of Normanby and Fergusson, the pivot of the Kula Ring and a strategic position the Dobuans used to advantage. Malinowski explained:

> From this island, in olden days, fierce and daring cannibal and headhunting expeditions were periodically launched, to the dread of the neighboring tribes. The natives of the immediately surrounding districts, of the flat foreshore on both sides of the straits, and of the big neighboring islands were allies. But the more distant districts, often over a hundred miles away by sail, never felt safe from the Dobuans.

We are taken in hand by Jenevi, the lady pastor whose large mission school occupies the sandy spit close by. Grade three children strike up in welcome, to the tune of "Here we go round the mulberry bush":

The school triton bell, Dobu

Yumi go round de pawpaw tree,
de pawpaw tree, de pawpaw tree,
yumi go round de pawpaw tree…

Pijin thrives on the smallest possible number of root words. You-me, *yumi*, does service for both "we" and "us."

The Kula Ring

281

Long-drops at Dobu

Several families in Dobu, a major Kula center, possess *soulava* and *mwali*. The traditions, however, seem to be weakening in some respects. Kula men no longer bother to dress in traditional pubic leaf, nor the ladies in grass skirts—both of which in the old days always had to be sparkling new for a Kula arrival. Nor can we find anywhere a proper oceangoing sailing canoe highly decorated for Kula, though people say there is one in some far-off village—mebbee.

We dive off *Nereus*, for the sea is clear and the coral looks good. Right below the boat a cluster of lionfish hovers motionless by a coral spur, their extraordinary fins hung out like the feathers of barnyard hens in a fluster, serving to conceal venomous spines. I am pestered for half an hour by a little remora, a sleek black-and-white suckerfish with a pad on the top of its flat head by which it tries to attach itself to my air bottle in the hope of scraps as I feast on other fish.

Lionfish

Reach for Paradise

AMPHLETTS

North of the d'Entrecasteaux Islands lies a small group of rocky islets called the Amphletts, famed for the making of clay pots. They have no clay, however. It has to be fetched fifty miles from Fergusson Island, one of the d'Entrecasteaux. Such is the specialization in New Guinea, what has been made in one village for hundreds of years is still made, and the next village will not challenge a monopoly or even consider it is something they might get into. Fergusson provides the clay, but does not manufacture pots. A careful look at the chart reveals about a hundred miles of nerve-wracking shoal-girt passages if we were to route via the Amphletts to Kiriwina in the Trobriands, our next target. I regret this, for the women of the islands make these clay pots by hand, without a wheel. Thin, strong and finely decorated, they are renowned far and wide.

"A woman of the Amphletts who does not learn to make good clay pots will not find a husband," Jenevi says. The Amphletts became a trading *entrepôt* on the basis of their clay pots, which were exported throughout the Kula area. "The whole gives a feeling of perfection and elegance, unparalleled in any South Sea pottery I know," wrote Malinowski.

The alternative course is well out to the east, an overnight sail through an expanse of ocean shown by the charts as "unsurveyed." Though the water looks deep enough, the area is full of *vigias*, shoals or discolored water reported some time over the past century and a half, but whose existence remains unconfirmed. We set out in a mild southeasterly, which quickly increases to twenty-five knots, driving us north faster than expected. At two o'clock in the morning, we nose gingerly into a shallow indentation in the straight coast where the radar indicates the village of Kaibola might be. As we are closing the beach, a squall hits the island and lashing rain obliterates everything. There are distant shouts and a signal fire on the beach, and someone in a canoe strikes a few matches. With no indication whether this signifies help to an anchorage or imminent danger, we retreat to open water, close down the engine and await dawn, drifting idly to the west.

First light reveals a canoe already expecting us, well out to sea. Lukas introduces himself, ties his canoe astern, and pilots us to a narrow strip of sand anchorage just outside the reef fringing the beach in his bay. We would not easily have found this spot by ourselves, even in daylight.

KIRIWINA

Scepters carved in Kiriwina

Eyes are watching from the bush. Carvers from far and wide observe our approach. The coconut wireless is buzzing: "A boat with *dim-dim*s is come in." The canoe line starts to build. Pleading fatigue, we arrange a "sight"—the diamond term seems appropriate—on shore after lunch. Asking prices are quite high, but the carvings are exquisite. Each is the product of hundreds of hours of skilled whittling and inlaying, working the beautiful grain of classic ebony, queen ebony, rosewood or kerosin. The succession of canoes continues while we remain in Kaibola. Each time we land, more carvers lie in wait at the top of the beach, often having journeyed many hours to seek us out. These are bush people, who seem to be looked down on by our new friends dwelling on the strand. Their supreme carving skill is not reflected in language ability; I guess most have learned to carve instead of attending school. It is heartrending to have to disappoint them, for we are the only *dim-dim*s on the island, again the sole market outlet for local wares.

With the day's trading completed, we walk inland along the narrowing remains of a wartime military road, one often traveled by Gordon in his days commanding a fighter-bomber wing in the island half a century earlier, five squadrons operating against the Japanese from two Kiriwina airfields, with their thousands of personnel. "The forward airbase at Kiriwina," Gordon explained, "was developed as essential for refueling of US Lightning fighters from the mainland of PNG to enable them to escort the raids of 100 B24 bombers, which eliminated Japanese offensive capability from their huge base at Rabaul. MacArthur was then able to bypass Rabaul and land in the Admiralty Islands."

A quarter of an hour inland lies Kaibola proper, a village I delightedly recognize as sprung to life from the woodcuts and engravings to be found in the earliest printed stories of South Seas exploration. A tightly clustered group of

Kaibola

sleeping huts, thatched in many layers of unruly pandanus and with walls of woven leaf, is interspersed higgledy-piggledy with open-sided day-huts containing platforms three feet off the ground where people with little to do perch on colorful woven mats, passing the time. Store huts have walls of thin poles spaced apart to let the wind blow through, while the occasional yam houses are tall, elegant structures of logs laid alternately on adjoining sides, topped by a fine carved roof befitting the storage of Melanesia's most venerated produce. The ground is beaten earth. Round about, green bush presses in on all sides. Chickens and pigs roam freely.

A letter arrives for us, apparently from the Chief:

To Whom Concern
Kaibola Village
Principle Resource Owner

Dear Sir

I principle Resource Own and chief of the village, Mr Tony Taori, would warmly WELCOME you to my village island. Please you are invited to make your holidays here and see my people etc. My son is there with your note, just to come for a honor visit to me and village. I am old to come over to your yacht, please forgive.

Thanks – T Taori

Lukas, who has appointed himself our minder, cautions us against the chief's son, Buonamata, the bearer of the note to *Nereus*, who wasted no time in asking for a contribution of rice, flour and money "for a memorial feast in a village an hour's walk away."

"This Buoni no good," warns Lukas. "He always ask people for something with some reason. He keep it for himself. You got to watch out for him."

As Buoni is seated in the village on our arrival, the afternoon of the memorial feast, it is likely that our rice and flour—we had jibbed at the money—has traveled no further than his kitchen.

Lukas, as the old chief's senior nephew on his sister's side, is in line to be chief, something we imagined Buoni might resent, though we are told this is normal. Buoni's reputation is corroborated by many people, including a delightful family who live in a huddle of leaf houses by our beach.

"He is a con man," says our closest neighbor, Emanuel, without pulling any punches about the son of his chief. "He is always trying to get something from the *dim-dim*s who stop here with some story which is not true."

Boki comes by in a canoe to ask if we can give him a lift to Rabaul. He is also a son of chief Tony.

We explain that it will take four days to get there, which doesn't discourage him. We ask whether he has any seagoing experience.

"I worked on a boat," he replies. "I was steward on a passenger boat so I have been on the sea plenty time."

I check him out with Emanuel, who grins. "You know, Boki is the same as Buoni, he is con man too. I laugh because when he worked on this boat, he was sent away after short time for taking the things from the passengers."

As I had indicated to Boki that we would take him and he would accordingly have the run of the boat for several days, this was bad news.

We have now been in betel nut country for a while. When Emanuel dips into his *bilum*, the colored raffia bag everyone carries, and digs out a nut, instead of banning chewing on the boat as usual, I quiz him how the various ingredients of a good chew come together.

"First, we have to make the lime," he says. "This is a very white coral, which we wrap up in coconut leaves and cook on the fire for a day. Then we leave it about a month. When we come to take it, is a white powder like this."

He shows me his small lime-pot full of fine white powder with a little spatula attached. Then he selects a nut, shucks off the rind and puts it in his mouth.

Chief Tony, Boki and AR

"We use a little of the lime, you see how it changes the nut," he says.

Indeed, we see the nondescript nut is going bright red. "Then we eat some mustard. It doesn't matter if it the root or the leaf or the seed of the mustard."

He shoves a few leaves in to join the mastication process now well under way, and looks happy. "It make me feel good, and not like some people I don't spit it out and make mess around the place."

It is apparent from our books that the routine of betel nut chewing is unchanged from the first voyage to these islands by the Europeans in the sixteenth century, and no one knows how old beyond that. Antique lime-pots come in gold, pearl and ebony, elaborately crafted. Early European travelers recorded that the natives wore no clothes at all, but always carried lime-pots. There's a twelfth-century Sanscrit text that lists betel nut as one of the nine enjoyments of life, along with unguents, incense, women, clothes, music, sleep, food and flowers. Much earlier, in the sixth century, it was written that "betel stimulates passion, brings out the physical charm, conduces to good luck, lends aroma to the mouth, strengthens the body, and dispels diseases arising from the phlegm." It's almost as comprehensive a panacea as the noni. But they omitted to mention that it turns teeth black, and rots them.

We are not in Kiriwina long enough to form a view about girls' morals, research that Robin would have banned despite my cogent arguments about its anthropological value. I assume missionaries put a stop to the fun they used to have. Malinowski concluded:

> Chastity is an unknown virtue among these natives. At an incredibly early age they become initiated into sexual life, and many of the innocent looking plays of childhood are not as innocuous as they appear. As they grow up they live in promiscuous free love, which gradually develops into more permanent attachments, one of which ends in marriage. Before this is reached, unmarried girls are openly supposed to be quite free to do what they like…

Well before dawn one morning, a raging tempest hits us without warning. As a vicious squall cell moves through, the wind has backed, bringing sheeting rain off an angry sea. We banish sleep and climb up to the cockpit to find water boiling on the rough fringing reef a few yards astern. We are now hanging off a most evil lee shore, the anchor chain wound into coral and the boat yawing and bucking as each threatening wave breaks with a crash, sucking us into the maelstrom. The world is reduced to roaring surf capped with flying froth, the nearby shore invisible though we feel its horrible proximity. We can hardly hear each other shout against the elemental clamor. The depth gauge has dropped from forty to twenty feet, and the GPS shows that we have moved nearer the rocks. With the engine idling, ready to abandon the anchor at any moment, we spend two hours monitoring each few feet of *Nereus'* position, until at last the squall cell moves on and the wind backs to bring her parallel with the reef and out of immediate danger. With sea room, seas however rough do not inspire such dread as this morning's menace of a rocky fate.

Once the capricious ocean is calm and all made safe, another letter over the Chief's name arrives by canoe:

> Sir Please,
>
> I would not be able to come over to your boat, because you may acknowledge my health, as you've met me. I need to come over, however instead, purposively to seek your utmost financial assistance for my need accordingly.
>
> I would need some cash and other items 5 kg rice, 2 kg sugar, 4 tins of meat, oil and flour. Mr Lukas can explain.
>
> Yours T. Taori

I read it aloud to Lukas who, dismayed, can provide no explanation. Puzzling over it, Emanuel thinks it Buoni's letter, and says Chief Tony probably does not even know about it. We don't mention it when Buoni paddles by in the evening, wanting batteries for his son-in-law's underwater flashlight so he can get us a crayfish. Knowing that loaned batteries never come back and the crayfish is unlikely, I lend him a flashlight. As if an afterthought before leaving, he asks Robin to pay one of his children's school fees. We let it all go for the moment, determined to make our thoughts plain to old Chief Tony and his grasping sons later.

Stephen's truck is the only public transport on Kiriwina, trundling around the cracked roads with no set schedule, the back festooned with people clinging on like burrs. An hour's drive along the military road brings us to Bweka, the house of John Kasaipwalova, to whom we bear messages.

Greeted courteously by John and his Chinese wife Mary, we are seated on a verandah of his house, which, though huge by local standards, was built in nineteen days flat, he tells us, for a meeting of Melanesian prime ministers and foreign secretaries in 1998. John is a poet, a playwright, and another old friend of Gordon.

"We will have many things to talk about," he says gravely, after chatting a while. "But, first, would you like to refresh yourselves in my cave?"

We follow him a short distance through the lush garden and twenty feet down a steep coral path into a declivity where he leaves us in front of the entrance to a high-ceilinged, natural grotto. The light is pouring in onto crystal clear water, and stalactites drip from the roof. Robin hears me exclaim that it is the most perfect natural swimming pool I've ever seen. It looks like a place of much magic for John's clan, which he confirms when we rejoin him. We strip off and swim naked in the soft water for a long while, lit by reflected ripples on the ancient stone.

Along the road we passed several picture-book villages with people walking purposefully between them, the ladies carrying packages on their heads and the men bearing yams, bananas and coconuts hung from a stick slung across their shoulders, milkmaid fashion. I ask John about the huge baskets burdening some of the women, fully five or six feet wide and three in height, sagging outward from their heads so they can only see a little ground around their feet.

"Ah, these are the *sagali* baskets," he replies. "They hold money."

"How do you mean, money?" I ask.

"Banana leaves. This is the currency in the villages. The women use banana leaves for exchange and for buying and paying obligations. They know exactly the exchange rate for kerosene, for fish, pigs or yam."

"But bananas are growing everywhere. Anybody can pick as many as they want."

"No, these have to be the leaves of only one type of banana tree. The people who have these trees sell the raw leaf. Then they are dried and very carefully stamped with a special process and then made into bundles, all laid flat."

He went to fetch some pale dun strips each about an inch wide, bound together in foot-long bunches of a hundred or so, embossed with markings like a stencil.

I couldn't resist it: "So after years of searching," I say, "I have found a spot where money does grow on trees?"

John must have heard the joke before, but he laughs and continues. "When there is a *sagali*, all the women bring their banana money and anything they want to trade, and it becomes a ready-made market. They use the occasion to pay any debts or make gifts. The *sagali* is a ceremonial food distribution usually on the occasion of a memorial feast for someone who has died, and often held months or years after his death, once it has been possible to collect all the food and the gifts that are needed for the *sagali*."

John Kasaipwalova with banana money

I bring John a message from Gordon, with which he is delighted. He answers with an e-mail for me to send off. Then we produce photographs of Faiteli's collection of *soulava* and Tomanboitomanguadi.

"The old bugger," John says, grinning widely. "He has been sitting on these *soulava*, the whole circle has been gummed up." Clearly he has great respect for Faiteli, no pushover in Kula negotiation, but always fair, he says.

After Mary has produced a lunch of yam, rice, green stuff and a dessert of pounded taro, he shares his thoughts. "I think this message you have brought from Faiteli is very important, more important than you can know. There have been some other chiefs who have been trying to mess around with the established partnerships, and some of the *bagi* in Faiteli's possession were given to him by people who are competing for Tomanboitomanguadi. I thought at first he was playing them off against each other by hesitating."

Talking to John, subsequently reading his fine book about Kula, and having assimilated more of Malinowski's *Argonauts*, I begin to appreciate how Kula forms an extraordinarily comprehensive tradition. The customs, myths, magic, history and practice of Kula appear as embracing and intricate as those of the Catholic church, or the rules and habits of Freemasonry. John is a pivotal figure, having inherited the mantle from his uncle Nalubutau. He knows all the main players and through the coconut wireless—his intelligence network—where most of the *soulava* and *mwali* are at any moment. "The jam caused by Faiteli sitting on a pile of *soulava* is echoing on to Woodlark and even Budibudi, which being the eastmost point of the circuit is known as 'the end of the world', where there's a big pile-up of *mwali*."

"You know that these things tend to travel in batches," he explains. "I think what Faiteli has been doing is to collect enough *soulava* to make one or two good baskets. A basket is full when you have five *soulava*. My uncle Nalubutau, the last chief of my clan, was a very important Kula figure, and Faiteli is making one or two baskets of *soulava* that include some necklaces my uncle himself made. He is perhaps going to bring these to his *sagali*."

John generously presents us with his book *Kula*, and inscribes it. "I did not know I had a copy left," he says. "But, just now, I went to find you towels to dry after your bathe in my cave, and there in the linen cupboard was this copy. It is clear to me that you are meant to have it."

"We will treasure this," I tell him.

He is proud to relate that he presented the first copy of *Kula* to the Queen of England.

We are watching people fishing the reef by crushing a poisonous herb from the pea family into the water when Boki arrives. "Has Lukas been telling you stories about me?" He asks.

Robin swallows hard, decides to come clean, and tells him that Lukas said nothing one way or another, but that we checked his references and they were not very good.

She remains admirably forthright while I cower below, fearful of offending the Chief's family in case they put a sorcerer on to us.

"No," Robin says, "we cannot take someone into our home for four days if there is any doubt, so, very sorry, we have decided that we cannot give you a passage to Rabaul."

We both regret not being able to take him, me most of all because this was the first chance of carrying a steward on *Nereus*. Improbable visions of an iced whisky and soda arriving on a silver tray as the sun sinks over the yardarm are abruptly erased.

Later, a canoe with both Buonamata and Boki aboard glides alongside. At the risk of stirring up a hornets' nest of recriminations in the village, I tell them, fairly straight, what we feel, which stimulates weak denials and attempts to put the blame onto our friend Lukas. I have to hope that Lukas can look after himself and that the Buonamata faction will not send the sorcerer after him. John has confirmed that there are still sorcerers around; indeed his eldest brother was poisoned by one. Rather like lawyers in the West, sorcery is a parasitic and self-perpetuating profession, for it is universally agreed that the only way you can combat a sorcerer paid to poison you is to employ another sorcerer in your defense.

Malinowski described how Kiriwina's paramount chiefs built on matrilineal tradition to develop a system worthy of feudal kings. The big chief would take as wives women from the families of lesser chiefs in each of the island districts. He derived great advantage by this, for it became the duty of the brothers of these wives to support him with munificent contributions to his fund of pigs, yams, and custom money. Malinowski estimated that Kiriwina's paramount chief, the chief of the central village of Omarakana, who had (when he researched his book in 1917) sixteen wives, down from forty in older times, commanded by this magnificent ploy more than half of the entire production of the island. This bounty he dispensed as gifts or used for trade. It gave him enormous power.

"I thought the missionaries had stamped polygamy out. How does the church accept that the Chief has several wives?" I ask John.

This turns out to be delicate ground. "No, no," he says. "The early ministers and priests were very hard and tried to change everything, but now they are much more flexible and mold the ways of the church around our traditions. I myself have three wives."

"You mean three wives all at the same time?"

"Yes, you have met Mary, my Chinese wife who is here. In Alotau I have a Trobriand wife, and another Trobriand wife who is here too."

We are invited to attend the piling of the yams, for it's harvest time. This proves a fascinating induction into a living tradition of an ancient culture, as well as an antique illustration of Parkinson's Law.

I am curious about the supreme position yams have in the rituals and traditions of most Pacific islands. "The traditional importance is that of life," John asserts, "for it is yams on which we have survived. I have observed that some people can grow yams, while others with exactly the same soil and seed crop fail; and that this success or failure reflects their ability to do well in life. The people with lots of yams are respected, for it is a matter of care and understanding that makes them successful. The yam house in a village is a sort of social security. It belongs to one family, usually the chief's, and it stores only their yams, but they do not eat the yams, which are kept for people who have no food later in the season when nothing is growing. It is considered wrong to take a yam from your own yam house."

"If you see a painted yam house, it must belong to a chief," he adds. His own splendid yam house, hard by Bweka, is a polychrome pile of interlaced poles under its steep eaves, topped by an elegant roof.

We acquire a giant trevally from a village fisherman, which Lukas smokes overnight. John's cousin, Morris, collects us from the beach in a truck that appears resurrected from the breaker's yard, and drives us to a garden in the countryside near the paramount chief's village and the island's rough airstrip, the remains of one of Gordon's busy fighter bases. Morris explains that the land was leased by his brother-in-law Thomas from the chief in return for a tithe on the produce, that Thomas will give him the yams once the harvest is correctly piled, and that having got them to the village he will in turn be presenting them to John Kasaipwalova. Eight field hands have been hired to carry yams and build the pile.

"The yams have all been dug up," Morris says, "and have been piled in these first piles."

He takes us to a yam heap about five feet high. "Now we must put this pile together with our other pile, and four men are the experts from our village who know how to do this."

The initial pile is shaded from the sun by a flimsy structure roofed in pandanus fronds; thirty paces away they have built a more substantial shelter of coconut-wood uprights, with a sturdy cross piece through the middle about four feet off the ground on which the builders will perch when the pile gets higher. Men are

The Kasaipwalova family yam house
RR Acrylic on canvas

dismantling the first pile. The four experts are laying out the foundation for the next pile, discussing technicalities. Thomas and Morris stroll around the fields with us, inspecting and explaining other gardeners' yam piles, which are ahead of theirs, reminiscent of the TV chef who tells viewers "and here is one that we prepared earlier." In addition to yams, the gardens produce taro, bananas, tapioca, ginger, pandanus, tomatoes. Where yams were dug up, sweet potatoes are planted.

"This garden is very good soil," Morris states. "It is eleven years since the last yam crop here. Now we should let the ground rest again for ten years. For three years we can grow taro and sweet potatoes, and then it will return to bush until it is ready for yams again."

"Kiriwina is only a reef," John remarks later, "a reef with six inches of soil on top of the coral. It is difficult to preserve the fertility of the soil."

Morris and Thomas stand together in front of one of the finished secondary yam piles with their arms stretched out, touching fingers. "The way we measure is in arm's lengths round the base of the pile," they say. "This pile is a five, and they go as much as seven or even eight. Always one man in the village do the measuring, we choose a man with arms that are not very long."

The measurement is made at ground level where the first four courses of yams are retained by wooden stakes hammered into the ground. Above them, the heap is constructed so that it bulges outward, like a beer belly hanging over a belt, and then it is tapered in a cone shape to a rounded top, about seven feet high. John has not accompanied us, explaining that this would not be polite if his yam house is to be the ultimate destination of the yams.

He tells us later, "A yam pile of four is small and the gardener will earn derision, but of six the gardener can be proud and will be respected as a good farmer. Seven starts to be politically dangerous, for the high chief will hear of it, and eight is near suicide. So if a farmer is in danger of having a yam pile that is too big, there are tricks he can use like subdividing the garden with his son-in-law and making separate piles."

Back at Thomas's pile the carriers have ceremoniously transported about fifty baskets to the new site where the builders squat, constructing the core of the pile amid a growing number of yams. Once the core, a cone some three feet high and six across, is complete, a serious debate gets going.

"Now we have to decide," Morris says, "if it will be a five or a six, and the experts advise on this, but Thomas have to take the final decision. If it is wrong, and there is not enough yams, we have to take it down and start again. Of course we have a trick for this one. We can use a reserve heap of yams if we have one to make the number up, and my son say we can use his yams for reserve. But if we are wrong the other way, and there is too many yams, everybody lose respect for the gardener, they laugh at him and of course we have to take it all down and do it again."

After half an hour of earnest discussion, and several trials laying yams out on the ground in a circle around the core cone, it is decided it will be a five. The circle is marked with a stick and the soil within it covered with yams, most carefully placed. The surrounding heaps of raw material continue to grow while the four

Starting a yam pile

experts start on the construction of the pile, large yams around the perimeter and average sized ones within. Each has to be precisely laid; deconstruction and rebuilding of sections is frequent.

"Only the experts can do this," admits Morris. "I tried once, and the whole pile collapsed in the night."

Meanwhile, as I wander into fringing bush to gather a bunch of red orchids for Robin, the ladies prepare lunch. Younger girls grate coconuts and peel fresh yams of different varieties while the great fish we contributed is prepared and installed in a large pot and enveloped in vegetables and coconut cream. A fire is made from old yam poles, and cooking commences.

Having eaten well, we take a final look at the near-complete yam pile, which now has some of the longer, thinner yams set so that they protrude from it, their ends marked with cinders from the cooking fire.

"These signs signify that the pile belongs to a chief," Morris tells us.

Thomas looks on, strained and preoccupied; it's a nerve-wracking time waiting to see if the assessment works out correctly.

"I can think of nothing closer to this process than the construction of a dry-stone wall," Robin observes as we returns to Morris's ancient truck. "Except that a dry-stone wall is meant to last for centuries, whereas these yam heaps built with enormous effort

Measuring a finished pile

and care are due to be torn down in a week. It must be one of the biggest wastes of time ever."

More surprising yet, we learn that what we are seeing is only one of five processes in transferring the yams from the ground to their final store. After this, the second piling, they will be carried in baskets to the village during a week of festivities, singing and dancing—the great harvest celebration of the year, the *Milamala*. There they will be piled once more, each pile larger than the last as families' and then clans' yams are amalgamated. The two final stages involve moving the yams to the yam house, making a pile, and then stacking them within the yam house. At each stage, similar care has to be exercised in constructing the pile. Magic will often be invoked, though the most potent garden magic still in use is kept for planting time. The hereditary Garden Magician holds a position of clan importance outranked only by the Chief and the Sorcerer.

The work involved in all this is immense. "If time was money here, these yams would be unaffordable," Robin notes practically.

But time has little value in the islands. Where living is easy, society has evolved rites, traditions and obligations that would be impossible in a harsher climate.

Malinowski remarked: "War, dancing and the Kula had supplied tribal life with its romantic and heroic elements. With clan

The Kula Ring

warfare prohibited by government, with dancing discredited by missionary influence, the Kula alone remains."

His summation of the Kula remains as true as when he penned it more than eighty years ago:

> The Kula exchange has always to be a gift, followed by a counter gift; it can never be barter, a direct exchange with assessment of equivalents and with haggling. There must be always in the Kula two transactions, distinct in name, in nature and in time. The exchange is opened by an initial gift, and closed by a final or return present. They are both ceremonial gifts, they have to be accompanied by the blow of a conch shell, and the present is given ostentatiously and in public. The native term "to throw" a valuable well describes the nature of the act. For, though the valuable has to be handed over by the giver, the receiver hardly takes any notice of it, and seldom receives it actually into his hands. The etiquette of the transaction requires that the gift should be given in an offhand, abrupt, often angry manner, and received with equal nonchalance and disdain.
>
> The opening gift of the exchange has to be given spontaneously, that is, there is no enforcement or any duty in giving it. There are means of soliciting it, but no pressure can be employed. However, the valuable gift which is given in return for the valuable gift previously received is given under the pressure of a certain obligation.
>
> The net result will be the acquisition of a few dirty, greasy, and insignificant looking native trinkets, each of them a string of flat, partly discolored, partly raspberry pink or brick-red discs, threaded one behind the other into a long, cylindrical roll. In the eyes of the natives, however, this result receives its meaning from the social forces of tradition and custom, which give the imprint of value to these objects, and surround them with a halo of romance.

Kula girl
RR Acrylic on canvas

Reach for Paradise

While the beaches are no longer alive with a hundred ornate canoes of a major Kula expedition and some of the magic, tradition, and force of the Kula has been eroded by the insidious Western pressures affecting every remote village, the Kula has somehow survived and seems to be evolving. Perhaps another Malinowski will arrive to maintain the record.

The Bismarck Sea

18

NEW IRELAND

A fine reach in gentle trade winds up the North Solomon Sea deteriorates in a trough of squalls to heavy rain, the wind fluctuating in direction and strength from nothing to a near gale. One gets little rest in such conditions, trimming and reefing sails repeatedly while at the mercy of a big, confused sea. Eventually the winds settle into a zephyr too light to sail, and we motor the final hundred miles to New Ireland, making landfall at dawn on a rugged, high jungle coast cloaked in heavy cloud. We drop anchor in an uninhabited bay charted as English Harbor. Thick bush crowds the enfolding shoreline, and green mountains soar to two thousand feet close by.

This place has not always been so empty and quiet, for it was the site of a cruel scrap of nineteenth century history. The so-called Marquis de Rays, who was in fact a mere viscount from Brittany with a history of failed enterprises, circulated France and neighboring countries with a prospectus for a new colony, a South Seas paradise. Upon those who purchased estates he conferred dukedoms in Nouvelle France, of which he was to declare himself King Charles I. From 1877 to 1881 he dispatched four vessels loaded with gullible immigrants to what he called

Port Breton. He had troubled neither to visit New Ireland to see the territory, nor acquire title to any of it. Naturally, the natives disapproved of the interlopers' intention to take over their land, and accordingly ate a number. It was quickly apparent that de Rays had selected an atrociously unsuitable place. Malaria proved an immediate killer, the rainfall was appalling, and the people were pathetically badly provisioned to cope with a savage tropical shore on which nothing useful seemed to grow. They had brought massive quantities of equipment to process their inappropriate crops, boxes of knives and axes with no handles. 180,000 bricks were sent to build a cathedral. Cargo holds included three thousand dog collars and twenty cases of stationery embossed with the royal crest. They arrived with a statue of the Madonna, but no quinine and little food.

Each succeeding shipload lasted a few weeks, and then the disillusioned survivors abandoned the place as best they could.

The affair would have been excellent material for a musical comedy had not de Rays, who made the equivalent of more than $2 million out of the scam, condemned more than 300 cheated French and Italians to miserable deaths. In return for passage to Australia, the last survivors traded their ships and remaining equipment with an extraordinary figure called Queen Emma. She was the daughter of a Samoan princess, one of dozens of children sired by an American cabin boy called Jonas Coe who was cast up in a storm on Samoa. Emma built up a successful trading empire that she ran from her palace in Kokopo. She was known, far and wide, as the Queen.

Nothing remains as evidence of the 610 hopeful immigrants who landed in English Harbor save a couple of small stone cisterns and their useless millstone, brought to process grain, which could never grow. It was retrieved to decorate a Rabaul street, itself desolate since eruptions in 1994. De Rays was charged for the swindle after some years, and jailed in France.

A night in English Harbor is enough. Was its name a Gallic attempt to saddle the English with the cause of their discomfort, much as syphilis, "the French disease," was known to Frenchmen as *le mal Anglais*? The mountains rise steeply from the beach, leaving only a small shelf of ground for cultivation, and the moisture-laden trades feel the high ground and unload up to a foot of rain in a day. We pick grapefruit in an abandoned orchard, but find them full of maggots. As we sail out into a misty sea, this land of misery dissolves and is lost to sight within the first hundred yards.

NEW BRITAIN

Fifty soaking miles further north, when we can at last see more than a few cables, we round a cape and turn toward New Britain and the large bay sheltering Rabaul.

A little girl, arriving in 1920 at the spacious town laid out to last by the Germans in the early years of the century, wrote this: "Waking up early in the morning entering Rabaul harbor, I thought I'd gone to heaven, it was so beautiful."

Now, three destructions later, *sic transit gloria mundi*: In less than sixty years, Rabaul has been obliterated once by bombs and twice by tectonic paroxysms.

I've been in e-mail correspondence for the last couple of months with my cousin John, of whose existence I did not know until another cousin came up with the news that here, in this distant place, lived a relative. There was some sort of bitter division in my father's family two generations before him, and knowledge of my less immediate paternal relatives was thin. John has worked in Rabaul for twenty years, bridging the cataclysmic simultaneous eruption of Rabaul's volcanoes, Vulcan and Tavurvur, in 1994. Now he is reconstructing the devastated town and its facilities, a project funded by AusAID, the World Bank, the European Union and others. Most businesses and people have relocated fifteen miles down the bay to Kokopo, the site of Queen Emma's rule—far enough to be free of risk of further eruptions and the sulphurous ash issuing from vents in the rumbling mountains. John e-mailed me to drop anchor by a little guesthouse. There I meet my new cousin for the first time as he brings his Swiss wife aboard for a drink, clutching a bunch of flowers from their garden. We give them a fine barracuda we've caught on the way and dine together, reconstructing family connections late into the evening.

"This is one of the most seismically active spots on earth," John says, "the junction of three great tectonic plates. There have been eruptions on average every fifty years and the instruments show that there are about 150 mini-earthquakes every day. Rabaul harbor is one caldera, there is another just to the south of it, and out to sea is one ten times the size of both of these."

On his office wall hangs a montage of satellite photos showing the three older volcanoes, the Mother, the North Daughter and the South Daughter, clustered on the peninsula that curves around like a hook to form the seaward side of the bay, next to Tavurvur, one

Tavurvur volcano, Rabaul

of a pair of newborn *enfants terribles*, a menacing heap of smoking black ash. Three miles across the harbor on the landward side looms Vulcan, which did not exist a hundred years ago. The half of Rabaul standing in the morning shadow of the Mother and her Daughters was completely wiped out by the weight of ash spewed out in 1994. It's now a moonscape, abandoned to the attempt to fix the dusty ash with the planting of a hundred thousand trees.

"There were only a handful of deaths," John says: "It was quite extraordinary. The old people who lived in the villages near Vulcan, and at the same time old people in Matupit village by Tavurvur, noticed that the megapode birds had all gone. Do you know about megapode birds?"

"Yes," we chorus, remembering the megapodes that dug their nests in the never changing 33°C soil of volcanoes in the Solomon Islands.

"Anyway, the old people saw that the megapode birds had disappeared, and they started walking away from Vulcan and from Tavurvur. As they passed round the harbor, other people joined them. Although the government radio station announced that there seemed no immediate threat, a great wave of people were on the move, gathering more as they went. When the first eruption happened, quite suddenly, at four in the morning, no one was left there."

These volcanoes growled on for ten years, but they are again quiescent, perhaps for another fifty years or so. Sometime there will again be a huge eruption as an earthquake breaches an empty magma chamber deep underground, the sea rushes in and encounters the thousand degree temperatures, and the mountain explodes. Or the movement of the plates, miles below, creates a weak spot through which gigantic pressure thrusts. Next time could even be worse. Vulcan, which had been but a pinhead islet in the harbor with a quarantine station on it, grew four hundred meters high like a hideous, black boil in just two and a half days in 1937. Another new mountain might well appear.

The Empire of Japan invaded in force in 1942 to grab the finest harbor in this part of the Pacific. An all-out attack on Australia was expected, based on Rabaul, and the harbor served to supply Admiral Yamamoto's celebrated Tokyo Express, the destroyer convoys that rushed troops and *materiel* down the Solomons Slot to the six months' pitched battle for Henderson Field on Guadalcanal.

The women and children had been shipped out by the extraordinarily unprepared Australians just in time to avoid capture by invading Japanese armies. Of the men who were subject to the 1942 proclamation on the next page, only a handful survived

For three years until the 1945 surrender, the occupation army had to withstand relentless blanket bombing by the American and Australian air forces. The Japanese constructed a vast underground city to withstand the fury raining down on them, and they were never driven out. Wrecks still litter the harbor, and more than three hundred miles of tunnels honeycomb the hills. Everywhere, Rabaul reveals crumbling martial remains. The aftermath of war must have been a scrap-dealers' paradise.

We are for the first time in the area of past German influence, though German colonial aspirations were brought to an abrupt halt after only thirty years by the Great War that broke out in 1914. Kokopo, then known as Herbertshöhe, served as the capital of Bismarck's burgeoning Pacific empire. New Britain was Neu Pomerania to the German colonists, and the area is still the Bismarck Archipelago in the Bismarck Sea.

Queen Emma's palace, Gunantambu, stood on the hill next to Herbertshöhe. R. W. Robson, in his book *Queen Emma*, left this description:

> All surviving records extol the beauty of the embowered Gunantambu, high on a point overlooking the blue bay. Extending southwards along the terrace, almost to Herbertshöhe, was a series of pretty bungalows, set amongst flower and colorful shrubs and surrounded by green lawns. There was a broad path through the lawns in front of Gunantambu, to the edge of the terrace. From there, between two ornamental pillars, a cement staircase 20 feet wide

TO ALL AUSTRALIAN MILITARY AND CIVILIAN PRISONERS OF WAR ON THE ISLAND OF NEW BRITAIN

It will be appreciated by all sections of the Community that it is necessary to elaborate on the reason why a state of war exists between the Great Empire of Japan and Britain, particularly when the conflict is now at its height, but is desired to take this opportunity to bring to the notice of both soldiers and civilians the following.

In pursuance of her National Policy of bringing eternal peace into the Orient, Japan has roused herself to action against the co-ordinated powers of Britain and U.S.A. who intend to besiege Japan and to interfere with her sacred Enterprise in Asia.

Japan's mission is first to accomplish the establishment of a great mutually prosperous Asia, then to contribute greatly toward the peace and happiness of all mankind.

It is your misfortune that you have been forced to surrender or have been captured but, no doubt, you already appreciate the advantages of being under Japanese military discipline during continuance of the conflict.

The Imperial Japanese Army is commanded by His Majesty the Japanese Emperor, in the shortest possible time it has proved to be the greatest and best disciplined army in the world.

Although drastic action will be taken against those who resist, every consideration will be shown to those who surrender, and there need be no fear of insult or ill treatment.

It is hoped that an early arrangement can be made for release of civilian prisoners and that, after the termination of the war in the near future, all prisoners will be permitted to return safely to their own country.

In conclusion it is recognized that you are prisoners who surrendered without resistance and you will be treated as such. It is for you now to comprehend the mission of the Imperial Japanese Army, and by observing its discipline your lives will be guaranteed. If on the contrary you make false statements or associate with any action calculated to hinder or resist the army you will be liable to capital punishment in accordance with Military Law and Discipline, as to the strict enforcement of which orders have already been given.

Dated 3rd February in the Japanese calendar year 2602
By Order Japanese Commander in Chief

descended gently to a carriage road, built along the lower face of the terrace. Every morning the Queen, usually attended by a secretary and a native footman, walked down the steps to her waiting rickshaw, and was drawn by two Buka boys along the seafront road between banks of brilliant flowers and crotons to her office. It was a sight to be remembered and it added mightily to her prestige.

After a drink in the Ralum Club, which occupies the site of the totally destroyed Gunantambu, we step down the wide stair that still descends gently to the carriage road, now cracked and rough, imagining past glories, flowered terraces and respectful buka boys bowing beside a waiting rickshaw.

In 1914, the arriving Australians immediately threw the Germans out and, once the war was over, accepted a League of Nations mandate to run the colony of New Guinea, which was later amalgamated with the British protectorate of Papua forming the southeast of the big island together with the outlying eastern islands. Independence was granted to the enlarged Papua New Guinea in 1975. The Dutch colony of Irian Jaya occupied the remainder of the big island, the western third.

John shows us where he used to work in the smart area of downtown Rabaul. "You see the remains of that frangipani?" he says. "My office was there."

There is nothing. A black ash plain with fine dust blowing in little streams across it is dotted with a few scrappy surviving trees. The weight of ash and rain-driven lahars from Tavurvur's vents caused the collapse of everything except a hotel that survived through the efforts of the owner, who kept shoveling the ash off his roof throughout the many days of eruption. No other building remains save the vaults of three banks, sticking up like the stubby supports of a concrete bridge under construction. Some of the wreckage was buried, the rest scavenged for new huts and houses. The city is gone. We drive across the ridge running between the Mother and the North Daughter, past sites where fine houses used to stand overlooking the beautiful bay, collecting the breeze. The road is crazy, eroded into a canyon overhung several meters by bits of the old tarmac, or buried under a heap of ash and mud. Only the wild gardens hint that this was not so long ago a leafy suburb echoing to nightly parties and the chattering of Rabaul's society.

Later, John shows us a video of the eruption. We see devastated scenes of surreal beauty, but not the beauty that astonished the little girl in 1920. Instead, there's a backdrop of mountains, trees and ocean, all a whitish gray monochrome of ash and pumice, set off by a green umbrella in the foreground. The slopes are covered in smooth snow with the coconut trees standing like scattered snow-laden pines in the Alps, the ash several meters deep in places. The angry white plume from Vulcan writhes against a blue sky to 70,000 feet, shot through with multi-flashes of lightning. The harbor is like a frozen lake under a blanket of floating pumice.

MANUS

William Dampier, 1651–1715

The stretch of water off Rabaul is known as the Dampier Channel. William Dampier was the first European to sail this way, and it was he who bestowed the names New Britain and New Ireland on the large islands to either hand. When Dampier sailed to explore New Holland and neighboring areas in 1699, he was briefly in the employ of the British navy. This was somewhat surprising, as his book *A New Voyage Round the World* revealing his exploits as a pirate had just been published to great acclaim. The reluctant navy had given him a decrepit ship, crewed by ruffians, which had sunk in the South Atlantic on the way home. Court-martialed and slung out of the navy again, Dampier returned to piracy. *A New Voyage* was unusual in being both a rollicking tale of high-seas adventure and brigandage and the first meticulous description of the peoples, plants and animals encountered in the far reaches of the globe. It became, deservedly, a best-seller. Among his shipmates was a Scot called Alexander Selkirk who, at his own request, was marooned on the lonely South Seas island of Juan Fernández in 1705. On his last voyage, four years later, Dampier's ship rescued Selkirk, now clothed in goatskins and "looking wilder than the original owner of them." In 1719, Daniel Defoe published Selkirk's story with some embellishment, which he called *Robinson Crusoe*. A quirky humor comes through in *A New Voyage*; Johnny Depp's character in *Pirates of the Carribean* seems less improbable after reading it, for though a fine sailor and navigator, Dampier's adventures appeal to a sense of the absurd, such as when combing the coast of

Panama for Spanish gold, he found he'd captured thirty tons of quince marmalade.

The last leg to Manus threads through the Admiralty Islands, marked on our charts as unsurveyed seas. This is surprising, as the huge Seeadler lagoon was a major Japanese and, after a bloody battle, American base in the war; hundreds of warships and a million GIs passed through. Maybe the US hydrographic authorities have continued to classify modern surveys as sensitive. Its name, Sea Eagle, is the only memory of German times. Now the shoreline has returned to bush, the busy installations have shrunk to decaying villages, the wartime jetties are decrepit and the colonial buildings rotted, for government failure has ensured that none of the expensive inherited infrastructure has been maintained.

We have been at anchor only a few hours when a family from a nearby hamlet, constructed on a solid base of metal war junk at the top of the beach, paddles over to warn us that the harbor isn't safe. The last yacht to anchor in Lorengau was badly robbed, they say, a Swedish boat nine months before us, and the yacht preceding that was attacked by rascals as well. In Rabaul, our predecessor yacht had also been robbed two months before us, but the culprits were quickly caught. Here the "rascals," as criminals in this part of the world are known in Pijin, have not been arrested according to most reports, though the mayor's wife, with an eye to PR or perhaps lulling us into carelessness, insists they are safe in jail. It was the mayor's driver who did the robbing, say some.

I ascribe our winter in PNG without seeing another yacht to the general impression that there is no law and order in the country and occasional reports of attacks on yachts on cruising websites. This is the first time we have been faced with an articulated threat. Perhaps we should have taken notice of the words of Sir Hubert Murray, Governor of Papua from 1920 to 1934 and a lawyer, who wrote of the Papuans: "Murder...in their eyes is, as a rule, not a crime at all; sometimes it is a duty, sometimes a necessary part of social etiquette, sometimes a relaxation."

We don't much fancy falling victim to etiquette or someone's idea of a leisure activity, but having declined to go alongside the horrible bunkering facility in Rabaul, we need fuel. It takes two days arranging with Shell, the harbormaster, and the mayor's wife, who owns the only road tanker, to berth to an old stone wall in a secluded backwater and take a load on board. We are a bit jumpy by now, and there doesn't seem much reason to linger longer in Lorengau, whose sole remaining claim to notice is its noisy chauka bird. Without allowing the local rascals more time to assemble their forces, we quietly move on.

HERMIT

Debouching from the last of a chain of lagoons that protect Manus's north shore, we are again facing the wide ocean. After many weeks winding among Papua New Guinea's islands, we both enjoy a sense of freedom in the limitless sea room and empty horizons ahead, an encompassing blue on the chart punctuated only by pinpricks. We feel a charged anticipation like starting on the voyage of life yet blessed with the perspective of age and experience. Even the added apprehension of evil weather as we approach the equator and enter the low-latitude zones of inter-tropical convergence seems a fair analogy of launching oneself on the world once school is done, the world an adolescent thinks he knows but knows in his heart he does not know.

A hundred miles overnight brings us to the isolated little Hermit group, a perfect atoll with a scattering of motus around its outer reef and a huddle of islands in the center where the single village, Luf, straggles along a thin sand isthmus between two high hills. By a narrow dogleg pass through the outer reef that is charted fully a mile and a half from its actual position, a banana boat awaits. A substantial man in a smart blue shirt calls to us. "I'm Bob," he says. "I saw you coming. I'll guide you in." He jumps aboard to take us through the reef and shows us a place to anchor in the deep bay.

Luf proves another Seventh-day Adventist village. Bob, one of its two ministers, invites us to hear him preach on Saturday, the Sabbath. A large church under construction for five years is still a skeletal frame, so the whole adult population of around a hundred crowds into an open-sided building with a high leaf roof and swept sand

Reach for Paradise

Luf village and island, Hermit

for the floor. My mind wanders while Bob indulges his hour of spiritual flagellation, drifting between the stresses of past life and the sensory delights of the present. It's curious that while I do not like the SdA regimentation of its people, I do not object to it. Without this relatively mild organization, human nature would hatch some other set of rules and beliefs to fill the vacuum, perhaps more oppressive.

We are each armed with a stick to prod away the foot-wide black and yellow spiders spinning stringy traps across the trail as we take an evening walk up through the village gardens and the flowering bush to the top of a hill. It's the cool of a midwinter evening in, yet the shade temperature is in the mid–nineties. Here we are only a single degree south of the equator.. Bob catches up near the crest. He pulls out of his *bilum* and with a two-foot bush-knife cuts the sweetest pineapple I ever ate.

In 1903, a German adventurer named Rudolph Wahlen built himself a fine castle on a hill on nearby Maron Island, rounding up the Hermit islanders for his labor force and omitting to pay them. By 1909, he'd also acquired Queen Emma's palace, Gunantambu. He lived with a succession of mistresses in magnificent style on the income of a gold mine, extensive copra plantations and other tropical enterprises. Nati, Wahlen's daughter, who learned about her parents only from a friend, has this to say about her father as quoted in Jan Roberts' *Voices from a Lost World*:

My mother was one of his young virgins—all Germans did that, all the colonial white men, and they had to be virgins... They went to the village chiefs and they would buy them, usually two or three at a time—often swapped them for an ax or a gun. Those bloody Germans, they had the time of their lives, five or six women waiting on them, and the women liked saying they "belonged to So-and-So Master," and getting new things.

Wahlen was chased away with the other Germans at the outbreak of war in 1914, his castle and plantations confiscated. The subsequent Australian owner, one McEvoy, failed to leave quickly enough once the Japanese had launched the Pacific war, was caught by a warship and, like many people unfortunate enough to find themselves prisoners of the imperial Japanese, was never heard from again. The castle still stood, however, until in 1968 an Australian manager of the plantation, hearing that PNG was to be granted independence, pulled the whole thing down, again making the village people work without payment.

Maron Island is now deserted, except for Alwin's dog.

Alwin has built himself a house among the rotting plantation buildings by Wahlen's little beach, and he rides there in the dinghy with us. The dog spots us a mile away and dog-paddles out to meet us, ears pricked, woofing excitedly. Alwin cheerfully says it has not been fed for days. We struggle up through triumphant bush to the top of the hill to find no more than the overgrown foundations of the *schloss*, a few barely discernible pillar stubs and some cisterns. One man's paradise, once magnificent, has been expunged. Plants have taken over the terraces, the broad verandahs,

Alwin and dog, Maron

The Wahlenburg shortly before demolition

the tennis court and the sweeping gardens. The superb views once embracing the whole island group and its lagoon are everywhere blocked by vines. Nothing significant remains of what was, in my experience, the only old attempt to create a great European house on a small Pacific island. Gordon later sends me a photograph of the stone *schloss,* and it was indeed impressive.

Jan Roberts, in *Voices from a Lost World,* wrote: "Wahlenburg… was a European man's nirvana, a coral atoll with imported horses, deer and fish that were fed on butterflies, immaculate lawn courts for croquet and tennis, telephones, electricity and air conditioning, a pet shark, and an endless supply of old wine and young women."

There's one surprising legacy. The horses, donkeys and cows Wahlen brought to his Wahlenburg are gone. But the deer he introduced have thrived, and every so often the islanders canoe over with children and dogs to drive them to the narrow waist of the island where they trap some in nets. "If so successful here without any husbanding at all," Robin remarks, "it's odd they haven't been introduced in other Pacific islands." We find out later that they were indeed brought to Hawaii, where they have become a pest.

As we depart the Wahlenburg's pathetic remains, Alwin's dog, still unfed, swims after us far out into the lagoon with pleading eyes. Robin claims she detects German Shepherd blood surviving from Wahlen's kennels.

There's said to be a cleaning station on the way back to Luf, a sort of piscatorial barber shop. Here, in a reef pass, specialist wrasse offer manta rays their services in removing encrustations and parasites. Just as we are putting flippers and masks on to check how the appointment system works, there's a swirling surge of the surface. One of the great beasts jumps clear of the water toward the dinghy and belly-flops with a resounding smash, sending a tsunami into the dinghy. Any closer and the manta would have sunk us.

"We lost our language long time ago," they tell us in the village. "Now we speak Pijin together." Hermit has also lost most of its population, apparently reduced from more than two thousand since the beginning of the last century by internal squabbles and battles with the neighboring atoll, Ninigo, a day's journey to the west. Several people assure us that no missionaries got to Hermit to tell them to mend their ways before 1950, when the SdA arrived to impose their ideas. "Before then we had no religion," they claim. I suspect the SdA has successfully obliterated memories of traditional beliefs.

As the days drift by, our symbiotic relationship with the islanders develops in many ways. They bring us fruit and vegetables, pilot us around the lagoon, dive with us, lend children to guide us through the bush, and take us to Bird Island on the outer reef, where the bushes are alive with nesting terns and fluffy booby chicks and we get buzzed by several thousand black noddies. We re-glass the shattered stern of a banana boat, mend a radio, get wheelbarrows back on the road, invite groups to watch DVDs on board, provide tools and fasteners and find appropriate presents from our stores, including much appreciated reading glasses. Robin's architectural skills are in demand. She does a sheaf of designs for the detail of the half-built church, consults on materials, and drafts plans for several houses. Our old genoa, given to make some canoe sails, is first put to use as a tent for a few boatloads of visitors from Ninigo arriving for some festivities. There is enough material for three or four canoe sails. "I hope this may prove a stimulus to build a large sailing canoe once more," I tell Bob, for with the coming of outboard motors the tradition of sailing has fallen into disuse.

We arrived well stocked with food, and at first gently refuse the many offers of provender. Then it starts arriving—drinking coconuts, giant clams, lobsters, two dozen varieties of fish, sweet potatoes, yam, beans and green leafy stuff, and those wonderful pineapples. One day we're given a brace of sand bugs, caught in an underwater snare resembling the sort an old poacher would set to catch a rabbit. These are entirely new to us, a foot-long version of a mantis shrimp. We eat magnificently of the bounty of the sea, and sympathize once again that the tenets of the Seventh-day Adventists deny them the pleasures of their crustacean Eden.

A change of wind prompts a move from our pool on the east of the village around the bottom of Luf, stopping off the far coast of the village close to an arc of coral, which falls away quickly to deep water. We swim without a care until, one evening, Bill arrives for a third consultation with Robin about his new house. He mentions that crocodiles living in our crescent were parading through the middle of the village the previous night, hunting for dogs to eat. Alerted, I see one swim by *Nereus* in the soft dawn light, on its way home, its surreptitious movements only detectible in flat calm water when its presence is betrayed by the faintest of ripples and the momentary appearance of an inch of nostril.

"These is big crocs, mebbee ten meters long," Namo claims later.

Enoch brings a live coconut crab one evening. As dinner is already planned around some giant clams we've harvested from a mid-lagoon reef, I house him in a bucket in the cockpit for the following day. He quickly escapes and finds his way down the companionway and into the galley. Replaced in the bucket with a heavy lid to keep him in, this time he cunningly waits until we're in bed, knocks it off, gets out of the bucket and somehow scales the cockpit side. Towards 3:00 A.M., I'm woken by furtive scrabbling over our heads and climb on deck to find the crab about to dive through the aft hatch, where he would have landed on Robin's bunk.

She turns pale when I confess next morning. I am firmly chastised for being an incompetent jailer: "You really mustn't trifle with a crab that's capable of opening a coconut," she mutters grimly. Forgiveness is several days in coming.

We loiter many days in Hermit, wondering if this might be close to the paradise we seek through Western eyes. Despite what we perceive as the misdirected fervor and heavy hand of the Adventist ministers, from the privileged platform of our boat the atoll is close to faultless, an emerald in an azure ocean.

Sand bugs, Hermit Islands

Bismark's Sea

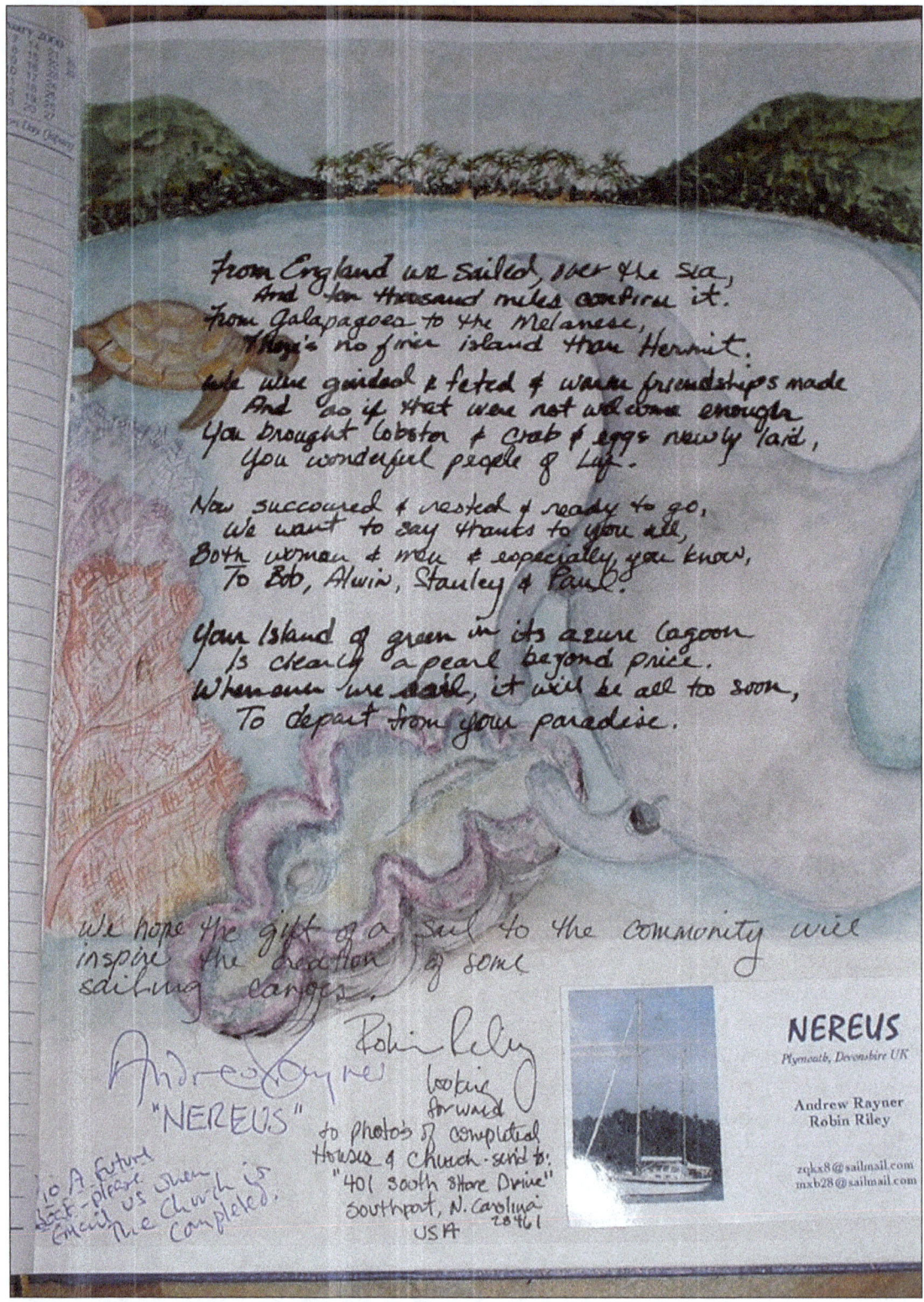

19

A Pacific Festival

PALAU

Our Pacific valediction is a mistreated small island group in the far northwest of the ocean. The brutal Japanese occupation was at its longest in Palau, and since liberation it has suffered the excessive generosity of close association with the United States. This is apparent in a number of ways, including a plethora of attorneys, that make it less interesting to a seeker of unspoiled islands, but its past is intriguing.

> From these islands, presently in discovery of us, came a great number of canowes, having in each of them in some four, in some six, in some fourteen or fifteen men, bringing with them coquos, fish, potatoes, and certaine fruites.... The people themselves have the neather parts of their eares cut round or circlewise, hanging downe very low upon their cheeks, wherein they hang things of a reasonable weight: The nailes on the fingers of some of them were at least an inch long, and their teeth as blacke as pitch; the color whereof they use to renew by often eating on an herbe, with a kind of powder, which in a cane they carrie about them to the same purpose. The first sort and company of those canowes being come to our ship very subtilly and against their natures, began in peace

to traffique with us, giving us one thing for another very orderly, intending (as we perceived) hereby to worke a greater mischiefe to us: Intreating us by signes most earnestly to draw neerer toward the shore, that they might (if possible) make the easier prey both of the ship and us. But these passing away, and others continually resorting, wee were quickly able to guesse at them what they were: For if they received anything once into their hands, they would neither give recompence nor restitution of it, but thought whatever they could finger to bee their owne: Expecting always with browes of brasse to receive more, but would part with nothing: Yea, being rejected for their bad dealing, as those with whom we would have no more to do, using us so evilly, they could not be satisfied till they had given the attempt to revenge themselves, because we would not give them whatsoever they would have for nothing: And having stones good store in their canowes, let flie a maine of them against us. It was farre from our Generals meaning to requite their malice by like injure. Yet that they might knowe that he had the power to doe them harme (if he had listed) he caused a great peece to be shot off not to hurt them but to affright them. Which wrought the desired effect amongst them, for at the noise thereof they every one leaped out of his canow into the water, and diving under the keele of their boates, stayed them from going any way till our ship was gone a good way from them. Then they all lightly recovered into their canowes, and got them with speed toward the shoare.

Notwithstanding other new companies (but not all of the same mind) continually made resort unto us. And seeing that there was no good to be got by violence, they put on a shew of seeming honestie, and offering in shew to deale with us by way of exchange; under that pretence they cunningly fell a filching of what they could, and one of them puld a dagger and knives from one of our mens girdles, and being required to restore it againe, he rather used what meanes he could to catch at more. Neither could we at all be ridde of this ungracious companie, till we made some of them feele some smart as well as terror: and so we left that place by all passengers to bee knowne hereafter by the name of the ISLAND OF THEEVES.

Thus was reported the first landfall of Francis Drake, sixty-eight days after leaving California (which he had named New Albion) in the year 1579, on the voyage that would make him the first captain to circumnavigate the globe.

Then the island was lost.

Over the centuries the location of this Island of Thieves evolved into a fascinating riddle. Scholars argued for an array of northwestern Pacific islands with elaborate proofs and equal conviction. It did not help that Drake had made a gift of his voyage journal and the sketches done along the way to Queen Elizabeth I, without keeping copies. These disappeared into the royal collection, and have not been seen since. The enigma appears to have been answered by an ethnological sleuth, William Lessa who, in his book *Drake's Island of Thieves,* proves it to be Palau.

After Drake, it was one hundred thirty years before the next European visitor to Palau provided another shiplifting opportunity. In 1710, a Spanish captain named Padrilla called in the *Santissima Trinidad* and deposited two Flemish priests, who were probably murdered within days. He left hastily when a swarm of locals descended and pilfered powerfully. A rescue vessel sent to look for the priests two years later was similarly chased away, and for many decades no one else hove over the horizon of what were now spoken of as *Las Islas Encantadas,* which translates better as "accursed" than "enchanted."

Johann Forster's view in 1775, reflecting reports from the *Santissima Trinidad* and the *Santo Domingo,* was no more complimentary than Drake's: "The inhabitants of Panleu or the Palaos are like negroes, savage and barbarous; they go naked, and are cannibals; and are for that reason detested by the inhabitants of the Caroline Islands, who look upon them as dangerous to deal with, and the fiends of mankind."

The Palau Visitors Board has been slow to use these few scraps of history in their publicity. Though, to be fair, all early sailors' reports complained bitterly about pilfering and thieving from one coast of the Pacific to the other, failing to accept that the concept of individual property was unknown. Fifty-eight years before Drake, Magellan had already labeled Guam his Island of Thieves, and Cook routinely took the local chief hostage until stolen goods were returned. By my voyage, ways have changed; we leave the boat unlocked, we have hundreds of Pacific people aboard, and nothing is taken.

In the nineteenth and twentieth centuries, the little archipelago of Palau, which sits on a lonely western Pacific reef 250 miles from its nearest inhabited neighbor and 550 miles from anywhere substantial, had successively Spanish, German (the Germans purchased it from the Spanish for 25 million pesetas along with the rest of the Caroline Islands and the Marianas), Japanese and American masters. Its eighteenth century population of some 60,000 was reduced to less than 4,000 by the European contact, and was at times heavily outnumbered by colonists. There were 25,000 Japanese on the island in 1935. It has now recovered to about a quarter of the previous tally, including a lot of people of mixed blood. The number of its villages has been reduced rather more, as nearly all the people now live on one small island, Koror, where we tie up after negotiating a long, curving passage through the inner reef.

In a roundabout way, the English seem responsible for the population concentration in Koror. The East India Company vessel *Antelope* was wrecked on Palau's outer reef in 1783. While the crew was constructing a new ship from the *Antelope*'s timbers to sail back to Macao, its captain, Henry Wilson, with a few men and muskets had helped the clans of Koror defeat the numerically superior people of the far bigger island, Babeldaob, just to the north. A hundred and fifty war canoes would not have overcome the Babeldaob forces, but supplemented by ten armed sailors and, on one occasion, a swivel gun, each battle was a walk-over. The Ibedul (high chief) of Koror was therefore a most welcoming host, and entrusted his son, Prince Lee Boo, to Wilson to sail away and learn the ways of the white men, after Omai only the second Pacific islander to be seen in London. To thank him for his friendship and his help sending Wilson and his crew home safe and sound, the grateful "John Company" dispatched a ship to Palau with muskets, powder and shot, which the Ibedul promptly used to dominate the entire group much as King Kamehameha used Western arms to conquer and unify Hawai'i. The population of the big island has never recovered.

Palau is well off the ocean tracks, and remained unaffected by missionaries and other imports (except viruses and the muskets) for a long time. The 1832 journal of another wrecked captain, the whaler Edward Barnard of Nantucket, whose ship *Mentor* struck the northern reefs of Belau, as it is alternatively known, when he thought himself to be one hundred fifty miles away, provides an unvarnished picture of a primitive place: "A number of larger [canoes] well maned made their apperance and came directly toward us having from five to ten men in each all armed yet naked the head one was conducted by what I then thought one of the most savage looking beings I ever beheld on getting along side we found him all that his looks bespoke."

That Barnard escaped immediate murder and after initial terrors was befriended and eventually helped to leave was solely due to the northern peoples' expectation of a cargo of firearms, like Koror fifty years before.

This was a fascinating place to aim for.

Besides, we heard that a rare Festival of Pacific Arts was to happen in Palau.

KOROR

Happy that the tedious eight-day passage through the difficult weather of the inter-tropical convergence zone bordering the equator is over, we clear in with a swarm of officials waving sheaves of forms to be completed. They remove every last vegetable leaf and fruit pip. We have successfully avoided areas of US influence until now, a happy thought as we suffer silly levels of formality and learn that law is the growth industry of Palau. A stout American yachtie in a passing dinghy advises us to anchor at Sam's, a couple of miles on in a hole clearly shown on our chart to be inaccessible. The chart turns out to be about seventy years out of date, though recently bought at a high price in Australia. A narrow channel blasted through a reef brings us into a beautiful little anchorage enclosed by high, wooded coral cliffs where we tie to one of Sam's moorings and use his "Royal" Belau Yacht Club with its humming bar as shore base. Only three overseas yachts have made it to Palau for the Festival—the result of fear of typhoons, worries about security in PNG and the Philippines, and an adverse monsoon to sail on west.

Koror is now connected to Babeldaob by a fine suspension bridge, a gift of Japan who named it—perhaps in face-saving apology for Japan's appalling behavior fifty years before—the Japan Palau Friendship Bridge. Here, at dawn, while brightly dressed Micronesian bands play island music on percussion and strange string instruments, a signal of colored smoke rises in the dim, early light. A fleet of canoes approaches between far-off islands, spreading out to cover the lagoon in a re-creation of olden days, drawing nearer as the sun climbs over the coconut trees and landing their painted captains at the steps where a dozen troupes in national grasses await to dance a welcome.

The peripatetic four-yearly Festival of Pacific Arts always opens thus. The Arrival of the Canoes is a recognition that canoes are everywhere fundamental to both Pacific life and art. The spirit, the *mana*, of the Pacific is embodied in the canoe above all.

The smallest one is a pretty, much-decorated white canoe without outrigger, piloted by a solo paddler from Taiwan. Then comes a fleet of inshore sailing canoes, followed by war canoes each propelled by about eighteen warriors. Proudly bringing up the rear, and most significant place, are three voyaging canoes, the symbol of Pacific history and culture, the last working craft in direct line of descent from the great double-hull canoes that carried Polynesians and Micronesians on extraordinary voyages of discovery and settlement over three thousand years.

Two voyaging canoes have arrived just in time from Saipan in the Northern Marianas and Yap, the nearest Caroline Island, sailing the 250 miles of open ocean from Yap using only traditional navigation. That means no charts, no GPS, no compass, sextant or other instruments, and no radios. Nothing was read, or written down. The sun and the stars were largely obscured by cloud, so the navigators steered by the swells, winds and expanded indications of land, such as refracted waves, cloud reflections and the flight of birds. These are not the *vaka* of Polynesia, but more compact traditional Micronesian craft with a single outrigger and woven platform on which a small shelter is perched. Nor are they of plastic or GRP, like reproductions sometimes seen in Hawai'i, but are properly constructed of forest materials. Navigating the Saipan canoe are two sons of the greatest contemporary Pacific navigator, Mau Piailug, whose fame covers fully a quarter of the globe though he hails from a miniscule Micronesian atoll, Satawal.

War canoe, Palau

Mau navigated the first modern canoe to make the 2,250-mile voyage from Hawai'i to Tahiti using traditional navigation, something most people considered impossible. He was imported from his faraway microdot of land because, in all of Polynesia, not one single master navigator remained.

"It's quite the wrong season for this voyage. We were blown right past Palau by terrible weather," Henry Piailug says. "So we made our landfall from the northwest when they were expected us from the southeast." Part of the knowledge of navigation is the "when" to travel a route, so it was with great misgivings that the canoes set out in defiance of tradition.

Henry is one of Mau's sixteen children. Sometimes I'm tempted to see the Pacific islands as the unchanging habitat of Rousseau's noble savage, that misleading notion eagerly adopted by the chattering classes of the Age of Enlightenment. Then I pinch myself. The island people, though innocent of much despoliation of the planet unlike their continental cousins, are well marked by the nineteenth and twentieth centuries. Mau's family is a signal of how things have changed; that a remote Pacific islander with sporadic access to modern medicine can raise sixteen healthy children while, two hundred years earlier, in the most advanced society on earth, the European master navigator James Cook's six children were all dead before producing him a single grandchild.

To witness traditional voyaging canoes at work is in a way the culmination of my Pacific voyage, for there are barely a dozen now in the entire ocean. Voyaging canoes express what it is to be an islander; they symbolize all that is special in this ocean; they

A Pacific Festival

Voyaging canoes from Saipan

embody a world spirit threatened with extinction. Yet the skill to make and dedicate voyaging canoes has faded, and trees good enough have become as rare as snow in the tropics.

Like the construction of canoes, nearly all islands have lost the skill of navigation, but efforts are afoot to educate young people in a few places. That this is onerous was reflected in an answer Nainoa Thompson gave when asked how he would train a young man.

"He must start when he is four years old," he said. "His grandfather should take him down to the beach and show him the stars. By the time he is eighteen years old, if he is a good learner he may know enough to be a navigator."

Nainoa Thompson, a Hawaiian, was instructed by Mau. He piloted the reproduction Hawaiian canoe *Hokule'a* on a 12,000-mile voyage around the Polynesian triangle in 1985 to 1987, arriving without charts or instruments accurately in New Zealand, Tonga, Samoa, Cook Islands, the Tuamotos and back in Hawai'i. This was the journey that demolished for ever Thor Heyerdahl's famous theory that Polynesia must have been colonized from the Americas.

A Micronesian navigator is known as *palu*, a title of extreme eminence. His initial qualification takes place at the intricate *pwo* ceremony. No more than a handful of living navigators have become *pwo*—in most islands no one still around has even witnessed a *pwo*. It was bitterly related that one church actually stole the ceremony, disused in that particular island for fifty years, to give its priest status: a sky navigator, perhaps. Later it transpired that it was the consecration of a Jesuit priest with the participation of Mau Piailug himself that had stirred up the backbiting.

In *The Last Navigator,* an American Stephen Thomas, who was privileged to be accepted as a pupil of Mau, explained the use of ocean swells, the technique the canoes had practiced to reach Palau from Yap:

> In the tropical Pacific, where the steady tradewinds blow from the easterly quadrant for most of the year, the wind pushes up long, low groundswells that march across the sea in steady lines. The vector of the swells' march remains steady, enabling the skilled palu to maintain his direction by keeping a constant angle between the swells and the canoe. Where two or three swell systems interact, the navigator will steer by what are called "knots," the peaks the swells make as they come together, like the converging wakes of two motorboats. At dusk and dawn he must check the swells' vector against the stars. At night, if the sky is overcast and there is no moon to light the swells on the ocean, he must steer by the pitch and roll of his canoe in the seaway. Navigators are taught to recognize "waves" from each octant of the compass. The most dominant are the swells from the north, north-east and east that are created by the strong winter tradewinds.

I knew the theory, but over thousands of miles of ocean passage no amount of staring at the passing waves has enabled me to distinguish and untangle the various swells pushing through the water, let alone interpret them, and I have encountered no cruising yachtsman who can. Yet a traditional navigator can identify, read, and use up to eight intersecting swells.

At a seminar on traditional navigation held as part of Festival proceedings, some of the handful of remaining navigators exchange thoughts of how the knowledge and practice might be preserved in an age of creeping westernization. An American takes the floor to suggest that the detail must be formally recorded, possibly using the Honolulu planetarium or professional astronomy software to preserve the vast amount of star-path data that must be learned by a Master Navigator.

This is met by a vehement response: "I feel my blood starting to get hot. This knowledge must be taught from a very early age, so that it becomes a part of the navigator. It cannot be conveyed any other way. It is not something which can be learned like a language."

Behind this stance, widespread among the few cognoscenti, is a feeling that traditional navigation represents intellectual property of a sort, one small part of the culture of the great ocean that can be protected from western rip-off, degradation and erasure. Since ancient times navigators have held paramount status in their clans, the repositories of immensely important, jealously guarded knowledge. In effect, this was similar to and quite as valuable as the early maps that enabled Western nations to find and grab new territories as the known world grew larger, and which spawned a vast international espionage industry as the Portuguese, Spanish, British, Dutch and French vied for sailing information through the seventeenth and eighteenth centuries. Navigation is a body of arcane knowledge that endows its few possessors with an aura of reverence, an initiation to an elite freemasonry of the sea.

Festival organization is anarchic. Whatever was scheduled is changed and changed again with little dissemination of the final truth. The information booth gives up trying after a few days. Navigating one's way to the different venues in the near total absence of signage is challenging, making me wish I could read a star path. When it's too wet to use our bicycles, we hitchhike. The first Palauan car along always stops and drives us wherever we want to go.

The Festival has slots for a wide variety of artistic activities, among which cooking is happily recognized. Long before the emergence of the cult of celebrity chef, I was convinced it was the most important of the lot. Stands offer intriguing dishes: strange fruits from the bush, unaccustomed vegetables and the inhabitants of exotic shells. Yams, manioc and taro *poi* are used to create delicious puddings and cakes with unrecognizable flavors. Elsewhere, exhibitions of photos, paintings, leaf-house architecture, museum artifacts and traditional products, canoe making and log carving, kite flying and other island skills and custom activities are spread all over town. Twenty-eight visiting states and territories and all provinces of Palau have built pavilions to exhibit their weaving, tattooing, music and crafts and to sell their products. Bands play extraordinary arrays of percussion, theater groups perform, poetry is recited and Pacific films run nonstop in a schoolroom.

Papuan musicians
RR Acrylics on canvas

All of this pales into insignificance beside the dancing. From wild war dances to gentle seated ballets of the arms and hands, there are expositions of dancing as varied as might be expected from peoples living throughout one-third of the world, coming from a dozen ethnic groupings and speaking a thousand languages. Large teams from Fiji, Tonga, Samoa and Vanuatu with swirling grasses and oiled bodies yield to more than sixty Papua New Guineans in full war dress festooned in huge, bright feathers plucked from their birds of paradise. Then we are entertained with the traditional dances of Tokelau, Tuvalu, Niue, Wallis and Futuna, and the scattered Marshall Islands. French Polynesia has scraped a dozen people together at the last moment after the recently displaced outgoing administration sourly vetoed funds for a delegation, but New Caledonia makes up for this with a troupe of more than fifty. The girls of Rapa Nui, as Easter Island is known throughout Polynesia, undulate in minimal grass attire. Australia has sent Aboriginal dancers from tiny islands to its north.

Painted pointy-hatted spirit-men accompany them on didgeridoo and bone-tipped boomerangs. From its dependency Norfolk Island comes a folk group comprised of the fifth to the ninth generations of descendants of Fletcher Christian, the leader of the *Bounty* mutineers. The dancing of Guam and the Northern Marianas is of clear Spanish provenance, for nothing much of the indigenous Chamorro culture survived the long Spanish occupation. Also from Micronesia come representatives from Pohnpei, Yap and Kosrae. The better funded neighbors, Hawai'i, Indonesia, American Samoa and Taiwan, give superb professional performances. Among the best are the girls from Aotearoa (the Polynesian name New Zealand bore long before Abel Tasman named it for part of the Netherlands), manically twirling snowballs on sennit cords as they writhe to the compelling beat of Maori music.

But the dancers to see again and again are from Isabel Island in the Solomons and Aitutaki in the Cook Islands. We already met the Solomons team in Guadalcanal and are not surprised that, even among the ocean's best, their wild gyrations as they play elephantine bamboo pan pipes produce huge applause. The Aitutaki performers are a mad oiled-brown-flesh whirl of knee-scissoring men and bottom-gyrating girls in polished coconut shell bosom holders and bright green swirling grass skirts. Aitutaki prides itself as the home of the ocean's best dancing—and may be right.

Dancers from Aitutaki, Cook Islands
RR Acrylic on canvas

The only no-show among the nations of the Pacific is the world's smallest republic, Nauru, which has somehow blown the phosphates fortune that made its citizens easily the richest of the entire ocean. In their heyday, Nauruans had the highest per capita income in the world. Neighbors from Kiribati were brought over to do the work, exporting two million tons of island each year, while the few thousand Nauruans swanned along their short road in shiny new cars, growing so fat that Air Nauru had to install the largest seats of any airline to contain their burgeoning butts. Someone has collected figures showing that 94 percent of Nauru people age fifteen and up are obese. The remaining 6 percent are probably ill. Investing in musicals caused some of the loss, as the national Trust Fund shrunk by nine-tenths. It's a horrible reflection on modern civilization that these islanders, pitched into the twentieth century utterly unprepared and unable to cope with unscrupulous financiers, are now impoverished after the destruction of four-fifths of their land by the mining operations as they expire of heart disease and diabetes.

ROCK ISLANDS

The ten days of festivities draw to a close with a final ceremony driven into a gym by torrential rain. Speechifying dignitaries and under-rehearsed schoolchildren tend to monopolize these occasions, so we flee with some new Kiwi friends aboard to Palau's extraordinary Rock Islands. Keeping a careful eye on the plentiful reefs dotting the big lagoon, we pick our way to a long thin island shaped like an open wishbone, in the crook of which lie another fifty smaller islands. Most are tiny and around one-hundred-feet high. Some of these islands are themselves wrapped around enclosed bays, forming lagoons within lagoons within lagoons.

I have seen no more lovely stretch of water. We see islands in every direction. When a vista opens between two of them as we paddle about in kayaks, we see more islands, sometimes a corridor of islands lining a reach like a row of green mushroom pillars. The calm blue waters occasionally continue right through an island, a natural arch framing a glorious panorama. The bays are sweet with the scent of scaevola, its tiny white flowers hanging down over the undercut, brushing our hair as we pass.

The Rock Islands are precipitous, uplifted coral, undercut at sea level by up to thirty feet, a hollowed-out girdle making landing impossible without climbing equipment, serving as total protection. The cause is not the abrading action of the sea, for the undercut is no greater where an island is exposed than in a sheltered spot. The chiton seems responsible. Flat, armored marine bugs, chitons look like zillion-year-old trilobite fossils or giant Jurassic lice. They eat microbes and chew their way through limestone, if given a few million years to do it. They are assisted in achieving a mushroom effect by acid produced by the reaction of rain with the rotting greenery on the top of each island, which floats on the seawater around the waterline.

We stay a few days and then drop off our guests and return toward this implausible seascape. Now we head for a secret bay hidden by high cliffs, entirely enfolded within an island. Its narrow entrance is invisible from our anchorage; we are floating inside a castle keep where the spirits of tropical gardeners have been busy. Birds are everywhere. White terns, prettier even than fairy terns, flit around the mast. Flashes of red are cardinal honeyeaters, and, of blue, pairs of collared kingfishers. Dusk brings the most exotic chorus imaginable from cockatoos, terns and noddies of various sorts, fruit doves, bush warblers, whistlers, hooters, and honkers echoing within the walls of our fortress. The tropic birds make a curious clicking chatter as they fly, and then emit a range of harsh noises from a branch somewhere. Megapodes, which stew their eggs in maturing compost here because there are no hot volcanic soils, have a three-note whistle, each lower than the last in pitch and volume. Owls and a jungle nightjar keep up the island music till late.

The national flower of Palau is the rur, a lilaceous-looking long white trumpet on a shrub that grows only on bare bits of the Rock Islands, just above the undercut. Balancing on tiptoe on the highest point of the dinghy at high tide, I can just reach up to pluck a bunch for Robin.

Toward the south of the huge lagoon, within a grouping of several dozen Rock Islands in the shape of a large *U*, is one of Palau's several inland marine lakes. Though totally landlocked, it's connected to the sea by porous limestone systems that allow salt water to filter through with the tides. Known simply as Jellyfish Lake, this is a wonder. Carrying snorkeling gear over a short hill, we plunge in to find ourselves among a vast concourse of yellow, bell-shaped jellyfish. Because of their separation from whales and the sea fish that like to dine on them, over the eons these jellyfish have lost their sting; we can swim among them, even handle them, unharmed. Their only predators are an array of white anemones stationed in ranks around the lake's rim awaiting unwary jellyfish for supper. Somebody has estimated there are fourteen million jellyfish in the lake.

As an impressionable boy growing up in my Devonshire home, roaming the woods, sailing small boats on the English Channel, and consuming volumes of boys' literature of derring-do, though I was never much bothered about spiders and serpents on land I suffered the usual water phobias of sea snakes, sharks, fathomless deep ocean and crocodiles. Drifting across the Pacific Ocean has served to deal with these hang-ups, one by one. Jellyfish were the last and cringe-worthiest of all. Swimming through a stellar firmament of jellyfish, one clasped gently in each hand, proves successful therapy for this one, too.

BABELDAOB

Palau has a prehistory that is not much understood. Hills were shaped into terraces by forgotten tribes, very old stone heads of enormous size lie in the bush, pottery shards are scattered about, and squared stone pathways connect prehistoric sites. Some dating has been done to 5,500 years ago, but no one knows what peoples may have found these islands in such distant times. At the intersection of two magnificent stone paths is a stone rotary. Did Chinese or Egyptian ancients design roads with roundabouts? Or could this be the first one? At Airai stands the only old *bai* still in use, the meeting house that in times past was the focal point of all Palauan villages. Besides its function for chiefs' business, this pavilion was a place for the young men to hang out, complete with teenage girls kidnapped from other villages. Thus a major part of young men's education was under the direct eye of the elders. The *bai* is a solid structure some forty paces long set on a broad stone platform, steeply roofed in pandanus and richly decorated with symbols and legends etched on a white background in browns and black. To reach it, we ascend a wide stone way, which may have been a thousand years old or more. Other raised stone paths radiate into the hills, skillfully built to last for centuries.

Sticking up on a round hilltop, surrounded by virgin bush and miles from previous development, is a grandiose colonnaded structure in a building site, topped by a fine dome. It looks like a nipple on a teat. This is the new capitol of Palau, the Pacific's own Brasilia, expensively funded by aid, gleaming in the sunshine, misplaced and unloved. It seems to personify the failure of Pacific communities to absorb only what they need from the West when exposed to aid in all its guises, their inability to reject the temptations of progress, the mirage of aggrandizement. People naïve in the ways of the developed world need a degree of insulation, yet what they are usually offered is a sort of political and economic seduction, leading inevitably to corruption of soul and tradition.

Departure to the Philippines marks the limit of *Nereus'* Pacific quest. We are tempted to turn around and sail back east to explore new islands and revisit friends. Toward the Hawaiian chain stretches the great expanse of Micronesia, an area larger than the continental United States containing more than two thousand five hundred islands with an average size of half a square mile. In Pohnpei, the mysterious ancient city of Nan Madol crumbles away on eighty artificial islands contained within basalt walls, the enigmatic Venice of the Pacific; nothing is known about the peoples who built it. Kosrae, too, has a ruined stone town, perhaps constructed eight hundred years ago and still thriving when Dumont D'Urville put the island on European charts before its population was nearly wiped out. The downward spiral has been from stone to leaf houses, and then to concrete. Truk or Chuuk, the spelling seems optional, is eternal home to a powerful Japanese fleet caught by US air power, a mecca for wreck divers; more than fifty ships were sent to the bottom of its shallow lagoon by Operation Hailstorm in 1944. Sadly, perhaps the legacy of rule by Japanese and Americans, the Chuukese do not manage affairs well; the land area is reported as rubbish-strewn and rather lawless, and it cannot have helped its slim forces of order that in 2003 two policemen actually managed to shoot each other dead in an argument. Yap is famed for its round stone money the size of truck tires, far too heavy for a man to carry yet imported over typhoon-swept seas in frail sailing canoes from quarries two hundred miles away. Saipan, the site of a huge 1944 battle to dislodge Japanese forces so its airfield could be used for the final assault on Japan, remains heavy with war junk. Its near neighbor, Tinian, was turned into a forty-thousand-man airbase with six two-mile runways, whence Little Boy and Fat Man were dispatched to rain destruction on Nagasaki and Hiroshima.

These little islands receive generous flows of US largesse, much of which feeds local officialdom without improving the lot of the inhabitants or improving the welcome accorded to visitors. Sometimes these and even tinier islands are visited by cruise ships. While a small yacht and its few crew can be absorbed into village life, the arrival of a cruise ship disgorging perhaps hundreds of tourists pointing cameras and goggling at the locals and their topless womenfolk for a few hours leaves lasting disturbance to the rhythm of life. Payments are usually made to the chief, who may feel no need to spread the money around, causing discontent and envy. Yachts that are asked for payment by a village chief can pull up their anchor and go elsewhere. They usually do, preferring to make their gifts personal.

Nevertheless, among the myriad islands of Micronesia there are said to be gems like Lamotrek where unspoiled, friendly people will appreciate the occasional visitor and welcome him as one of the extended family. But to spend longer in this ocean seeking fragments of perfection would seem like simple hedonism. Robin and I reluctantly persuade each other we have more to do with our lives than float around pieces of paradise practicing boat maintenance. It's agreed that the Festival is the grand finale to our extraordinary Pacific years. We know we have been privileged to touch the best this globe has to offer.

Reflection

ISLANDS THE WORLD OVER seem to imbue in islanders a fiercely independent spirit. There's a remarkable self-reliance from the Scottish Hebrides to New Zealand to Japan's outliers.

This is equally true of the people of small Pacific islands. But, protected as they have been by a unique combination of distance and time, they have something besides, something that, at the risk of dreadful generalization, I think of as a beautiful innocence. This is not the innocence of not knowing, but the joy of not caring; an insouciance to a multitude of shortcomings and sins of civilization.

Despite twenty centuries of European incursion in Asia and Africa, the Great Ocean remained *Terra Incognita* long after Balboa crossed Darien. Even two hundred fifty years ago, nearly all of it was a guess, its jewels guarded not by weather, armies or frontiers, but by isolation itself. Colonial desires and the tentacles of diplomacy on the far side of the world briefly intruded and the islands suffered grievously. But once empire-building countries' passing craze for overseas possessions had its day and the violence of the Second World War had passed, the islands were largely left in peace. When France has evaporated from its Pacific territories, as it surely must, and the USA at last leaves its family of islands to stand on their own feet, interference will be down to a modest, perhaps tolerable, level. In anywhere less blessed, UN income statistics of a few dollars a day would draw hordes of well-meaning NGOs to apply hopeless nostrums for the relief of poverty. But figures are meaningless where gods smile and money is rare.

People question whether Pacific islanders can preserve this rich way of life. Will they get sucked into the twenty-first century, to suffer like the Nauruans a destructive exposure they are perhaps not ready to resist? There are some useful negatives: Most islands receive little corrupting aid, and where they do it doesn't percolate far. The insulating distances will get no less daunting. Political and military attractions are unlikely to reemerge in the foreseeable future to bring increased Western or Asian involvement. The last Pacific empire may be dismantled for, apart from *la gloire*, there is no discernible reason for the continuing drain of French and EU resources. Nuclear testing is unlikely to be reinstituted. Other existing interference will probably recede, too, though there will be episodes of altruistic or even self-serving intervention where island governments fail and law breaks down, prompting increased immigration pressures on the rim or threatening an overspill of crime. The size of most islands will not support an airport or the development of a deep-water harbor even if their topography could, and their economies cannot generate the cash to buy a westernized life. Outside a few small trouble spots, there is no apparent stimulus to terrorism, insurrection, jihad or increasing lawlessness.

That is not to suggest a shortage of threats in addition to ever-present danger of cyclones, tsunamis, earthquakes and rotten government. As elsewhere on the globe, there are plenty, varying from island to island. The most immediate is demographic: population growth on islands that appear to be up to capacity already. Emigration, largely to Australia and New Zealand, relieves pressure, but I fear there might be a Malthusian solution to some of it. Other islands are losing their populations, but nature abhors a vacuum and I suspect habitable territory will somehow continue to be inhabited.

Logging old rainforests is a disaster, damage that is nearly complete. No one can know for sure, but tree lovers have estimated that 70 percent of the great tree species have been exterminated in the Pacific. It's easy to blame the devastation of the Philippines, Borneo and much of the Pacific on the loggers, but that's to look the wrong way. As it is the nature of a fox to kill, logging companies exist to fell valuable trees. Trying to persuade them is like talking to foxes, it doesn't work. Only guarding the chicken coop will preserve the chickens, and this is what governments have signally failed to do. Most even feed the foxes. It's too late to preserve an adequate portion of old growth forest, and corruption and incompetence still generally prevents it being made a priority where there is anything left to save.

Overfishing on the other hand will surely get worse as worldwide fish stocks dwindle. No independent Pacific Ocean country seems able adequately to police its fishery or receive its value, and the fishing fleets of Taiwan and Japan will be hard to contain. A great number of people depend on the Pacific for food. Curtailing the large foreign boats that employ modern methods to vacuum up entire shoals of fish, educating people to stop dynamiting and poisoning reefs, and controlling exploitation of reef and lagoon fish are necessary, but unlikely to be effectively implemented.

There are a bunch of threats to coral, thus to the complex systems that nurture the ocean harvests for island villages. Coral is sensitive to temperature, and a direct symptom of warmer water is the bleaching of reefs. Pollution is the other great enemy, for coral needs salt water of the right temperature and depth not only unsullied by filth and chemicals, but free of fresh water and sediment as well. Soil erosion from logging and misguided farming methods causes run-off that can blanket a reef and destroy it fast.

Tourism is inflating rapidly, but will in general stay confined to enclaves as it is now, and even dip in response to escalating fuel costs. Even on the most crowded resort coasts of the world it is usually possible to drive a few miles to tranquility inland or up-anchor and escape the sheen of sun-oil on the sea surface around the headland. Cruise ships, however, are penetrating further each year. The United States and Australia are building more, many more, floating beds, and populous Southeast Asia won't be far behind as incomes grow. Neither the lack of a harbor nor the protection of a reef will prevent a tour company crossing the open ocean and depositing a few hundred whistle-stop visitors for a few hours in places too fragile to shrug off the impact, risking damage to the essence of that which they have come to experience.

These things are sure. The degree and impact of climate change is less clear. There have been many historical cycles of sea-level change. Only 20,000 years ago, because of lower sea-levels about half the thousand Solomon islands formed a single island. Atolls sink anyway. It's a late stage in their life cycle, and islands go up and down on their own elevators with local adjustments of the earth's crust. Coral cannot build in air, thus only when an atoll is inundated can coral extend its height, ready for the next time waters recede and soil can accumulate. Despite the view of the Intergovernmental Panel charged with keeping tabs on the climate, a body of serious opinion holds that the precise effect of human interference with our sphere is far from proven, that political action is adopted on shaky grounds. But to islanders, whether the cause is burning fossil fuel, cows' flatulence, forest clearance, volcanic activity or sunspots doesn't matter much. It's the measure of any effect that's vital. When seawater expands as it heats, if glaciers and icecaps melt, then tropical waters must inevitably rise (albeit slowly) when the climate warms, as has happened many times through the earth's four-billion-year history. If we are in a warming phase, existence on atolls like Palmerston, the Tuamotus and the many islands of Kiribati is then doomed along with the Maldives and many others. Already, plenty of atolls are occasionally swept by raging seas driven by tropical storms. It would take a very small rise in sea level to make them uninhabitable, even where they appear to remain viable in normal weather. Then destruction of crops and pollution of the freshwater table by seawater, or perhaps an increase in the impact of cyclones in response to higher sea-surface temperature, will occasionally inspire a brief paragraph on news pages as atolls become unfit and are abandoned. How many inches ice melt will add to sea levels as the years pass, how fast the equally dire threat of ocean acidification can result in serious reductions in calcification and thus threaten shellfish and coral and the many species that depend on it, whether higher sea temperatures will affect the incidence of revolving tropical storms or extend the hurricane belt and the season, or not, it all seems fragile science so far. There's not much flood insurance available in Tuvalu, though.

It was a joy to find enlightened people who knew they had the finest lifestyle on earth out in the Pacific, a standard of living inexpressible in statistics or in cash. For, like most of mankind whose grass is less green than the neighbor's, the pull of the gold-paved streets of Brisbane and Auckland and Honolulu, a hankering after cars and casinos and better boom boxes than the next guy, exposure through videos and DVDs to society's "advances" does nothing for the stay-at-home satisfaction quotient. There seems to be little re-emigration after islanders have shipped off to Australia or New Zealand, where they now number about the same as the native Maori.

Though the legacy of a few centuries of outside meddling is ineradicable, I nevertheless suspect the world has nothing better to offer a pilgrim searching for paradise through the filter of Western education and city life than the deep Pacific.

A paradise to be looked upon, tasted, smelled and drunk in deep draughts.

To be treasured and protected. But perhaps not adopted unless of an especially hardy nature like the New Zealander, Tom Neale, who spent six years alone on Suvarov atoll. D. H. Lawrence wrote a cautionary novella on the subject entitled *The Man Who Loved Islands*. The fate of his hero, who tried three islands on a diminishing size basis, might fall upon one who tried to live the dream too long. He ended up marooned on the island that is madness.

Thanks

I AM DEEPLY GRATEFUL to the people of small Pacific Islands. It has been a joy and an education to know a few of you, to experience your handsome welcome wherever I have wandered. Without you this book would be unwritten and my life would be immeasurably poorer. Your lifestyle is unparalleled, your generosity magnificent. To John Kasaipwalova, Kubha, Kerely, John Wayne, Anitelu Fisi, the Marsters family, the people of Luf, chiefs of villages and many more I send aloha and mahalo.

Inspiration and practical help has flowed in tides from reading the many authors who have contributed research, interpretation and imagination to the lore of the Pacific. To those quoted, those listed in the bibliography and others I am much indebted.

As a rookie author, I leant on friends to guide me. Many thought the task hopeless, but invaluable advice was provided by Gloria Riley in North Carolina, John and Anne Marie Edwards in London, Tad Bartimus, Dean Warriner and Sybil Chapellet in Hawai'i, Aviva Riley in the Bahamas, Gordon Steege in Australia, David Tonge and Emine Usakligil in Turkey, Lucretia Hedinger in Spain, and my new cousin John Eddison in Papua New Guinea. Editor Deb Strubel and indexer Kathleen Strattan of Pennsylvania have ensured that the mistakes are only those I insisted on, and in Vermont John Reinhardt has marshalled my ramblings into a proper book.

In spite of the sea-changes since boats were of wood, sails of canvas and dependable engines but science fiction, there is still a conspiratorial fellowship among small-boat sailors, who may be the only ones to understand each others' passions. Those who have become friends and those who helped *Nereus* on her way, I thank. Supreme among them, and a powerful support in times of nautical or literary doubt as well as the creator of the maps charting this journey and the fine paintings illuminating it, is Robin, my mate, my adviser, my companion, my wife.

Andrew Rayner
Hana, Hawai'i

Glossary

ahu — Raised platform commanding a marae, roughly equivalent to the chancel of a church

atoll — Island(s) formed by coral on the rim of an ancient volcano that has sunk beneath the sea, usually leaving a ring around a lagoon

arii, alii — Priestly or princely caste in Polynesia

bagi — Handmade string of cut, polished and pierced shell, PNG (see below)

bai — Village meeting house in Palau, highly decorated

bakslida — Dropout from one of the fundamentalist protestant sects. Pijin

banana boat — Longboat made of plastic or aluminum, powered by an outboard

banyan — Large, parasitic tree of the fig family, elsewhere balete, strangler fig

bêche-de-mer — Sea slug, trepang, sea cucumber

betel nut — Fruit of the areca palm, chewed in many islands once mixed with coral lime and a bean-like vine-fruit called daca, mustard or pepper

bislama — The Pijin spoken in Vanuatu, a corruption of bêche-de-mer

black tip — Common reef shark

blackbirder — Pacific slaver, labor recruiter, usually for sugar cane industry in Australia or Peru

bommie — Isolated coral outcrop or rock (an Australian term)

booby — Pelagic seabird of mallard size. Species include masked, red-foot, blue-foot and gray

bronze whaler — Large potentially dangerous shark

butanding — Whale-shark, the Filipino name for the largest fish in the ocean, up to 50 feet long

caldera — Volcano crater, usually the result of an explosion

cassava — Tapioca, manioc; all the same food plant

casuarina — Tree with needles like pine, also known as ironwood

ciguatera — Poisoning resulting from consumption of larger reef fish in certain areas. Cause is unknown.

coastwatcher — Spy secreted far behind Japanese lines to report on ship and aircraft movements in Pacific war

copra	Coconut flesh sun- or fire-dried
coral trout	Reef fish, no relation of freshwater trout
cyclone	See typhoon
dim-dim	White man, a PNG word
dugong	Large marine vegetarian mammal, closely related to manatee
el nino	Weather following periodic changes in the southern ocean oscillation, sea temperature change bringing drought to wet areas and unusual storms. Lit: The Christ child. Also ENSO
fakaleiti	Men living as women, Tonga
fale	House in Tahitian, in other Polynesian countries fare, are, hale etc.
fetch	Distance the wind blows over water. A longer fetch produces larger waves
filariasis	Nasty tropical disease caused by parasitic worms, otherwise elephantiasis/elephantitis
flic	Policeman, cop in French slang
frangipani frigate	Plumeria, Large pelagic bird, aka man-o-war bird. Species include magnificent, great and lesser
genoa	Largest foresail
gmelina	A very fast-growing tropical tree, now widely planted for lumber
gnatu	Cloth made from tree bark used for tapa
gorgonian fan	Fan form of soft coral, can be several feet wide
GPS	Global Positioning System, a network of around thirty earth satellites from which a processor can deduce exact position anywhere on the face of the planet as well as groundspeed and direction
GRIB	Weather chart showing forecast windspeed and direction receivable by radio e-mail
haka	Polynesian dance
halyard	See typhoon
hurricane	ail hoisting rope or wire.
kai, kaikai	Food
kastom	Tradition, or traditional, in Melanesia; Pijin from "custom"
kava	Beverage made from the root of a particular member of the pepper family, essential part of ceremonial and social life in Samoa, Vanuatu, Fiji and Tonga
kerosin	Wood used widely for carving in Melanesia, mid-brown with a fine pronounced grain, kou
kina	Unit of currency of PNG
knot	One sea mile per hour, about 15 percent faster than 1 mph.
kula	The ancient trading ring of some of the eastern islands of PNG
kumala, kumara	Sweet potato grown widely in Pacific islands
kutnut, cutnut	Nut from a variety of Barringtonia tree
laplap	Sarong, a Melanesian word. Also Pareu in Polynesia, lavalava in Cook Islands

laplap	Pudding made from roots (manioc, taro) in Vanuatu
lei	Necklace of flowers or leaves
mahi-mahi	Pelagic fish, delicious, also known as dorado or dolphin-fish, but no relation of dolphin
mahu	Men living as women, Society Islands
mako	Large and occasionally dangerous shark
mana	Spirit, life force, innate power which seems to vary with the seniority of a chief. Common people are presumed to have little or none
manioc	See cassava
marae, me'ae, malai	Polynesian temple platform, heiau in Hawaii
megapode	Bird dwelling on volcanoes or places where it can lay its eggs in a high and stable temperature to hatch on their own; incubator bird
meke	Fijian entertainment, singing, dancing and acting
mile	"Mile" denotes a sea mile when the context demands; about 15 percent greater than a statute mile. A sea mile is one minute of surface latitude, thus the distance between the poles is (180x60) 10,800 sea miles
mizzen	The aft mast of a ketch, or the boomed sail thereon
moa	Chicken. In New Zealand, the large emu-like bird extinct since the sixteenth century
moai	The stone tiki statues of Easter Island
monoi	Scented oils made from copra in Polynesia
mother hubbard	The tentlike dress worn by women subject to extreme missionary/minister disapproval of any sign of female flesh or shape. Mu'umu'u in Hawaii
motu	Island formed on a barrier coral reef or on an outcrop in a lagoon
mud crab	Large black crab found throughout western Pacific, excellent eating
mud-map	Hand-drawn informal chartlet of a marine feature, usually an anchorage, passage or reef
mwali	Kula-quality arm-bracelet centered on a large white cone-shell
nakamal	Village meeting house in Vanuatu
namba	Penis covering in Vanuatu, usually constructed of bits of tree and leaf
nangol tower	Tower made of timber from which Vanuatu land-divers launch themselves
nipa	Dwarfish palm tree grown for thatch, wall-panels and general weaving
ni-Vanuatu	The people of Vanuatu
noni, nono	Fruit used for medicine
no-see-um, nono	Tiny to invisible biting sand flies that produce red weals that itch for several days

nsu nsu	Stylized carving, originally for the prow of a canoe in Solomon Islands
nudibranch	Marine creature, seldom more than an inch long, of wondrous patterns and colors
pa'anga	Unit of currency of Tonga
palangi, palagi	White men in parts of Polynesia
palu	Traditional, formally qualified, navigator. Micronesia
pamplemousse	Citrus fruit related to pomelo of SE Asia and, more distantly, to grapefruit (grapefruit in French)
pandanus	Tree yielding leaves valuable for weaving, roofing etc, the screwpine, boiboi in Fiji, hala in Hawaii
pareu	see laplap
pawpaw, papaya	Same fruit, alternative names
pay-back	Vendetta system practiced in Melanesia
pelagic	Pertaining to the open ocean
Pijin, Pisin, Pidgin	Compound language developed by islanders from Vanuatu, PNG and Solomons working in Queensland. Now the common language of these countries
pikinini	Child, any race
PNG	Papua New Guinea
pwo	The ceremony of qualification of a traditional navigator in Micronesia
rae rae	Mahu (see above) prostitutes
rascal raw fish	Criminal (PNG). Poisson cru, ceviche, fish pickled in lime, lemon, or calamansi, onions and coconut milk. Prepared throughout the Pacific
reach	Fastest point of sailing, with the wind on the beam
resort	Seaside hostelry or hotel, usually with four to twelve beds
sagali	Memorial feast in Trobriand Islands
scrimshaw	Decorative etching on ivory or bone of whale, sea lion, dugong etc.
SdA	The Seventh-day Adventists
sennit	Woven coconut fiber cordage
sevusevu	Gift of yaqona offered to a chief on entering a Fijian village
sheet	Sail control line
soulava	Kula-quality bagi with additional decoration
SSB	Short-wave radio operating on a single sideband
star path	Navigational tool of Pacific voyagers: The series of stars known to rise or set sequentially near a certain point of the horizon in a given season
tabu, tapu,	Forbidden; sacred; reserved for priests or chiefs. Kapu in Hawaii
tamtam	Wooden slit drum, up to several feet long
tamure	The rapid and erotic dance of Tahiti

tapa .... Cloth made from tree bark, usually the paper mulberry or the breadfruit, and decorated with bush dyes in stencil patterns

taro .... Staple root crop, dalo in Fiji, kalo in Hawaii. The young leaves are eaten as greens

tiare .... White flower of the gardenia family, used commonly in the Society Islands for lei, or worn above the ear (left if booked, right if free)

tiki, ti'i .... Stylised stone or wood carving representing god or spirit figure in Polynesia

trevally .... Coastal South Pacific fish, good eating

transit .... Useful navigational alignment of two fixed objects, giving a bearing

trochus .... Spiral shell used in the button industry

tuba, toddy .... Drink made from sap of particular palm trees, which soon ferments

tuna .... Of the several species of tuna, the yellowfin (ahi) and Bluefin are the best eating. Others include albacore, skipjack and bonito

typhoon .... Rotating tropical storm exceeding 64 knot windspeed, known as a hurricane around N America, a cyclone south of the equator, and a typhoon in the northwestern Pacific and Indian Ocean

Umu, imu .... An earth oven. A hole in the ground where cooking is achieved by surrounding food wrapped in leaves with stones heated in a fire

uru, ulu .... The breadfruit tree or its wood

vahine .... Woman in Polynesian languages

Vaka, va'a .... Canoe

vanua .... Land. The basis of Vanuatu's name

vatu .... Unit of currency in Vanuatu

vigia .... Reported possible oceanic hazard to mariners, noted on a chart but unconfirmed

wahoo .... A pelagic fish, good eating. Ono

wantok .... Any group of clans in the Solomons united by language (one talk)

white tip .... Common reef shark

williwaw .... A sudden, strong gust off a mountain

yam .... The staple edible root of a climbing plant, central to much Pacific ceremonial

yankee .... High-cut foresail

yaqona .... The Fijian word for kava, pronounced as below

SHORT NOTE ON PRONUNCIATION

In Polynesian languages, vowels are pronounced separately, no matter how many are consecutive, and an apostrophe denotes a glottal stop or okina.

Consonants are often indistinct, with no regular difference between p and b, t and k, or l and r.

Glossary

As consonants must be separated by vowels, missionaries invented an artificial spelling for some letter combinations; in Fijian, for example, see below:

b is pronounced "mb"; i.e., tambu is written tabu
c is pronounced "th"; i.e., then is written cen
d is pronounced "nd"; i.e., Nandi is written Nadi
g is pronounced "ng"; i.e., Pango Pango is written Pago Pago
q is pronounced "ngg"; i.e., yang-gona is written yaqona

Sources

And Some Other Interesting Pacific Books

EARLY VOYAGERS

First Voyage around the World, translated by J. A. Robertson
 Filipiana Book Guild, Manila, 1969, Antonio Pigafetta. 1527

Drake's Island of Thieves
 University of Hawai'i Press, William Lessa. 1975

A New Voyage Round the World, ed. Sir Albert Gray
 Argonaut Press, 1927, rep'b 1936, William Dampier. 1697

Dampier's Voyages
 Grant Richards, Ed John Masefield. 1906

Account of the Discoveries made in the South Pacific Ocean before 1764
 Alexander Dalrymple. 1769

A Historical Collection of the Several Voyages and Discoveries in the South Pacific Ocean
 Alexander Dalrymple. 1770–1771

Voyage Autour du Monde en 1766–1767
 Louis Antoine de Bougainville. 1772

An Account of the Voyages Undertaken by the Order of His Present Majesty for Making Discoveries in the Southern Hemisphere, and Successively Performed by Commodore Byron, Captain Wallis, Captain Carteret, and Captain Cook, in the Dolphin, The Swallow, and the Endeavour
 John Hawkesworth. 1773

The Journals of Captain Cook on his Voyages of Discovery (2 vols.)
 Cambridge University Press, J. C. Beaglehole. 1955–1961

Captain Cook's World: Maps of the Life and Voyages of James Cook
 Random House, John Robson. 2000

Captain Cook: Obsession and Betrayal in the New World
 Random House, Vanessa Collingridge. 2002

Joseph Banks: A Life
  Collins, Patrick O'Brian. 1987

Observations Made during a Voyage Round the World
  University of Hawai'i Press (1996), Johann Reinhold Forster. 1778

The Bounty: The True Story of the Mutiny on the Bounty
  Viking, Caroline Alexander. 2003

An Account of the Pelew Islands (and the Wreck of the Antelope in 1783)
  George Keate. 1788

Lee Boo of Belau
  University of Hawai'i Press, Daniel J. Peacock. 1987

NINETEENTH CENTURY

Naked and a Prisoner: Captain Barnard's Narrative of Shipwreck in Palau 1832–1833
  Trust Territory, Saipan, ed. Kenneth Martin. 1980

The Marquesas Islands
  Institute for Polynesian Studies, Rev. Robert Thomson. 1841

Typee
  New York, Herman Melville. 1846

Moby Dick
  New York, Herman Melville. 1851

Melville's South Seas
  Hawthorn Books, ed. A Grove Day. 1970

The Marriage of Loti, 1976 translation
  University of Hawai'i Press, Pierre Loti. 1880

In the South Seas
  Chatto and Windus, Robert Louis Stevenson. 1896

Robert Louis Stevenson in Samoa
  Mutual of Honolulu, Richard A. Bermann. 1937

The People from the Horizon: An Illustrated History of the Europeans among the South Sea Islanders
  Phaidon Press, Philip Snow and Stefanie Waine. 1979

Missionary Adventures in the Pacific
  Tuttle. 1967

Rascals in Paradise
  Random House, J. Michener and A. Grove Day. 1957

Thirty Years in the South Seas
  Richard Parkinson. 1909
  (Despite his name, Richard Parkinson was German. His book was published in German and appeared in English in 1999.)

Voices from a Lost World
   Millennium Books, Jan Roberts. 1996
Queen Emma
   Pacific Publications, R W Robson. 1965
Noa Noa
   Noonday Press (1957 translation), Paul Gauguin. 1901

MODERN TIMES and GENERAL

The Circumnavigators
   Constable & Co., Derek Wilson. 1989
Argonauts of the Western Pacific
   Dutton, Bronislaw Malinowski. 1922
Island of Desire
   Online at www.gutenberg.net.au, Robert Dean Frisbie. 1944
Betel Chewing Traditions in South East Asia
   OUP, Dawn F. Rooney. 1993
The Trembling of a Leaf
   Doubleday, W Somerset Maugham. 1921
South Sea Tales
   Hutchinson, Jack London. 1911
Tales of the South Pacific
   Macmillan, James Michener. 1947
Return to Paradise
   Random House, James Michener. 1951
Hawai'i
   Random House, James Michener. 1959
A Pattern of Islands: We Chose the Islands
   John Murray, Sir Arthur Grimble. 1952
The Blue of Capricorn
   Houghton Mifflin, Eugene Burdick. 1961
The Missionaries
   McGraw-Hill, Norman Lewis. 1988
Lonely Vigil: Coastwatchers of the Solomons
   Viking, Walter Lord. 1977
The Happy Isles of Oceania
   Hamish Hamilton, Paul Theroux. 1992
Coral Sea Reef Guide
   Seachallengers, Bob Halstead. 2000
The Great Pacific Rip-Off
   Follett, Robert Wenkam. 1974

Kula
   Cowrie Books, Australia, Jutta Malnic and John Kasaipwalova. 1999

Guns, Germs, and Steel
   W. W. Norton, Jared Diamond. 1997

Collapse
   Allen Lane, Jared Diamond. 2005

We, The Navigators
   University of Hawai'i Press, David Lewis. 1972

The Last Navigator
   Random House, Stephen Thomas. 1987

Sailing in the Wake of the Ancestors
   Bishop Museum Press, Honolulu, Ben Finney. 2003

South Pacific Handbook
   Moon, David Stanley, regularly revised.

The Pacific
   Hutchinson, Simon Winchester. 1991

The South Pacific
   Institute of Pacific Studies, Ron Crocombe. 2001

Fatu Hiva: Back to Nature
   Harper Collins, Thor Heyerdahl. 1975

The Fatal Impact
   Hamish Hamilton, Alan Moorhead. 1966

A Fragile Paradise
   Collins, Andrew Mitchell. 1989

Among the Islands
   Atlantic Monthly, Tim Flannery. 2011

Index

(Italic page numbers indicate illustrations.)

A

Aboriginal peoples, 40, 45, 151, 265, 327
Academy Bay, Galápagos, 14
Adams, John (*Bounty* crew member), 89
Admiralty Islands, PNG, 44, 284, 309
Adventure (ship), 69
Agnes Lodge, Munda, 224
ahu, 46, 70
aiguilles, Marquesas, 33
Airai, Babeldaob Island, 331
Aitutaki, Cook Islands, 97, *328*
albatross, 17, 156
Aldio, Pita, 217–22
Alexander, Caroline, 61–62
Alotau, PNG, *266,* 270–73, 277, 292
Alwin (Maron Island), *312*–13
Amagiri (Japanese destroyer), 224
Ambae Island, 170, 176
Ambrym, Vanuatu, *157,* 164–71
American Memorial, Guadalcanal, 200
American Samoa, 44, 98, 328
Amphlett Islands, PNG, 283
Andihite, Chief (Madou), 227–28
anemones and anemone fish, 225, 277, 330
angel fish, 67, 78
Anitelu (Nuapapu), 120–24
Ansanvari, Maewo, *174*–75
Antelope (ship), 320
Aotearoa, 45, 328
  See also New Zealand
Aranui (supply vessel), 33–34
archery, 68
Aremiti, 74
Argonauts of the Western Pacific (Malinowski), 267–68, 291
  See also Malinowski, Bronislaw
arii, 24–25, 31, 62
Astrolabe Reef, 137–41
Astrolabe (ship), 137–*38*
atolls, 41, 47, 51, 55, 132, 337–38
Atuona, Hiva Oa, 23–24
Auckland, New Zealand, 144–45
Austen, Mount, 204
Australia, 19, 44–45, 259–60, 306

  See also New Holland; Norfolk Island; Queensland; *specific topics,* e.g., Aboriginal peoples; emigration
Austral Islands, French Polynesia, 20

B

Babeldaob, Palau, 320, 331–33
Bagaman Island, PNG, 251–54
bagi necklaces, 251, 265, 272, 278, 291
Baie des Vierges, 20, *22*
Baie du Controleur, Nuku Hiva, 34
Baie Maitira, Bora Bora, 78
bakslidas, 210, 219
Balboa, Vasco Nuñez de, 41, 305
Bali Ha'i, 176–77
banana leaf money, 289–*90*
Banks, Joseph, *43,* 63–64
Banks Islands, Vanuatu, 183, 187
banyan tree, 32, 171
Baret, Jeanne, 249
Barnard, Edward, 321
barrier reefs, 41, 127–28, 150, 250, 260
  See also coral
basket weaving, *103,* 109, 212
bats, 25, 139, 238
  See also "flying fox"
Beaglehole, J. C., 64
the *Beagle* (ship), 16
bêches-de-mer, 194–95, 257
Becke, Louis, 39
Bensley (Simbo), 236–38, *242*–44
betel nut, *191*–92, 236, 255, 265, 272, 286–87
Beveridge Reef, 138
The Big Blow (cyclone), 94–95
Bilikiki (dive boat), 207–8
Bird Island, PNG, 314
bird's nest soup, 48–49
birds of paradise, 281
Bishop Museum, Honolulu, 277
Bislama (Pijin), 160
Bismarck Sea, 301–16
blackbirders, 28, 46, 69, 160–61, 237–38
black pearls, culturing, 56
Bligh, William, 43, 61–62, 87–*89,* 130, 134
Bloody Ridge, Guadalcanal, 200, 239

353

blue-foot booby, 13, 16
  See also booby
Blue Lagoon restaurant, Foeata, 117–18
Blyth's hornbill, 208, 211, 214
Boia Boia Waga Island, PNG, 273–76
Bonaire, 219
Bonechea, Domingo de, 87
booby (gray, masked, red-foot, blue-foot), 9–13, 16, 18, 314
Bora Bora, 74–78
Borneo, 212, 275, 336
Boso, Nelson, 227–29
bosunbird, 96
Botany Bay, 87
La Boudeuse (ship), 249
Bougainville, Louis-Antoine de, 43, 49, 63, 85, 249
Bougainville, PNG, 44, 48, 235, 249
bougainvillea, 249
the *Bounty*, 43, 48, 61–62, 87–89, 130, 134, 147–48, 328
Boyowa Island, PNG, 278
bracelets. *See* mwali
breadfruit, 36, 61, 83, 87–88, 166
bride price, 169–70, 180, 187–88, 198–99, 236
Britain, 40–41, 44, 97, 165
  See also specific topics, e.g., colonialism
British Phosphate Commission, 131–32
British Solomon Islands Protectorate, 238
Brooke, Rupert, 64–66
Budibudi, PNG, 245–48, 291
Bundaberg, Australia, 259–60
bungy jumping, 171–72
Buruku, Solomon Islands, 221
butanding, 275–76
butterfly, world's largest, 280
butterfly fish, 67, 78
Bwagaoia, Misima, 248–49, 262, 267
Bweka (house of John Kasaipwalova), 289, 293
Byron, Admiral John, 43, 85

C

calderas, 17
Calliope (ship), 97
Calvados Chain, PNG, 251–52
cane. *See* sugar cane
cannibalism, 30, 36, 48, 69, 109, 112, 120, 133–34, 181–82, 196, 198, 219, 281, 319
canoes, 84, 193, 267, 269, 321–26
  See also outrigger canoes; *vaka*
Cape Horn. *See* Horn, Cape
cargo cult, 155–56
Caroline Islands, 132, 319–20, 322
  See also specific locations, e.g., Yap
Carteret, Philip, 43, 85, 88
carving, 27, 40, 166, 180, 207–10, 212, 234, 272–73, 284

cats, feral, 15, 46, 240
Cavalli Islands, New Zealand, 145–46
Cavendish, Sir Thomas, 43
caves, cave diving, 100–101, 226–27
chambered nautilus, 174–75
Chamorros, 42, 328
Chatham (island), 83
Chatham (ship), 62
Chile, 44–45
China, 40, 45, 48–49, 68, 194
  See also specific topics, e.g., shark fin soup
chiton (marine bug), 329–30
Christian, Fletcher, 43, 87–88, 130, 147–48, 328
Christianity, Christian churches, 76–77, 107–8, 120, 178, 210, 219–20
  See also missionaries; *specific denominations*, e.g., Seventh-day Adventists
Christmas tree worms, 71
Chuuk (or Truuk), 332
ciguatera, 48
circumnavigation of the globe, 12, 43, 249, 318
clams. *See* deo clam; giant clam
Clark, Dr. Eugenie, 278
Clay, Warwick, 208
Clerke, Charles, 163
Cliffs of Lekine, Ouvéa Island, 152
climate change, 47, 127, 131–32, 337–38
  See also sea-level change
clown triggerfish, 253
coastwatchers, 200–201, 210, 217
coconut crab, 230–31, 315
coconuts, 73, 166, 225–26
See also copra
coconut wood, 210, 293
Coe, Jonas, 302
Collapse (Diamond), 191
colonialism, 39, 47, 62, 97, 305, 312, 335
Columbus, Christopher, 42, 47
Commerçon, Philibert, 249
"The Condominium," 165
Conflict Lagoon, PNG, 267
convergence zones, 179
Cook, James, 43–46, 48, 58–59, 63–64, 69–70, 75, 87–88, 93, 99–101, 105, 110, 112, 128–30, 163, 320, 323
Cook Islands, 44–45, 91–97, 324, 328
  See also Palmerston
Cook Pines, 150–51
Cook's Bay, 66
Coolidge (ship), 177–78
copra, 29, 94, 166, 181, 194, 201
coral, coral reefs, 41, 47, 126–28, 138, 195, 210, 273–75, 277, 295, 337–38
Coral Sea, 147, 259–60, 278
Cormorant Passage, PNG, 250
corruption (government), 29, 47, 196, 201, 336–37

Coward, Noël, 26–27
cows, 169–70, 180
crab, coconut. *See* coconut crab
crocodiles, 163, 194, 206–7, 217–18, 315, 331
crown-of-thorns starfish, 127–28
cyclones, 94–95, 98, 120, 127, 143, 145, 157–58, 185, 191, 260, 336, 338

D

Dampier, William, 15–16, 43, *308*–9
Dampier Channel, 308
damselfish, 67, 250, 262
dancing, 113, 187, 297, 327–28
"The Dangerous Archipelago." *See* Tuamotu Archipelago
Daniel's Bay, Nuku Hiva, 37–38
Darwin, Charles, 13–14, 16
Darwin Research Institute, 14–15
Darwin's finch, 12, 14, 16
Deboyne Lagoon (Louisiades), 249–50, 267
deer, 313
Defoe, Daniel, 308
d'Elcano, Juan Sebastian, 43
dengue fever, 48, 55, 137
d'Entrecasteaux Islands. *See* Entrecasteaux Islands, (d')
deo clam, *206*
Déta and the one-string trashcan, 72–73
diabetes, 61, 329
Diamond, Jared, 191
Diamond Narrows (Solomon Islands), 226
"dildoe-tree," 16
Dillon, Peter, 190
Discovery (ship), 62
diseases, imported, 15, 25, 28–29, 38, 47–48, 53, 62, 161, 237–38
Dobu Island, PNG, 266, 281–83
dogs, 15, 76, 78, 83, 107, 110–11, 180, 265, *312*–13, 315
dolphins, 18, 23–24, 248
Dolphin (ship), 85–87
Drake, Sir Francis, 43, 84, 103, 318–20
Drake's Island of Thieves (Lessa), 319
The Duff (ship), 29
dugong, 160, 162–63, 175
d'Urville, Dumont, *137*–38

E

eagle ray, 16, 79
earthquakes, 41, 168, 303–4, 336
Easter Island (Rapa Nui), 27, 44–46, 83, 89, 160, 327
East India Company, 320
East Indies, 85
ebony wood, 40, 207, 209–10, 212, 272–73, *284*, 287
Ecuador, 15, 44–45
  See also Galápagos Islands

eel, ribbon. *See* ribbon eel
Efate, Vanuatu, 156–61
d'Elcano, Juan Sebastian, 43
Elizabeth I, Queen of England, 319
Elizabeth II, Queen of England, 105, 172, 291
El Niño/ La Niña, 127, 157
emigration, 102–2, 336, 338
Emma, Queen, 302–3, 305, 311
Las Encantadas (Melville), 15
Engineer Group Islands, PNG, 265, 270
English Harbor, New Ireland, 301–2
d'Entrecasteaux Islands, PNG, 41, 44, 265–66, 269, 271, 276–83
Epi, Vanuatu, *157*, 162–63
Espiritu Santo, Vanuatu, *157*, 177–80
Essex (American naval frigate), 29
Essex (whaleship), 29
Euakafa Island, Tonga, 116–17

F

Faa'a (airport suburb of Papeete), 75
Faaaha, Taha'a, 75
Faiteli (Normanby), 276–79, 290–91
fakaleiti, 113
Fakarava, Tuamotu Islands, *54*, 56–58
Faraway (Irvine), 193
Fatu Hiva, Marquesas Islands, 19–22, *26*
feather dusters, 199, 277
Ferdinand of Spain, King, 41
Fergusson Island, PNG, 281, 283
Festival of Pacific Arts, 321–29, 333
Fiji, 40, 44, 77, 83, 103, 112, 116, 119, 125–26, 130–41, 158, 160, 183, 237, 327
"finning." *See* shark fin soup
First World War, 64, 69, 305, 314
fishing industry, 48, 201–2, 337
Flinders, Matthew, 87
"flying fox," 139, 281
flying witches, 266, 281
Foeata Island, Tonga, 116–19
Following The Equator (Twain), 131
Fongataufa Atoll, Tuamotu Archipelago, 57
Forster, Johann Reinhold, 63–64, 75, 110, 319
Fortune, Leo, 266
The Fo'ui Tree (Tongan folk tale), 116–17
France, 40–41, 44–45, 165, 335
  See also specific topics, e.g., nuclear testing
French Polynesia, 20, 23–24, 44, 55, 71–72, 78, 80, 327
  See also Marquesas Islands; Society Islands; Tuamotu Archipelago
"The Friendly Isles," 128–29
frigate bird, 9, 11–*12*, 17–18, 216, 245
Frisbie, Dean, 39
Frum, Jon, 155–56
Furneaux, Tobias, 69–70
Futuna, 44, 327

Index 355

G

Galápagos Islands, 9–18, 29, 44–45
Galloping Horse Ridge, Guadalcanal, 204
Gambier Archipelago, French Polynesia, 53
Gaua Island, Vanuatu, *157,* 179–82
Gauguin, Paul, 20, 24, 39, 62–63
genealogies, 280
Genovese, Galápagos Islands, 11–14
Gerbault, Alain, 64
Germany, 40, 97, 165, 305
    See also specific topics, e.g., colonialism
ghost pipefish, 277
giant clam, *55,* 225–26, 236, 250, 253–54, 277
giant giant clam, 253–54
giant tortoise. *See* tortoises, Galápagos
Gigilia Island, PNG, 253–55
Gina (cyclone), 157–58, 185
Gizo, Solomon Islands, 192, 233–34
global warming, 127
    See also climate change
gnali nuts, 242
gold mining, 190, 248–49, 267, 273, 311
gorgonian fan, 216, 225
Graciosa Bay, Solomon Islands, 190, 193
Grande Terre, New Caledonia, 41, 150–51
Great Barrier Reef, Queensland, 127, 150
Great War. *See* First World War
Greenpeace, 145–46
green turtle, Pacific, 16, 224–25, 227
Guadalcanal, Solomon Islands, 190, 195–206, 217, 239, 305, 328
Guadalcanal Liberation Army (GLA), 196, 198, 203
Guam, 40, 42, 44–45, 320, 328
Gunantambu palace, 305, 307, 311

H

Ha'apai Islands, Tonga, 125–30
Hakatea, Nuku Hiva, 37–38
Hakehau, Ua Pou, 33
Hall, James Norman, 39
Halstead, Bob, 278
Hammerstein, Oscar, 176
Hanamenu, Hiva Oa, 31–32
Hanavave, Fatu Hiva, 20–21
The Happy Isles of Oceania (Theroux), 206
Harold, Chief (Simbo), 243–44
Havannah Harbor, Efate, 159, *161*
Hawai'i, the Hawaiian chain, 21, 39, 40, 43, 45, 74–75, 83, 102, 106, 113, 130, 313, 321, 328
Hawaiian language, 75, 233
Hawai'i (Michener), 108
Hawaikinui, 74
headhunting, 48, 210, 215–17, 219, 221, 234, 243, 281
Hele Bar, Solomon Islands, 222
Henderson airfield, 200, 305
Hepworth, Diane, 193
Herbertshöhe, 305, 307
Hermit Islands, PNG, 310–16
Hessessai Bay, PNG, *253,* 255–59, 261
Heyerdahl, Thor, 27, 83, 324
Hill 27, Guadalcanal, 204
Hiva Oa, Marquesas Islands, 22–33, 36
Hobuk primary school, Pana Tinani, 255–57, 261–62
Hog Harbor, Espiritu Santo, 179
Hokule'a (Hawaiian canoe), 324
Holmes, Oliver Wendell, 174–75
"Holy Mama" (Kolombanggara), 231
Homo Bay, Vanuatu, 172
Honiara, Solomon Islands, 48, 192–94, 196, 199–200, 202–3, 205–7, 222
Horn, Cape, 12, 42, 87
hornbill, 208, 211, 214
Huahine, 69–72
Hummock Island, PNG, *266*–70
humpback whales, 115, 117

I

iguana (land, marine), 9, 11, 16–*17*
Île de Pins (Isle of Pines), New Caledonia, 150–51
Indian Ocean, 168
Indonesia, 17, 45, 167–68, 211, 328
International Date Line, 103–4, 114
invasive species, 46, 66
Irian Jaya, 307
Iron Bottom Sound, Guadalcanal, 200, 202, 206
Irvine, Lucy (*Faraway*), 193
Isabela, Galápagos Islands, 17–18
Isabel Island, Solomon Islands, 215, 243–44, 328
Isla Genovese, Galápagos Islands, 11–14
Island of Thieves, 318–20
Isla Santa Cruz, Galápagos Islands, 14–17

J

Japan, 19, 39, 132, 337
    See also specific topics, e.g., Second World War; Tokyo Express
Japan-Palau Friendship Bridge, 322
Java, Indonesia, 167
Jellyfish Lake, 330–31
jewelry. *See* bagi; mwali; soulava
John Wayne (Marovo), 212, 214–15
Jones, Tristan, 184
"Jon Frum," 155–56
Juan Fernández (island), 44, 189–90, 308

K

Kaibola, Kiriwina, PNG, 283–85
Kamehameha, King (Hawai'i), 321
Kanaks; Kanaky, 151–52
Kao Island, Tonga, 129–30

kapok, 120
Kasaipwalova, John, 278–79, 289–95
Kasko (magic figure), 234–35, 246, 260–61
kastom, 180
kava, 109–11, 132, 139, *158,* 171, 175, 187–88
Kavala Bay, Kadavu, 139
Keke, Harold, 198, 203
Kellum, Marimari, 68–69
Kennedy, Donald, 217
Kennedy, John F., 222, 224
Kenyatta, Jomo, 108
Kerely (Vanua Lava), 182–83
kerosin wood, 40, 207, 209–10, 234, 284
kingfisher, 116
Kipling, Rudyard, 77
Kiribati, 44, 114, 131–32, 328, 338
Kiriwina, PNG, 40, *266–67,* 272, 278, 283–99
Kitava Island, PNG, 278
Kokopo, East New Britain, 302–3, 305, 307
Kolombanggara, Solomon Islands, 229–33
Kon-Tiki, 27, 83
Koro, Sea of, 131
Koror, Palau, 320–22
Kosrae, Caroline Islands, 328, 332
krait, sea, 137
Krakatoa, Mount, 167–68
Kubha (Kadavu), 139–*41*
Kula (Kasaipwalova), 291
Kula Ring, PNG, 263–99
Kulo Island, Tonga, 114, 116
kutnut, 214, 217

L

Lakona village, Gaua Island, 179
Lambeti, Solomon Islands, 223
Lamen Bay, Epi, 162
Lamotrek, Caroline Islands, 333
Land of Men. *See* Marquesas Islands
land tenure systems, 101–2
La Niña/ El Niño, 127, 157
Lapérouse, Admiral le Compte de, *189–90*
Lapita People, 83
laplap, 170, *180–81*
Lapulapu, Chief, 42
Las Encantadas (Melville), 15
The Last Navigator (Thomas), 325
Lata, Santa Cruz Province, 191, 193
Laughlan Atoll. *See* Budibudi, PNG
Lau Group, Fiji, 130
Laval, Father Honoré, 53
Lawrence, D. H., 339
Ledyard, Patricia, 108–9
Lee Boo, Prince (Koror), 320–21
Legana village, Simbo, 235, *237*
Le Maire, Jacob, 85
Lenakel, Tanna, 156
Leoncico (Balboa's dog), 41, 46

Lessa, William, 319
Lever Brothers, 230–31
Lewis, Norman, 108, 220
Lilo, Reuben ("The Honorable," Simbo), 239
lionfish, *282*
lobster, Pacific painted, *120*
"lobtailing," 125
logging, 47, 49, 140, 150, 201–2, 216, 218–19, 228, 230–31, 336–37
London, Jack, 39, 133–34, 196
London Missionary Society, 29, 48, 108
longline fishing, 48
Lorengau, Manus, PNG, 309–10
Loti, Pierre, 36, 39, 62
Loudon (Dutch ship), 168
Louisiade Archipelago, PNG, 44, 248–62, 265
    See also Misima Island
Loyalty Islands, New Caledonia, 151
Lucas, Chief (Marovo), 210–11
Luf village, Hermit, PNG, *310–11,* 313, 315
Luganville (Santo), Vanuatu, 178–79
Lukas (Kiriwina), 283, 285–86, 288–89, 291–93

M

Madou, Vona Vona, 227–29
Maeva, Huahine, *70–71*
Maewo, Vanuatu, *157,* 173–78
Magellan, Ferdinand, 42–43, 46, 84, 103, 320
mahu, 61, 72, 113
Baie Maitira, Bora Bora, 78
Makemo, Tuamotu Islands, 52–55
Makira Island, Solomon Islands, 194
Malaita Eagle Force (MEF), 198
Malaita Island, Solomon Islands, 197–200, 222
malaria, 48, 209, 237, 302
Malaysia, 45, 49, 216, 218
Malekula, Vanuatu, *157,* 163–64
Malinowski, Bronislaw, 267–68, 270, 281, 283, 288, 291–92, 297–99
mana, 30, 41, 198, 322
Mangareva, Gambier Islands, 53
mangrove clams, 206
mangrove oysters, 257
manioc, 121, 181, 185, 326
manta ray, 14, 23, 37, 48, 134–35, *260,* 313
Manus, PNG, 308–10
The Man Who Loved Islands (Lawrence), 339
Maoris, 40, 46, 83, 151, 328, 338
Maori wrasse, 253
marae, 53, 70–71, 74
Marau Sounds, Solomon Islands, 196, 199
Marcellin Champagnat, St., 231
Le Mariage de Loti (Loti), 36
Mariana Islands, 40, 44–45, 320, 322, 328
marine iguana, 11, 16–17

Mariner, William, 43, 111–12, 128, 134, 190
Marist Brothers, 230–31
Maron Island, PNG, *312*–13
Marovo Lagoon, Solomon Islands, 40, 208–22
Marquesas Islands, 19–38, 45, 51, 56, 62–63, 83
The Marquesas Islands (Thomson), 36
Marshall Islands, 44, 327
Marsters family, Palmerston Island, 91–97
Marula trees, 25
Marum, Mount, 165, 168–69, 173
Mary Island, Solomon Islands, 207–8, 211
Mary (Louisiades), 255–57, 259–62
Masefield, John, 148
Maskelyn Islands, 163–64
Mataniko Falls, Guadalcanal, 203–5
Matavai, Tahiti, 62
Matikuri Island, Solomon Islands, 221–22
matrilineal inheritance, 224, 236, 271, 279–80, 292
Maupihaa, Society Islands, 20, 80
Maupiti, 78–81
Mbareho, Solomon Islands, 217
Mbatuna, Solomon Islands, 212
Mbili, Solomon Islands, 208, 234
Mbuinitusu, Solomon Islands, 216
Mead, Margaret, 98, 266
me'ae, 34
megapode, 202–3, 206, 239–41, 246, 304, 330
Melanesia, 45, 110, 113, 133, 136–37, 151, 163, 178, 187, 212–13, 238, 241, 285
Melinda Lee, 146
Melville, Herman, 15, 29, 34–35, 39
Mendaña, Álvaro de, 21, 48, 84, 190–91
Mendoza, Garcia de, 21
Mentor (ship), 321
Michener, James, 39, 66, 108, 176
miconia (invasive species), 66
Micronesia, 84, 113, 137, 322, 324, 328, 332–33
Micronesia, Federated States of (FSM), 44–45
migration, 40, 45, 163
Milamala festival, 297
Million Dollar Point, 178–79
Milne Bay, PNG, 270, 273, 277
Mindeminde Islands, 216
Minerva Reef, 138
Misima Island, PNG, 248–49, *253*, 262, 263, 265, 267
missionaries, 20, 28–30, 35, 47–48, 108–9, 288
The Missionaries (Lewis), 108, 220
missionary pot, 69
moa (extinct bird), 46
moai, 46
Moby Dick (Melville), 29, 114

money. *See* banana leaf money; shell money
Moorea, 66–69
moray eel, 56, 72, 250
Mormons, 47, 108, 120, 125
Moruroa Atoll, Tuamotu Archipelago, 48, 57
Moso Island, Vanuatu, 161
Mosquito Bay, 194
the Mother (volcano), 303–4, 307
Motorina Island, PNG, 251
Mount Onemanu, 75
mudskipper fish, 262
Munda, Solomon Islands, 222–26
Murray, Sir Hubert, 309
Mushroom Island, Solomon Islands, 224
mwali, 265, 279, 282, 291
My Tongan Home (Ledyard), 108–9

N

"namba," 163, 173
Nambas, Big and Little (Malekula tribes), 163
nanghol, 171–72
Nan Madol, Pohnpei, 332
native populations, annihilation of, 28–31, 47–48, 62, 237–38, 320–21, 332
A Naturalist Among the Headhunters (Woodford), 238
Nauru, 44, 328–29, 336
nautilus, chambered, 174–75
navigation, navigators, 84, 322–26
Naviti Island, Fiji, 134–35
Neale, Tom, 339
necklaces. *See bagi; soulava*
Neiafu, Tonga, 105, 111, 112, 119, 123
Nelson, Chief (Maewo), *158,* 173–74, 176
Nende, Santa Cruz Islands, 189
Nereus (Greek mythology), 4–7
The Netherlands, 45, 106, 328
New Britain, PNG, 303–8
New Caledonia, 40–41, 44–45, 80–81, 83, 143–53, 160, 163, 184, 327
New Georgia, Solomon Islands, 208, 216, 224
New Guinea, large island of, 39, 45, 307
See also Papua New Guinea
New Holland (Australia), 87, 308
New Ireland, PNG, 301–2, 308
A New Voyage Round the World (Dampier), 308
New Zealand, 39–40, 44–46, 75, 93, 96, 98, 101–3, 109, 136–39, 143–47, 167, 196, 324
See also Aotearoa; emigration; Maoris
ngali nuts, 211, 214
Nguna Island, Efate, 159
Nicholson, Chief (Ureparapara), 184–88
Ninigo Atoll, PNG, 314
Niuatoputapu, Tonga, 105
Niue, 44–45, 49, 97, 99–104, 327

Nivani Island, PNG, 249–50
Noa Noa (Gauguin), 62
nomela (palm), 182
Nordoff, Charles, 39
Norfolk Island, 44, 147–48, 328
Normanby Island, PNG, 269, 276–81
Noro, Solomon Islands, 226
the North Daughter (volcano), 303–4, 307
North Island, New Zealand, 143
Noumea, New Caledonia, 45, 150–52, 160
nsu-nsu, 210, 215
Nuapapu Island, Tonga, 119–24
Nuapapu Lagoon, 114, 119
nuclear testing, 47–48, 53, 57, 145–46, 336
nudibranch, 216, 224–25, 277
Nuku'alofa, Tonga, 105, 113–14
Nuku Hiva, Marquesas Islands, 26, 29, 34–38

O

Ocean Island, Kiribati, 131–32
octopus, 158, 175, 234
Olmsted, Francis, 109
Omai, 69–70, 320
Omarakana, Kiriwina, 292
Omsk, Siberia, 12
Onemanu, Mount, 75
Operation Hailstorm, 332
Opunoha Bay, 66–68
opuntia (tree cactus), 16
outrigger canoes, 84, 150, 161, 322
Ouvéa, New Caledonia, 151–53
Ove volcano, Simbo, 239–41
owl, short-eared, 13
oysters, 56, 199, 257, 265, 278

P

Pa'ao, 74
Pacific Island Countries and Territories, 44
Pacific painted lobster, *120*
Pacific Ring of Fire. *See* Ring of Fire, Pacific
Padilla, Captain, 319
Pago Pago, American Samoa, 45, 98, 348
palangi, 106
Palau, 44–45, 317–33
Palmerston, 91–97, 191, 338
palu, 324–25
pamplemousses, 21
Panaete Island, PNG, 267, 269
Panama, 10, 41, 308–9
Panapompom Island, PNG, 250, *253*
Panasia Island, PNG, 250–51, *253*
Pana Tinani Island, PNG, 255–57, 261–62
Pana Wina Island, PNG, 258
pandanus, 92, 94, 109, 113, 120, *123*, 239, 268, 285, 293, 331
"The Pandemonium," 165
Pandora (ship), 62
Papeete, French Polynesia, 45, 53, 59–62, 64, 66, 74–75

Papua New Guinea (PNG), 44–45, 48, 166, 202, 233, 244–316, 327
A Paradise Is Dead (Gerbault), 64
parrotfish, 78, 92–*93*, 96, 207
Pau Island, Fiji, 134
pearls, culturing, 56
Pentecost, Vanuatu, *157*, 171–73
Pépérou, 25–27, 30
Peru, 15, 21, 28, 83, 87, 190
Philippines, 39, 42–43, 45, 212, 322, 332, 336
phosphate, 40, 131–32, 328
Piailug, Mau, 322–25
Picasso triggerfish, 67–*68*
Pigafetta, Antonio, 42
Pigeon Island, Solomon Islands, 193
pigs, 111–12, 170, 180, 269
Pijin language, 160–61, 180, 213, 219, 228, 232–33, 270, 281, 309, 314
Pines, Isle of (Île de Pins), 150–51
pirates, 6, 15, 22, 43, 308
    See also Dampier, William
Pitcairn Island, 41, 44, 85, 88–89, 147–48
Pizarro, Francisco, 47
plagues. *See* diseases, imported
Plum Pudding Island, 224
PNG. *See* Papua New Guinea
Pohnpei, Caroline Islands, 328, 332
pollution, 47, 126–27, 337
Polo (Simbo), 236, 239–42, 244
polygamy, 292
Polynesia, 4, 19, 29, 40, 45, 70, 83–84, 96, 116, 137, 187, 198, 212–13, 322–24
    See also French Polynesia; *specific locations*, e.g., Tahiti
Polynesian languages, 75
Pomare of Tahiti, Queen, 29
Popao guesthouse, Tonga, 116
population growth, 15, 46, 238, 336
populations, annihilation of native. *See* native populations, annihilation of
population statistics, 44
"Port Breton," 301–2
Port Moresby, PNG, 48, 248
Port of Refuge, Tonga, 105
Port Vila, Efate, 156–57
pottery, 83, 283
President Coolidge (ship), 177–78
prostitution, 61–62
PT109 (ship), 222, 224
Puamau, Hiva Oa, 25, 27–28
Puerto Ayora in Academy Bay, Galápagos, 14
Puerto Villamil, Isla Isabela, Galápagos, 17
puffer fish, 135
Pyle, Richard, 277

Q

Quattorze Juillet festivities, 75–76
Queen Alexandra's bird-wing (butterfly), 280
Queen Emma (Robson), 305, 307

Queensland, Australia, 127, 150, 160, 237
Quirós, Pedro de, 84, *190*–91

R

Rabaul, PNG, 284, 302–5, 307–9
Rabi Island, Fiji, 131–32
rae rae, 61
Raffles, Sir Stamford, 167
Raiatea, 74
Rainbow Warrior, 145–46
rainforests, 47, 49, 182, 204, 336–37
Ralum Club (East New Britain), 307
Rangiroa, Tuamotu Archipelago, 57
Ranongga Island, Solomon Islands, 234, 243
Ranvetlam, Ambryn, 164, 166
Rapa Nui. *See* Easter Island
Rarahu (Tahitian girl), 62
Rarotonga, Cook Islands, 93–96
Ray (Ambrym), 165, 168–70
de Rays, Marquis, 301–2
red-foot booby, *10*–11
  See also booby
Reef Islands, Solomon Islands, 193
remora (fish), 282
Rendova Island, Solomon Islands, 229
the *Resolution, 88,* 130
Return to Paradise (Michener), 66, 176
Reynolds, Sir Joshua, *69*–70
ribbon eel, 80, 277
Ring of Fire, 4, 41, 165, 167
Roberts, Jan, 311–13
Robinson Crusoe (Defoe), 308
Robson, R. W., 305, 307
Rock Islands, Palau, 329–31
Rodgers, Richard, 39, 176
Roggeveen, Jacob, 46, 85
rosewood, 27, 166, 209, 273, 284
Rotoava, Fakarava, 56
Roughing It (Twain), 140
Roviana, Solomon Islands, 221, 224
rugby, 109
rur (flower), 330
Russell Islands, Solomon Islands, 198–99, 206–8

S

sagali baskets, 289–90
sago palm, 212, 214
sailfish, 254
Saipan, Northern Marianas, 322, *324,* 332
Salote of Tonga, Queen, 26–27, 105
Samoa, 40, 44–45, 83, 97–98, 113–14, 160, 302, 324, 327–28
  See also American Samoa
Sampson Eli, Chief (Legana), 235
sandalwood, 47, 150, 194
sand bugs, 314–*15*
Sandi, Chief (Efate), 158
Santa Cruz, Galápagos Islands, 14–17
Santa Cruz Islands, Solomon Islands, 189–93, *195*
Santissima Trinidad (ship), 319
Santo. *See* Espiritu Santo, Vanuatu
Santo Domingo (ship), 319
Satawal, Caroline Islands, 322
Savage Island, 99–100
Savari, PNG, 258
Savo Island, Solomon Islands, 202, 206
Savusavu, Fiji, 131, 133
Scorff Passage, 177
scorpionfish, 277
"screwpine," 94
scurvy, 59
Sea Eagle, 309
sea horse, 215–16, 225, 277
sea krait, *see* sea snake
sea-level change, 46–47, 132, 337–38
sea lion, 9, 11, 14–18
sea slug. *See* bêches-de-mer
sea snake, 137, 225
Second World War, 47, 177–78, 208, 234, 271, 306, 332, 335
  See also specific locations, e.g., Guadalcanal; Kiriwina; Saipan; Solomon Islands
Seeadler Lagoon, Manus, PNG, 309
Seghe, Seghe narrows (Solomon Islands), 217
Selkirk, Alexander, 189, 308
Seventh-day Adventists (SdA), 210, 213, 215, 219, 310–11, 314–15
shark fin soup, 23, 48, 194
Shark Point, Munda, 225
sharks, 23, 102, 257
shark-worship, 199
Shcherbakov, Sergey, 12
shell money, 198–99, 236, 242
Shibumbum Island, PNG, 259
short-eared owl, 13
Shortland Islands, Solomon Islands, 238
Siberia (boat), 12
Sieling, Dirk, 212
Simbo, Solomon Islands, 234–44
Skull Island (Madou, Vona Vona), 227–29
Sleavin, Judith, 146
"sleeping snake," 226
the Slot, Solomon Islands. *See* Solomon Islands "Slot"
smallpox, 47, 237
snakes. *See* sea snake; "sleeping snake"
the *Snark* (ship), 196
Society Islands, 20, 45, 51–81
Sola, Banks Islands, 183, 185
Solomon Islands, 44–45, 83, 85, 166–67, 176, 188–244, 263, 304–5, 328, 337
Solomon Islands "Slot," 197, 201, 305
Solomon Star, 235
Solotavui, Kadavu, 139
Somosomo, Taveuni, 132–33

The Sorcerers of Dobu, 266
sorcery, 266–67, 281, 291–92, 297
soulava, 265, 268–70, 272, 278–79, 282, 290–91
South America, 4, 6, 9, 19, 42, 83
the South Daughter (volcano), 303–4
the Southern Cross, 22, 38, 148, 187
South Island, New Zealand, 144
South Pacific Anchorages (Clay), 208
South Pacific Handbook (Stanley), 193, 203
South Pacific (musical), 176
South Sea Tales (London), 133–34
Spain, 40–43, 328
Speight, George, 133
Spice Islands, 42
spondylus shell, 265
sponges, 195, 225, 277
squid, 258
St. Patrick (ship), 190
starfish, 127, 225
Steege, Gordon, 271, 276, 284, 289–90, 293, 313
Stevenson, Robert Louis, 39, 97–98, 131
stonefish, 66, 80, 272–73
sugar cane, sugar plantations, 40, 132–33, 160–61
Sumatra, Indonesia, 17, 167–68
Sumbawa, Indonesia, 167
Sunda strait, 167
surfing, 64
Suva, Fiji, 48, 136–37
Suvarov Atoll, 339
sweetlips (fish), 67, 253
swiftlet, 48–49
syphilis, 29, 48, 237, 302

T

Tagula Island, PNG, *253,* 259–62
Taha'a, 72–75
Tahanea, Tuamotu Islands, *54*–56
Tahiti, 2, 29, 33–34, 51–66
Taiji, Japan, 23
Taiohae, Nuku Hiva, 35–37
Taipivai Valley, Nuku Hiva, 34
Taiwan, 45, 48, 322, 328, 337
Takiriki, 133–34
Talafaiva, Princess (in Tongan folk tale), 116–17
Talava Arches, 101
Tales of the South Pacific (Michener), 176
tamarind, 140
Tambora, Mount, 167
Tangaloa (Tongan mythology), 105–6
Tanna, Vanuatu, 155–57
Taori, Chief Toni (Kaibola), 285–89
ta'ovala, 113
tapa, 70, 113, 120–*21,* 123
Taputapuatea marae, 74
Tasman, Abel, 45, 106, 328

Tasmania, 45
tasseled wobbegong, 277
tattooing, art of, 27–28
Tavanipupu Island, 196–97
Taveuni Island, Fiji, 131–33
Tavurvur (volcano), 303–*4,* 307
tectonic plates, junction of, 168, 303, 305
Te 'Enua Enata, 21
Tehura (Paul Gauguin's girlfriend), 20
Telina Island, Solomon Islands, 212–13
Telita (boat), 278
Temetiu, Mount, 24
Temple Protestant de Vaitape, 76–77
"The Tension" (Solomon Islands), 196–98, 200, 204, 222
Theroux, Paul, 33, 106, 206
Thieves, Island of, 318–20
Thomas, Stephen, 325
Thompson, Nainoa, 324
Thomson, Rev. Robert, 36
Three Sisters Islands, Solomon Islands, 194–96
tiger shark, 257
tikis, 25, 27–*28, 29,* 31, 34–35
Tikopia Island, Solomon Islands, 191
timber. *See* logging
Timor, 88
Tinian, Mariana Islands, 332
Toba, Lake (Indonesia), 17
Tofua Island, Tonga, 129–30
Tokelau, 44–45, 101, 327
Tokyo Express, 197, 200, 305
Tomanboitomanguadi, *279,* 290–91
Tonga, 26, 39, 43–44, 48, 88, 103, 105–41, 146, 158, 324, 327
Tongatapu, Tonga, 105
Tonsa (carver), 210, *234*
Tony, Brother, 230–33
Torba, Vanuatu, 187
Tordesillas, Treaty of, 42
tortoise, Galápagos, 14–15
Tour d'Auverne (ship), 95
tourism, 337
  See also specific locations, e.g., Galápagos Islands
Traitors' Bay, 25
transvestites, 61, 72, 113
triggerfish, 67–*68,* 225, *253*
triton bell, *281*
Trobriand Islands, PNG, 44, 265, 273, 283–99
  See also Kiriwina
trochus shells, 45, 257
Tropic of Capricorn, 147
Truuk (or Chuuk), 332
tsunamis, 41, 167–68, 336
Tuamotu Archipelago, 20, 38, 41, 45, 51–59, 83, 85, 338
Tubetube, PNG, *266,* 270–78

tufa rock, 251
tupapau, 20
turtle, green. *See* green turtle, Pacific
Tuvalu, 44–45, 327, 338
Tuvaruhu village, Solomon Islands, 204
Twain, Mark, 131, 140
20,000 Leagues Under the Sea (Verne), 190
Typee (Melville), 34–35

U

Ua Pou, Marquesas Islands, *26,* 30, 33
unicornfish, 67, 102
Unilever, 231
United States, 44–45, 97, 332–33, 335
    See also specific topics, e.g., Second World War
Uoleva Island, Tonga, 129
Upi lagoon, New Caledonia, 150
Ureparapara, Vanuatu, *157,* 184–88
d'Urville, Dumont, 137–*38,* 332
Utapua Island, Solomon Islands, 163
Uturoa, Raiatea, 74

V

Vaekehu, Queen of Nuku Hiva, 36
vaka, 74, 84
Valeti's tapa, 120–*21*
Vancouver, George, 62
Vanga Point, Kolombanggara, 230–33
Vangunu Island, Solomon Islands, 212, 214, 216
Vanikoro Island, Santa Cruz Group, 189–90
vanilla vines, 71
Vanua Lava, Vanuatu, *157,* 182–84, 187
Vanua Levu, Fiji, 133–34
Vanuatu, 44, 153, 155–88, 191, 201–2, 232–33, 327
Vava'u, Tonga, 105–17, 125, *127*–28
venereal disease, 47, 62
    See also diseases, imported; syphilis
Victoria, Queen, 30, 93
Vierges, Baie de, 20, 22
vigias, 283
Viti Levu, Fiji, 136–37
Vittoria (ship), 43
Voices from a Lost World (Roberts), 311–13
volcanoes, 10
    See also Ring of Fire, Pacific; *specific names and locations,* e.g., Rabaul
Vona Vona Lagoon, Solomon Islands, 226–30
Vulcan (volcano), 303, 304–5, 308

W

Wahlen, Nati, 311–12
Wahlen, Rudolph; Wahlenburg, 311–*13*
Wallis, Samuel, 43, 85–*86*
Wallis (island), 44, 327
wantok system, 228
Waterfall Bay, Vanua Lava, 182
"water music," *180*–81
Wayne, John (Marovo), 212, 214–15
weaving, 40, 326
    See also basket weaving; pandanus
Wesleyans, 108–9, 120
West Indies, 6, 42, 87, 158, 193
whalers, whaling, 15, 21, 23, 28–29, 46, 48
whales, 114–15, 117, 125
whale-shark, 275–76
Willie, Chief (Pentecost), 172
Wilson, Henry, 320
witches, 266, 281
Woodford, C. M., 238
Woodlark Island, PNG, 265, 269, 278, 291
World War I. *See* First World War
World War II. *See* Second World War
wrasse, 67, 78, 253, 313

Y

Yabon, Esther and Joe, 271, 276
Yamamoto, Isoroku, Admiral, 305
yams, importance of, 285, 293–97
Yanuca Island, Fiji, 136
Yap, Caroline Islands, 322, 325, 328, 332
Yasawa Islands, Fiji, 134–35

www.ingramcontent.com/pod-product-compliance
Lightning Source LLC
Chambersburg PA
CBHW080724230426
43665CB00020B/2607